W9-AAT-146

Creativity
and the **Arts**
with **Young Children**

SECOND EDITION

Join us on the web at

EarlyChildEd.delmar.com

Creativity and the Arts with Young Children

SECOND EDITION

Rebecca T. Isbell, Ed. D.
Director, Center of Excellence in Early Childhood Learning
and Development
Professor of Early Childhood Education
East Tennessee State University

Shirley C. Raines, Ed. D.
President
Professor of Curriculum and Instruction
University of Memphis

THOMSON

DELMAR LEARNING   Australia Brazil Canada Mexico Singapore Spain United Kingdom United States

THOMSON

™

DELMAR LEARNING

Creativity and the Arts with Young Children, Second Edition
Rebecca T. Isbell and Shirley C. Raines

Vice President, Career Education SBU:
Dawn Gerrain

Director of Learning Solutions:
Sherry Dickinson

Managing Editor:
Robert L. Serenka, Jr.

Senior Acquisitions Editor:
Erin O'Connor

Editorial Assistant:
Stephanie Kelly

Director of Production:
Wendy A. Troeger

Production Manager:
J.P. Henkel

Production Editor:
Amber Leith

Technology Project Manager:
Sandy Charette

Director of Marketing:
Wendy E. Mapstone

Channel Manager:
Kristin McNary

Cover Design:
Judi Orozco

Composition:
Interactive Compostion Corporation

COPYRIGHT © 2007 Thomson Delmar Learning, a division of Thomson Learning Inc. All rights reserved. The Thomson Learning Inc. logo is a registered trademark used herein under license.

Printed in Canada
1 2 3 4 5 XXX 08 07 06

For more information contact Thomson Delmar Learning,
Executive Woods, 5 Maxwell Drive, Clifton Park, NY 12065-2919.

Or find us on the World Wide Web at www.thomsonlearning.com, www.delmarlearning.com, or www.earlychilded.delmar.com

ALL RIGHTS RESERVED. No part of this work covered by the copyright hereon may be reproduced or used in any form or by any means—graphic, electronic, or mechanical, including photocopying, recording, taping, Web distribution or information storage and retrieval systems—without written permission of the publisher.

For permission to use material from this text or product,
submit a request online at
http://www.thomsonrights.com

Any additional questions about permissions can be submitted by email to
thomsonrights@thomson.com

Library of Congress Cataloging-in-Publication Data

Isbell, Rebecca T.
  Creativity and the arts with young children / Rebecca T. Isbell, Shirley
C. Raines. -- 2nd ed.
    p. cm.
  Includes bibliographical references and index.
    ISBN-13: 978-1-4180-3072-8 (alk. paper)
    ISBN-10: 1-4180-3072-4 (alk. paper)
    1. Arts--Study and teaching (Early child-hood) 2. Creative ability in
children. I. Raines, Shirley C. II. Title.
    LB1139.5.A78I73 2009
    372.5--dc22
                                    2006004018

NOTICE TO THE READER

Publisher does not warrant or guarantee any of the products described herein or perform any independent analysis in connection with any of the product information contained herein. Publisher does not assume, and expressly disclaims, any obligation to obtain and include information other than that provided to it by the manufacturer.

The reader is expressly warned to consider and adopt all safety precautions that might be indicated by the activities herein and to avoid all potential hazards. By following the instructions contained herein, the reader willingly assumes all risks in connection with such instructions.

The Publisher makes no representation or warranties of any kind, including but not limited to, the warranties of fitness for particular purpose or merchantability, nor are any such representations implied with respect to the material set forth herein, and the publisher takes no responsibility with respect to such material. The publisher shall not be liable for any special, consequential, or exemplary damages resulting, in whole or part, from the readers' use of, or reliance upon, this material.

The authors and Thomson Delmar Learning affirm that the Web site URLs referenced herein were accurate at the time of printing. However, due to the fluid nature of the Internet, we cannot guarantee their accuracy for the life of the edition.

Brief Table of Contents

Table of Contents

Foreword

Rebecca Isbell and Shirley Raines have presented us with a wonderful book on creative arts with young children. As they state, the creative arts are a powerful tool when used with young children. It accommodates to their needs and means of instruction. I do not know why we have had so little of this kind of education. When I was in Japan in 1979 and 1980, I visited some 25 preschools where the curriculum was built on the arts: music, literature, drama, folktales, and the like. While the curriculum in the primary schools was less creative, the evidence showed that children maintained the creativity that had been cultivated in the early years.

Another important point that the authors make is that creativity and the arts are not alone for the gifted and talented, but are for all children. As I have studied creativity, I have become aware that some children of only ordinary intelligence are highly gifted in one or more of the arts, and this fuels their learning.

The authors have had rich experiences in working with the creative arts and draw on this broad experience to give us a very worthwhile book. As children themselves, they experienced plays, drama, dance, and music, and were entertained and enriched by this. They also found that they could introduce creative ideas into the regular curriculum in science, social studies, and the language arts.

The authors use separate chapters in addressing specific areas of the creative arts: art, music, movement, drama, and literature. They use inspiring quotations from artists, philosophers, and creative teachers throughout the book to promote new ways of thinking about creativity in the arts. They also use pictures, open-ended activities, and children's literature to stimulate creativity and imagination. I feel confident that readers in the early childhood education field will find many helpful ideas in this book for developing creativity.

E. Paul Torrance (1915–2003)
Georgia Studies of Creative Behavior

Preface

INTRODUCTION

This is both an exciting and a challenging time to be an early childhood teacher. So much is known about how young children develop and learn in their diverse environments. National and international interest in the capabilities of young children has grown in recent years as new research has identified enormous possibilities. This increased interest in young children has inspired the design of appropriate early childhood curricula, as well as the development of standards and testing that challenge our beliefs about how young children learn.

Today's world is filled with new challenges of global issues, concerns about safety, and expanding technology. Never before has there been such a need for creative thinking by both teachers and young children. An early childhood educator must create a supportive environment for young children that accepts them as they are and nurtures them so they can reach their potential. The early childhood classroom should be filled with meaningful learning experiences, intriguing materials, emergent literacy, and opportunities to be creative investigators. To meet these diverse expectations, an early childhood educator must understand the holistic nature of children's development and be able to design an environment that matches their unique ways of learning.

Our world is often at its best when people are playing, painting, singing, dancing, and creating. Important elements of civilization and culture are often preserved in literature, art, drama, music, and dance. These creative arts, which were so important in ancient times, must continue to be powerful influences in the lives of young children. The creative arts remain a basic and essential form of communication and an avenue for building understanding of one's self as well as the people of the world. The arts help us make meaning of our deepest feelings, share our significant thoughts, and organize our thinking.

The creative arts, defined as visual art, music, drama, and movement/dance, are powerful tools that inspire children to use their intelligence, think in unique ways, work together, and make connections across content areas. Participation in the arts gives young children the opportunity to discover the world around them and provides ways to expand into new areas that are both enjoyable and challenging. For this to occur, teachers must develop their own creative thinking and value the inclusion of the creative arts as an essential part of their classroom. This textbook is designed to help teachers discover and gain information that will help them integrate creativity and the arts into their early childhood classroom.

THE VALUE OF THE ARTS FOR THE AUTHORS

The arts have been an integral part of the authors' lives since childhood. Rebecca was raised in a home filled with music, sparking a lifetime interest in music. In school, she participated in madrigal groups, choral ensembles, and dramatic productions. These experiences built her self-confidence and provided a strong foundation that helped her deal with the challenges of professional and family life.

Rebecca has had varied experiences with children. She has taught music for K–5, worked with a gifted and talented program, directed an early childhood program, and was a teacher of children two to five years of age. In each of these experiences, she found that creative thinking and the arts were critical tools to inspire, challenge, and gain knowledge. These years were filled with opportunities to deal creatively with diverse children, collaborate with teachers, and gain knowledge about implementing the arts. During these experiences, Rebecca continued to learn that the arts could enrich children's lives, inspire investigations, and provide an avenue for personal fulfillment.

When Rebecca began teaching early childhood courses in the university setting, she found that few classes addressed creative thinking or the creative arts. In response to this identified need, she developed a course that focused on "Creativity and the Arts with Young Children." This textbook is based on many years of teaching that creativity course at both the undergraduate and graduate levels. The content included in this text, the examples shown, and the activities provided for students have been developed and refined during this process.

Rebecca believes that creative classrooms begin with a teacher who is knowledgeable about the creative process and can effectively integrate all of the arts into a program that engages and inspires young children. The content of this textbook is designed to help early childhood educators in this exciting adventure.

Like Rebecca, I have had the joy of teaching children and teaching adults who will eventually teach children. Few experiences can compare to the creativity of the young child and the ingenuity of those who teach. My years of study and work in the field of early childhood education have convinced me that the ways we organize classrooms, provide materials, and open our minds to children's inventiveness are key factors in fostering creativity.

Growing up in a rural community with a large extended family, I learned that music was a link to our shared heritage and a fun way to spend Sunday afternoons with guitars, pianos, and family members singing harmony. No one had to convince me of the value of music: I lived it. Play, drama, dance, and using my imagination entertained me and occupied the attention of my cousins and the younger children.

As a teacher, my classroom came alive with activity when children were free to choose their own expressive arts, and when I added creative ideas to the regular curriculum in science, social studies, and language arts. Children thrive in classrooms where the arts are a way of life. Invitations to be creative have structures beneath them such as resources, time, and ways of engaging children's thinking. The delight in the arts begins with the young child and lasts for a lifetime.

My husband is an artist and sees the world through an artist's eyes. His stained glass art in several churches and his paintings are evidence of the artistic process, but the great joy of his artistic life is much like what I feel when I see children painting, making collages, or dancing. The ability to express one's self and to enjoy the process of creating has applications to the artist's life, but it also has applications to life in general. Children and adults compose their lives. I am still in the process of the composition, as I enjoy the music. This book is jointly composed, but it is Dr. Isbell who is the maestro. I have learned a great deal from her about how one supports creativity because my colleague has supported me in my own composition.

Rebecca Isbell
Shirley Raines

How to Use This Book

This text is a practical introduction to the creative arts in early childhood. It is designed to nurture the creativity of new or experienced early childhood teachers. The first chapter provides the background for understanding creativity. It discusses theories, research, and environmental issues that help recognize the significance of the creative process. Chapter 2 explores the potential for creativity that exists in each person. The focus is on the creative possibilities that are within each early childhood educator. The next chapter examines the importance of play in the development of young children and its relationship to creativity. Teachers can design play environments that will nurture young children's creative endeavors in the early childhood classroom.

The chapters that follow address specific areas of the creative arts such as art, music, movement, and drama. Each chapter includes what, why, and how the art form should be included in early childhood programs, and gives specific ways to enrich their development. Chapters 9 and 10 provide insight into the meaningful integration of the arts across the curriculum. These chapters include developmentally appropriate approaches for making the arts an important component of the classroom content.

SPECIAL FEATURES OF SECOND EDITION

Observation of Creativity with Reflections. Each chapter begins with the description of an experience that demonstrates the creative child or adult, doing his best work. The episode is

followed by a discussion of what can be learned from observing creative moments that occur throughout the day. At the end of each chapter, questions are posed to assist readers in reflecting on the episode and identifying the creative aspects of their observations.

Quotes. The powerful words of artists, philosophers, and creative teachers provided throughout the book promote new ways of thinking about creativity and the arts. These quotations provide inspiration to teachers for including the arts in programs for young children.

Increased Number of Pictures and Drawings. For many people, visual images provide important connections for learning. Throughout this book, wonderful images of children and adults are included that demonstrate active participation in the arts. In addition, specific examples of children's work are included to show the range of creative possibilities across the early childhood period. These provide another way of understanding the creative potential of young children.

Expanded Research. Each chapter includes new research and publications related to the creative arts, visual arts, music, movement, and drama.

Possibilities for Adult Learners. At the end of each chapter, there are several examples of activities that can be used with adults. These activities provide opportunities for students in college courses to experience the power of the arts and the creative process for themselves. Adults learn and enjoy active participation almost as much as young children do. The activities that are included should be expanded and enriched to match the needs of the specific class and the interest of the adult students.

Open-Ended Activities for Young Children. Each chapter includes open-ended activities for young children. Examples are provided for both PreK–K and primary grades so adult students can recognize opportunities for the creative arts across the early childhood developmental span. The focus of these activities is on diverse and unique responses instead of on "cute products." None of the activities are meant to be prescriptive or replicated. Teachers should adapt and shape the ideas for their specific group of children and add their own creative touch.

Additional Reading. This section at the end of each chapter provides references for additional reading on the chapter's topic. These sources are for students who want to expand their knowledge of a subject or search for additional information on these topics.

Application of Theory. Chapters include examples of thematic units, centers, projects, and activities related to the application of theory.

Children's Literature. Children's books are a resource that provides additional support for learning about the arts and creative thinking. Each chapter includes recommended and recently published books to extend children's understanding and provide a literary connection to the arts. An annotation is included so the teacher can make appropriate selections for the specific needs of children in the classroom.

Expanded Helpful Web Sites. An expanded listing of Internet resources is included in the Online Companion (see next section). These online resources can provide additional information related to the content of each chapter and identify other avenues for obtaining current information. Because of the dynamic nature of the Internet, remember that Web sites are subject to change at any time.

Appendices. Much of the information contained in the appendices of the first edition has been incorporated into the chapters. The appendices of this second edition provide a great deal of practical information for the teacher to use in early childhood classrooms. The busy student–teacher or experienced teacher often does not have time to find rhymes or finger plays that they would like to use. The appendices also provide stories for dramatizing and a creative unit to demonstrate some unique possibilities. The appendices are a resource for educators and provide new materials that will enrich classroom offerings.

Key Terms and the Glossary. When a new term or concept is introduced in the text, it will appear in color print. The bolded terms are listed at the end of each chapter and defined in the glossary at the back of the book. Terms used by artists in their field also are included. These terms and definitions can be used to expand the vocabulary of early childhood teachers and may be used with children as they participate in the arts.

ANCILLARIES

INSTRUCTOR'S MANUAL

The instructor's manual includes questions for review and discussion, multimedia resources, and other references to support instruction. One of the goals of the updated Instructor's Manual is to guide instructors in nurturing the creativity of their own students so that they will become early childhood educators who are willing to venture into new dimensions with their students. Each chapter in the manual works to achieve that goal by providing Learning Objectives for the students, a chapter outline, suggested approaches for instruction, methods for evaluation, and figures or visuals, including content that could be used for transparencies, that reinforce chapter concepts.

ONLINE COMPANION™

The Online Companion™ to accompany this text has been revamped and expanded to further support the needs of instructors. There are four main components:

- Personal Creativity Journal: to record your thoughts as you read, observe, and reflect on the content of the text and the class. It is recommended that students find 15 minutes of quiet time each day to reflect on their journey into creativity and the arts. Since there are a variety of configurations for college courses, this journal form follows the chapters of the text rather than specific days.

- The Children's Literature Connection: recommended books to extend children's understanding and provide a literary connection to the arts. An annotation is included, so the teacher can make appropriate selections for the specific needs of children in the classroom.

- Additional Materials: including samples of art, photographs, learning webs, and units of study to provide support for students as they move into a more in-depth study of the arts.

- Helpful Web sites: An expanded listing of Internet resources is included for each chapter. These online resources can provide additional information related to the content of the chapter and identify other avenues for obtaining current information. The descriptions are taken from the Web sites. Due to the dynamic nature of the Internet, remember that Web sites are subject to change at any time.

In addition, users will find a survey of the text, where they can provide feedback to the authors regarding the usefulness of the text and these supplements and suggestions for how to improve future editions.

You can find the Online Companion™ at www.earlychilded.delmar.com and click on online companions. This text will be listed and you can access the online information from the site.

Acknowledgments

This book was created with the support of many different people, with a wide range of capabilities and talents. Stacy Larsen was an essential person in making sure that the early childhood content was accurate and appropriate. Sarah Hackney assisted in the final stages of the first edition, to refine and check details to improve the book. Throughout the revision process, Aimee E. Mullins has assisted in a wide range of ways, from checking references to securing photo permissions. Her work has had a positive impact on our second edition. Michael Talley has worked diligently to get just the right picture that effectively demonstrates the young child in creative activities; a very difficult job that he has accomplished with great skill. Su Lorencen contributed many wonderful photos of very young children; her eye for observing and recording children's creative moments has added a special view into the world of infants and toddlers. Mary Myron, Susan Lachmann, and Stacy Larsen also contributed some photographs. Our thanks also go out to J. C. Mills for his wonderful drawings of the puppet stages, which have been used in both editions. Sheila P. Smith has worked with us on each step of the first and second edition manuscript processes, editing with a focus on details and making sure that the work followed the established guidelines. Her contribution has been invaluable.

Several additional people have been involved in the refinement of this second edition. Sue Price and Kathryn LaGuardia have assisted in finding new references and publications that were essential to this expanded edition. Linda Hammons has been our resident librarian, helping us find wonderful current children's books for our second edition. Rae Pica was instrumental in the revision of the chapter on movement. As a nationally recognized expert in this field, Rae's insight was extremely beneficial for early childhood educators. Jane Broderick reviewed and added new sections to the visual arts chapter. Since she is both an artist and early childhood educator, her involvement strengthened this section and gave it the artist's touch. Graduate students, Kendra Hice, April Teilhet, and Aleksandra Vukosavljevic, contributed to units of study in the expanded art chapters. The Renaissance School provided the beautifully designed art center, and Holly Barnett and Noell Brickell shared wonderful work in their study of photography. The expanded second edition was possible because of the many dedicated people who were willing to work and contribute to this book that focuses on the importance of the arts for young children.

Many of the photographs have been taken in the Child Study Center, a component of the Center of Excellence in Early Childhood Learning and Development on the campus of East Tennessee State University in Johnson City, Tennessee. The director, teachers, and children allowed us to observe, photograph, and retake pictures. They have welcomed us into the center, even at the most inopportune times. We thank them for collaborating with us and supporting our efforts to include visuals that effectively represent the creative children in their environment.

Most photographs of primary-grade children were taken at the University School located on the campus of East Tennessee State University. The principal and talented early childhood teachers welcomed us into their classrooms to observe and record the many creative happenings that occur in these settings.

During some of the difficult moments encountered in the writing of a textbook, we have had supportive family and friends who have assured us repeatedly that we could make it happen. We could not have created this book without their personal support and tolerance.

For over 20 years, we have had the joy of working with many amazing early childhood students. Our experiences with them in creative arts classes, and later in their early childhood classrooms, have convinced us that it is possible to become more creative and to use these approaches with young children. These interactions with creative teachers have helped us continue to grow and to challenge the limitless possibilities that creative thinking provides. It is our hope that this textbook will help you enrich your own creativity, and that you will pass it on to all the children that you inspire.

Rebecca T. Isbell
Shirley C. Raines

Reviewers

The authors and Thomson Delmar Learning would like to thank the following reviewers for their valuable comments and suggestions.

Kathleen Cummings, M.S.
Suffolk County Community College
Riverhead, NY

Alison Paul, M.A.
Hartnell College
Salinas, CA

Pamela Davis, Ph.D.
Henderson State University
Arkadelphia, AR

Karen Ray
Wake Technical Community College
Raleigh, NC

Adrienne Edlen, M.Ed.
Truman College, City Colleges of Chicago
Chicago, IL

Hilary Seitz, Ph.D.
University of Alaska–Anchorage
Anchorage, AK

Regina Fontana, Ed.S.
Seminole Community College
Longwood, FL

Nancy Wiltz, Ph.D.
Towson University
Towson, MD

To Ben and Bob,
our husbands whose creativity
and love of beauty
have brought joy to our lives.

About the Authors

Dr. Rebecca Isbell is Director of Tennessee's Center of Excellence in Early Childhood Learning and Development and professor of Early Childhood Education at East Tennessee State University, where she received the Distinguished Faculty Award for Outstanding Teaching.

She is a former teacher of preschoolers and gifted–talented children in elementary school, and has been a director of programs for young children. Dr. Isbell has developed undergraduate and graduate programs in Early Childhood Education that have received NAEYC approval. Her specific areas of interest are creativity, environments, and literacy development. Dr. Isbell has authored a number of books, including *The Complete Learning Center Book* and co-authored *Stories: Children's Literature in Early Education.*

Dr. Shirley Raines is President of the University of Memphis and professor of Education. She is a past President of the Association for Childhood Education International (ACEI), and a former classroom teacher, Head Start director, and child care center director. Dr. Raines has taught undergraduate and graduate courses in the creative development of young children at a number of universities and colleges. She has been a strong advocate for quality programs for all young children. Dr. Raines has many publications, including the *Story S-t-r-e-t-c-h-e-r-s* series for preschool and primary children, and co-authored *Stories: Children's Literature in Early Education.*

CREATIVITY

This chapter explores creativity and the importance of the creative arts in early childhood education. Theories that relate to young children's creative development will be examined, including constructivism, multiple intelligences, and humanism. The inclusion of creativity and the arts during the early years of a child's life is seen in relation to the development of the "whole child."

After studying this chapter, you will be able to:
- **Define creativity and the arts.**
- **Demonstrate the creativity of young children.**
- **Identify theories that relate to creativity in the early years.**
- **Recognize that teachers' questions can help children think creatively.**
- **Describe the four dimensions of creativity that are frequently studied.**
- **Explain the importance of including creativity and the arts in programs for young children.**

OBSERVATION OF CREATIVITY

Jamil was working in the art center of his kindergarten classroom. He was cutting tiny pieces from colored construction paper. Jamil was very intent on the task, even though cutting with scissors was very difficult for him. After he had cut several pieces, he collected them into a small pile. He began carefully gluing a small piece of yellow paper to the design that he was creating on a heavy sheet of cardboard. He continued to cut pieces and attach them to the cardboard base. He selected a piece of foil from the display on the art table and added it to the design.

When his teacher began to sing the "clean-up" song, Jamil's facial expression clearly demonstrated that he was upset. He did not want to stop his work. Jamil placed his hands on the side of his head and called to his teacher, "I can't stop now. My head is too full of ideas."

His observant teacher recognized his intense interest in creating his design. Since she valued children's creative effort, she allowed Jamil to continue working. After a while, Jamil triumphantly declared, "I'm done!" He stood back from the table and admired his work. He proudly showed the colorful design to his friends, who were circled around him watching him create.

WHAT WAS OBSERVED?

Jamil was a creative young child with specific ideas of what he wanted to make. In this classroom environment, Jamil was able to use his ideas to create an intricate mosaic. His teacher, who understood the creative process, supported Jamil's effort, by providing unique materials, sufficient time, and a place where his creativity could be nurtured.

The world is changing at an incredible pace and is filled with new technologies. This expansion of knowledge has brought about a great deal of discussion concerning preparing today's children for the future. Many educators, scientists, and philosophers have recommended that today's children should learn to be thinkers. Specific facts and memorized information that have long been major components in the educational system are no longer useful to children who will live their lives in this expanding world. Rather, children must be able to solve problems, be flexible in their thinking, and be willing to venture into new areas of study that have yet to be discovered. Today's children must be creative thinkers.

As we begin our study of creativity, it is important to build a framework for understanding the nature of this complex process. What is creativity? Who has it? Can it be taught or nurtured? Can it be identified in young children? These are recurring questions asked by those seeking to understand the creativity process, and the answers to these and other questions can provide information for those venturing into the land of creativity as they chart a new course for themselves and the children whose lives they touch.

In this chapter, you will examine factors that help explain the creative process. You also will learn how specific theories and models assist in understanding the intricate operations that are at work during creative thinking. And you will investigate the unique features of the creative development of young children. Chapter 2 explores

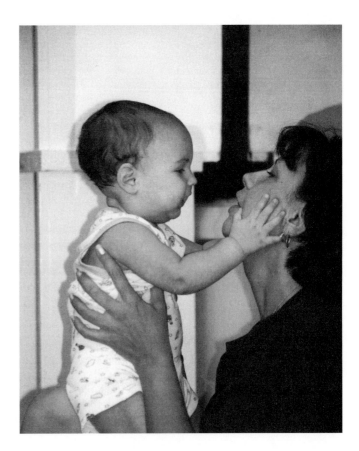

This infant is learning by interacting with a responsive caregiver.

creative teachers and the critical influence they have on the development of young children. The chapters that follow focus on the creative arts and the important connections to these areas that should be established during the early years of children's lives. The creative process is interwoven with the arts and the integrated curriculum that is appropriate for young children.

✥ WHAT IS CREATIVITY?

There are many different ways to define **creativity,** and the definitions are as varied as the people who developed them. Some say creativity is doing things in a unique way. Others believe that creativity requires the person to move out of a pattern of sameness. Creativity has been described as "thinking outside the box." Some believe that creativity is flexible thinking, whereas others see it as a special type of problem-solving. Still others believe that creativity must generate a useful or appropriate product. And creativity has been described as the production of novel thoughts, solutions, and/or products based on previous experience and knowledge (Hendrick, 1986). These definitions do not explain fully the intricate nature of the creative process or list ways to determine when creativity has occurred; you must examine all the components of creativity to find a clearer view. Although many definitions of creativity have been given, we will define it in the following way: Creativity is the ability to think in unique ways, produce unusual ideas, or combine things in different ways. In 1992, E. Paul Torrance's artistic definition of creativity stated that:

> Creativity is digging deeper.
> Creativity is looking twice.
> Creativity is crossing out mistakes.
> Creativity is talking/listening to a cat.
> Creativity is getting in deep water.
> Creativity is getting out from behind locked doors.
> Creativity is plugging in the sun.
> Creativity is wanting to know.
> Creativity is having a ball.
> Creativity is building sand castles.
> Creativity is singing in your own way.
> Creativity is shaking hands with the future. (p. 5)
>
> (Courtesy of Dr. E. Paul Torrance)

✥ CREATIVITY AND YOUNG CHILDREN

In the massive amount of literature on creativity, young children frequently are mentioned as examples of creative thinkers because they play with ideas and exhibit characteristics often found in creative individuals. Albert Einstein (Schilpp, 1949), the renowned scientific thinker, said he was most creative as a young child when he played with ideas.

A toddler is using her senses to explore pieces of wet yarn.

E. Paul Torrance (1964) said we are most creative at four years of age. If this is true, it might be interesting to examine the characteristics of young children that demonstrate they are creative. What special qualities do they possess that can help us understand their unique way of experiencing the world?

Many four-year-old children are:

- independent
- curious
- uninhibited
- interested in learning new things
- active participants
- playful
- adventurous

Many young children who have lived their first years in supportive environments naturally exhibit the characteristics of creative individuals. However, by adulthood, many have learned to camouflage these qualities and perform in more expected ways to conform to the expectations of the society in which they live. Their early creative abilities seem to have been lost in an environment that does not value doing things differently.

If young children are naturally creative, how can the environment be designed to support this ability? How can creativity be nurtured so it is maintained throughout their lives? Perhaps a good starting point is to develop an awareness of the complex process of creative thinking. Creativity is very difficult to understand. It often is unobservable and may not have a finished product to evaluate. For these reasons, it is necessary to look at the components of creativity and identify observable features.

DIMENSIONS OF CREATIVITY

In an attempt to understand creativity, four specific dimensions are frequently studied.

1. The creative person.
2. The creative process.
3. The environment that nurtures creativity.
4. The product of the creative act.

The study of each of these dimensions has contributed to our knowledge of creativity. It is important to remember that most of these aspects have been investigated as they relate to adults. This information, however, can be transferred into what is known about young children and their creative activities. At the beginning of each chapter, you will find specific creative episodes, including adults and young children, which demonstrate children's development and help establish a relationship with the creative process.

The Creative Person

Many believe that creativity is a gift only a few people possess. Highly creative individuals have had a tremendous impact on our world. Ben Franklin's work with electricity, Galileo's study of astronomy, Picasso's use of cubes, and Frank Lloyd Wright's architectural designs are examples of the work of creative geniuses. They are only some of the creative people who have had a tremendous impact in their field and on our way of thinking.

In the past, investigations have focused on highly creative adults who have produced great works of art, designed unique buildings, or made important scientific discoveries. Determining the common characteristics of creative people has provided insight into personal traits and attributes that frequently occur within this special group.

Although studies are interesting and provide insight into the uniqueness of creative adults, they do not truly define what creativity is, especially as it relates to young children. It is interesting to note, however, that many of the characteristics of creative adults are the same as those identified by Torrance and are recognizable in young children (Table 1–1).

Case studies of creative individuals provide a framework for seeing creativity in a more personal way. In addition, teachers can begin to identify some of these characteristics

The child finds a new use for a plastic knife—cutting clay.

TABLE 1–1 Comparison of Creative Adults and Young Children

Characteristics of Creative Adults	Characteristics of Many Four-Year-Olds
Curious	Curious
Expressive	Language explosion
Spontaneous	Uninhibited
Self-confident	Independent
Playful	Playful
Adventurous	Adventurous
Open-minded	Inquiring
Intrinsically motivated	Active participants

in people and perhaps recognize them in themselves. It is helpful to make the distinction between cultural creativity and personal creativity to begin to recognize that creativity is possible for both adults and children and is not limited to a few talented people whose contributions have changed the world.

Cultural Creativity

Cultural creativity is seen as an act, idea, or product that has an impact on the world or how it is viewed. Some writers have identified this type of creativity with a capital "C." This indicates the creativity that brings something new into existence that has an impact on society or a culture. This type of creativity is rare. For example, twentieth-century creative thinkers would include physicist Albert Einstein, social reformer Mahattma Gandhi, modern dancer Martha Graham, composer Igor Stravinsky, and writer Virginia Wolf (Fowler, 1990). These creative people thought in new ways and challenged others to question traditional thinking in their fields. Most created an exceptional product, and their creativity influenced their fields of expertise as well as the thinking of a broader group of people and society.

Only a few highly talented individuals, whose innovative ideas have challenged traditional views, have accomplished cultural creativity. Often, they were viewed as weird and their ideas were ridiculed by their peers. They met this adversity and continued to work in new ways. These creative people and their ideas literally changed the world.

The teacher is guiding toddlers to use a tree trunk for a rubbing.

Personal Creativity

Personal creativity is doing something new—something you have never done before. This personal creativity can be identified with a small "c," and involves ideas that are new for the person, but may not be new for others. This type of creativity can be seen in everyday events and accomplished by ordinary people. Examples of personal creativity include making a flower arrangement, finding a new route to a friend's house, or modifying a recipe to create a dish made for the first time. Personal creativity is expressed when doing new or different things. David Perkins (1981), author of *The Mind's Best Work,* explains that creativity is not some peculiar gift or mysterious process, but is best understood in terms of everyday experiences.

The concept of personal creativity is especially valuable in the world of young children. For example, the first time a young child paints the traditional symbol for a tree, he is being creative. He never had drawn two sticks for the trunk of a tree or a circle for the branches before. This is new for him. The teacher who has observed many children **painting** a tree in this way may overlook the "new" representation for this child. However, this painting of the tree is significant for this child and is a personally creative act.

This view of personal creativity also can be applied to the work of a teacher. For example a teacher may choose to cover his blackboard with woven fabric so there is more **display** area for the children's work. Although this may have been done in other classrooms, it is the first time this teacher has tried the technique. An interesting fabric is chosen and creative problem-solving is used to determine how to attach the material to the board.

The Creative Process

The **creative process** refers to a creative act and the methods or procedures that are used during this activity. When the process is valued, a person can be engaged in the creative act even when there is no final product (Schirrmacher, 2006). The emphasis is on the thinking and doing during the creative experience. Often, when young children are exploring materials and techniques, there is no finished product. The creative process mesmerizes them. Tasha, using white glue, is involved in the creative process. She focuses on the properties of the glue and the changes that occur when it is piled high. She explores the unique physical properties of the glue, such as its smoothness and responsiveness. When she finishes her adventure with the glue, it dries to a clear, invisible form and no product exists. But observations of Tasha during the process clearly demonstrate that she has been creative in her experimentation with glue.

A curious preschooler is learning about the properties of glue.

In the study of creativity, many writers and researches have described the creative process as developing in steps. Insight into these steps is another way to understand the complex workings that occur during creative thinking.

THE WALLAS MODEL. The traditional model developed by Wallas (1926) defines four steps in the creative process (Table 1–2).

Note that these steps are similar to those used by researchers in scientific studies. A scientist identifies a problem and, after some time, forms a hypothesis that is then tested and verified. The same procedures are used in the early childhood classroom. For example, the problem might be, "How do you display the natural materials collected during a walk?" Possibilities are discussed and explored with the children. The next day, a decision is made to place the items in plastic bags and hang them on a display board. Together, the children determine how the natural items will be displayed. Using this systematic approach, the students find a creative solution to the problem.

TABLE 1–2 Four Steps in the Creative Process

Preparation	Exploring and looking for the real problem. This can include gathering information, finding available resources, and getting acquainted with the problem or issue.
Incubation	During this step, the problem is not considered; instead there is a period of abstinence from mental work.
Illumination	This is often described as the moment of "Aha!" or "Eureka!" A new idea or combination appears that meets the requirements of the problem. This step is also referred to as the "light bulb" effect.
Verification	Trying out the solution and determining if the idea will work.

Creative Problem-Solving

Another way of explaining the creative process was developed by Osborn (1963) and Parnes (1967). They spent many years studying and teaching creativity in workshops, seminars, and college classes. Their **Creative Problem-Solving (CPS) model** focuses on the generation of creative ideas.

A unique feature of the CPS model is its emphasis on **divergent thinking.** For many years, education has focused on getting the right answer through **convergent thinking.** For example, when a teacher asks, "What color is this apple?" he is expecting to hear the answer "Red." The CPS model stresses the need to produce many ideas or divergent thinking. Instead of asking about the one right color, the question might be, "How many different colors do you see on the apple?" Open-ended questions encourage a variety of responses and ideas. By using divergent questions and open-ended activities, the teacher allows children to think in different ways instead of trying to figure out the "correct" answer. Many possibilities exist when questions are posed in a manner that encourages diverse responses.

Brainstorming

Osborn also developed procedures for **brainstorming.** This technique is widely used today as a way of producing many options in business, education, and scientific study. Brainstorming provides an environment where all ideas are accepted and judgment is

Leaves are being collected for display in the classroom.

deferred during the generation process. Only later are the ideas critiqued and/or selected for implementation. This free-flowing process provides unique ideas that might not have been contributed if evaluated during brainstorming.

Brainstorming can be used in early childhood classrooms to produce many possibilities. For example, a parent brings in a large bag of paper towel rolls. How can these be used in the classroom? Children can come up with unique suggestions when encouraged to brainstorm ideas. Some suggestions for the rolls might include adding them to the art area, building with them along with the blocks, attaching them to space helmets, cutting them into smaller pieces for jewelry, and making tunnels for the guinea pig. Participation in the process gives children empowerment as well as an experience that demonstrates their ideas are valuable.

Basic Rules for Brainstorming

1. Quantity of ideas is important. Later, possibilities can be evaluated.
2. Do not criticize the ideas of others or yourself.
3. The combination of ideas is encouraged; one idea can spark another.
4. Wild and imaginative ideas are valued in brainstorming.
5. It is okay for the group to have times of silence.
6. The group leader or facilitator is responsible for establishing and maintaining the basic rules.
7. Brainstorming works best in groups of three to eight children or adults.

Young children are very good at brainstorming. They can learn to abide by the rules involved in the idea-generating session.

Adapted from the work of Osborn, A. F. (1963). *Applied imagination.* New York: Charles Scribner's Sons.

Torrance's View of the Creativity Process

E. Paul Torrance (1964, 1969), one of the most prolific writers on creativity in education, identified four components of the creative process.

1.	**Originality**	The idea that is truly unique. It is not like any other product; it is a one-of-a-kind idea.
2.	**Fluency**	The generation of many different ideas. The emphasis here is on the number of ideas produced.
3.	**Flexibility**	The ability to change direction or think in another way.
4.	**Elaboration**	Taking an idea and expanding it to make it more intriguing and complex.

Originality can be observed as a young child builds a structure from pieces of cardboard cutouts. In each of the circular openings, he glues brightly colored tissue paper. On the top are flags made out of pieces of colorful fabric. He names his interesting structure, "the house of colored lights." Although many children have built cardboard structures before, this is an original interpretation using a variety of materials.

Young children also elaborate on the ideas of others. Jessica is making a paper chain out of construction paper. Leonard, seeing this chain, proceeds to make a

"The best way to have a good idea is to have a lot of ideas."
L. Pauling, 1961
(in Applewhite, Evans, & Frothingham, 1992)

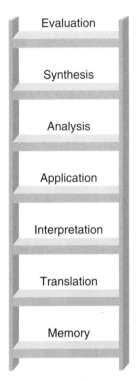

Evaluation

Synthesis

Analysis

Application

Interpretation

Translation

Memory

Ladder of Thinking
(Bloom et al., 1956)

chain from strips of ribbon left from holiday wrapping. He has taken an idea and elaborated on it to produce a different kind of chain. A teacher also elaborates, or piggybacks, ideas when she takes the idea of another teacher and does it a different way. Angelo adds real musical instruments to the classroom center. Lucretia sees the real musical instruments in the classroom and this inspires her to bring in her kalimba and some music recordings. Sometimes, this elaboration is not considered creative; "I got the idea from Angelo." But Lucretia added her own interpretation and included an instrument that had not been in her classroom previously.

Levels of Questioning

Benjamin Bloom identified different types of thinking. The lowest levels relate to recalling information that is repeated back to the teacher. Higher levels of thinking require children to use the information in a new situation or put ideas together in a different way. These higher levels of thinking seem to relate to creative thinking by asking children to use information they have gained in new ways (Bloom, Englehart, Furst, Hill, & Krathwohl, 1956).

Sanders (1966) built on Bloom's taxonomy and suggested ways for teachers to construct questions that encourage children to think in more complex ways. These carefully structured questions extend from the knowledge level, which require the child simply to remember information that has been given, to higher levels of thinking that ask the child to apply or critique the information. This technique can help teachers develop and use more questions that will challenge children to think at higher levels and creatively.

A toddler is experimenting with paint by brushing it on his hand.

The Environment That Nurtures Creativity

Although these views of the creative process focus on an organized approach to thinking, they can be applied to young children as they investigate problems and find solutions. The teacher can use them as he plans, selects materials, and designs the classroom environment. Theories and models also can assist in the design of an environment that will nurture young children in their creativity.

The Product of the Creative Act

One way of examining creativity is to focus on what is created, or the final product. The creative product could vary from a shaded watercolor painting to a musical composition or dramatic performance. It is possible to evaluate the creative product by determining its uniqueness or usefulness. For the product to be truly creative, it must be different, original, or use innovative methods.

Emphasizing the end product of creativity may limit, or even exclude, the work of young children. During the early years, most young children show little interest in the final product; they are focused on the process of creation. The young child is more interested in mixing colors than in the final hue that appears on the paper. They want to explore how glue works instead of how the picture looks when they are finished attaching cutouts to the panel.

In the primary grades, some children become interested in the final product and want to represent their ideas realistically. Older children may want to make their clay models look like real horses. But the transition from process orientation to product focus should follow the developmental interest of the child, and not be imposed by adults or teachers. Early emphasis on the product can discourage the creative efforts of young children. Amabile (1989), in her book *Growing Up Creative,* cautions that "children's motivation and creativity can be destroyed if evaluation, reward, and competition are misused" (p. 69).

THEORIES AND MODELS

Theories and models can provide other ways to understand creativity. A number of theorists have discussed the process of creative thinking. The next section will discuss these theories and describe their application to young children and their teachers.

Psychoanalytic Theory

One early theorist who discussed creativity was Sigmund Freud (1964). He believed that creativity was the result of a subconscious conflict between the sexual urges (libido) of the id and the influences of the social conscience (superego). He also suggested that childlike regression and free play are creative activities. There have been several interpretations of this **psychoanalytic theory,** each with its own variation. But the interpretations each share the common belief that conflict and difficulties provide motivation for creative acts. The manner in which subconscious thought influences creativity and the illumination of wonderful ideas is still debated.

Behaviorist Theories

Behaviorist theories provide little insight into an understanding of creativity. Behavioral theorists believe in the importance of reinforcement (reward) in learning responses to particular stimuli. Behaviorists also offer different interpretations of the effects of reward on behavior or the nature of the stimulus–response (S-R) relationship. For example, Skinner (1971) explained that the behavior of a creative person is the product of his genetic and environmental history. This view sees the environment as a critical element that reinforces creative activity or diminishes the possibility that it will occur.

According to the behaviorist interpretation, in a creative environment where making music is rewarded, young children will be more interested in participating in musical activities. The teacher, a musical person, uses music throughout the day and rewards children who display special musical talent. Music becomes very important in this classroom environment, and musical talent is encouraged. When the parent or teacher values the creative arts, the young child will be rewarded for her effort. Of course, when the adult values conformity and strict compliance with rules, the young child may be rewarded only when this behavior is exhibited. Therefore, the child will be less likely to try creative activities because these are not rewarded. He will attempt to act in the way that produces a positive response and avoids negative consequences.

For example, when William came into our preschool program, he was unwilling to participate in painting. He would stand and watch the other children paint. At our fall conference, his mother explained, "I can't believe you're letting him paint and use markers. I could never do that—he would get too messy." Obviously, his mother was rewarding him for staying clean. We realized that we would need to help William understand that he could get messy at school, and it was okay.

The behaviorist theory also emphasizes the importance of the adult "model." Children who observe influential adults involved in creative arts are more likely to imitate this behavior, particularly if it is encouraged. A mother who is an artist may set up an easel for her son beside her own easel. The teacher who creates an attractive display of the children's work allows his students to see that aesthetics are valued in his classroom. Both are powerful role models for the children with whom they work.

The right costume can support participation in a drama.

Psychologically Safe Environment

Carl Rogers (1962) and Abraham Maslow (1970) believed that creativity was obtainable for most people. Rogers described the ability to be creative as an attribute that every individual possesses but that may be buried under layers of psychological defense. Rogers's and Maslow's work contributed to the concept of the **psychologically safe environment** that is so important during the early years of children's development. This is where there is freedom to think creatively and take intellectual risks. In such an environment, individuals are accepted unconditionally and allowed to follow specific interests. The psychologically safe environment is a critical feature of programs that serve young children. Early childhood classrooms must meet the child's basic needs, support ideas, and respect individual differences. It is an environment where risk can be taken and interesting materials explored without fear of criticism or ridicule. This psychological safeness is an essential ingredient of an environment designed to nurture children's cognitive and social–emotional development, as well as their creative abilities.

While visiting a kindergarten classroom, I observed the positive benefits of a safe, supportive environment. Three children were playing rhythm instruments in the music area. They were excluding Mary Ann, who obviously wanted to play an instrument, too. The sensitive teacher entered the area and asked Many Ann to help her play the bongo drum, to accompany the other children. The children readily accepted the bongo drummers. The teacher's actions helped Mary Ann to safely enter the music-making group.

Humanistic Theory

In the **humanistic theory,** the creative person is viewed as a self-actualized person. He uses his talents to become a fully functioning and mentally healthy person. Self-actualization is seen as the highest level of personal development that can be reached only after basic needs are met (physiological needs, safety needs, the need for love and belonging, and self-esteem). Maslow's pyramid (Figure 1–1) illustrates the basic needs that form the foundation necessary to move to higher levels of personal fulfillment (Maslow, 1970).

Maslow's information on needs-based motivation suggests that children who are hungry or worried about their home life will have difficulty engaging in art activities that focus on higher-level esthetic needs. Understanding this means the teacher of young children must consider if these basic needs are being met. If a child arrives at school hungry, it is important to provide breakfast or a snack. Physical and psychological safety can be met by establishing an environment that respects children, accepts mistakes, provides choices, and supports all levels of accomplishment. In the arts, where doing things differently is valued, children must feel safe to try new things and to venture into unexplored territory.

Maslow defines the **self-actualized** person as becoming what one is capable of being. It is interesting to note that a goal of most early childhood programs is to "help each child reach his or her potential." For many children, the nurturing of creativity and enrichment with the arts may be the best way to reach this important goal. It may be the spark that lights the interest of a child or helps find a new possibility for joyful participation.

Maslow further explains that self-actualized people often live productive lives and tend to do things in a more creative manner. He explains that art education is important, not so much to develop an artist or a product, but to develop better

Maslow's Hierarchy of Needs

Self-fulfillment:
Self-actualized person

Esthetic needs for beauty and order

Knowledge and intellectual needs

Approval and recognition from others

Belonging, love, and acceptance of others

Physical and psychological safety

Survival needs: food, clothes, water, shelter

FIGURE 1–1
Maslow's Hierarchy of Needs

people. For children to become full human beings, they have to move toward actualizing their potential. Education, through the arts, works to meet these goals. Instead of being regarded as a frill, art education should be taken seriously and recognized as the way to develop educational potential (Maslow, 1970).

Carl Rogers (1962) added some important conditions that are believed necessary for creativity to occur.

1. Psychologically safe environment. This is an atmosphere where ideas are accepted and people are respected.
2. Internal locus of evaluation. This refers to the personal characteristics of self-confidence and independence. The individual makes a decision and is willing to accept responsibility for the outcome.
3. A willingness to play with ideas and possibilities. This characteristic allows the individual to demonstrate playfulness.
4. Openness to experience. This is seen as an attraction to new experiences and receptiveness to new ideas.

The humanistic theory provides insight into environments that encourage creativity in young children. Such environments must be psychologically safe to support the efforts of each individual. This theory also identifies the need for the individual to become self-confident and independent. Included in this interpretation is the need to be playful and participate in new experiences. Although these conditions are necessary for becoming self-actualized adults, they also support the development of psychologically healthy children.

Constructivist Theory

The **constructivist theory,** postulated by Jean Piaget (1960), focuses on the development of cognition. According to the constructivist theory, individuals are active participants in the construction of their own knowledge. Knowledge is constructed by the assimilation of information into existing **schema** (frameworks or outlines). As the child actively engages his environment, new schemas are built as understanding expands. A classic example of this progression in thinking is observed when a young child sees a zebra for the first time. Carla calls out, "horsie." She knows what a horse is, but she has never seen a zebra. As she gains more experience with zebras, she begins to understand that they are different from horses. She forms a new category for large four-legged striped animals and calls this zebra. This process of **assimilation** (taking in information from the world) and **accommodation**

The light table provides a different way to view colored blocks.

(applying new information to aid ideas or schemas) continues as she is introduced to other animals.

According to the constructivist theory, development occurs through predictable stages. During the infancy stage, sensorimotor learning is of critical importance. Preschoolers in the preoperational stage are developing important symbolic representations in their play. Only later, in the formal operations stage, are children able to construct understanding by using abstract thinking.

Constructivists believe that learning is accomplished through exploring, experimenting, and manipulating objects or materials. This theory directly relates to the development of creative thinking and the necessity for active participation in the process. Using the constructivist theory as a basis for environmental design, the classroom should contain a variety of materials that can be explored and combined in many different ways. Active learning and social interactions are encouraged throughout the day. Individual interests of the child will be identified to provide opportunities for group work and long-term projects. The constructivist's curriculum is child-centered and based on the interests of the individuals who make up the group.

Social Constructivism

Vygotsky's (1962) **social constructivist theory** is built on the belief that learning is too complex to be studied in a vacuum. Instead, it must be studied in the social and historical context in which it occurs. He describes socially meaningful activity as the way we learn about ourselves as we interact with others. Vygotsky's **zone of proximal development (ZPD)** is a well-known concept. He believed that a gap exists between the child's level of actual development (what can be done independently) and her potential level of development (what can be accomplished with

Children share ideas as they experiment with dirt.

assistance). He further explained that this gap could be filled by the supportive collaboration of an adult or capable peer. This interpretation recognizes the importance of support, guidance, and interactions as children move toward their potential (Dixon-Krauss, 1996). Appropriate social interactions with both adults and peers can enrich and expand the creative possibilities for young children participating in the arts.

Collaboration is a tool used to assist children in working together on projects, sharing ideas, clarifying thinking, and mediating problems. In the search for information, the teacher poses questions, guides thinking, and challenges the children to think in new ways. For example, in a collaborative group, the students work together to determine how to combine pieces of fabric and make a classroom quilt. Laurie suggests gluing the pieces, Rhonda thinks tape might work, and Andrew shares how his grandmother sews quilts together. He explains to the group how this is done and the tools that are used. They are very interested in the quilting frame that his grandmother uses and how many people work together to make beautiful hand-sewn quilts. Andrew's knowledge about quilt-making has extended the understanding of the individuals in the group. Small cooperative groups work well in the early childhood classroom and support the development of independence.

Theory of Multiple Intelligences

"What the child can do in cooperation today he can do alone tomorrow."

L. S. Vygotsky, 1962

In 1983, Howard Gardner published the first edition of *Frames of Mind: The Theory of Multiple Intelligences*. In this book, Gardner suggests there are at least seven different types of intelligence. More recently, he added an eighth—naturalistic—and is now working on a ninth, the existentialist intelligence (Gardner, 1993). These different types of intelligence have added new dimensions that specifically relate to the creative arts and creative thinking. Gardner believed only two forms of intelligence were emphasized in most schools: verbal-linguistic and logical-mathematical. As a result, Gardner suggests that many of the other areas of intelligence have been undervalued and have the potential to be lost.

According to Gardner, the nine intelligences include the following.

1. **Verbal-Linguistic:** Related to words and language; producing language with sensitivity to the nuances, order, and rhythm of words.
2. **Logical-Mathematical:** Includes deductive or inductive reasoning; recognizing and manipulating abstract relationships.
3. **Musical:** Deals with the recognition of tonal patterns, environmental noise, and sensitivity to rhythm and beats; responsiveness to the emotional implications and elements of music.
4. **Visual-Spatial:** Relies on the sense of sight and the ability to visualize an object; creating visual-spatial representations of the world, and transferring them mentally or concretely.
5. **Bodily-Kinesthetic:** Includes physical movement and awareness and/or wisdom of the body; the body is used to solve problems, make things, and convey ideas and emotions.
6. **Interpersonal:** Deals with person-to-person relationships and communication: working effectively with others; understanding people; and recognizing their goals, motivations, and intentions.
7. **Intrapersonal:** Involves self-reflection and metacognition; understanding one's own emotions, goals, and intentions.

Interpersonal relationships are built as these girls communicate about a project.

8. **Naturalistic:** Capacity to recognize flora and fauna, make distinctions in the natural world, and use this ability productively.

9. **Existentialist:** The ability and tendency to consider questions about life, death, and basic truths.

Gardner's theory of multiple intelligences identifies a variety of ways in which we learn and may excel. For example, a person with a high level of linguistic intelligence might become a poet, a dramatist, or a lawyer. Another person with exceptional kinesthetic intelligence may become a dancer or athlete. Gardner also recognized that artists might use several of these areas in combination. A dancer may use bodily-kinesthetic, musical, and spatial intelligence to perform effectively.

This theory provides support for a much larger role for the arts in the school curriculum. The different kinds of intelligence point to a variety of ways of knowing. Teachers should encourage students to use their individual strengths, which may be in music, movement, or drawing (Fowler, 1990). And teachers must provide various learning opportunities to meet the needs of their students' different learning styles. Teachers should try new ideas, approaches, and techniques so they move "out of the box" and create an environment that inspires problem-solving.

A classroom for young children working with this model will provide opportunities for the development of all areas of intelligence. Children can participate in visual-spatial, kinesthetic-movement, and musical activities, as well as the more traditional areas of language, science, and math. Using this model to plan curriculum ensures that a variety of intelligences are used throughout the classroom and that children's different ways of learning are supported through appropriate activities.

For example, when a project is developed by a group of children, they can choose how they will share the information they have collected. They may use a dramatic presentation, a mural, a dance performed to music, or a computer presentation. Providing options from different intelligences supports the varied ways children learn while building on their personal strengths. Gardner (Durie, 1997), in an interview, explained that if material is taught in only one way, only certain children will be reached. The more we can match children to congenial approaches to teaching and learning, the more likely these individuals will be to achieve educational success.

Brain Development

For many years, the brain has been thought to be composed of two separate hemispheres, having different functions and specializing in different types of learning. The right hemisphere controls the left side of the body and operates in a nonverbal, intuitive, and global way, while the left hemisphere controls the right side of the body and provides the functions of verbalizing, analyzing, and logical thinking. New information now stresses that the two hemispheres can and do work together. On some activities, they work in concert, benefiting from a combined effort. In other experiences, each hemisphere works separately, doing what it does best (Schirrmacher, 2006).

Sometimes, people will identify themselves as "right-brained," indicating that they are creative, imaginative, and value personal feelings. Others may indicate that the left part of the brain influences their behavior. They believe that they are logical thinkers, are rational, and have strengths in the cognitive area. This is certainly an oversimplification of the complex workings of the brain. In fact, most people use both hemispheres of the brain, and many activities require that the two parts work together to complete a task successfully.

Some educators believe that the school curriculum and many activities focus on what has been identified as left-brain functions. In these schools and classrooms, the teaching is focused on getting the right answers (convergent thinking). Reading, writing, and math are the subjects stressed in these environments. Administrators and teachers who consider the whole brain, including the right hemisphere, will provide opportunities for art, music, movement, and creative (divergent) thinking within the curriculum. A model school, using the holistic approach, provides an environment where both hemispheres are challenged and children with strengths in the academic areas and/or the arts will have opportunities to be successful. In our preschools and elementary schools, we should provide opportunities to develop, use, and extend different ways of thinking and processing information. If both the academic content and the arts are integrated into the curriculum, children will be able to work in ways that match their strengths and expand their experiences in a positive manner.

New brain-imaging technologies have enabled scientists to investigate how the brain develops and works. This fascinating area of research has stimulated new dialog between neurologists, developmental biologists, psychologists, and educators. These neurological findings have increased interest in the amazing capabilities of young children. Articles in national publications and presentations at international conferences have focused on the significant learning that occurs during the early years of a child's life. This information has supported what early childhood educators have believed for many years: the early years are a critical time of development, and experiences during this period impart lifelong learning. This knowledge about early brain development and the widespread interest in the early years can be used to support efforts to create quality programs for young children (Jensen, 1998).

> "If in early life, children have the opportunity to discover much about their world and to do so in a comfortable, exploring way . . . they can draw on it in later life."
>
> *H. Gardner, 1993*

When a child is born, the brain contains trillions of neurons. Connections between neurons and synapses are formed as we learn. Positive interactions with caring adults and meaningful experiences can stimulate a child's brain profoundly, causing synapses to grow and strengthening existing connections. The synapses that are used in a child's brain tend to become permanent fixtures. Brain cells that are not used or developed tend to be eliminated as the brain effectively "prunes" itself into an efficient, information-processing system (Healy, 1994).

If a child receives little stimulation during the early years, synapses will fail to develop and the brain will make fewer connections for learning. Brain research emphasizes that experiences, particularly during the first three years of life, are decisive for children to reach their full potential. Neurological plasticity, the brain's ability to adapt with experience, confirms that early childhood sets the stage for how children will continue to learn throughout life.

These neurological studies have increased our understanding of the "windows of opportunity" or **critical periods** in children's lives. Critical periods are sensitive times when the brain is primed for certain types of learning to take place. Language development, for example, begins in infancy, long before verbal language appears. Between three and twelve years of age, children are capable of developing an enormous vocabulary of 50,000 to 100,000 words. Some children in language-rich environments learn 50 words a day (Arcangelo, 2000). The window for beginning interest in musical sounds and composition is between three and ten years of age. It has been found that few professional musicians begin their study after this important period of development. Knowing about this critical period of musical development emphasizes the need to include music in the lives of young children. Identifying windows of opportunity can assist teachers in developing an appropriate curriculum that capitalizes on these intense periods of learning.

Brain research does not suggest that children learn through drill or rote memorization. Instead, it supports the principles of developmentally appropriate practices that include meaningful experiences matching the child's level of development. The best learning for young children is active, hands-on, meaningful, integrated, and responsive. Active learning experiences, including the visual arts and music, can establish connections in the brain that will last a lifetime.

Eisner (2003) provides a different way of looking at brain development. He suggests that infants come into the world with a brain, but without a mind. The task of education is to provide experiences that will transform the brain into a functioning, thinking mind. Curriculum, teaching, and experiences shape the mind and expand capabilities. Decisions about curriculum and teaching approaches will have a profound effect on how children think and what they do. The arts must be an essential part of the curriculum and should be integrated into learning. These experiences refine sensibility, provide content for representation, and develop the capacity to think creatively.

Affective Development

It is important to consider the emotional development of both teachers and children. We know that affective development can have an impact on all areas of development: cognition, language, and social, as well as the creative arts. Many scholars have emphasized the need to consider the affect and its impact on development. Gardner (1991) urged teachers to use approaches that provide opportunities for affective expression. Wood (1996) views affective education in schools as one of the critical factors in development. Edwards (2002), in her review of the literature on the topic, concludes that many research studies indicate the need to include affective education in the curriculum.

The arts provide the perfect avenue for affective development. In the arts, there are opportunities to talk about feelings, identify personal attitudes, and learn ways to cope with emotions. Beating a drum when you are angry provides an appropriate outlet for these feelings. Listening to calming music when you are upset provides a way to deal with these feelings. Dancing around the playground provides a way for the child to express his excitement after seeing a caterpillar on a leaf.

Holistic Development

Although many theories focus on one aspect of development, it is important to understand that children do not develop in unconnected parts. The different areas of development interact and allow the child to develop in a **holistic** way. In the field of early childhood education, there is a shared belief that young children should be provided opportunities to develop in all areas: physically, cognitively, socially, and emotionally. Creativity and the creative arts are components essential to the development of the whole child.

Musical experiences help a child remember melodies (cognition), move to rhythm (physical), and identify the cover of a favorite recording (literacy). When she participates in circle time, the child sings songs with peers (social), and at rest time, she relaxes with quiet music (emotional), so that, when she goes home, she shares a new song with her father (emotional confidence/self-confidence). These experiences with music enrich the life of the child and stimulate her development in all of these domains.

> "Early experiences have a decisive impact on the architecture of the brain and on the nature and extent of adult capabilities."
>
> M. McCain & F. Mustard, 1999

Outdoor play provides an opportunity to interact with friends.

The Study of Creativity

Many years ago, J. P. Guilford (1956) wrote that creativity played a critical role in reaching a person's potential. He concluded, however, that research on creativity had been sadly neglected, and suggested that creativity should be seen as a separate domain, different from the construct of intelligence. He believed that important information could be gained by studying creative people and creative productivity. From these recommended studies, he determined that new knowledge would be gained, which could be used to develop creativity in children. Since that time, there has been a significant increase in the research related to creativity in many fields, including education, science, business, and the arts. The research has investigated creativity, creative thinking, creative people, and the environmental features that support creative development in adults and children.

Expanding Understanding

E. P. Torrance, an important researcher of creativity, conducted a 30-year study that followed individuals who made remarkable creative achievements in specialized areas (Torrance, 1993). He found that these creative people shared many personal characteristics, such as enjoying thinking, tolerating mistakes, having a sense of purpose and mission, and accepting being different, and they did not feel uncomfortable being the only person interested in something. Based on this research, Torrance and his colleagues suggested that children should be able to pursue their interests and work in their areas of strength. In addition, it would be helpful if they learned to be interdependent, learned to evaluate their own work, and tried to find mentors to support them. Programs emphasizing these skills and building strong relationships with mentors could be places where creativity would grow.

With the increase in research, there have been many findings that can assist us in learning about creativity. Some of these studies provided important **empirical evidence** for behaviors that teachers and employees have observed in adults and children for many years. Other research studies provide new ways of looking at creativity. From this vast number of existing studies, we have selected several to provide an overview of the kind of work that is being done with regard to creativity. A study by Diamond and Hopson (1999) concluded that children have active imaginations. Many educators have observed the vivid imagination of young children, and this research supports that conclusion.

Several studies have identified that when people are involved in creative projects, they are very focused—often losing track of time while they work (Kashdan & Fincham, 2002). Csikszentmihalyi (1997), a scholar who studies creativity, refers to this intense focus when things are going well, as the "**flow.**" He concluded that this creative process was so satisfying that a person would work in this way even if there was no reward for the effort. An example of "flow" can be observed when a young child is intensely involved in a personally meaningful activity. In the creative episode at the beginning of this chapter, Jamil was focused on his work and persisted until his mosaic was complete, with little concern for the time or difficulty involved. In the language of Csikszentmihalyi, he was in the flow.

Teresa Amabile, at the Harvard Business School, has been studying creativity for many years. In her studies (1983, 1996), she investigated the daily journal of 238 people who worked on creative projects. The 12,000 journal entries of these individuals are still being studied; however, some initial findings are intriguing.

In the work environment, she found that some factors supported creativity while others hindered the development of new ideas. She and other researchers concluded that anyone with normal intelligence is capable of doing some degree of creative work. They suggest that creativity depends on a number of factors: experience (including knowledge and technical skills), ability to think in new ways, and the capacity to continue to work during difficult periods. She also found that **intrinsic motivation,** which prompts people to work on something that provides no external reward, was the most critical factor influencing the creativity process. Her findings support the idea that everyone can be creative. This fosters the view that creativity is not limited to a few talented people, but can be found in many people. Teachers and young children are capable of being creative, if the environment supports this process. Creative opportunities should be available to every child, not just to those children who seem to demonstrate special talents.

A thought-provoking finding from this study was that creative people persist on a task, even when the going gets rough. How can we design an environment that gives children the opportunity to persist on an activity over time? One possible way is to incorporate more long-term projects and activities into the classroom curriculum. Rather than providing an activity that is done in one day, a project may be developed and refined over an extended period. This longer time frame allows children to build on their learning experiences and gives depth to their understanding. For example, the study of bugs can continue for several weeks and include many opportunities for children to follow their interest, build understanding, and think creatively. The arts can be integrated into this study, as bugs are constructed (art), bug songs are sung (music), and children move like different bugs (movement). This bug study will support a long-term investigation and will help children persist on the task involved.

Amabile (1983, 1996) also found that collaboration was more supportive of creative thinking than was competition. In the study, people were more creative when they collaborated than when they competed on a project. This supports the belief by early childhood educators that young children should not compete against each other for a prize or reward, but rather learn how to work together, cooperate, and assist each other. This favors the use of small groups and collaborative teams working together in early childhood classrooms. In these small groups, children are able to expand their thinking, generate more ideas, and learn to develop social skills that are beneficial throughout their lives. Amabile's findings indicate that teachers may be more creative when they work together as teams than while working in isolation. Experienced teachers can provide ideas about what works in the classroom, while new teachers can share ideas from their recent academic experience. In this collaborative effort, each member's ideas are valued. By working together, the team creates possibilities and appropriate practices that might not be identified by a teacher working alone.

Other Important Developments

There are two journals published that are composed largely of research studies related to creativity, *Journal of Creative Behavior* (begun in 1967) and *Creativity Research Journal* (begun in 1989). Many other professional journals include articles and studies that relate to creativity. The National Science Foundation funds grants to study creativity in children and adults, as is the case with other agencies and foundations. These developments show the interest in creativity and the importance of studying this area.

✺ RELATING CREATIVITY TO PROGRAMS FOR YOUNG CHILDREN

Most definitions, theories, and models focus on the adult's ability to create. However, it is important to recognize the differences between a creative adult and a creative child. Adults have more experiences and their work styles are often rigid. Children have unique ways of thinking, exploring materials, and creatively playing with ideas. If one is trying to understand creativity as it occurs during the early years, it is important to study the development of young children. How do they grow and develop in the dimension of creativity? Are they naturally creative, or does the environment nurture or delay this development?

Observing Creativity in Young Children

Creativity can be seen in many different forms during the early years. It can be observed when a toddler uses the handle of a push toy to get the teddy bear that he wants from behind the storage cabinet. It is observed when a preschooler designs a menu to add to the restaurant center. Creativity is observed when a kindergartner retells a favorite story with new elements and a surprise ending. These behaviors can be identified as creative. Although these actions are not new to the classroom, they are new for the individual child at that specific time.

> "Creative behaviors abound in young children."
>
> *F. E. Williams, 1982*

For many years, the accepted view in early childhood education has been that the process is more important than the product. Teachers who observe children exploring and experimenting with materials support this conclusion. They see the creative process in action and the unique combinations that occur during each activity. Can young children who may not create a product be identified as creative? Yes! The observant and knowledgeable teacher can recognize creative acts as they occur, and support their value. The preschooler using colored yarn and white glue demonstrates creativity in an open-ended art activity as he experiments with color and shape. He is focused on the changes that occur when he glues more yarn to the art-board. Finally, the paper is a mass of glue and yarn. He demonstrated creativity while working on the art but the final product is unrecognizable. When working with young children, it is essential to understand that at different times and in particular activities, the process may be more important than trying to make a recognizable finished product.

Some children become interested in the product as they become more skilled in the use of varied materials and techniques. For instance, Mia, a first grade child, works on cutting small and intricate parts for her mask. She stands back and looks at her work. She is personally evaluating the product. Does it look the way she wants? Should she add another feature? For this child, the end product is important, but it is self-imposed and not demanded by the teacher. As in other areas of development, it is important to follow the lead of the child and assist her in the process as needed.

Barron (1988), a scholar of creativity, wrote about some variables that relate to creativity. The creative potential of young children can be seen when observing this process. Some of the attributes Barron discussed include taking risks, making connections and associations, and seeing things in new ways. If trained to see these indicators, teachers will begin to observe the creative process as it occurs. As a preschooler tries to find foil to add to his cardboard building, she is making new associations. When the kindergartner pours sand into his container of tempera paint, he is taking a risk. Will it work? How will it go on the paper? What will the

A roller stimulates a toddler to think about painting in new ways.

teacher say? If the teacher understands the creative process, he will interpret this as creative experimentation and not mischievous behavior.

Young children are sensitive to internal and external stimuli, lack inhibition, and have the ability to become completely absorbed in an activity (Holden, 1987; Isenberg & Jalongo, 1997). These are characteristics that are often found in the highly creative individual. An example of sensitivity to stimuli can be seen when observing a toddler playing outside. He collects smooth stones, crunchy leaves, and prickly cones. These treasures are placed in a bag and examined again and again. His interest is maintained for an extended period because the collection is meaningful to him. The teacher is sensitive to the collecting toddler and allows him time to explore and select the natural items that are of interest to him.

It often is said that young children have a short attention span. Children's attention depends on their interest and absorption in the materials. If it is meaningful, they have a longer attention span. The child who truly is focused on something interesting has an amazing ability to stay with the project for a long time. During the early years, finding engaging and challenging things is a substantial task for teachers, parents, and caregivers. In many cases, what is required is the ability to observe and follow the "real" interest of the child.

Imagination

In the study of creativity, one characteristic often identified as essential is an active **imagination.** Imagination is the ability to form rich and varied images or concepts of people, places, things, and situations when they are not present (Isenberg & Jalongo). The imaginations of young children are highly developed and frequently used in play and art. Imagination is at its peak during the early years. As children grow, they modify their behavior and become less willing to move out of traditional boundaries. In pretend play, the young child is able to create roles, settings, and events without concern for realism. A dog can be as big as a bear, a house can be a castle filled with jewels, and a special friend can be invisible. Young children seem to think with more creative freedom than older children. They alter reality to their own needs as they experiment with life through play (Piaget & Inhelder, 1969). This imaginative play helps children create a better understanding of their world.

Playfulness

Play often has been referred to as the "work" children do. Early childhood experts throughout the world recognize the importance of play. In 1991, the National Association for the Education of Young Children (NAEYC) issued a position paper concerning appropriate programs for children three to eight years of age. In this landmark document, they stated that one of the reasons play is so important is that it allows children to develop their imaginations and creativity (Bredekamp, 1993).

The relationship between play and creativity has been examined in hundreds of research studies. Kagan (1984) found that open-ended play provided more opportunities for creative behavior. Games with rules allow little flexibility and few opportunities for make-believe, fantasy, or symbolic play. In play, children are in a risk-free environment where there is no evaluation or fear of failure. Playing with objects is often a part of the experience, and is believed to be fundamental in the development of young children's thinking and imagination (Trostle & Yawkey, 1982).

Imagination comes alive as transformations evolve in play. Play allows children to invent many different ideas (divergent thinking) and ultimately decide which to use in a specific situation (convergent thinking).

Hats inspire role-playing.

Aesthetics

Aesthetics can be defined as the means for organizing, thinking, feeling, and perceiving the world. Learning to see and value these elements can help us have a richer life that includes an appreciation for the beauty of things in our environment. This sensitivity to the environment can be developed through the senses: sight, sound, touch, and taste. Sensory experiences expand the way the world is viewed and understood.

Young children learn to recognize and enjoy the beautiful things that exist in their environment when provided with experiences that nurture the senses. Children love to go on nature walks, during which they can touch moss, see a spiderweb, or hear birds singing. A teacher can help identify these features as they walk though the park, increasing children's awareness of the special elements. Young children are excited when a teacher brings a bouquet from her flower garden. They want to explore the flowers through their senses by touching, smelling, and admiring the arrangement. They may choose to represent the bouquet with paints in the art area, working to match the colors they have seen. They may talk about the smell and how it made their noses tingle. Or, they may choose not to do any of these things, and simply enjoy the flowers. Any of these approaches is appropriate for young children and should be appreciated.

Each person must determine what they appreciate and value. It is the individual who decides what is beautiful or touches her heart. Young children should be allowed to determine what they find beautiful and experience it in a way they find meaningful. The teacher and parent can help the child question, wonder, and enjoy the things around them. By drawing attention to the pattern of the footprints in the snow or the stack of beautiful stones on a wall, adults help children "see" these wonderful elements, and help them be sensitive to their environment (Mayesky, 2006).

An early childhood classroom should include opportunities for children to see and touch beautiful things. When a teacher includes a poster of the painting, *Mother and Child,* by Mary Cassatt on the board in the classroom, some children will pose questions and enjoy the artwork. When an African drum is added to the music center, some children will enjoy both the sounds it produces and the texture of the tough leather that is strung around the opening. These thoughtful additions, selected by a knowledgeable teacher, provide the stimulus for aesthetic development in the early childhood classroom.

Assessment of Creativity

In 1966, E. Paul Torrance developed a series of tests to measure creativity, *Torrance Tests of Creative Thinking: Technical Norms Manual.* After years of use, this multifaceted instrument seems to have validity and reliability. Since it is individually administered, it is not frequently used in early childhood classrooms. Today, assessment is viewed as the process of observing, recording, and documenting children's work and abilities. This information can be used to make curriculum decisions, determine progress of individual children, identify learning problems, and help a child evaluate his own progress (Crosser, 2005; Katz, 1997).

Creativity and the arts are very difficult to assess using tests. Rather than test, in creativity and the arts, appropriate assessment should include **observation,** documentation, collections of student work, photographs, checklists, event sampling, and language samples. These items can be included in portfolios, and demonstrate growth and understanding of the child in these areas. Additional information about assessment is included in the chapters related to play, art, music, movement, and integrated curriculum.

Young Children's Creative Abilities

❝The creative mind plays with the objects it loves.❞
C. Jung, 1921
(in Fitzhenry, 1993)

All children are creative during their early years of development. It is up to parents, teachers, and caregivers to support their creativity so that as they grow older, they can continue to be creative and self-actualized people.

Examples of creativity in young children include:

- inventing songs or using new words to familiar songs (music).
- painting different lines, shapes, and colors (art).
- experimenting with building different types of structures (blocks).
- using movement to express a feeling or thought (movement).
- taking on roles and acting out events (play).
- concentrating on a project for a long period of time.
- organizing or grouping items in their environment (math).
- using expressive language and creating new words (language).
- telling a story (drama).
- creating a dress-up outfit (art and play).

These behaviors are active, child-initiated, and displayed by most children at various times during the early years of development. Torrance (1969) believed that everyone is creative if given the opportunity.

It is impossible to identify all the characteristics of creative children and the many different combinations that exist. These observable behaviors help us recognize creativity in young children and appreciate their special abilities. However, these characteristics alone do not provide a total understanding of the complex workings that occur in the creative mind.

❀ INDIVIDUAL DIFFERENCES

Although creativity is part of the developmental process, children express creativity in individual ways. The process is influenced by the unique characteristics that emerge from each child. There is no profile that fits all creative children. Instead, each creative child possesses attributes that are combined in a special way. The environment in which the child lives interacts with individual abilities to produce even more variations (Tegano, Moran, & Sawyers, 1991). In this reciprocal relationship, the child influences his environment and, in turn, the environment affects the child.

A young child may be visually oriented and fascinated by shapes, patterns, and colors. If this child lives in a home where the father is a sculptor, the combination of her visually oriented traits and the opportunity to live in an artistic environment certainly will have an impact on the child's visual arts development.

Early childhood is characterized as a highly creative period. It is perhaps the most creative phase in human development. All races and all people share this creative time (Cobb, 1977). Unfortunately, the creativity seen in preschoolers often is not maintained throughout life. Torrance (1962) reported a decline in creativity when children enter kindergarten. He also noted a significant slump between the third and fourth grade, and another between seventh and eighth grade. For many children, changes in the school environment can inhibit the growth of creative thinking instead of maintaining the momentum that was present in the early years.

A variety of dress-up clothes in a center encourage pretend play.

Torrance also observed that the two most powerful inhibitors to creativity during the early years seemed to be a premature attempt to eliminate fantasy and/or play and the practice that allows children to learn only what is expected.

✿ ENVIRONMENTAL CONDITIONS FOR CREATIVITY

The environment consists of people, places, objects, and experiences. All of these elements can have an impact on the development of young children. Children need real experiences as well as sources of inspiration to develop creatively. For example, the young child who has been to a home repair center with his parents can collect new ideas to use in the woodworking center. Or the child who has helped his dad prepare dinner will have more ideas for creating snacks. Children can use these real experiences to enrich their participation in the classroom.

An analogy that clarifies the relationship between the environment and creativity is a kaleidoscope (Parnes, 1967; Schirrmacher, 2006). The more colorful pieces included in the drum of a kaleidoscope, the greater the variety of possible shapes, colors, and patterns. In creativity, the more experiences a child has with people, places, or materials, the more possibilities will exist for use in creative activities. Young children's worlds should be filled with interesting experiences that build on their level of development. These should include many opportunities to experiment and combine a variety of materials and objects in different ways, and should allow them to make choices and work on projects across time.

In the classroom, an environment that will foster creativity should include the following elements (Fleith, 2000):

- providing time to think creatively
- rewarding creative ideas and products
- providing choices in activities and materials
- encouraging sensible risks
- accepting mistakes
- providing opportunities to explore the environment
- looking at others' views
- finding individual interests
- questioning ideas and problems

✿ THE IMPORTANCE OF THE CREATIVE ARTS

The creative arts have been an important part of many early childhood programs for a long time. In the early 1900s, Patty Hill Smith blended Froebel's methods and John Dewey's philosophy to create a curriculum that provided the foundation for kindergarten practice in the United States. One of her major contributions was the founding of the laboratory nursery school at Columbia University Teachers College, which became the model for training early childhood educators. Her second innovation was organizing the National Association for Nursery Education, which led to the development of today's early childhood professional organizations. From that time until the present, the arts have been viewed as important to the development of children. Many globally recognized experts strongly support the inclusion of play and the creative arts in programs for young children.

Kieran Egan (1997) wrote about "The Arts as the Basis of Education." He challenges educators to "stimulate thinking" through the use of the creative arts. Lella

Gandini, representative of the highly acclaimed Reggio Emilia schools in Italy, provides support for the integration of the arts into early childhood programs. The Reggio Emilia program demonstrates the importance of the arts and their effective integration throughout the early years. Italian children's in-depth projects, often lasting for more than a month, have served as an inspiration for early childhood programs around the world. These amazing projects demonstrate the unique capabilities of young children.

In 1990, the Association of Childhood Education International (ACEI) published *The Child's Right to the Expressive Arts: Nurturing the Imagination as Well as the Intellect,* a position paper written by Mary Renck Jalongo. This paper, endorsed by an international group of educators, focused on the rights of children to participate in the expressive arts. In 2003, ACEI published another position paper focusing on *The Child's Right to Creative Thought and Expression* (Jalongo, 2003). The professional organization endorsed the belief that "creative expression depends not on talent alone, but also on motivation, interest, effort, and opportunity. The creative process, contrary to popular opinion, is socially supported, culturally influenced, and collaboratively achieved."

The 2003 ACEI position paper defined creativity and the need to expand related experiences based on current theory and research. The position paper explained that "creative expression depends not on talent alone, but also on motivation, interest, effort and opportunity. The creative process, contrary to popular opinion, is socially supported, culturally influenced, and collaboratively achieved" (Jalongo, 2003, p. 218). Some challenges to the development of creativity are identified as redefining creative teaching, providing students with role models who are persistent in creative thinking, and encouraging educational institutions to focus on creative thinking that children will need in the future.

The position paper concludes by saying that every child has a right to creative experiences. If creativity is included in programs for young children, they will develop connections between imagination, thought, and creative expression. This powerful paper provides research, writings, and interdisciplinary examples that demonstrate the essential need for the inclusion of creative thinking in programs that serve young children. The entire paper, *The Child's Right to Creative Thought and Expression,* written by Mary Renck Jalongo (2003), is included in Chapter 10.

Across the nation, teachers are beginning to promote creative thinking. According to Amabile (1989), teachers who encourage creative thinking in children are helping them become lifelong problem-solvers. This will help society progress, as they come up with new and better ways to solve problems.

A report by the J. Paul Getty Trust (Wolfensohn & Williams, 1993) concluded that the arts contribute to an overall culture of excellence in schools. They provide an effective way of connecting children to each other and understanding the creative people who came before them. The arts help to establish relationships across traditional disciplines and to connect ideas.

Professionals recognize the importance of providing opportunities for young children to develop in all domains: socioemotional, psychomotor, and cognitive. The creative arts, music, drama, movement, and the visual arts are essential in nurturing development in early childhood education (Fox & Diffily, 2000).

Visual Arts support symbolic representation and thinking, by using varied techniques and materials. This art provides a way to communicate ideas, express feelings, and challenge thinking by combining materials in two- and three-dimensional ways.

> "Teachers in Reggio Emilia believe that all children have the right to quality programs that promote aesthetic and creative development."
>
> *R. New, 1995*

Music provides the sounds, rhythms, melodies, texture, and form that are used to create songs. Music engages the affective domain with cognition and often includes the psychomotor domain. It connects people, as they gain understanding of their culture and the culture of others.

Drama includes the opportunities to pretend, role-play, create scripts, and participate in meaningful enactments. This creative art can be used to encourage self-confidence, while group dramatic experiences can encourage collaboration with others.

Movement encourages the use of the body, supports physical development, and includes opportunities to use creativity in a different way. The bodily-kinesthetic intelligence is essential to learning.

Each of these creative arts provides a unique way to learn, use problem-solving, and identify personal strengths. The creative arts can be studied as unconnected identities or interwoven into a fabric that is composed of many different ways of learning and finding personal fulfillment. When the creative arts are integrated into the curriculum and units of study, it is essential that each art retain its integrity and not be absorbed into the academic content. The arts have and will make the following three important contributions to people's lives (Eisner, 2003):

- The arts provide a way to express meanings. A monument to the Holocaust victims and the Vietnam Wall are examples of art being used to express deep emotional feelings.

- The arts provide distinctive ways to think in unique ways through sight, sound, and movement. A painting by Van Gogh, an opera by Puccini, and a Scottish fling are all unique ways of experiencing the world.

- The arts improve the quality of experiences, by appreciating aesthetics. Appreciating the beauty of the wildflowers along an interstate highway, the smile of a baby, or cactus in the dessert, add new dimension to life.

The arts provide a special way of seeing, enjoying, and experiencing what is uniquely positive for a developing person or learning child.

Several groups have developed standards for arts education. The Kennedy Center has created national standards for the arts, specifically for K–4. These competencies are described as "What every young American should know and be able to do in the arts." The K–4 National Standards for Arts Education in dance/movement, music, dramatic arts, and visual arts are included at the end of Chapter 10.

At a time when there is a push for higher academic standards and more testing, it is important to recognize the importance of the arts. What is required for workers at all levels is that they be creative thinkers who can work well independently and with others. Schools can no longer train people for specific tasks. Instead, education must provide training for solving problems, skills, and strategies. No person can know all that is important. We must encourage the development of active learners who know how to work collaboratively, have the courage of their convictions, and are willing to try new things. The arts can help develop these abilities (Perrin, 1994).

Critical Time

It is important to develop creativity during the early years of a child's life. The attitude of being creative—finding the unknown challenge, coming up with many ideas, persisting on a difficult task, and having original thoughts—is established early in life. It appears that these attitudes, once established, will continue later in life (Lowenfeld & Brittain, 1987). Over 20 years ago, Scott was in my preschool classroom. He was always building unusual and intricate structures in the block center. On one occasion, he used wooden twigs that he had collected for his forest ranger station. He covered the floor of the station with scrap pieces of cardboard. Today, Scott is an architect who creates environment-friendly buildings.

Eleanor Duckworth (1996), the author of *The Having of Wonderful Ideas: And Other Essays on Teaching and Learning,* asked what kind of people we want to live with in our society. She concluded that if we want people who are confident, who think about what they are doing, who see potential and possibilities, and who ask questions rather than simply follow commands, then we must create an environment that nurtures these qualities. To have adults who demonstrate these capabilities, we must provide opportunities for this development during the early years. If children are given challenging activities, interesting materials, and meaningful opportunities, they will come up with creative ideas. As they grow and develop, they will continue to come up with wonderful ideas and learn that they have their own way of doing things. These early experiences provide the foundation for developing children and, later, adults who can respond to the challenges and rewards of society (Duckworth, 1996).

Personal Development

The arts provide another way of learning about the world. They provide the opportunity to explore and examine art materials, to recognize the capabilities of the body in motion, and to enjoy the sounds of music. The arts allow us to discover new ways to feel good about ourselves in a rich and varied environment. The open-ended nature of the arts allows us to work at a level that is personally satisfying, and to find success and enjoyment in an important area of development.

Cultural Diversity through the Arts

Play and the arts provide a way to communicate across cultures and regions. **Multicultural education** often includes race, values, parenting styles, food, and

A sticky wall invites a child to attach leaves for a display.

clothing. Music, visual arts, dance, and drama provide an avenue for appreciating and understanding others. These various art forms provide a vehicle for young children to communicate in a nonverbal way. Creative experiences from various cultures provide a supportive environment for children less familiar with the classroom community. The arts can help children from different ethnic groups feel accepted by their peers as they play, dance, make music, or use puppets (Tubba, 1992). The arts help us understand how we are different as well as how we are the same.

Goldberg (2001) developed principles that focus on making connections between multicultural education and the arts. They relate to both the content and process of creativity, and can guide the many ways the arts influence learning for all children:

The following points illustrate some of the connections between multicultural education and the arts.

1. The arts expand the expressive opportunities and range of learning approaches to children.
2. The arts provide freedom of expression for second-language learners.
3. The arts are an avenue for building self-esteem.
4. The arts encourage collaboration and group harmony.
5. The arts empower students and teachers.
6. The arts develop a teacher's awareness of the different abilities of children.
7. The arts provide authentic cultural voices that support learning.

In addition, the arts provide opportunities for individual development and build a sense of community where all are respected. Because the arts are expressive, they bring new understanding to people and events being studied. They provide documentation for struggles, celebrations, and living together in our diverse and global world.

Working together on art projects builds a sense of community.

SUMMARY

In a rapidly changing world, we must develop programs for young children that include the competencies they will need now and in the future. The experiences provided should nurture the child and include all domains important for total development. Each domain offers special features that contribute to the enrichment of the environment and the experiences of young children. The creative arts provide an avenue for learning and experiencing that is uniquely different. Their inclusion, during the early years of children's lives, establishes a rich foundation that adapts to change, provides joy, and inspires involvement. An appropriate, well-designed program will encourage each child to reach his potential in an environment that is interesting, challenging, and supportive of individual creativity.

 KEY TERMS

accommodation
aesthetics
assimilation
behaviorist theory
bodily-kinesthetic intelligence
brainstorming
collaboration
constructivist theory
convergent thinking
Creative Problem-Solving (CPS) model
creative process
creativity
critical periods
cultural creativity
display
divergent thinking
elaboration
empirical evidence
flexibility
flow
fluency
holistic
humanistic theory
illumination

imagination
incubation
interpersonal intelligence
intrapersonal intelligence
intrinsic motivation
logical-mathematical intelligence
multicultural education
musical intelligence
naturalistic intelligence
observation
originality
painting
personal creativity
preparation
psychoanalytic theory
psychologically safe environment
schemas
self-actualized
social constructivist theory
verbal-linguistic intelligence
verification
visual-spatial intelligence
zone of proximal development (ZPD)

 REFLECTION

1. What is cultural creativity?
2. What is personal creativity?
3. Compare process and product as they relate to creativity.
4. Identify the steps that often are included in creative problem-solving.
5. What are the components of creativity as describe by E. Paul Torrance?
6. How do theories contribute to your understanding of the nature and importance of creativity?
7. Explain how the theory of multiple intelligences emphasizes the different ways children and adults learn.

8. Are young children creative? Describe how you support your belief.

9. What has caused the renewed interest in young children and their participation in the creative arts?

THINKING ABOUT THE OBSERVATION OF CREATIVITY

1. What observation of Jamil demonstrated his creativity?

2. Can you determine how this classroom environment nurtured Jamil's development?

3. How did Jamil's teacher respond to his individual needs?

POSSIBILITIES FOR ADULT LEARNERS

Activity: Theory to Practice

Goal: To determine the usefulness of theories as they relate to understanding creativity in young children.

Materials: Paper and pencil.

Procedure:

1. After reflecting on the many different theories discussed in this chapter, determine the one that provides the most insight for you.

2. Describe ways this theory could influence your teaching in an early childhood classroom.

3. Write a scenario that demonstrates this application of a theory.

Activity: Creative Child

Goal: To observe young children and recognize the creative behaviors they exhibit.

Materials: Paper and pencil.

Procedure:

1. Observe young children in a natural setting such as at home, in child care, or on a playground.

2. Record the behaviors that demonstrate creative abilities or problem-solving skills.

3. Share these observations in class.

Activity: *The Ducks That Could Not Swim* Story

Goal: To recognize that learned behavior could restrict thinking.

Materials: *The Ducks That Could Not Swim* (Appendix A).

Procedure:

1. Read or tell *The Ducks That Could Not Swim* to the class.

2. Pose questions such as:
   - Why did the ducks not swim in the pond?
   - How did they come to believe they could not swim?

• Why were the ducks unable to change their behavior and swim?
• Why is it difficult to think in new ways?

OPEN-ENDED ACTIVITIES FOR YOUNG CHILDREN

PreK–K

Activity: Box Possibilities

Goal: To develop flexible thinking using literature as a stimulus for the process.

Materials: The book *Christina Katerina and the Box* and three cardboard boxes.

Procedure:

1. During group time, discuss the cardboard boxes that you have brought. Include questions, such as:
   • What might have come in the box?
   • How did the box get to your house?
   • What could you put in the box?
2. Read the book *Christina Katerina and the Box* aloud.
3. Reflect on how Christina used boxes in different ways.
4. How would you use a box? Brainstorm a list of ideas with the children.
5. Pose the question, "What could you create if you used two boxes together?"
6. Ask the children to sketch their ideas on paper.
7. Place boxes and various containers in the art center for the children to construct their ideas in three-dimensional form.

Primary Grades

Activity: Squiggly Lines

Goal: To elaborate on a form created by another child while using art materials.

Materials: Art paper, magic markers, crayons, chalk, watercolors, and scrap colored paper.

Procedure:

1. Give each child a piece of art paper.
2. Ask each child to draw a squiggly line on the paper with a dark marker.
3. Let the children exchange sheets of paper.
4. Suggest that each child incorporate the squiggly line on the paper into a drawing, or to create an object, place, or collection.
5. Provide time for the thinking and creating processes to occur.
6. Have the children share their creations with others.
7. A display can be designed for "Our Creations from Squiggles."

ADDITIONAL READING

Berk, L., & Winsler, A. (1995). *Scaffolding children's learning: Vygotsky and early childhood education.* Washington, DC: National Association for the Education of Young Children.

Blythe, T., & Gardner, H. (1990). A school for all intelligences. *Educational Leadership, 47*(7), 33–37.

Campbell, L., Campbell, B., & Dickinson, D. C. (1996). *Teaching and learning through multiple intelligences.* Needham Heights, MA: Simon & Schuster.

Chenfeld, M. B. (1995). *Creative experiences for young children* (2nd ed.). Fort Worth, TX: Harcourt Brace Jovanovich.

Cohen, M. D., & Hoot, J. L. (1997). Educating through the arts: An introduction. *Childhood Education, 73*(6), 338–341.

Davis, G. A. (1992). *Creativity is forever.* Dubuque, IA: Kendall/Hunt.

Edwards, C. P., & Springate, K. (1995). The lion comes out of the stone: Helping young children achieve their creative potential. *Dimensions of Early Childhood, 23*(4), 24–29.

Edwards, L. C., & Nabors, M. L. (1993). The creative arts process: What it is and what it is not. *Young Children, 48*, 77–81.

Eisner, E. (1992). The misunderstood role of the arts in human development. *Phi Delta Kappan, 73*(8), 591–593.

Fowler, C. (1990). Recognizing the role of artistic intelligences. *Music Educator's Journal, 77*(1), 24–27.

Haiman, P. E. (1991). Developing a sense of wonder in young children. *Young Children, 46*(6), 52–53.

Hoffman, S., & Lamme, L. L. (1989). *The expressive arts: Learning from the inside out.* Wheaton, MD: Association for Childhood Education International.

Hughes, F. P. (1998). *Children, play, and development* (3rd ed.). Boston: Allyn & Bacon.

Isaksen, S. G. (1992). *Nurturing creative talents: Lessons from industry about needed work-life skills.* Buffalo, NY: The Creative Solving Group.

Rankin, B. (1992). Inviting children's creativity: A story of Reggio Emilia, Italy. *Child Care Information Exchange, 85*, 30–35.

Torrance, E. P. (1987). Teaching for creativity. In S. G. Isaksen (Ed.), *Frontiers of creativity arts: Beyond the basics* (pp. 189–215). Buffalo, NY: Bearly Limited.

 ## CHILDREN'S LITERATURE CONNECTION

Gauch, P. L. (1971). *Christina Katerina and the box.* New York: Coward, McCann & Geoghegan, Inc.
Christina finds many uses for the large box that housed the new refrigerator. (PreK–2)

Hoban, T. (1988). *Look! Look! Look!* New York: Scholastic.
Photographs of familiar objects are viewed through a cutout hole, then in their entirety. Children can use problem-solving skills as they decide what the mystery object is. (PreK–1)

Pfanner, L. (1989). *Louise builds a house.* New York: Orchard.
Louise builds a marvelous fantasy house full of things she loves, then gives it to her sister. (PreK–1)

Pfanner, L. (1990). *Louise builds a boat.* New York: Orchard.
Louise imagines building her own boat with a wooden deck for games, a crow's nest for watching dolphins, and a figurehead to paint. (PreK–1)

Pinkwater, D. M. (1977). *The big orange splot.* New York: Scholastic.
When a splot of orange paint accidentally lands on his home, Mr. Plumbean is inspired to repaint his house and his neighbors can't believe their eyes. (K–3)

Rubin. C. M., & Fowler, C. (2003). *Eleanor, Ellatony, Ellencake, and me.* Columbus, OH: Gingham Dog Press.
The various members of Eleanor's family give her very creative nicknames, but she finally decides on one of her own. (K–3)

Shaw, C. G. (1947). *It looked like spilt milk.* New York: Scholastic.
A mystery book for young children presents a continuously changing white shape silhouetted against a blue background that challenges readers to guess what it is. (PreK–1)

 For additional resources involving creativity and the arts with young children, visit our Web site at **www.earlychilded.delmar.com**

✹ REFERENCES

Amabile, T. M. (1983). *The social psychology of creativity.* New York: Springer-Verlag.

Amabile, T. M. (1989). *Growing up creative.* New York: Crown.

Amabile, T. M. (1996). *Creativity in context: Update to the social psychology of creativity.* Boulder, CO: Westview Press.

Applewhite, A., Evans, W. R., III, & Frothingham, A. (Eds.). (1992). *And I quote.* New York: St. Martin's Press.

Arcangelo, D. (2000, November). How does the brain develop? A conversation with Steven Peterson. *Educational Leadership, 58*(3), 68–71.

Barron, F. (1988). Putting creativity to work. In R. J. Sternberg (Ed.), *The nature of creativity* (pp. 76–98). New York: Cambridge University Press.

Bloom, B., Englehart, M., Furst, E., Hill, W., & Krathwohl, D. (1956). *Taxonomy of educational objectives: The classification of educational goals. Handbook 1, Cognitive domain.* New York: Longmans Green.

Bredekamp, S. (1993). *Developmental appropriate practice in early childhood programs serving children from birth through eight.* Washington, DC: National Association for the Education of Young Children.

Cobb, E. (1977). *The ecology of imagination in childhood.* New York: Columbia University Press.

Crosser, S. (2005). *What do we know about early childhood education? Research based practice.* Clifton Park, NY: Thomson Delmar Learning.

Csikszentmihalyi, M. (1997). *Creativity: Flow and the psychology of discovery and invention.* New York: HarperCollins.

Diamond, M., & Hopson, J. (1999). *Magic trees of the mind: How to nurture your child's intelligence, creativity, and healthy emotions from birth through adolescence.* New York: Penguin Group.

Dixon-Krauss, L. (1996). *Vygotsky in the classroom: Mediated literacy instruction and assessment.* White Plains, NY: Longman.

Duckworth, E. R. (1996). *The having of wonderful ideas: And other essays on teaching and learning.* New York: Teachers College Press, Teachers College, Columbia University.

Durie, R. (Spring 1997). An interview with Howard Gardner. *Mindshift connection.* Tuscon: Zephyr Press.

Edwards, L. (2002). *The creative arts: A process approach for teachers and children.* (3rd ed.). Upper Saddle River, NJ: Merrill Prentice Hall.

Egan, K. (1997). The arts as the basics of education. *Childhood Education, 73*(6), 341–345.

Eisner, E. W. (2003). The arts and the creation of mind. *Language Arts, 80*(5), 340–344.

Fitzhenry, R. I. (Ed.). (1993). *The Harper book of quotations* (3rd ed.). New York: HarperCollins.

Fleith, D. S. (2000, April). Teacher and student perceptions of creativity in the classroom environment. *Roeper Review, 22*(3), 148.

Fowler, C. (1990). Recognizing the role of artistic intelligences. *Music Educator's Journal, 77*(1), 24–27.

Fox, J. E., & Diffily, D. (2000). Integrating the visual arts—building young children's knowledge, skills, and confidence. *Dimensions of Early Childhood, 29*(1), 3–10.

Freud, S. (1964). *An outline of psychoanalysis: Standard edition of the works of Sigmund Freud.* London: Hogarth.

Gardner, H. (1983). *Frames of mind: The theory of multiple intelligences.* New York: Basic Books.

Gardner, H. (1991). *The unschooled mind.* New York: Basic Books.

Gardner, H. (1993). *Creating minds: An anatomy of creativity seen through the lives of Freud, Einstein, Picasso, Stravinsky, Eliot, Graham, and Gandhi.* New York: Basic Books.

Gardner, H. (1993). *Multiple intelligences: The theory in practice.* New York: Basic Books.

Goldberg, M. (2001). *Arts and learning: An integrated approach to teaching and learning in multicultural and multilingual settings* (2nd ed.). New York: Addison Wesley Longman.

Guilford, J. P. (1956). The structure of intellect. *Psychological Bulletin, 53*, 267–293.

Healy, J. M. (1994). *Your child's growing mind: A guide to learning and brain development from birth to adolescence.* New York: Doubleday.

Hendrick, J. (1986). *Total learning: Curriculum for the young child.* Columbus, OH: Merrill.

Holden, C. (1987). Creativity and the troubled mind. *Psychology Today, 21*(4), 9–10.

Isenberg, J., & Jalongo, M. R. (1997). *Creative expression and play in early childhood.* Upper Saddle River, NJ: Merrill.

Jalongo, M. R. (1990). The child's right to the expressive arts: Nurturing the imagination as well as the intellect. *Childhood Education, 66*, 195–201.

Jalongo, M. R. (2003, Summer). A position paper of the Association for Childhood Education International: The child's right to creative thought and expression. *Childhood Education, 79*(4), 218–228.

Jensen, E. (1998). *Teaching with the brain in mind.* Alexandria, VA: Association for Supervision and Curriculum Development.

Kagan, J. (1984). *The nature of the child.* New York: Basic Books.

Kashdan, T. B., & Fincham, F. D. (2002). Facilitating creativity by regulating curiosity. *American Psychologist, 57*(5), 373–374.

Katz, L. G. (1997). *A developmental approach to assessment of young children.* ERIC Digest (ERIC Document Reproduction Service No. ED 407172).

Lowenfeld, V., & Brittain, W. L. (1987). *Creative and mental growth.* New York: Pearson Education.

Maslow, A. (1970). *Motivation and personality.* New York: Harper & Row.

Mayesky, M. (2006). *Creative activities for young children* (8th ed.). Clifton Park, NY: Thomson Delmar Learning.

McCain, M., & Mustard, F. (1999). *The early years report.* Ontario, Canada: Reference Group Report to the Minister Responsible for Children, 28.

New, R. (1995). *Contributions from Reggio to issues of advocacy and social policy in the United States.* Presentation in Connection with The Hundred Languages Exhibit. Chicago, IL.

Osborn, A. F. (1963). *Applied imagination.* New York: Scribner.

Parnes, S. J. (1967). *Creative behavior guidebook.* New York: Charles Scribner's Sons.

Perkins, D. (1981). *The mind's best work.* Cambridge, MA: Harvard University Press.

Perrin, S. (1994). Education in the arts is an education for life. *Kappan, 75*(6), 452–453.

Piaget, J. (1960). *The child's conception of the world.* Totowa, NJ: Littlefield, Adams.

Piaget, J., & Inhelder, B. (1969). *The psychology of the child.* New York: Basic Books.

Rogers, C. R. (1962). Toward a theory of creativity. In S. J. Parnes & H. F. Harding (Eds.), *A source book for creative thinking* (pp. 63–72). New York: Scribner.

Sanders, N. M. (1966). *Classroom questions: What kinds?* New York: HarperCollins College Division.

Schilpp, P. (1949). *Albert Einstein: Philosopher scientist.* Evanston, IL: Library of Living Philosophers.

Schirrmacher, R. (2006). *Art & creative development for young children* (4th ed.). Clifton Park, NY: Thomson Delmar Learning.

Skinner, B. F. (1971). *Beyond freedom and dignity.* New York: Knopf.

Tegano, D. W., Moran, J. D., & Sawyers, J. K. (1991). *Creativity in early childhood classrooms.* Washington, DC: National Education Association.

Torrance, E. P. (1962). *Guiding creative talent.* Englewood Cliffs, NJ: Prentice-Hall.

Torrance, E. P. (1964). *Creativity: Progress and potential.* New York: McGraw-Hill.

Torrance, E. P. (1966). *Torrance tests of creative thinking: Technical norms manual.* Lexington, MA: Personnel Press.

Torrance, E. P. (1969). *Creativity.* Belmont, CA: Fearon.

Torrance, E. P. (1969). *Dimensions in early learning: Creativity.* Sioux Falls, SD: Adaptation Press.

Torrance, E. P. (1992). Creativity. Cited in R. Hill, *Finding creativity for children.* Paper prepared for Leadership Accessing Symposium, Lafayette, IN.

Torrance, E. P. (1993). The beyonders in a thirty-year study of creative achievement. *Roeper Review, 15*, 131–134.

Trostle, S. L., & Yawkey, T. D. (1982). Creative thinking and the education of young children: The fourth basic skill. *International Journal of Early Childhood, 14*(2), 67–71.

Tubba, J. (1992). *Cultural diversity and creativity in the classroom.* Flagstaff, AZ: World Organization for Early Childhood Education.

Vygotsky, L. S. (1962). *Thought and language.* Cambridge, MA: MIT Press.

Wallas, G. (1926). *The art of thought.* New York: Harcourt, Brace & World.

Williams, F. E. (1982). *Developing children's creativity at home and school. G/C/T (Gifted, Creative, and Talented), 24*(1), 2–6.

Wolfensohn, J. D., & Williams, H. M. (1993). *The power of the arts to transform education.* Los Angeles: J. Paul Getty Trust.

Wood, S. J. (1996). Implementing a successful affective curriculum. *Theory and Practice, 33*(2), 126–128.

THE CREATIVE TEACHER

CHAPTER 2

This chapter examines the relationship between the creative teacher and the classroom that nurtures creativity in young children. Characteristics of creative teachers will be investigated, along with the impact of these factors on environmental design. Included are examples of teachers who have taken "creative risk" and tried doing things in different ways. The results of their adventures and the effects on young children's thinking will be explored.

After studying this chapter, you will be able to:
- **Identify the characteristics of a creative teacher.**
- **Name the elements of a classroom that nurture creativity.**
- **Use phrases that encourage children's creativity.**
- **Describe the value of using open-ended activities and materials with children.**
- **Plan an effective physical environment that encourages creativity and includes the arts.**

OBSERVATION OF CREATIVITY

Marie is a kindergarten teacher in an urban elementary school. Today, she arrives at her classroom early so she can add potting soil and hand gardening tools to her new greenhouse center. Marie has been planning this greenhouse center for several weeks. She asked parents to bring seeds, plant supplies, and garden catalogs for the area. She collected plastic tubs, pictures of flowers, plastic plants, and a roll of plastic sheeting to create a canopy over the center. She is excited about the new center and is anticipating how the children will respond to the area.

During circle time, Marie reads *Planting a Rainbow* by Lois Ehlert (1988). The children discuss the interesting plantings that are illustrated in the book. Several children are intrigued by the flowers that come from bulbs and ask questions about the process. Marie makes a note of which children are interested in bulbs. She shares with the class that a dogwood tree is blooming at her home and that she has brought some branches for them to enjoy. After the new greenhouse center is introduced, the children make their choices and go to work.

During their time in the greenhouse center, Marie moves around the classroom, writing notes on her clipboard about specific

WHAT WAS OBSERVED?

Marie demonstrated her creativity in the design of her classroom environment. She added a unique center to her classroom, included interesting props, and added beautiful items. She also noted the specific interest displayed by the children and planned ways to incorporate their ideas. Her flexible thinking allowed her to blend her plans with the emerging interests of the children. She reflected on the children's involvement and was able to generate several ideas to make changes that will enrich their experiences. Marie is a teacher who is modeling creativity. She has developed an interesting environment that will inspire the young children in her classroom to think and participate in new ways.

children's participation, language use, and developing skills. Later, she will add these annotations to the children's portfolios. She also observes the play that is going on and thinks of ways to extend or enrich the activities with props or other materials.

At the end of the day, Marie reflects on the activities of the day. She thinks about the greenhouse center and how the children participated. She asks herself, What materials were most interesting? What learning was occurring? What could be changed? How could more literacy be included? She also recalled that several children were interested in bulbs during circle time. Tomorrow, she will bring some bulbs to add to the center, building on that interest.

The world today represents the products of many creative people interacting with a changing environment. These changes are complex and challenge us in many different ways. Torrance (1992) stated that never before has there been such a need to create a climate that encourages the development of creative and inventive talent. Currently, many companies have responded to this growing need by offering **creativity training** to their employees. They believe that creative thinking is essential to being globally competitive and able to develop new technology.

Society needs people with creative problem-solving abilities and strategies to address the ever-increasing issues of society, education, and technology. Creative thinking can help adults achieve satisfying lives (Kerka, 1999). Our schools must lay the foundation to equip our children with the capability to deal with complex problems and solve them in creative ways. During the early years, children need opportunities to develop ingenuity and the capacity to creatively problem-solve. This can only occur if we have creative teachers working with young children during this critical period of development (Abdallah, 1996).

EARLY CHILDHOOD TEACHERS

Early childhood teachers are the most important element in making the classroom a wonderful learning place. The effective teacher learns about her children, shapes the curriculum, sets up the environment, and encourages the learning that she values. Most early childhood teachers are dedicated to nurturing the development of the **whole child,** which includes creativity and the creative arts. Central to the development of creativity is a teacher who realizes that creativity is not narrowly defined as an art or music program, but is much broader and can be nurtured in every area of learning. Teachers who understand the importance of creativity and the arts design their classroom so these areas are an essential part of the environment and are integrated across the curriculum.

Creativity can occur as children use paper-towel rolls to build a castle or as they choose musical instruments to accompany a story they are telling. Creative thinking occurs when children write a story, determine a way to measure the growth of plants in the greenhouse, or find a new way to use an art medium. Interactions within the creative environment are a powerful way to nurture creativity in children (Mellou, 1996). Teachers who understand the benefits of promoting creativity, as well as the barriers that stifle creative development, can design a supportive environment.

Teachers are being asked to use more creative approaches to facilitate learning with this new generation of children. Many old methods of rote memory or direct instruction are no longer effective tools. There is a new emphasis on the importance of child-directed learning and the design of classroom environments. When creativity is studied and understood, the guiding principles can give teachers valuable tools that can be used to make their classrooms exciting learning places (Simplicio, 2000).

Teaching methods have changed and so has the relationship between teacher and pupil. Generally, approaches are moving from predominantly teacher-directed or teacher-controlled practice toward a teacher and pupil interactional system in which discovery learning is an integral part of the process. In the past, many teachers controlled the delivery, pacing, and content presented. There was little variation for individual needs or interest, and two concerns have led to significant changes in these practices.

1. Great numbers of children were not learning how to think; they were unable to generalize from the specifics they were taught.

2. The burst of information has expanded the need to know into many different directions; no one is sure what the basics are.

It is obvious that new methods are needed. The focus has now shifted to helping children use creative thinking skills to

An interested teacher poses questions to toddlers about a small flower.

help them understand how to learn in a rapidly changing world (Torrance & Safter, 1986). Teachers cannot make children be creative. However, the teacher can provide a classroom that includes the ingredients that nurture children's unique abilities.

Teachers Can Be Creative

Creative teaching starts with the power of the teacher to be creative. Jeanrenaud and Bishop (1980) concluded that in order to promote creativity in others, we must be creative ourselves. Most early childhood teachers are creative, although they may not recognize this ability in themselves. Over the years, some teachers may have fallen into meeting expectations of conformity and compliance. As a result, they do not see themselves as creative people. But many teachers are very creative. For example, on a typical day, an early childhood teacher will choose appropriate books to read during group time, plan an interesting follow-up activity, add new items to spark center play, and decide what work will be included in a child's portfolio. All of these activities require creative thinking, flexibility, and elaboration. In the field of early childhood education, teachers have many opportunities to

"Children's creativity will be enhanced if teachers believe that children should be active learners with a sense of ownership and pride in their classroom."
T. M. Amabile, 1989

"The creative individual can not only have a new idea but he can appreciate such an idea."
J. Haefele, 1962

Sometimes, the creative teacher is playful with the children in her class.

nourish their own creativity and use the arts to expand their possibilities. Early childhood teachers who may feel they are not creative, can recapture their "creative spirit" as they work with young children. They can observe the children's creative activities, notice how they experience the world, and celebrate their vast capabilities for investigating.

Learn to Be a Child Again

We know that young children see and enjoy the world in special ways. You can be more creative if you use these child-like qualities. You can discover how to let your playful spirit grow and blossom again. Young children represent and typify total "aliveness" and a joy of living. Think about young children when you are around them. Are they cheerful, alert, eager, and open? Are they energetic, sensitive, friendly, and inquisitive? Are they also playful, expressive, spontaneous, and loveable? These child-like qualities are magical and are essential elements for a creative life.

THE ROAD TO CREATIVITY GUIDED BY YOUNG CHILDREN. How do these qualities match your attitudes about yourself and life?

Living in the moment. This is an incredible quality inherent in young children. They center on what they are doing and focus on the immediate situation. They have the ability to make the most of what they have at the current time. Permit yourself to experience the excitement of the moment and enjoy the everyday things you do.

Acceptance of the world. Children are unbelievably accepting and have the ability to take things as they come. As adults, we face many challenges and often wish things were different. Sometimes things can be changed or improved, but other times it is important to accept the way they are and do the best you can in the situation.

Sensitivity to the world around you. Young children are excited and interested in the smallest items in their world: the leaf on the ground or the stone on the sidewalk. There are many wonderful things in your world. Are you enjoying them? Do you notice the colors in the sunset or the dew on the pampas grass? Take a moment to watch a young child examine and experience the dandelion on the playground.

Happiness, laughter, and smiles. Children are usually happy people. And many adults have positive attitudes, too. Children are sometimes silly, make jokes, and laugh. Some adults take themselves too seriously and have forgotten to see the humor around them. Many believe that one of the most important qualities of a healthy life is a sense of humor.

Playful attitude. Young children play with ideas and experiment with materials. Adults need to nurture their playfulness. Take time to experiment or play with possibilities. Fool around with clay, walk in the woods, dress up in fun clothes, or play a board game. Take a fun break and the creative ideas will flow.

Think you are creative. Roger VonOech, author of *A Whack on the Side of the Head,* is a well-known business consultant on creative thinking. In his work, VonOech (1983) discovered one trait that distinguished creative employees from others: creative people thought they were creative.

Prize individuality. Notice creative ideas and unique individuals. What is special about these actions and people? How can you appreciate these differences and learn from the experiences and interactions? What are your unique talents? And are you nurturing those interests?

Take a risk. Young children are afraid of very little. Most of them jump into new experiences with little concern about possible failure. Try something different, and do something you have never done before. Taking these risks will stimulate your creative thinking, expand your interest, and allow you to venture into new areas.

Studies have found that children are more creative when working with creative teachers. Torrance (1965) found that kindergarten and primary school children made the most significant gains in creativity when they worked with creatively motivated teachers. The creative teacher who recognizes the importance of creative thinking can have a positive impact on the development of creativity in the classroom.

A child discovers that a ball can be created using tissue paper and glue.

❝The teacher, with the knowledge and attitudes about guiding the creative process, is the most important part of the environment.❞

R. S. Zener, 1995

✿ CHARACTERISTICS OF A CREATIVE TEACHER

The creative teacher understands children's development and uses this knowledge to make decisions about activities and materials that will be included in the classroom. He observes children and knows when to ask divergent questions or add unique materials to a work area. The creative teacher is playful and experiments with new ideas, materials, and approaches. Interactions with children and their developing projects are unpredictable, and teachers are often in the mist of ambiguity. Creative teachers are comfortable with temporary confusion and enjoy anticipating how the project will evolve (Tegano, Groves, & Catron, 1999). He encourages divergent and messy activities because he understands their importance. He searches for **novel** toys and activities that elicit interest and questioning. He provides choices for himself and the children. He is supportive of children's efforts and provides encouragement, rather than praise. For example, an encouraging comment might be, "You are really working hard on your mask," rather than, "Good job." He values children's unusual ideas. He asks questions that provide provocation and encourage thinking. The creative teacher finds ways to nurture this important ability, even in an environment that seems to stress teaching to a standardized test. He recognizes that competencies can be gained through creative activities and that these activities can produce children capable of solving difficult problems.

Many teachers in the **Reggio Emilia** school, reported to be the best early childhood program in the world, listen to, observe, and understand children. They serve as resources, and provide occasions of discovery and learning for the children in the Italian schools. Gandini (1992) explains that Reggio teachers are partners in the children's learning process. The Italian teachers enjoy discovering together with the children. The role of the teacher is both observer and learner who provides a wonderful model for the children to emulate.

The creative teacher is intrinsically motivated and interested in growing as a teacher. He is committed to attending conferences or seminars, reading a new book on teaching, or taking additional classes. He knows professional development leads to making changes within the classroom. Creative teachers are constantly looking for and trying out new approaches and ideas that will help improve their classrooms and the children's learning. For example, Joseph attends a conference and chooses sessions especially related to art. He collects several new recipes for clay and learns about a simple drying rack that he can add to the art center.

In a study by McGreevy (1990), a group of high school students were asked to identify the most creative teacher they had ever had. When analyzing their choices, some interesting patterns emerged. These students believed teachers were the main source of recognition for their creative abilities and talents. Many students identified the creative classroom environment as comfortable and where ideas flowed. Students frequently mentioned that creative teachers were funny and had a sense of humor. Other qualities mentioned included an open and accepting mind, a willingness to share their personal side, spontaneity in the classroom, and an understanding of and caring for individual students. They also mentioned that creative teachers managed to find unique ways to present material and that students were given choices in implementing assignments. Many of these characteristics are the same ingredients good teachers incorporate into their classrooms today.

Good and creative teachers are seldom satisfied with the way things are. They understand that past accomplishments do not guarantee future success. Creative teachers are constantly seeking new ways to improve their abilities, and they eagerly explore different avenues that lead to greater insight.

Poole (1980) identified several important roles the teacher can play in fostering creativity in children. These roles include teacher attitudes, communication, classroom atmosphere, and the teacher's ability to design a creative classroom.

TEACHER DISPOSITIONS

Characteristics of a Creative Teacher
(Teachers may possess some or all of these.)

- self-confident
- willing to try new ideas
- interested in many things
- flexible
- concerned about children's feelings
- appreciates beautiful things
- has a sense of humor
- reflects on his/her actions
- has many ideas
- may appear disorganized
- is a lifelong learner
- enjoys novel items and experiences
- not bothered by change
- persistent
- enjoys working with children

Building Trust

The teacher's attitude of trust is essential to developing creativity. She believes that children can choose activities that will interest and engage them. The teacher believes that children can participate in these activities without a great deal of adult-imposed regulations. Her focus is on the children becoming competent decision-makers and allowing them to become fully engaged in what interests them (Kamii & DeVries, 1978). The children know they are trusted to choose an activity and to work on it at their level. The teacher sees the children in the classroom as capable, and they respond by being competent.

This supportive attitude is demonstrated when the teacher follows a **teachable moment.** When children find an idea intriguing or look for expansions, she follows their lead. Support is not indiscriminate praise, but encouragement of the individual and his or her efforts (Shallcross, 1981). For example, when Jowanda brings an African flute into the classroom, all the children rush to examine the instrument. The observant teacher joins the group and poses questions about the flute. How is it played? Can Jowanda or a family member play the flute? What could the students use to make a flute? While this is happening, the teacher makes a mental note to bring in some books about African instruments to expand this budding interest of the children. She collects materials in the room that could be used to make a flute

> "Creativity is not a gift that few teachers possess and others envy. It is an ability that can be acquired and nurtured."
> *J. S. C. Simplicio,*
> *2000*

and adds them to the music center. The teacher recognizes that the children's interest in African musical instruments can be enjoyed and expanded into the study of music from another culture.

Caring Person

Linda Edwards (2002) conducted a long-term research project with her students who were studying to be early childhood educators. Over a 15-year period, she asked them to identify the characteristics of their favorite teacher. Her results indicated that her students' favorite teachers display positive affective characteristics, including caring, concern, interest, respect, and positive attitudes. Attributes related to knowledge and content information, although always included, were low on the list of words used to describe their favorite teachers.

Other researches have identified that effective teachers possess more warmth and empathy than ineffective teachers (Himsl & Lambert, 1993; Stout, 1999). In one study, effective and ineffective teachers were compared. The effective primary-grade teachers were enthusiastic, used more diverse techniques, and frequently encouraged children in their specific accomplishments. In these classrooms, the teacher helped children learn to be independent and able to do things on their own. Not surprisingly, the children in these effective classrooms were more engaged in meaningful activities and achieved more. The important conclusion from these research studies is that young children are more likely to exhibit positive growth and feel more positive about themselves if a teacher is enthusiastic and caring. Since effective teachers used diverse approaches that were challenging, the children in their classrooms were more engaged and self-regulated (Bohn, Roehrig, & Pressley, 2004).

To extend this farther, teachers who see children in a positive way, as capable and loveable, create more pleasant environments for their students. These environments help children feel comfortable and make them willing to take risks and think in different ways. For instance, a child may be building a runway for landing hot-air balloons or adding pieces of sandpaper to a mural to create a texture for touching. He knows that these "different" ideas will be accepted and valued by his teacher in this classroom.

Communication

The creative teacher communicates to children that they can try new things and that unconventional work is valued. Young children may not have the vocabulary needed to describe their thinking when working creatively. However, children can be helped to put their ideas into words. If the teacher describes a building structure as

The teacher observes when help is needed.

"unique," she can explain that the cardboard cylinders added a special dimension to the top. Later, she will hear the children describing their work as "unique." They begin to understand that ideas can be original and that words can be used to express the special qualities.

A teacher encourages students to think and express themselves creatively. Her confidence in the child's ability to think in new directions will influence the child's estimation of her own creative abilities (Mellou, 1996). The climate of the creative classroom is positive, and supports collaboration between teacher and children and children and children. The teacher works to establish this sense of trust over a long period of time. Each successful experience and interaction builds the feeling of trust within children in the classroom as they grow in confidence.

Classroom Atmosphere

Children benefit from an **atmosphere** that is relaxed and based on respect. The classroom atmosphere communicates to children that it is all right to take a risk or make a mistake. In this place, no one puts down another person's ideas or unusual answers. The children are able to explain what it is they are trying to do without being criticized or ridiculed. It is essential for them to develop an internal sense of worth in order to feel secure, take risks, try new things, or venture into the unknown. Therefore, the atmosphere needs to provide opportunities for children to govern their own behaviors and make choices. In this setting, children will develop self-confidence and begin to take risks regarding creative problem-solving, and in other areas of the curriculum.

Because each child is unique, the classroom climate must reflect an atmosphere of acceptance for each person's individuality. Most young children are active and curious, but a very creative child may have a well-developed sense of humor that could be viewed by others as odd. In an atmosphere of acceptance, the child is appreciated without criticism and allowed to work in her own special way. The teacher sets the tone of respect, helps the child through difficult times, learns from these moments, and then goes on with life. The teacher's respect of all children demonstrates that each person is valued and treasured for her uniqueness in this diverse classroom community.

The Creative Environment

The early childhood **environment** plays an important role in enhancing or inhibiting creativity in children. Over a hundred years ago, nursery schools and kindergartens provided children with experiences that would develop perceptions, cognitive structures, and social interactions. Children were encouraged to experiment with the sand and water, to explore shapes with modeling clay, and to participate in play that allowed them to imagine. These experiences continue to be in evidence in appropriate early childhood classrooms today.

The caring teacher listens and respects a child's unique ideas.

The school environment is important in the development of creativity in both children and adults. Environments that encourage creativity provide time and resources, develop expertise, give positive and constructive feedback, and encourage a spirit of play and experimentation. They provide children from diverse backgrounds with opportunities for group interaction, create a safe place for risk-taking, allow for choices, and encourage intrinsic motivation instead of controlling behavior (Kerka, 1999). Children are important members of the school community and should have a voice in their classroom design. Providing opportunities to talk with children about things they would like to add to the classroom or particular aspects of the environment they like makes them contributing members of the community. By inviting them into the discussion, you help them feel more ownership in the space and materials.

Communities and schools are a collection of personalities and educational styles. Teachers wishing to be creative should collaborate with others to gain new insights and identify new approaches to facilitate learning. Collaborative efforts between teachers, parents, and the community broaden possibilities, open a network for brainstorming, and provide stimulation for creativity. For example, a group of early childhood teachers have been studying their environment. They want to create a more home-like atmosphere in their center. In a group meeting, they discuss ways to improve the environment. They brainstorm possibilities and are careful to value each of the ideas contributed. Some ideas include uncluttering the rooms, adding plants, bringing in soft items, providing new light sources, adding curtains to the windows, and placing a couch in the parent area.

At the next group meeting, the teachers invite several parents to attend and share their goals for creating an inviting center. Parents provide additional suggestions that include area carpet pieces, wallpaper borders, beanbag chairs, and soft pillows. Two parents volunteer to begin collecting old pillows that can be

Teachers collaborate to generate more ideas and possibilities.

reconditioned. At their next session, the teachers determine which items can be added quickly and which may require more time. Together, they begin their plan of action to create a wonderful environment for children, teachers, and families.

Primary teachers will benefit from being part of a team or working with a partner. In these combinations, teachers are able to share success stories, ask questions, and find support for their work. No longer are teachers working in isolation, but rather, they are discovering that a team can provide many positive benefits for both beginning and experienced educators. In business, many CEOs have found that groups can generate more ideas and find unique solutions to problems that an individual working alone is not able to accomplish. In the elementary school, leaders are finding that teams can solve problems, develop curricula, and even manage their own site (school) operations. For the beginning teacher, it is important to find a person or team that will serve as a mentor, by providing support, suggesting ideas, and giving instruction on how to meet the challenges of inclusive classrooms.

For instance, in a small elementary school in a rural area near my community, there is only one classroom for each grade level. The four primary teachers, K–3, have a weekly planning meeting where they work together. Sometimes they work on continuity of the curriculum, other times they plan parent communications, and sometimes they simply talk about issues that are of concern to them. Together, they are able to find solutions, plan expanded activities, and have a shared voice for parents and administrators. At a working session early in the year, the teachers shared their concerns about pressure they were receiving to narrow their curriculum to include only the elements that were being tested. The teachers feared that the test, rather than what children were learning, had become the focus. As a group, they decided that they would not eliminate the arts, but rather they would find ways to demonstrate how experiences with the arts were strengthening the children's capabilities. Together, they brainstormed about how the visual arts related to the achievement test the children would be taking in the spring. Each teacher contributed ideas related to the arts, such as "the children will be able to draw a more detailed portrait of themselves if they have experience with art tools," "the arts will help the children recognize similarities and differences," and "vocabulary will be expanded through the introduction of new materials." Armed with these ideas, they were able to document ways the visual arts could support better test scores, whereas individually they may have been unable to defend the use of the arts. Learning to work together and support other teachers is an important skill that must be developed by early childhood educators as they work in collaborative settings.

In the study of creativity and collaboration, it is helpful to investigate how ideas are discouraged. It can happen to your ideas or you may squelch the ideas of others. In a nurturing environment, creative ideas are encouraged; but in some places, comments can make you hesitant to share your great idea.

These third graders are participating in a group meeting, during which they plan their day.

The following are some ways to encourage and to discourage creative ideas or new projects:

Encouraging Creative Ideas	Discouraging Creative Ideas
You did it!	It can't be done.
What a great possibility.	We don't have the money.
That is a very special idea.	Let's form a committee to look into it.
Tell me more.	It's never been done before.
That could work.	It won't work.
Great question.	I have a friend who tried it and it
Let's use it.	didn't work.
Very interesting!	Are you serious?
Let's talk about that one.	Interesting. . . .
I wish I had thought of that.	What will the parents think?
Amazing idea!	Where did that idea come from?
You got it.	What does everyone else think?
Let's build on that.	We tried something like that once.
Follow that thought.	It will take too much work.
Where might that lead?	That is really weird.
Good thinking	I am uncomfortable with that.
(child's name).	Let's talk later.
Let's find out more about that.	Moving right along. . . .
Write that down.	Maybe we could do that next year.
You are on a roll.	Let's get back to that.
Another good one.	Can you think of anything else?
Wow!	Hmmmmmmmmm.

Have any of these statements discouraged you from trying new things or suggesting possibilities? Have you ever used these phrases with others? Think of ways you can support new ideas and teachers who are being creative. For some reason, it seems easier for teachers to be supportive of children than of other adults. In a community of learners in which collaboration is valued, a supportive environment should be developed for both children and teachers.

> "Everyone is creative: we are born not only ready but anxious to act upon the creative proclivity within us."
>
> *M. Goldberg, 2000*

✺ | VALUING CREATIVITY

To encourage creativity, teachers acknowledge the individual child's contribution to a particular idea or product, validate their unique and sometimes outrageous ideas, and let the child know it is all right to move beyond the common and expected. The following scenarios demonstrate how early childhood teachers can encourage creativity.

A kindergarten child uses two materials in a different way. The teacher says, "Using that aluminum pie pan and the yarn was a very interesting way to make a puppet."

A first grader insists there are 100 different toppings on the pizza she has made. Children begin to laugh and tease her. The teacher asks, "You have used many different toppings on your pizza. What are some of them?"

A third grader wants more Popsicle sticks for his construction. He wants to build the tallest building in the world. The teacher responds, "You have a great idea and I will bring more Popsicle sticks for you to continue building tomorrow. Is there another building material you could use today?"

MAKING MISTAKES

During the creative process, there are often mistakes, retries, and failures. Teachers experience this when a great activity doesn't work or the plaster of paris doesn't harden. They learn to accept the trials that occur during the creative process. As the following examples demonstrate, innovative teachers can help children understand that mistakes and accidents can happen, and sometimes these can be turned into an advantage.

A kindergartner's box structure falls apart before the glue dries. The teacher sees the child's concern. She comments on the child's effort. "That is a very interesting **sculpture.** Is there some way you can support the structure until the glue dries?"

A second grader is working on a poster to demonstrate what she had learned in her study of rocks. LaDonna tries to attach a large rock to the poster board and it falls off. After repeatedly trying to attach the rock, she angrily walks away from the project. The teacher recognizes her frustration and says, "I can see you are very upset. What are you trying to show by attaching the rock to the poster?" LaDonna replies, "I want them to see the different kinds of rocks I studied." The teacher encourages her to think of another way of displaying the rocks so the children can see and also physically examine the rocks. LaDonna thinks for a moment and then concludes that she could put the rocks on a box in front of the poster. "Then the children could feel the rocks for themselves," she explains.

RESPECT FOR DIFFERENCES

Within every classroom, there are a wide range of abilities and talents. Children's work can be less advanced, more advanced, or from a totally different perspective. These variations are recognized and respected in a sensitive environment, and are shown in the following examples.

A kindergartner who is making a book, fills the pages with uncontrolled scribbles. When other children see his book, they tell him "that's not the way you do it." The teacher explains, "people make books in different ways; some use words and some use pictures. The ideas and thinking are the most important parts of creating a book."

A third grader creates a **mobile** with unusual items such as feathers, pinecones, and dried flowers, and hangs them from

Young children learn about respect, as they observe their teacher reading a story to a preschooler with special needs.

a small limb. This mobile is very difficult to balance while allowing the parts to move with the airflow. The teacher recognizes that this child is building a very complex mobile, and provides the time and support for her to finish her work of art.

COOPERATIVE AND INTERACTIVE THINKING

Teachers understand they can learn from others and that working together can expand their own thinking. They model this when they share with children that a wonderful idea came from a helpful book or that another teacher suggested an activity. Children need to experience sharing ideas and learning from others.

During circle time, preschoolers share items brought from home. Carlos shows a bridle. He tells the group he just learned to put the bridle in the horse's mouth. The teacher comments that she has learned something new from Carlos's explanation because she has never tried to put a bridle in a horse's mouth. She asks if other children have ever had this experience.

In the third grade, children are talking about their recent trip to see the *Nutcracker Suite*. The teacher encourages Sarah to tell the children about her experience dancing in the local production of the *Nutcracker*. At the conclusion of the discussion, the teacher comments, "Sarah, we have learned so much from you about dancing in the *Nutcracker*."

TEACHING FOR CREATIVITY

Trostle and Yawkey (1982) identified seven specific ways teachers can encourage creative thinking. These relate to curricular activities, classroom lessons, and teacher actions.

1. Facilitate creative thought in early childhood programs. In the early years, the teacher should encourage children to use physical objects in their own way.
2. Adult playfulness. The teacher is playful and serves as a model of a creative person.
3. Exploration. The teacher provides sufficient time in the schedule for children to investigate and explore objects and materials.
4. Oral cues. The teacher talks to the children while they are involved in creativity activity, thereby extending their thinking.
5. Verbal descriptions. The teacher helps children express their creative ideas as vividly and clearly as possible.
6. Modifying objects. The teacher changes familiar objects into unfamiliar ones by changing their physical characteristics.
7. Adding novel objects. The teacher adds unusual materials to the children's role-playing activities in order to extend their play.

STRATEGIES

There are a number of strategies for incorporating creative expression into the classroom. Strategies include problem-finding, problem-solving, project-based instruction, and reflective thinking.

Problem-Finding and Problem-Solving

Problem-finding refers to children identifying their own problems. They ask questions about the world and pursue what interests them. At least some of the time, children should have the opportunity to define their own issues, problems, and areas of inquiry. Teachers can initiate problem-finding by following the children's interests and posing provocative questions. The teacher becomes a resource and supports the child as she begins to solve her problem, and structures the day so there is sufficient time to work on solving problems.

This approach can be observed in the interactions of a teacher and a small group of children. The children have designed and planted a small garden on the playground. They are very concerned that birds are eating many of the seeds. The teacher poses the question, "How can we keep the birds out of our garden?" The children suggest several options, including moving the garden, taking turns guarding the plants, and making a scarecrow. The teacher talks further with the children about their ideas and possibilities. They conclude that a scarecrow would work best. Logan and Jay explain that it cannot be an ordinary scarecrow; it must be enormous and make loud sounds when birds approach the garden.

The children work several days on the design of the scarecrow. When the plan is complete, they construct a large stuffed scarecrow and attach foil pie plates on the hat, chest, and back. The plan came from the identification of the problem and the ideas of the children. The teacher asked provocative questions, helped collect materials, and assisted in the construction of the enormous, noisy scarecrow.

Teachers who value creativity recognize that curriculum can emerge out of the interest and investigations of children. To plan in this way requires that teachers become researchers, and focus on listening and observing instead of telling and demonstrating (Carter, 1992).

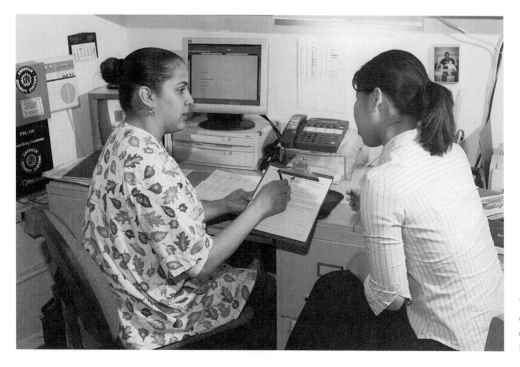

Teachers are discussing children's interest for future projects.

Projects

Project-based instruction engages children in long-term initiatives. In sustained projects, children participate as inventors and researchers. Children find out how plants grow by planting a garden on the playground. Over a period of time, they observe, record, and draw conclusions about resources that the plants need. They take pictures of the garden at different points in time. They determine which plants grew best and which did not grow as well. Projects allow children to work together to maintain interest and develop a new depth of understanding. The interest in the garden project is sustained over a three-month period with intense focus at certain times during the process.

Lillian Katz (1994), an expert on the project approach, describes how children's interest and questions are valued when using this method. She defines the project as an in-depth investigation on a topic that is usually undertaken with a small group of children. The project is a research effort to find answers to questions about the topic that are posed by the children, teacher, or a collaboration of the two. The focus is on learning more about the topic, instead of just finding the right answer (Katz, 1994; Maple, 2005).

Reflective Thinking

Another strategy that supports creative development is reflective **self-assessment.** Assessment is often thought of as the teacher evaluating children. This teacher-oriented assessment makes the child dependent on the feedback of others and does not prepare her for independent learning. Reflective thinking encourages children to assess their own work and to think about what they have done. This self-evaluation encourages children personally to determine the merits of their work. Four questions can help children think about their work.

1. What does the work look like? The children describe or evaluate their work.

2. What was it like to do the work? The focus here is on the process by which the work was accomplished.

3. How can the work be improved? What can be done to revise the product, story, or painting? This requires critical and creative thinking.

4. How can you share what you have learned with others? This asks the child to determine if the work is ready to be shown or if she wants to share this time.

Reflective thinking can be encouraged informally as the teacher walks around the room and poses questions, or more formally when older children can record their responses to these questions on paper (Torff, 2000).

❈ FOSTERING CREATIVITY WITH ACTIVITIES AND MATERIALS

Mayer (1989) describes three conditions for creative teaching.

1. The material must be meaningful to the children.

2. The children must actively engage in the learning process.

3. Evaluations of learning must include a measure of students' creativity.

Activities based on the interests of the children foster creativity. Young children can tell what they know about a topic, what they want to learn, how they want to explore the topic, and how they will share what they have learned. A nature item or new book brought to school by one child may cause other children to become interested and curious. Teachers who value and act on these interests give children a sense of ownership. Ownership leads to engagement that encourages creative behavior.

Open-Ended Activities

Activities that foster creativity should be **open-ended.** Instead of giving a model or telling what the product should be, give children reasonable control over deciding what materials they want to use and how they will approach the product. In the process-oriented class, the thinking that occurs during the work is as important as the final product. Children need to have a wide variety of materials available so they can select items that match what they are thinking or expand their existing ideas. Many possibilities and combinations allow children to think divergently. A number of studies have shown that children who are encouraged to use divergent thinking dramatically increase their ability to think creatively (Torrance, 1964; Chiatt, Shaw, & Sherwood, 1980).

Leaves, pumpkins, pinecones, and orange paint inspire a fall design on the light table.

EXAMPLES OF OPEN-ENDED ACTIVITIES.   The block center provides opportunities to use construction materials in many ways. The child can determine if the blocks will be a garage, a skyscraper, or a path to the housekeeping center.

- An art activity that provides a variety of materials can inspire ideas and original work. The availability of the varied materials provides choices that allow each child to create what he or she would like.

- A sociodramatic center that is set up as a fitness center is open-ended. The theme of the play is determined, while the area includes varied props: exercise outfits, musical recordings, an appointment book, exercise tapes, hula-hoops, and an exercise ball. The play requires the child to make choices. In this center, each child can determine how to get fit and what tools he or she will use.

- Music activities that include keyboard, guitar, and a collection of rhythm instruments inspire experimenting with sounds and rhythm. The child can use the instrument that interests him and play it in a way he feels accompanies the music.

These open-ended activities are beneficial, because there is no predetermined use. The child is able to control how materials are used, increasing their confidence in their capabilities and ultimately a willingness to try more challenging tasks.

"When children have the chance to notice, collect and sort materials, and when teachers respond to their ideas, the children become artists, designers, and engineers."

Topal, Gandini, & Golding, 1999

OPEN-ENDED MATERIALS AND ACTIVITIES. A key element needed for developing creative expression is the availability of open-ended materials like clay, paint, tools for drawing, and a variety of building materials. Reusable resources that children have not experienced provide materials that can be used in art, play, and construction. Scraps of wood from a woodworking shop or building site can stimulate children's thinking, as they manipulate the material and generate possible uses (Drew & Rankin, 2004).

EXAMPLES OF OPEN-ENDED COLLECTIBLE MATERIALS

Material	Source
Scraps of wood	cabinet shop, furniture factory
Pieces of plastic	packing store, computer store, furniture store
Branches, twigs, and bark	woods, forest
Cardboard boxes	grocery store, home improvement store, furniture store
Paper rolls (variety of sizes)	carpet store, wrapping paper
Electrical wire (variety of colors and sizes)	electrician, building site, power company
Telephone cable	telephone company, building site
Plastic pipe	home improvement store, landscaping company, plumber
Fabric	seamstress, garment factory
Variety of paper	computer paper, print shop, wrapping paper

These boys are trying to decide what they will cook for supper.

Children need opportunities to explore and manipulate a material before they actually use it in a project. This exploratory period is very important and leads to generating more ideas, some that are used and some that are not. The teacher can assist in the process, by posing questions and providing the time for this step to be completed. When children are given the opportunity to explore the ways materials can be used, and teachers respond to their ideas in a positive way, children will be more creative and take pride in their ideas (Topal, Gandini, & Golding, 1999).

Flexible Time

Children need time for uninterrupted work, investigation, and discussion. Flexible schedules and longer blocks of time allow children to see new concepts or make extensions. This allows them to work on a project or activity until they determine it is completed, instead of rushing to finish or even disband the work because there is not enough time. As the following scenario demonstrates, the gift of time encourages creative activity and more in-depth work.

> In the block center, several children are working on a structure to represent the new fire station that was built near their school. They have watched the construction, drawn pictures of the progress, taken photographs of the workers, and walked around the site. For several weeks, they have added parts to their own "work in progress." Just at the moment when center time is to be over, Jose has a great idea. The fire station needs a flying banner with a sign that says "Grand Opening." His teacher, who was moving around the room to encourage cleanup, sees Jose working frantically to make the sign and banner. She suggests that Will and Tara, who also have been working on the structure, help with the wonderful sign idea. They can come outside with the aide when they finish the banner. Together, the children create the sign and banner for the Grand Opening.

THE PHYSICAL ENVIRONMENT

The physical environment of the classroom can have a tremendous impact on the creative actions of young children. Some early childhood classrooms are so filled with equipment, materials, and supplies that they overwhelm the children. A well-organized classroom groups materials together and displays them for children to make their own selection.

The classroom should be aesthetically pleasing, with attractive elements included for the children to enjoy. Young children can appreciate a bouquet of spring flowers in a clay pot as well as a poster of a Monet painting. These additions to the classroom expose children to beautiful things, and provide opportunities to experience the color and texture of the flowers and the techniques used by the painter.

The physical arrangement of the space should include areas for both large and small group activities. A group meeting place encourages the sharing of ideas, learning from others, and building a sense of community. In this special area, stories are told, songs are sung, and projects are shared (Isbell & Exelby, 2001).

There should be places for small groups to work and play together. Learning centers or contained areas allow several children to interact frequently, shape their activity, and cooperatively carry the play to completion. Loud and active areas should be grouped together in a portion of the classroom so that quieter areas can function appropriately with a minimum of distractions. Included in the area is a space that provides privacy. In a busy classroom, young children need a place where they can escape to think or simply be alone. This private area can be created in a quiet corner with draped fabric, or in a large cardboard box with cutouts on the side and pillows inside.

A variety of spaces allow children to make choices and determine where they can work best on a specific day or on a special project. At another time, they may make different choices and participate in other activities (Isbell & Exelby).

✿ DISPLAYS

There should be many examples of children's work throughout the room. These examples reflect the individual creations of the children who work in this space. The work should be displayed in interesting ways and include a range of activities, not just art. Always ask the children if their work can be displayed and respect their decision. This will help them begin to evaluate work and determine which projects to share with others. Some children's work could be displayed on a large painted cardboard box that will add a three-dimensional look. Covering boards with textured fabric, contact paper, foil, or other materials can vary the display effects. Children's work can be matted or framed to enhance the presentation of materials. Simple frames can be made from cardboard, poster board, or art board and covered with foil, satin, small pinecones, buttons, and other items. When children see their work framed, they feel proud and know that it is valued in their classroom.

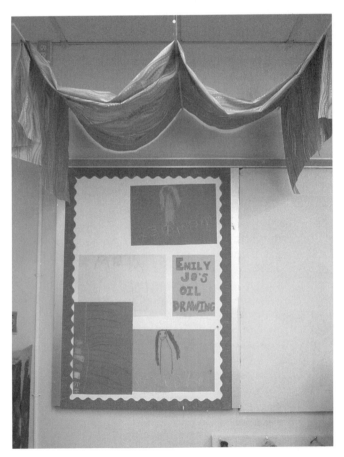

An attractive display with draped fabric demonstrates that this child's artwork is valued.

✿ ACCESSIBILITY OF MATERIALS

Basic art and construction materials should be visible and easily accessible for children to use spontaneously, as well as with teacher-initiated activities. This allows children to choose the materials they want to use independently, without asking the teacher for help. This communicates to children that they are capable of selecting and using the materials they need. This independence allows children to go forward with an idea instead of waiting until they are able to get help from the teacher. Their great ideas may be lost during the wait.

Novel Materials

Novel items capture the interest of young children. The novelty of a toy is a primary reason for children to explore it. Novel items force a child to think in different ways and invent possibilities that did not previously exist. Some novel items might include unusually shaped styrofoam scraps, industrial salvage, old postcards, hardware, maps, boxes, natural materials, recyclables, fabric, cork, buttons, old kitchen tools, antique/junk items, colored electrical wire, auto parts, wooden spools, building supplies, and discarded storage racks. Opportunities to work with novel materials can spark young children's creativity. Once exploration stops, there is a transition into play. In play, the emphasis changes from "What does this object do?" to "What can I do with this object?" (Frost & Klein, 1983).

A kindergartner was intrigued by the pieces of PVC pipe that the teacher added to the block area. She explored the properties of the plastic material. Then she began to construct with blocks. She built a submarine from the blocks and added the pieces of pipe for the periscope. The pipe resulted in a new structure that she had not thought of creating before it was added.

A first grader was very interested in the dulcimer his teacher brought in to play during group time. The experience with this new instrument inspired him to construct his own dulcimer from a cardboard box, complete with yarn strings.

Allow children to use materials in novel ways. Do not restrict them to using their resources in one prescribed way. This requires flexibility of thinking, an important component of creativity.

Grouping plastic food, including peppers and tacos, in the grocery store center encourages creative play.

✸ | SUMMARY

There are many ways to encourage creativity in adults and children, but strategies alone are insufficient. A creative classroom environment requires a teacher with courage, a willingness to try new things, and an ability to do things in a different way. A teacher can use creativity each day as he plans an interesting lesson, creates a new learning center, or designs an aesthetically pleasing place. Two sets of creative faculties are interacting in the early childhood classroom: the teacher's and the children's. If the teacher values and develops his creativity, the children will notice. If a teacher is enthusiastic, innovative, and tries new things—even if some ideas fizzle—children thrive because this is an exciting learning environment. Children in the creative classroom will be more adventurous and try doing things for themselves. Both the teacher and children gain from these creative encounters in an environment that encourages their personal growth.

A creative teacher and child enjoy playing with the idea of a "clay nose."

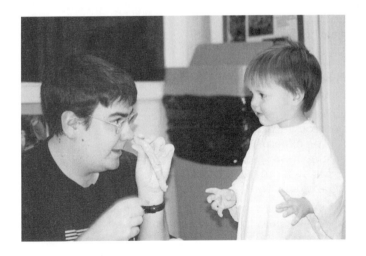

KEY TERMS

atmosphere
creativity training
environment
mobile
novel
open-ended

Reggio Emilia
sculpture
self-assessment
teachable moment
whole child

REFLECTION

1. Why is it important for a teacher of young children to be creative?
2. What are some of the characteristics of a creative teacher?
3. What is a value of collaboration for children and teachers?
4. Describe a classroom environment that nurtures creativity.

THINKING ABOUT THE OBSERVATION OF CREATIVITY

1. What were some of the ways Marie demonstrated that she was a creative teacher?
2. In what ways did Marie value the ideas of the children?
3. How will Marie determine other additions and expansions to the greenhouse center?

POSSIBILITIES FOR ADULT LEARNERS

Activity: The Most Creative Teacher
Goal: To recognize the characteristics of creative teachers.
Materials: Paper and pencil.
Procedure:

1. Think about the most creative teacher you have worked with during your academic career. List the qualities this teacher possessed.
2. Share these remembrances in class with other students.
3. Make a list of the characteristics that are shared, and determine the qualities that were identified most frequently in creative teachers.

Activity: Find Your Own Creativity
Goal: To recognize that each person is creative and demonstrates creativity in everyday activities.
Materials: Journal for recording creative moments and pencil or pen.
Procedure:

1. During the past month, identify something that you have done that was personally creative.
2. Think about the personal and professional activities that have allowed you to be creative, playful, or thoughtful.
3. Write a paragraph about these creative moments.

Activity: Brainstorming with Others

Goal: To experience how collaboration with others can extend creative thinking.

Materials: Basic Rules for Brainstorming (found in Chapter 1) everyday objects, chart paper for recording ideas, and markers.

Procedure:

1. Share the guidelines for brainstorming in Chapter 1.
2. Divide the class into small groups of four to five people.
3. Present an everyday object and ask the groups to list all the ways it could be used. Remember, the focus is on generating many ideas (fluency).
4. Give the groups five to eight minutes to produce a list of possibilities. When the groups seem to stall, encourage them to keep going and remind them that some of the best ideas come at the end of brainstorming sessions.
5. Share the number of ideas each group came up with, and ask them to identify the two or three most unusual ideas.

Activity: Recognizing the Beauty

Goal: To become more observant of beauty in the world around us.

Materials: Journal for recording creative moments and pencil or pen.

Procedure:

1. On the way home from class, notice creative things you may not have seen before such as a sign with a creative slogan, a beautifully decorated door, a flower arrangement in a florist's window, or reflections of light on the wet pavement.
2. Make a conscious effort to notice and appreciate creative things in your environment.

OPEN-ENDED ACTIVITIES FOR YOUNG CHILDREN

PreK–K

Activity: New and Improved

Goal: To identify ways that a familiar item can be improved (flexible thinking).

Materials: Teddy bear, chart paper, and marker.

Procedure:

1. Bring an old teddy bear to group time.
2. Lead a discussion about the teddy bear and ways it may have been used.
3. Divide the class into small groups and ask the children to think of ways they can have more fun playing with the teddy bear.
4. Allow about three to six minutes, depending on the developmental level of the children and their experience with this type of activity.

5. Return to the group and ask them to share their ideas. Record their suggestions on the chart paper as they are given.

6. Comment on the uniqueness of the ideas and how they would improve the teddy bear.

Primary Grades

Activity: Putting It Together

Goal: Combine unrelated objects to develop flexibility of thinking.

Materials: A plastic bag for each small group containing three unrelated items. Examples of items to include in the plastic bags are pieces of yarn, paper clips, a small paper cup, a button, a piece of wire, a sheet of paper, a section of newspaper, masking tape, and a toothpick.

Procedure:

1. Divide the class into small groups.

2. Ask each group to use the three items in its bag to make something that would be useful.

3. Allow 5 to 10 minutes.

4. Combine the small groups and share the inventions that were created.

Extension: Return the participants to the small groups, and ask each to write an advertisement or create a sign to sell the new products.

Venturing Outside the Box: *Environmental Sensitivity*

- What color was the sky at sunset last night?
- How do you feel when you hold a new baby?
- What pictures are on the bulletin board in your classroom?
- How did the last pizza that you ate smell?
- What patterns do the tires on your car make?
- What junk item could you add to the art center?
- How does an ice cube feel?
- When do you see your shadow?
- How many shades of green are the leaves on trees?
- What does sand feel like on your feet?
- Where can you find a smooth surface to touch?

 ## ADDITIONAL READING

Akande, A. (1997). Creativity: The caregivers' secret weapon. *Early Child Development and Care, 134*, 89–101.

Albert, R. S. (1996). Some reasons why childhood creativity often fails to make it past puberty into the real world. *New Directions for Child Development, 72*(1), 43–56.

Ashton-Warner, S. (1963). *Teacher.* New York: Simon & Schuster.

Byrnes, D. A., & Kiger, G. (1996). *Common bonds: Anti-bias teaching in a diverse society.* Olney, MD: Association for Childhood Education International.

Cecil, L. M., Gray, M. M., Thornburg, K. R., & Ispa, J. (1985). Curiosity-exploration-play-creativity: The early childhood mosaic. *Early Child Development and Care, 19*(1), 199–217.

Chenfield, M. (1991). Everything you need to know about being a creative teacher in four easy nudges. *Phi Delta Kappan, 73*(1), 332–334.

Colangelo, N., & Davis, G. A. (1991). *Handbook for gifted education.* Boston: Allyn and Bacon.

Craft, A. (1998). Educator perspectives on creativity: An English study. *Journal of Creative Behavior, 32*(4), 244–257.

Czikszentmihalyi, M. (1996). *Creativity.* New York: Basic Books.

Duckworth, E. (1996). *The having of good ideas and other essays on teaching and learning.* Olney, MD: Association for Childhood Education International.

Fisher, J. (1996). *Starting from the child.* Buckingham, PA: Open University Press.

Hoffman, S., & Lamme, L. L. (Eds.). (1989). *Learning from the inside out.* Olney, MD: Association for Childhood Education International.

Jalongo, M. R. (1999). How we respond to the artistry of children: Ten barriers to overcome. *Early Childhood Education Journal, 26*(4), 205–208.

John-Steiner, V. (1985). *Notebook of the mind: Exploration of thinking.* Albuquerque, NM: University of New Mexico Press.

Jones, C. F. (1991). *Mistakes that worked: 40 familiar inventions and how they came to be.* New York: Doubleday Books for Young Readers.

Keegan, R. T. (1996). Creativity from childhood to adulthood; A difference of degree not kind. *New Directions for Child Development, 72*(1), 57–66.

Powell, M. C. (1997). The arts and inner lives of teachers. *Phi Delta Kappan, 78*(6), 450–453.

Runco, M. A. (1996). Personal creativity: Definition and developmental issues. *New Directions for Child Development, 72*(1), 3–30.

Siegl, E. (1986). How to encourage creativity in teachers. *Roeper Review, 9,* 18–19.

Smith, M. K. (1996). Fostering creativity in the classroom. *Early Childhood Education Journal, 24*(2), 77–82.

CHILDREN'S BOOKS THAT BRING OUT THE KID INSIDE

Reading children's books also can help us become more sensitive to their way of experiencing the world. The following selections can help in this process.

Anholt, C., & Anholt, L. (1991). *What I like.* New York: G. P. Putnam's Sons.
    Rhymed text and illustrations describe a child's likes and dislikes and demonstrate each child's individuality.

Anholt, C., & Anholt, L. (1992). *Kids.* Cambridge, MA: Candlewick Press.
    Illustrations and rhyming text present the traits, activities, and feelings of many different children.

Baker, J. (1991). *Window.* New York: Hudson.
    A mother and baby look through a window at the beautiful wilderness and sky beyond their home. But as the baby grows into a boy, and then a man, the scene begins to change.

Borton, L. (1997). *Junk pile.* New York: Philomel Books.
    Helping out in her father's auto junkyard has taught Jamie to fix the school bus and construct wonderful works of art with junk, but the other children's teasing still hurts until she learns how to fix a friendship as well.

Johnson, C. (1977). *Harold and the purple crayon.* New York: HarperCollins.
    Come join Harold on an adventure with his purple crayon and see the many possibilities that exist.

Jonas, A. (1983). *Round trip.* New York: Scholastic.
    Start at the beginning and read to the end. Then turn the book over and begin again!

Lester, A. (1990). *Imagine.* Boston: Houghton Mifflin Company.
    This book invites the reader to imagine what it would be like to live in various locations such as a house, a jungle, and an icecap, and meet the animals that live there.

Shannon, D. (2004). *A bad case of stripes.* New York: Scholastic.
    In order to ensure her popularity, Camilla Cream always does what is expected. She is very, very worried about what other people think; so worried that she's about to break out in . . . a bad case of stripes!

Small, D. (1985). *Imogene's antlers.* New York: Crown.
> One Thursday, Imogene wakes up with a pair of antlers growing out of her head that cause a sensation wherever she goes.

 ## CHILDREN'S LITERATURE CONNECTION

Allard, H. (1977). *Miss Nelson is missing!* Boston: Houghton Mifflin.
> The kids in room 207 take advantage of their teacher's good nature until she disappears and they are faced with a vile substitute. (K–2)

Beardshaw, R. (2001). *Grandma's Beach.* New York: Bloomsbury USA Children's Books.
> Emily wants to go to the beach, but her mother can't take her. So, her grandmother creates a wonderful beach in her backyard. (PreK–2)

Finchler, J. (1995). *Miss Malarkey doesn't live in room 10.* New York: Walker.
> A first-grade boy is shocked, then pleased, when he discovers that his teacher has a life away from school. (PreK–2)

Glennon, K. (1990). *Miss Eva and the red balloon.* New York: Simon & Schuster Books for Young Readers.
> Miss Eva, an old-fashioned school marm, leads a routine life until one of her students gives her a magic red balloon. (K–3)

Henkes, K. (1996). *Lily's purple plastic purse.* New York: Greenwillow Books.
> Lilly loves everything about school, especially her teacher, but when he asks her to wait awhile before showing her new purse, she does something for which she is very sorry later. (PreK–1)

Houston, G. (1992). *My great-aunt Arizona.* New York: Harper Collins Publishers.
> An Appalachian girl, Arizona Houston Hughes, grows up to become a teacher who influences generations of schoolchildren. (PreK–3)

Lehman, B. (2004). *The red book.* Boston: Houghton Mifflin Company.
> This wordless picture book follows the adventures of a red book. An interesting touch is that the book itself is also red. (K–3)

Seuss, Dr., & Prelutsky, J. (1998). *Hooray for diffendoofer day!* New York: Knopf.
> The students of Diffendoofer School celebrate their unusual teachers and curriculum, including Miss Fribble who teaches laughing, Miss Bonkers who teaches frogs to dance, and Mr. Katz who builds robotic rats. (K–3)

Slate, J. (1998). *Miss Bindergarten celebrates the 100th day of kindergarten.* New York: Dutton Children's Books.
> To celebrate one hundred days in Miss Bindergarten's kindergarten class, all of her students bring one hundred of something to school, including a one hundred-year-old relative, one hundred candy hearts, and one hundred polka dots. (K–1)

Thaler, M. (2000). *The music teacher from the Black Lagoon.* New York: Scholastic.
> A boy contemplates all the horrible stories he has heard about the music teacher, Miss LaNote, and the ordeals she forces her students to endure. (K–3)

Weiss, L. (1984). *My teacher sleeps in school.* New York: F. Warne.
> Because Mrs. Marsh is always sleeping in her classroom before the students arrive and always stays after they leave, Mollie becomes convinced that her teacher has no home other than school. (K–2)

 For additional resources involving creativity and the arts with young children, visit our Web site at **www.earlychilded.delmar.com**

 ## REFERENCES

Abdallah, A. (1996). Fostering creativity in student teachers. *Community Review, 14*(1), 52–58.

Amabile, T. M. (1989). *Growing up creative: Nurturing a lifetime of creativity.* New York: Crown.

Bohn, C. M., Roehrig, A. D., & Pressley, M. (2004, March). The first days of school in the classrooms of two more effective and four less effective primary-grades teachers. *The Elementary School Journal, 104*, 269–287.

Carter, M. (1992). Training teachers for creative learning experiences. *Child Care Information Exchange, 85*, 38–40.

Chiatt, M. P., Shaw, J. M., & Sherwood, J. M. (1980). Effects of training on the divergent thinking abilities of kindergarten children. *Child Development, 51*, 1061–1064.

Drew, W. F., & Rankin, B. (2004, July). Promoting creativity for life using open-ended materials. *Young Children, 59*(4), 38–43.

Edwards, L. (2002). *The creative arts: A process approach for teachers and children* (3rd ed.). Upper Saddle River, NJ: Merrill Prentice Hall.

Ehlert, L. (1988). *Planting a rainbow.* San Diego, CA: Harcourt Brace Jovanovich.

Frost, J., & Klein, B. L. (1983). *Children's play and playgrounds.* Austin, TX: Playscapes International.

Gandini, L. (1992). Creativity comes dressed in everyday clothes. *Child Care Information Exchange, 85*, 26–29.

Goldberg, M. R. (2000). *Arts and learning: An integrated approach to teaching and learning in multicultural and multilingual settings* (2nd ed.). New York: Longman.

Haefele, J. (1962). *Management series: Creativity and innovation.* New York: Reinhold.

Himsl, R., & Lambert, E. (1993). Signs of learning in the affective domain. *The Alberta Journal of Education Research, 39*(2), 257–273.

Isbell, R., & Exelby, B. (2001). *Learning environments that work with young children.* Beltsville, MD: Gryphon House.

Jeanrenaud, C., & Bishop, D. (1980). Roadblocks to creativity. In P. F. Wilkinson (Ed.), *In celebration of play: An integrated approach* (pp. 73–84). London: Croom Helm.

Kamii, C., & DeVries, R. (1978). *Physical knowledge in preschool education: Implications of Piaget's theory.* Englewood Cliffs, NJ: Prentice Hall.

Katz, L. G. (1994). *The project approach.* Champaign, IL: Children's Research Center (ERIC Document Reproduction Service No. EDO-PS-94-6).

Kerka, S. (1999). *Creativity in adulthood.* Washington, DC: Office of Educational Research and Improvement (ERIC Document Reproduction Service No. ED 429 186).

Maple, T. L. (Spring 2005). Beyond community helpers: The project approach in the early childhood social studies curriculum. *Childhood Education, 81*(3), 133–138.

Mayer, R. E. (1989). Cognitive view of creativity: Creative teaching for creative learning. *Contemporary Education Psychology, 14*, 203–211.

McGreevy, A. (1990). Tracking the creative teacher. *Momentum, 21*, 57–59.

Mellou, E. (1996). Can creativity be nurtured in young children? *Early Child Development and Care, 119*, 119–130.

Poole, M. (1980). *Creativity across the curriculum.* Sydney, Australia: George Allen and Union.

Shallcross, D. J. (1981). *Teaching creative behavior.* Englewood Cliffs, NJ: Prentice Hall.

Simplicio, J. S. C. (2000). Teaching classroom educators how to be more effective and creative teachers. *Education, 120*(4), 675–701.

Stout, C. J. (1999). The art of empathy: Teaching students to care. *Art Education, 38*(2), 21–24.

Tegano, D., Groves, M. M., & Catron, C. E. (1999). Early childhood teachers' playfulness and ambiguity tolerance: Essential elements of encouraging creative potential of children. *Journal of Early Childhood Teacher Education, 20*(3), 291–300.

Topal, C. W., Gandini, L., & Golding, C. M. (1999). *Beautiful stuff: Learning with found materials.* New York: Davis.

Torff, B. (2000). Encouraging the creative voice of the child. *The NAMTA Journal, 25*(1), 10–14.

Torrance, E. P. (1964). Bringing creativity into play. *Education, 85*, 457–550.

Torrance, E. P. (1965). *Rewarding creative behavior.* Englewood Cliffs, NJ: Prentice Hall.

Torrance, E. P. (1992). A national climate for creativity and invention. *Gifted Child Today, 15*, 10–14.

Torrance, E. P., & Safter, H. T. (1986). Are children becoming more creative? *The Journal of Creative Behavior, 20*(1), 2–13.

Trostle, S. L., & Yawkey, T. D. (1982). Creative thinking and the education of young children: The fourth basic skill. *International Journal of Early Childhood, 14*(2), 67–71.

VonOech, R. (1983). *A whack on the side of the head: How to unlock your mind for innovation.* New York: Warner Books.

Zener, R. S. (1995). Nurturing the creative personality. *The NAMTA Journal. 20*(1), 13–29.

THE ROLE OF PLAY

CHAPTER 3

This chapter examines the different types of **play** and their relationship to the development of young children. The importance of play is studied as it influences the cognitive, social, and physical development of young children. It includes ways to develop playfulness and design environments that encourage creativity. During play, children construct and transform their world to be meaningful for them, and at their level of development.

After studying this chapter, you will be able to:
- Trace the historical trends in play.
- Understand how major theories explain the role of play.
- Support the importance of play during the early childhood years.
- Identify the qualities of play.
- Distinguish between the types of social play.
- Select appropriate learning centers for PreK through primary levels.
- Explain the teacher's role during children's play, indoor and outdoor.

OBSERVATION OF CREATIVITY

Niki, fourteen months old, is visiting in the home of her mother's friend. At first, her mother and Loretta play with Niki and encourage her to interact with them. As time passes, they begin to talk about adult subjects. Niki grows weary of all the talk and being ignored. She toddles around the room, obviously looking for something. She searches through a box of toys. She looks behind the furniture. Finally, Niki finds a small piece of fabric in the sewing area. She climbs up on the couch with the tiny piece of fabric in her hands. She closes her eyes, lovingly rubs the fabric, pretends to go to sleep, and snores, "Zzzzzz."

WHAT WAS OBSERVED?

Niki has created a symbol for her "blankie" using the small scrap of soft fabric. She pretends to be asleep by closing her eyes and adds to the play by making a snoring sound. Niki is playing and using symbolic representation. This is the beginning of symbolic play that will appear more frequently during the preschool years.

✿ | HISTORICAL PERSPECTIVE

As early as the time of Plato (427–347 BC), play has been seen as a part of childhood. Rousseau (1712–1778) wrote that work and play are the same for the child: he knows no difference. In the nineteenth century, Froebel (2003) saw play as the vehicle for unfolding the inner good of the child. The play Froebel described focused on active engagement through motor play and concrete materials that were manipulated easily by young children. Play with these materials provided its own reward for the child. Froebel's play materials included soft wool balls, sets of small unit blocks, and parquetry (geometrically patterned tiles). The play Froebel suggested with these materials included structured activities with specific goals. He believed that play was the highest expression of human development in childhood; play alone is the free expression of what is in a child's soul (Froebel, 2005; Brosterman, 1997).

During the industrial revolution and colonial period, play was not as valued. It was viewed as a frivolous waste of time. The work of notable theorists and important research studies reestablished the importance of play during the next century. In recent years, play has become an area of serious empirical research and scientific recognition (Elkind, 1987; Pellegrini, 1996; Sutton-Smith, 1979). This expanding research base supports the contention that play is a developmentally important and purposeful behavior. Many early studies concluded that play follows a developmental sequence, serves as a reflection of social and cognitive development, and strengthens developing skills (Quinn & Rubin, 1984). Later, Russ (1996) concluded that fantasy play is important in childhood because it facilitates many of the cognitive and affective processes related to creativity.

But even today, there remains some conflict over the value of play. This can be seen in the trend to push academic curriculum down to preschool levels and to introduce structured sports and competition during the early years of children's development. Often, these additions eliminate the time and opportunity for young children to be involved in play. Should play be included in early childhood

Kindergarten boys are using unique materials in their structure—metallic fabric, large cardboard tubes, and large wood turnings.

programs, and what are the benefits of this inclusion? In this chapter, we will provide support for the inclusion of play in early childhood classrooms.

✽ | WHAT ARE THE QUALITIES OF PLAY?

It is important to be able to identify play and the special characteristics of this activity. There is no simple definition of play because the borders between play, exploration, and work are not always clearly defined. A number of typical play features (Hughes, 1999; Nourot & Van Hoorn, 1991) can help in the recognition.

1. Play is intrinsically motivated. It is an end in itself. It is done for the sheer joy of doing it.

2. The child freely chooses it. In a study by King (1979), it was found that if the kindergarten teacher assigned a play activity to the pupils, they regarded it as work.

3. Play must be pleasurable. The child must enjoy the activity for it to be identified as play. The second grader who agrees to participate in T-ball because his parents insist fails to meet this requirement for play. He did not choose to do this and finds no pleasure in the activity.

4. Play may be nonliteral or symbolic. It involves an element of make-believe and allows the child to change reality. The child with a new brother at home is able to develop a play scenario in which she continues to be the star.

5. Play actively engages the child. In play, the child participates in an activity that is personally meaningful. It is based on his experience and provides an avenue for following these interests at this point in time.

✽ | THEORIES OF PLAY

Play has a central role in many theories that relate to early childhood development (Erikson, 1950; Montessori, 1964; Piaget, 1962; Vygotsky, 1976). Each theorist describes the role of play by focusing on a particular element of the process and providing an interpretation.

Herbert Spencer (1896) developed one of the earliest theories of play. His **surplus energy theory** explained that children release their excess energy through play. Spencer also believed that children's play is an avenue for developing behaviors that are essential for adulthood. This view of play supports the need for physical activity and outdoor play in early childhood programs.

The **relaxation theory** of G. T. W. Patrick (1916) explained that play was a way to recover from fatigue or hard work. Patrick felt that recreational play was beneficial and restored energy. This theory relates to the practice in early childhood of rotating the daily schedule between active and quiet activities.

In the **practice theory,** developed by Karl Gross (1916), play was described as an intrinsic activity. Gross believed that play began naturally and continued to develop as a child matured. The young child exercised in playful ways. He believed that children need a period of play in childhood to practice the skills that will be needed in adult life. Gross further extended his theory by proposing that play is a preparation for life or a strategy for practicing life skills in a safe way. Today, this explanation of play can be observed when young children dress dolls or play in the salon center (Hughes, 1999). Play leads to the mastery of self and environment that is related to personality and intelligence (Frost & Kein, 1983).

✿ MODERN THEORIES

Theorists involved in the psychoanalytic movement focused on the emotional aspects of development. Freud (1963) believed the primary motivation for play was the **pleasure principle.** He explained that pleasure is achieved through wish fulfillment in play. Play provides a release from repressed emotion and thereby reduces anxiety in the child. This interpretation can be seen when Cassandra becomes a nurse and gives the doll a shot again and again. At first, the doll cries loudly. After several shots, the doll cries very little. When the last shot is given, Cassandra explains that the baby is "very brave." For Freud, this play is valued because it provides an avenue for release of emotional feelings, an opportunity to remold past experience, and practice for future experiences.

For Erikson (1950), play has the role of cultural evolution and developmental progression, in which the child adds new and more complex understandings of the world. Erikson identified three ways this play may occur:

1. **Autocasmic play:** Self, people, and things.
2. **Microsphere play:** Small objects and toys.
3. **Macrosphere play:** Shares play with others.

Through play, Erickson believed, children develop cooperative relationships and gain mutual trust. He saw play as a vehicle that children use to find their identity and master the skills needed for everyday life. Solitary play is valued in this theory as a way for children to deal with emotions after difficult periods. In this process, the child plays alone. Play provides a vehicle to master anxiety and conflict.

A small train encourages microsphere play in the block area.

✿ CONSTRUCTIVIST THEORY

For Piaget, a cognitive theorist, play was viewed from a cognitive perspective. Piaget devoted an entire book to the development of play entitled *Play, Dreams and Imitation in Childhood* (1962). He believed that play was a mode by which children learn to understand their experiences. During the process, children are engaged in cycles of assimilation and accommodation. During these cycles, modifications are made in the child's operating schema as she makes sense of the world. Play is considered an interaction among children and the physical environment. Their action on the environment is the primary force for adaptation (Gehlbach, 1991). Play is described as a vehicle for children to use in communication, expression, and reasoning. Piaget identified four types of play that change over time and have different focuses. Although these stages of play can be seen across childhood, there is often a concentration of a particular approach during specific stages of development.

Sensory-Motor Play (Functional Play)

Sensory-motor play is the exploration of objects and materials in the child's environment. Very young children act on the materials, use their senses to examine them, and explore the properties of each item. For example, a group of bells are attached to elastic and hung on the baby's crib. First, the baby explores the bells through the senses: they are touched, mouthed, and visually examined. During this exploration, he is learning about the bells and their responsiveness to his actions. After this exploration, the infant intentionally hits the bells with a foot, hand, head, or another toy. This action on the bells is repeated again and again. The baby laughs out loud. According to Piaget (1962), he is now playing with the bells because he enjoys the activity. This enjoyment signifies that he has moved from exploration of the bells to play.

Hughes (1999) found that during infancy, the two most powerful predictors of intellectual development are parental involvement and availability of play material. Materials can be commercial toys or collected household items that the infant is able to explore and learn about. Infants and toddlers are very interested in materials and spend a great deal of time exploring them through their senses. Through manipulation and action, young children gain understanding of the objects that are in their environment.

Preoperational Play (Symbolic)

Preoperational play is dominated by the development of symbols. At first, the symbol must look like the object it represents, such as a toy telephone that stands for a real one. Later, the symbol can look less like the object it represents. The child can substitute a block for a race car or a stick for a snake. At a higher level of symbolic representation, the children are able to pretend that the real object exists. For example, they drink from a cup that is invisible and eat food that is not there. During the preoperational period, children move into sociodramatic play in which they take on

Ice is a new material that invites a toddler to participate in sensory play.

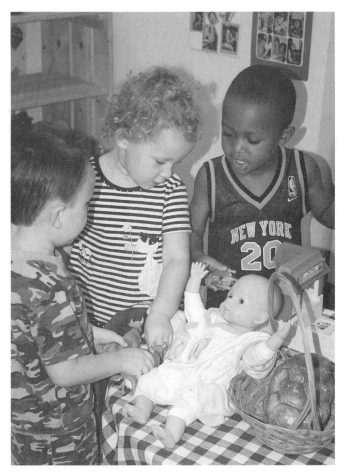

Three children are playing with baby in home living.

roles and are involved in a sequence of events with other children. In housekeeping, for example, Carla and Jose check the refrigerator and find it empty. They decide to go to the grocery store (the block area) to get some food. They cooperatively prepare a dinner of tacos and refried beans, then eat the meal. The two children even wash the dishes at the end of dinner. Carla and Jose have taken on the roles of their parents. The play has been sustained, lasting over 20 minutes. They have talked together, compromised on the food for the dinner, and participated in a sequence of events. This sociodramatic play demonstrates many of the qualities of higher-level preoperational play.

Construction Play

Piaget does not view **construction play** as a separate stage but rather as occurring across several stages. In this play, children build and construct using a variety of materials. The construction can be done individually or in social groups working together. Construction begins with the toddler simply stacking blocks and can progress to the third grader building a sailboat, complete with sail and rudder. Piaget believed that construction is uniquely positioned between play and intelligent work. This play can occur in a variety of settings with different materials, including blocks, woodworking, sand, and clay centers.

"Every time we teach a child something, we keep him from inventing it for himself."

J. Piaget, 1962

Games with Rules

This type of play usually occurs when children have moved into the concrete stage of cognitive development at approximately seven to ten years of age. At first, children construct their own rules that are strictly enforced: "You know the rule, the tallest goes first." If children do not abide by the rules, they are often banned from the play. Later, the rules become more standardized and associated with specific games: "You are out when you miss three times." These are the rules of the game and they are to be maintained during play. Piaget saw the role of play as being fundamental for intellectual functions. He viewed play as a strategy for children to transform the world and meet personal demands. As children move into higher levels of cognitive understanding, they begin to consider the rules imposed by others, and often associated with games and sports.

Piaget explained that children should be able to do their own experimenting and research in play. Teachers can guide or facilitate children's understanding by providing appropriate materials, but the child must construct and reinvent knowledge for himself.

Primary children are playing by the rules and keeping score with a magnet game.

SOCIOCULTURAL THEORY

Lev Semenovich Vygotsky (1896–1934), a Russian psychologist, developed his cognitive theory at the same time as Piaget in Switzerland. Vygotsky's (1978) theory, however, was very different from Piaget's. Vygotsky addressed the sociocultural and historical forces that he believed had an impact on the child's cognitive development. He also wrote that young children learn through interactions with their peers and the adults in their environment.

Vygotsky (1967) believed that children learn when they are in the **zone of proximal development (ZPD).** This is the gap between the point of being able to do something with the assistance of an adult or peer and the point of being able to do it alone. For example, Troy is trying to construct a complicated block structure, but he is unable to balance a large piece of plywood for the roof. His teacher, who is observing his frustration, helps him balance the piece and talks with him about the problem and possible solutions. Vygotsky might conclude that Troy is in the zone of proximal development. The teacher helped Troy balance the plywood; next time, he may be able to do it on his own (Sluss, 2005).

Vygotsky (1967) reasoned that a child in play is functioning above their daily developmental level. Play is in the zone of proximal development. Therefore, the child is learning through this involvement. In play, the child begins to use abstractions such as a block that stands for a baby. The child sees the block, but is able to pretend that it is a baby. According to Vygotsky, this indicates that the child is able to think independently.

Vygotsky concluded that play has two features that make it unique and essential in a child's development. First, representational play creates an imaginary situation that permits the child to explore unrealized desires. Second, it contains rules for behavior that the children must follow to be successful in the play situation. In dramatic play, children learn to respond to external stimuli but in accordance with internal ideas. A child who is imagining himself to be a father with a baby, conforms to the rules of parental behavior that he has experienced. According to Vygotsky, pretend play helps children separate meaning from objects, which is vital preparation for the later development of abstract thought (Berk, 1994).

✵ COGNITIVE ADAPTATION

The work of Jerome Bruner (1973) focuses on play as a way to promote cognitive adaptation. As children play, they try out roles and begin to work out problems cooperatively. Bruner explains that play nurtures the cognitive development of young children as they explore their world. He suggests that play provides a safe way to experiment with different behaviors, investigate how people respond, and learn about adult roles. In play, children try to understand their world and how people function within that arena. The later writings of Bruner investigate the importance of narrative development. According to Bruner, children's knowledge is organized as a narrative and displays features found in stories (Bruner, 1992). It has been further suggested that there is a strong connection between sociodramatic play and storybook enactment with literacy development (Fein, 1995; Pellegrini, 1996).

✵ THEORY OF THE MIND

In the past decade, the relationship between pretense play and the development of mental representation has been studied. The **Theory of the Mind (TOM)** suggests that pretend play uses mental representation and role-playing as a way of understanding others (Leslie, 1987). Saracho and Spodek (2003) conclude that collaboration between players with different views requires the child to think in two ways, real and pretend. In role-playing, children perform the actions of a person, while interpreting the emotions as they relate to the situation. Much of the research of this theory has been done in laboratory settings, although it is beginning to be studied in other settings. This research suggests that play may be an important factor in developing the child's perspective, and later, in abstract thought (Bergen, 2002).

✵ BRAIN DEVELOPMENT

Research on the development of the brain indicates that experience and opportunities during play are essential to the development of neural pathways. These connections are a crucial feature of brain development during the early years of children's lives. Play provides the context for experiences and is vital to the development of learning. There is an unprecedented explosion of information about the importance of play for brain growth and child development (Frost, 1998). Lack of experience during this time will result in underdeveloped neural pathways. These important connections are formed as children explore their environment, play, and form positive relationships with adults and children (Kieff & Casberque, 2000).

Shore (1997) developed broad guidelines based on brain research that support the link between play and healthy brain development. These guidelines can assist adults working with young children:

Respond to the children's clues.

Play with children and follow their lead.

Interesting props stimulate sustained play.

Move into play when children are interested; pull back when they have had enough.

Maintain an ongoing conversation about what they are doing.

Encourage play exploration.

Allow children to explore their relationships.

Arrange time for them to play with children their own age as well as other ages.

In both the psychoanalytic and constructivistic theories, the emphasis is on the self-directed nature of children's play. Play is viewed as self-developed when the child selects and participates in an activity. Both theories emphasize the need for children to control their own play if it is to achieve its purpose of supporting the development of cognition and positive mental health. Vygotsky added another important element needed in play: social interactions that occur between adults and peers.

IMPORTANCE OF PLAY

Play has been the focus of hundreds of research studies in early childhood. Findings from these studies have demonstrated the importance of play in children's development and has been acknowledged repeatedly as a primary vehicle for concept development and problem-solving. Play brings children into contact with multiple stimuli that support the development of categorization, generalization, and conceptual skills.

The importance of play has been emphasized by theorists and researchers, who clearly document the benefits. Many curriculum standards and professional guidelines emphasize the importance of play during early childhood. The NAEYC has taken a strong stand on appropriate practice for young children. In the guidelines for Developmentally Appropriate Practice, play emerges as a critical element in the appropriate early childhood environment. The NAEYC Position Statement (Bredekamp & Copple, 1997) stated:

> 9. Play is an important vehicle for children's social, emotional, and cognitive development, as well as a reflection of their development.
>
> Understanding that children are active constructors of knowledge, and that development and learning are the result of interactive processes, early childhood teachers recognize that children's play is a highly supportive context for these developing processes (Piaget, 1952; Fein, 1981; Bergen, 1988; Smilansky & Shefatya, 1990; Fromberg, 1992; Berk & Winsler, 1995). Play gives children opportunities to understand the world, interact with others in social ways, express and control emotions, and develop their symbolic capabilities. Children's play gives adults insights into children's development and opportunities to support the development of new strategies. Vygotsky (1978) believed that play leads development, with written language growing out of oral language through the vehicle of symbolic representation abilities. Play provides a context for children to practice newly acquired skills and also to function on the edge of their developing capacities to take on new social roles, attempt novel or challenging tasks, and solve complex problems that they would not (or could not) do otherwise (Mallory & New, 1994b).
>
> Research demonstrates the importance of sociodramatic play as a tool for learning curriculum content with three- through six-year-old children. When teachers provide a thematic organization for play; offer appropriate props, space, and time; and become involved in the play by extending and elaborating on children's ideas, children's language and literacy skills can be enhanced (Levy, Schaefer, & Phelps, 1986; Schrader, 1989, 1990; Morrow, 1990; Pramling, 1991; Levy, Wolfgang, & Koorland, 1992).
>
> In addition to supporting cognitive development, play serves important functions in children's physical, emotional, and social development (Herron & Sutton-Smith, 1971). Children express and represent their ideas, thoughts, and feelings when engaged in symbolic play. During play a child can learn to deal with emotions, to interact with others, to resolve conflicts, and to gain a sense of competence—all in the safety that only play affords. Through play, children also can develop their imaginations and creativity. Therefore, child-initiated, teacher-supported play is an essential component of developmentally appropriate practice (Fein & Rivkin, 1986, p. 14).

BENEFITS OF PLAY IN THE CURRICULUM

"The most creative artist living today is the young child at play."

Author Unknown

Children benefit in many ways from play. Researchers continue to document that learning occurs when children play (Berk, 1994; Isenberg & Jalongo, 2001; Isbell & Raines, 1994; Pellegrini & Boyd, 1993). Play provides children with opportunities for social development as they share materials, develop plans, negotiate differences, and cope with disappointments. Play helps build motor skills as children use eye–hand coordination, and engage in activities such as running, climbing, and throwing.

Play helps children's emotional development as they play out their fears and gain control of anxieties. Play is an integral strategy because it contributes to children's language, motor skills, and social, emotional, and intellectual development.

Measuring a block for possible use in construction requires concentration.

✿ PLAYFULNESS

There is another way of thinking about children's play. This interpretation breaks away from old strategies of defining play by focusing on the child's behaviors or what the child does. This contemporary approach focuses on play as an internal predisposition to be playful.

Lieberman (1966) was one of the first to suggest the existence of the playfulness trait in young children. She identified components of **playfulness** as humorous, emotionally expressive, novelty-seeking, curious, open, and communicative. These factors were later supported by the work of Singer & Singer (1976).

Lieberman developed a questionnaire that was revised by Barnett (1990) to help teachers identify playfulness in children. They believe that playfulness is comprised of five dimensions.

Dimension	Questions
1. Physical Spontaneity	How often does the child engage in physical movement during play? Are her movements well-coordinated?
2. Social Spontaneity	Does the child show flexibility in his interactions in the group? Does the child play cooperatively?
3. Cognitive Spontaneity	Does the child use imagination in dramatic play? Is the child spontaneous during dramatic play?
4. Sense of Humor	How does the child show a sense of humor during play? Does the child enjoy joking or clowning around?

5. Manifest Joy How often does the child show she enjoys the play activities? Does the child show enthusiasm during play?

These characteristics of playfulness provide another way of looking at the developing young child. They provide a way to assess play and the children who participate. Maintaining a playful attitude toward learning is an integral part of acquiring skills necessary to meet the challenges of the twenty-first century. Playfulness is an important part of learning to work with others and attaining flexible thinking, persistence, and commitment (Boyer, 1997).

Playfulness and imagination are influenced by experience and training. This development progresses through phases, three of which occur during the early years of children's lives. The early childhood phases include the following.

1. **Sensory Exploration** (approximately birth to age five). This is a playful time when children are flexible and enthusiastically examining their environment. Playfulness can be enhanced in this phase by using the senses to explore objects and materials. An example of an appropriate toy is a large textured ball made of a variety of fabrics that produces a bell sound when moved. The very young infant feels the ball, sees the variation of fabrics, and hears the sound.

2. **Egocentric Speculation** (approximately two to seven years of age). Fantasy and the exaggeration of intuitive impressions dominate this phase; the possibility of "magical powers" exists. Enhance playfulness in this period by providing opportunities for dramatic play. Dress-up clothes, including hats, men's and women's jackets, pocketbooks, wallets, shoes, boots, and scraps of fabric, encourage dramatic play. Placing these items in a housekeeping center sets the stage for sociodramatic play.

3. **Personal Experimentation** (approximately six to ten years of age). During this period (the early school years), there is a trial-and-error approach to the world. Enhance playfulness during this period by experimenting with visual and auditory images. In the primary grades, learning centers can match the interest and/or areas of study. For example, set up a Mexican restaurant center when studying Mexico or a fitness center to encourage increased physical activity. These centers provide opportunities to play and experiment within the curriculum framework.

The development of playfulness provides children with opportunities to think, plan, and enjoy life and all the changes and challenges that will come their way (Boyer).

> **"Play is a natural function, and the learning it leads to is achieved by the well-accepted process of 'doing'. Actual learning comes from doing."**
> *C. Cherry, 1976*

SOCIAL PLAY

Social play involves children's ability to interact with peers. Mildred Parten (1932) identified six types of play (which follow) that are developed during the early childhood years. These types of play begin with solitary play and progress to the more social level of cooperative play. Although originally viewed as developmental steps in social play, today these steps are viewed as descriptive of the different styles of play observed in children (Isenberg & Jalongo, 2001).

Types of Play

1. **Unoccupied Play**   The child is not engaged in play.

2. **Onlooker Play**   Watches others in play but does not enter the activity. May ask questions or make suggestions, but does not enter the play.

3. **Solitary Play**   Plays independently. Is not involved with other children. Pursues own activity without concern for what others are doing.

4. **Parallel Play**   Plays beside or near other children. Plays independently with toys and is not influenced by the play of others.

5. **Associative Play**   Plays with others in an informal way. Communicates about the common activity but there is no organization of the play.

6. **Cooperative Play**   Involves complex play with others, sharing goals and materials.

Knowledge of the types of social play provides the teacher with insight into the activity. It helps teachers appreciate play and the benefits play can provide for developing social skills. The teacher can understand that solitary play is very typical of the two-year-old, but is also important for the primary-grade child who needs privacy and/or time to develop creative ideas. The teacher can offer support for cooperative play as children attempt to organize their play by determining roles, themes, or events. There is agreement that children can develop from playing alone as well as playing cooperatively with others (Parten, 1932; Iwanaga, 1973).

A telephone invites children to use language in their play.

✿ SOCIODRAMATIC PLAY

Sarah Smilansky's work (1968) provides insight into the development of **socio-dramatic play**. She found that children around the world between the ages of two and eight engaged in different levels of social play. In dramatic play, the child takes on a role and pretends to be someone else. In this type of play, children imitate the person and often use props as they draw from personal experience. Dramatic play can begin as early as age two and develops at an accelerated rate from age four to six. It continues to develop in many children until the age of ten or older.

Sociodramatic play is more narrowly defined. It involves at least two children who interact verbally and cooperate in their activity, adjusting their roles in response to others. This play is more sustained, lasts for longer periods of time, and involves a sequence of events. In both pretend play and sociodramatic play, the child's experiences and play environment affect their imitation. Children often use make-believe or imagination to create the play episode. This element allows children to play in ways that represent reality instead of making it an exact replica. Make-believe play relies heavily on oral language and interactions. Children often say, "Let's pretend that this is a bus," or, "I am going to be the daddy, okay?"

Smilansky identified six elements that exist in sociodramatic play.

1. The child takes on a role.
2. The child substitutes an item for a real object (toy or open-ended object).
3. Make-believe is used in the play.
4. The play is persistent and the focus is maintained for a reasonable period of time (ten minutes or more is suggested).
5. There is interaction between two or more children.
6. There is verbal interaction between members of the group.

Sociodramatic play focuses on roles and themes instead of on the materials that were emphasized in the sensory-motor stage of development. Sociodramatic play stimulates emotional, social, and intellectual growth in children. In this type of play, children participate in problem-solving, developing social skills in meaningful activities, and using language to communicate with others. As children participate, they become more accomplished in sociodramatic play.

A number of studies (Lewis 1974; Smilansky, 1990; Smilansky & Feldman 1980) have found that there is a positive relationship between children involved in sociodramatic play and their ability to organize their thoughts through action and language. Smilansky concluded that role-playing was not the critical element for developing children's abilities. She believed it was make-believe (verbal and nonverbal) that was the most powerful element. Smilansky also believed that appropriate adult interactions and a stimulating environment could support sociodramatic play.

✿ SOCIODRAMATIC PLAY IN THE EARLY CHILDHOOD CLASSROOM

Historically, the housekeeping center (Wendy's Corner or home living) was recognized as an important feature in the early childhood environment. Reasons for the inclusion of this area vary. Some believe the housekeeping area is a secure place where children can make the transition from home to school. Others feel that the home is where children have had many experiences and, therefore, provides numerous themes for their play. Whatever the reason, this center continues to be included in most preschool classrooms. Although its use with older children is sometimes questioned, it is interesting to note that in multi-age classrooms, many older children choose to play in the housekeeping center. They continue to want to be involved in play related to home and family.

PLAY ENVIRONMENT

The environment of play is very complex, and is composed of both physical and social elements. The physical environment—variety of materials, space available to play, and sufficient time—can affect the development of the child's play. The social environment can be affected by parenting styles, interaction with peers, and feelings of support. These physical and social elements interact with the child's level of development, experiential background, time, and protected space. To see young children absorbed in their play is a joy, but it can happen only when sufficient time and space are provided (Balke, 1997).

Time and Space for Play

When children play, they need space and time that will not be interrupted. Play is a flowing, creative process. Children require time to become engaged in and to carry out plans. An adult's most important contribution to children's play is ample time. A flexible schedule that includes large blocks of time allows children to remain in play activities that are interesting to them. These blocks of time will vary, based on the developmental level of the children involved in the play; for instance, from a minimum of thirty minutes for toddlers to forty-five to sixty minutes for preschoolers. Primary-grade children who are focused on play may need an hour or more to bring their work to a conclusion. Otherwise, they should be allowed to continue the theme

A water trough inspires creative play.

on the following day. This time frame provides a smooth transition from activity to activity, following the interest and focus of the children. It provides the time needed to become engaged in play and to be involved in more complex activities.

Rooms filled with desks and chairs provide little space for play. Areas that encourage active learning include places that are designed to communicate to children that active, pretend, and construction play are welcome. For example, the block area should be clearly defined with open storage that displays the variety of materials available for building. Low shelf units distinguish boundaries for the area and help children identify specific centers. Children understand that play and building are acceptable activities in the block area.

Play Materials

The selection and regular rotation of play materials is an important consideration for appropriate activity to occur. Materials should be chosen that match the age, developmental level, and interest of the children who will be using them. For example, toddlers need large vinyl-covered blocks for building, whereas kindergartners often prefer snap-together blocks that allow for more complex structures. Primary-grade children may want to create the village they live in, complete with tiny homes, shops, and road signs. Play materials that relate to the culture and region in which the children live also can influence their involvement in a positive way.

In a cross-cultural study of play, Feitelson (1972) found that children's pretend play was richer and more complex when props and toys were provided that reflected the children's environment and were specific to their culture and experience. In one Native American center, the level of dramatic play increased significantly when a Native American doll family was added to housekeeping. The new play items connected to the children's culture and their experiences. When selecting toys and materials, be sure to take into consideration the experiences of the children who make up the classroom.

LEARNING CENTERS (PLAY CENTERS)

Young children are active learners who benefit from an environment that responds to their special way of acquiring knowledge. An appropriate learning environment for young children provides a place where they are challenged to reach their potential while providing opportunities for successful experiences at their developmental levels. **Learning centers** provide a wonderful match for active young learners and a responsive environment.

In learning centers, young children can select the activity that interests them. They can work at their own pace and participate in activities that allow them to be successful. Here, children are motivated to work on the tasks that are important to them and are able to shape what is happening. The effective center is designed to relate to the children's environment and planned to encourage their involvement. In this "center world," children can try out many ideas and rearrange the events to fit their level of understanding. In this social setting, children have opportunities to work together and get rapid feedback from their actions and language (Isbell, 1995).

There are many different types of learning centers that can provide opportunities for participating in sociodramatic play. Traditional centers include blocks, sand and/or water, housekeeping, library, and science and/or nature. Other centers are focused around specific themes and may take turns in the classroom for two to three weeks each. Such examples include grocery store, camping (indoors or outdoors), pet store, doctor's office, mall, and restaurant centers. These centers are equipped with props that support the development of themes and the related roles in play. The inclusion of unique centers in the classroom inspires new play and demonstrates that a creative environment can provide opportunities for change.

Ways to support play in centers include:

- allowing children to select the center where they play.
- providing sufficient time for children to move into roles and sequence.
- selecting equipment and props that are attractive and interesting.
- designing the areas so they are self-managing and do not require an adult in the area.
- changing the materials to stimulate new interests or expanded play opportunities.
- taking time to talk about center play after it is completed each day.

At the beginning of the year, it is helpful to introduce children to the traditional centers by visiting each and discussing the activities that can occur in these special areas. When a new center is set up in the classroom, have a "Grand Opening." During group time, talk about the area, some of the possibilities for play, and new props that are included. Children should choose the center that they would like to work in each day. This personal choice nurtures creative problem-solving and allows children to follow individual interests.

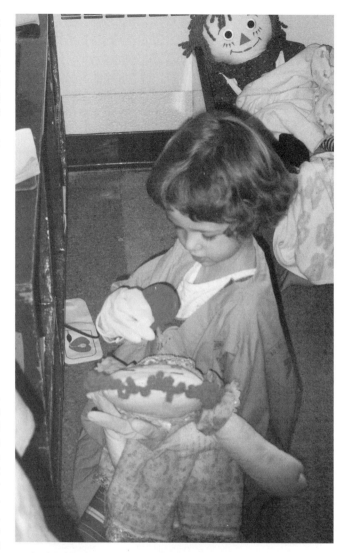

In the health clinic a "doctor" is examining her sick patient.

Blocks

One of the most appealing toys for young children is blocks, because they are versatile and appropriate for many different age groups. The toddler can stack four small cubes on top of each other; the kindergartner can build a sophisticated parking garage; and the nine-year-old can create a mall including a variety of stores, an atrium, and a food court. Children of all ages enjoy playing with blocks because their open-ended quality allows countless possibilities for construction and transformation. Blocks provide many learning opportunities, such as measurement, spatial relationships, and classification. Block centers also encourage language use as children talk about their building and ideas related to construction (Isbell & Raines, 1991). Children often progress in orderly steps as they use blocks in their play (Dodge, 1988).

1. Children carry blocks.
2. Children pile blocks and lay them on the floor.
3. Children connect blocks to create structures (enclosures, bridging).
4. Children make very elaborate constructions.

In the area of creativity, blocks can become anything the child wants. The diversity of blocks allows children to transform the materials in many different ways to follow their interest. Working with blocks encourages fluency and flexibility of ideas. Blocks can become a barnyard for horses, a bridge joining neighborhoods, or a landing strip for an airplane. These transformations and symbolizations encourage the child's creative and cognitive abilities.

There are many types of blocks available for young children including variations of size and material that can add challenges to the play. Different types of blocks include foam blocks, cardboard blocks, unit blocks, small cubes, bristle blocks, and hard plastic blocks that can be used outdoors. Wooden blocks can be made inexpensively from scraps of lumber and added to the area for little or no cost.

Block play can be enhanced by including novel items in the space. Some interesting additions could include cardboard cylinders, a variety of sizes of boxes, pieces of styrofoam, tree branches, pieces of plastic pipe, rulers and yardsticks, Plexiglas pieces, carpet scraps, string and yarn, blankets, plastic animals, miniatures of people, and duct tape. These items can be rotated into the block area on a regular basis so the area is changing, interesting, and challenging. Plastic containers can provide storage for small items and be visible for children to use in their play. These could include a collection of plastic farm animals, a collection of trucks, a multicultural family, and items that relate to a specific theme of study.

Foam blocks provide another material for building.

Water and Sand Play

Young children are drawn to natural materials such as sand, water, dirt, stones, and snow. These materials respond to children and give immediate feedback from their actions. This play can be at a water table, plastic tub, or in a puddle on the playground. Children explore the properties of a material to see how it pours, sifts, fills a cup, and spills on the floor. The young child's first experiences with these elements should be free and open for individual experimentation. Later, items can be added to sand or water for extensions of children's thinking, new combinations, and unique possibilities.

The sand/water table can contain different materials for toddlers to examine.

Items to Enrich Play

Sand: Different size shovels, cups, spoons, buckets, plastic wheeled toys, funnels, sifter, spoons, and ice cubes.

Water: Clear tubes, nested cups, clear bottles, funnel, plastic pump, small boats, plastic fish, spray bottles, medicine droppers, turkey baster, sponge, egg beater, tongs, and clear plastic tubing.

Have a broom or vacuum cleaner, dustpan, mop, bucket, and sponge near the area so children can be responsible for cleaning up when finished. Playing clean-up is a fun activity for most young children and involves them in the care of the area.

Extensions: Food coloring to change the color of the water or sand, soap to add bubbles and foam to the water play, and ice cubes with plastic items frozen inside.

Long-Term and Special Centers

Traditional centers such as blocks and housekeeping can remain set up in the classroom throughout the year, while others take turns in the area for a short period. Special theme centers add interest to the classroom and expand opportunities for learning (Tables 3–1 and 3–2). Since centers are open-ended, they allow children of varying abilities to work together successfully. In the music center, two children are playing tambourines to accompany a 1960s recording. Summer, a child with Down syndrome, is tapping the tambourine with her hand. Ronda, her friend, is creating a rhythm pattern by rotating her hand and elbow to create the sounds on the tambourine. Summer and Ronda are creating music

TABLE 3–1 Suggested Centers for Preschool and Kindergarten

Long-Term Centers	Special Centers
Blocks	Construction/Carpentry
Art	Fitness
Housekeeping/Home Living	Sensory Exploration
Library/Literacy	Drama/Puppets
Private Places	Pizza Parlor (Thematic)
Music/Movement	Beach (Thematic)
Nature/Discovery	Hair Salon (Thematic)
Writing/Illustrating	Camping (Thematic)
Manipulatives	Doctor's Office (Thematic)
	Grocery Store (Thematic)

TABLE 3–2 Suggested Centers for Primary Classrooms

Long-Term Centers	Special Centers
Literacy	Carpentry
Fitness	Drama
Discovery (Science and Math)	Projects/Thematic Centers
Math/Manipulatives	Literature-Related Centers
Blocks/Construction	Inventor's Laboratory
Author's Corner	Art Activities
Computer Area	Gardening (Thematic)

together in the center. Each child is working at her level of development and being successful in a musical experience.

A special/unique center can be added to the classroom for a short time. It will be set up in the classroom for two to three weeks. The best way to determine when to close the center is by watching the children's interest and play involvement. These changing centers provide new interest in the classroom and encourage children to stretch their thinking into new areas.

Learning centers provide many opportunities for integrated learning. For example, in the grocery store center, preschool children can use numbers and prices as they select and purchase products (math). They will see and recognize familiar labels on foods (literacy). In this center, they can try out different roles as the shopper, checkout person, or store manager (social development). The children can stack the cans, push the cart, or bag the groceries (physical development). In the arts, they might create displays or add decorations (art) (a more detailed example of a grocery store center follows). Figure 3–1 visually demonstrates some of the learning possibilities that can occur in the different areas of development.

The Grocery Store Center

Learning Objectives for Children in the Grocery Store Center

1. To learn about the world in which they live.
2. To use real experiences in their sociodramatic play.
3. To expand language as they use new vocabulary related to the grocery store.
4. To learn about the operation of a grocery store and work of the employees.
5. To recognized symbols and labels for food items.

Time Frame for the Grocery Store Center

The grocery store center is effective in the classroom for two to three weeks, although many children will enjoy it for a longer time. The amount of time should be influenced by the experiences and interests of the children in the classroom. Observe the children's activities, to determine when their meaningful play has been completed and the grocery store center should be closed.

Vocabulary

aisle	cereal	manager
bagger	checkout	meat
barcode	customer	poultry
bill	dairy products	price
bread	display	produce
canned items	frozen food	purchase
cart	fruit	stock

Teacher- and Parent-Collected Props for the Grocery Store Center

- cash register
- play money
- paper for making a grocery list
- plastic fruit and vegetables
- scale
- empty food containers (Be sure to include food items that are eaten frequently by the children in the class.)
  - boxes of pasta
  - canned food
  - frozen food containers
  - jugs
  - milk carton
  - plastic jars
- plastic baskets
- toy grocery cart
- cardboard boxes
- paper bags and plastic bags
- signs and displays from a grocery store
- newspaper advertisements for grocery stores
- children's books about shopping

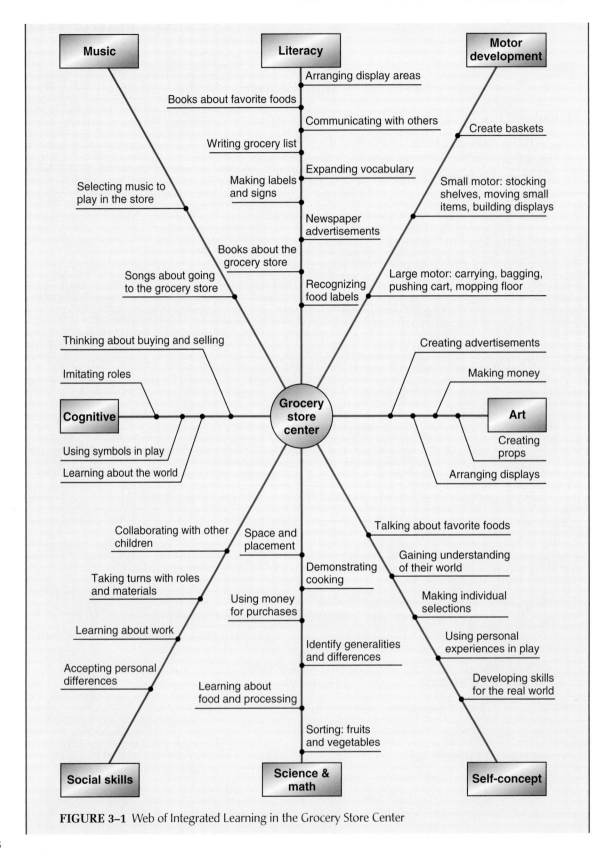

FIGURE 3–1 Web of Integrated Learning in the Grocery Store Center

Evaluation of the Grocery Store Center

1. Are children using their experiences in the grocery store center in their play?

2. Are children using new vocabulary as they describe their activities in the center?

3. Is sequential play being observed during the children's grocery store play (e.g., Going to the grocery store, making selections, paying for purchases, bagging groceries, etc.)?

4. Are children using the roles of grocery store shoppers and employees in their play?

5. Are children beginning to understand economic principles as they use money, run special sales, determine prices, and pay for the products?

(Adapted from *The Complete Learning Center Book* and *The Complete Learning Spaces Book for Infants and Toddlers*).

Literacy in Learning Centers

Centers provide a place to include literacy materials that children can use in their play. With today's emphasis on the development of literacy, centers can provide a way to experience reading and writing in "real" ways. Morrow (1991) found that by simply adding pencils and paper in centers, children significantly increase their writing. Each center can also contain books, magazines, and other printed material related to the area. In the home living center, include cookbooks, telephone books, and books about families to add new opportunities to learn about print. A pad and pencil can provide the props for writing a grocery list or leaving a note for Dad on the refrigerator. In the block center, books about construction, trucks, or cars can provide literacy enrichment. A blueprint with color pencils can encourage the redesign of a building.

These props increase the literacy possibilities that can occur in the centers. With these experiences, children use reading and writing in meaningful ways. Children actively construct their understanding of the forms and functions of the written word. Play provides a direct link to literacy skills. Their first experiences with reading and writing for many children is in dramatic play, where they read environmental print or make shopping lists (Isenberg & Jalongo, 2001).

❀ THE TEACHER'S ROLE IN PLAY

There are many different ways for teachers to encourage play. The teacher can provide options that match the activity of the children, their level of development, and their need for intervention.

Teacher As Planner

The teacher plans the environment so children will participate in play. He is knowledgeable of the background and experiences that the children in his classroom bring with them. This information provides ideas for centers, materials, and themes that build on children's unique interests and provide extension to their learning. The teacher designs the classroom space so that quiet activities are not placed next to the music center or other noisy areas. In planning, the teacher determines which objects and materials will stimulate play: a hard hat in the block area, fancy hats and purses for housekeeping, or a collection of different size balls for outdoor play (Isbell & Exelby, 2001).

Teacher's Role in Assessment

Observing children in their play is one of the most important roles of the teacher. Being attentive to the activity of the children, the language they are using, and the happenings in their play can provide a teacher with much information. It can help determine the interests of the children, materials that are working, and when assistance is needed. The teacher can observe the children's social, motor, and cognitive skills during meaningful activities. Annotations of these observations can provide a record of the child's involvement in play, language development, and ability to work with others. This information is more meaningful than results obtained from more formal methods of evaluation. These observations document the skills children are able to use rather than those they can perform on a test.

Observations of play have assisted many scholars and researchers in their understanding of how children learn and develop. Froebel (2005) observed mothers and children in play. Piaget (1962) observed his children and children all over the world. Parten (1932) studied children's social interactions through observation. Rubin and Daniels-Beirness (1983) also used this technique to develop a Play Observation Scale (POS). Pellegrini (1988) observed and concluded the benefits of rough-and-tumble play. Observation continues to be an appropriate way to study children's play as well as their individual development.

Today, teachers and researchers have new tools that can be used to improve their skills in observation. Video cameras and digital cameras help to study, revisit, and document play. Videos and photographs provide a way to look at a play sequence again and again. With repeated viewing of an episode, the teacher or researcher is

During center time, a teacher observes and documents the play of children.

able to determine exact language, social interactions, and skills that are being used in play (Sluss, 2005).

Teacher As Model

Sometimes it is appropriate for a teacher to actively participate in the play and model a particular behavior. Some children seem to have difficulty moving into play. The teacher can assist the child in this process by assuming a minor role in the play. But the teacher should remove himself from the play once the activity is underway. Teachers must be careful not to take over play or insert personal interests in the activity. Follow the lead of the children and their focus.

Teacher As Mediator

When young children are playing, there will be conflicts and disagreements. Often, these disputes are left for the children to work out. Sometimes, however, there is concern and the teacher may need to intervene to support a peaceful solution. In this role, the teacher helps children in their problem-solving while maintaining a playful attitude. For example, in the greenhouse center, Louie and Sarah both want to be the clerk at the cash register who takes the money for the sales. Debate between the two children continues for a long time with no solution in sight. The teacher may enter the area and ask how they could work together to collect the money from the sales. "What are some of the different ways people may pay for the plants?" After some discussion, the children, guided by the teacher, decide that Louie will take the cash sales and Sarah will take the credit card purchases. They make a credit card machine from some wooden blocks and add some paper for the credit card receipts. Together, they run the sales collection for the greenhouse center.

Teacher As a Resource

A new role for the teacher is that of a resource person for the children's exploration. In order to nurture thinking and problem-solving, children need to learn how to find answers for themselves. The teacher can assist in their research by suggesting references, books, or friends they may ask. But the teacher should not provide immediate answers or take away a child's opportunity to learn how to find answers alone.

A first grader brings an abandoned bird's nest to be placed in the discovery center. Several children are interested in the nest and begin to question what kind of bird might have built it. The teacher suggests that they find a book in the classroom library that can help them find the answer. Or the teacher and the children might use the Internet to find information including pictures of different kinds of bird's nests. These examples demonstrate how teachers can be a resource for information instead of being the person with all the answers. Together, the teacher and children learn about birds and their nests.

✿ | MULTICULTURAL CONSIDERATIONS

Play is universal and has no national or cultural boundaries. It is central to the transmission of cultures and heritage of families. Play enables children to learn who they are and expand their view of the world. If appropriate materials are provided, children who have lived in the desert will bring this knowledge and experience into their play. A young child who lived in China will bring special interest and information into his play. Props from this culture will help Chinese children make connections in their play. It is important to help children explore their own cultural backgrounds and those of others by providing appropriate centers and play materials. Children from all cultures will benefit from having their experiences and understanding expanded through play.

Cultural and racial issues also can influence children's play. In today's world, teachers need to be sure that culturally diverse materials are available for children's play. Is diversity represented in the puppets, dolls, and dress-up clothing? Are there images of the major racial and ethnic groups seen in the classroom? Are there books in the play areas that include children of different races? Is there a balance of images of women and men doing jobs at home and jobs outside the home? For example, are there dress-up clothes for both men and women in the housekeeping center? Are elderly people from different backgrounds shown in recreational as well as work activities?

Sparks (1989) described the challenge for early childhood educators to increase the materials used in their classroom that show children and adults of many different colors, and persons of different ages engaged in nonstereotypical activities. An environment that includes many possibilities for exploring race and ethnicity, gender, and special needs provides the tools for practicing play.

Dramatic play should include:

- diversity of gender play. Rooms of the house other than the kitchen; male and female clothing; pictures of both males and females; and pictures and books that show a diversity of family composition.

- cultural diversity. Foods, cooking utensils, work tools, and items that reflect holiday celebrations from different cultures. Purchased or homemade

Hardhats, tubing, and cylinders inspire these girls to create a complex machine.

dolls representing major ethnic groups, gender balance, and with different kinds of disabilities. Always begin with the diversity represented in your classroom and expand from there to other groups in the community.

- tools and equipment for people with special needs. Wheelchairs, walkers, braces, hearing aids, ramps, heavy glasses, books written in Braille, crutches, walking canes, magnifiers, and a respirator with mask.

CHILDREN WITH SPECIAL NEEDS

Play provides a wonderful way for all children to interact. Because play is open-ended and self-selected, all children can feel successful in their participation and involvement. An inclusive environment encourages children to interact in play, communicate, and develop an appreciation for the strengths of a child who may look different or use an unusual piece of equipment.

A beautiful example of how this can occur was observed when Paulette, a four-year-old child who was deaf, was in an inclusive classroom. Paulette and Vera frequently played together during center time, and they became very good friends. Vera was indifferent to the fact that Paulette was deaf. When watching the girls play, it was difficult to identify any differences between them except that Paulette wore a sound amplifier around her neck. During the holidays, Vera received a doll as a gift. When she returned to school, her treasured doll had a small box strung around her neck. Vera said, "My doll is deaf, just like Paulette. Isn't she beautiful?"

Another example was observed in the housekeeping center. Three children were cooking dinner. One prepared the lasagna and another was making the salad. The child making the salad named the ingredients he was including, such as lettuce, cheese, almonds, and tomatoes. Another child echoed the ingredients, "cheese and tomatoes." Although these children are at very different levels of language development, they interact and learn from the process. Each accepts the other's level of involvement and enjoys the participation.

Some children have difficulty entering and participating in play in their classroom or center. A teacher can assist these children in a number of different ways, based on their individual developmental level and specific needs. The teacher may enter the play episodes or stay outside the play (Johnson, Christie, & Yawkey, 1999). If the teacher chooses to enter, she can guide the play in four different ways.

1. **Parallel Play:** The teacher is near the child but does not participate in the child's play. In this role, the teacher can model play and stimulate ideas. This assists a child who is fearful or unable to participate in play.

2. **Co-Play:** In this situation, the teacher becomes a player with the child. She follows the child's lead and exits the episode, when it is appropriate. Co-playing can extend the play, introduce other roles, and expand interactions.

3. **Play Tutor:** A teacher in this role serves as the leader of the play. She guides and scaffolds the child to higher levels of play by modeling play and leading the child to more advanced play.

4. **Spokesperson for Reality:** In this play, the teacher can add statements that extend or stop the play. For example, a child has brought art scissors to the salon center. The observant teacher may say, "Julian, the scissors belong in the art center."

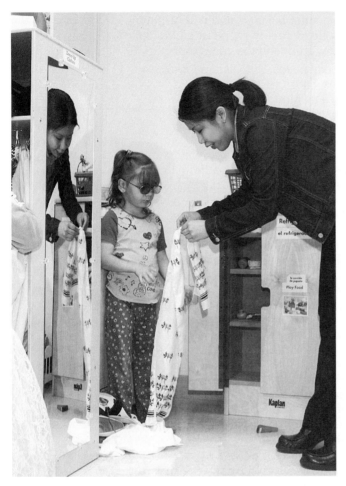

A visually impaired child gets appropriate assistance from her observant teacher.

Outside the play, the teacher can also guide children. In this situation, she does not enter the play, but rather offers a suggestion or intervenes. For example, the teacher may serve as a peacemaker helping solve conflicts (Sluss, 2005).

Outdoor Play

There are many ways to extend play outdoors. Although there is a need for unstructured, active play, other possibilities also can be offered on the playground. Dramatic or sociodramatic play can be moved outdoors by providing the props and setting for this type of activity. A camping center or a farm can be created on the playground for the children to use as a theme in their play and dramatizations. A raised area with arena seating, made from logs or landscaping timbers, can become a stage for performances or dramatic productions. Moveable parts encourage construction play that seems very different because it is done outdoors. Possible materials for construction include plastic milk crates, plastic blocks, wooden planks, pieces of plywood, plastic pipe with fittings, and cedar shingles. Riding toys, push–pull toys, and balls of varying sizes can encourage large motor activity and play.

A garden area can provide a place to plant, weed, and harvest a crop. Water and sand play also can move outdoors with an appropriate portable tub and the intriguing equipment that supports that play. It is helpful to view the playground and outdoor area as another place where play can occur.

WORKING WITH PARAPROFESSIONALS

Paraprofessionals sometimes serve as assistants or aides in early childhood classrooms. These individuals vary greatly in their training and experience with young children. It is often necessary for the teacher to help the aide gain an understanding of the value of play, as well as methods to use in encouraging young children's involvement. It is helpful to talk with paraprofessionals about children's play and identify children's activities that demonstrate their learning, so they can begin to recognize these behaviors. For instance, when a child is taking an order in the restaurant center, she is learning about "writing." When a boy is rocking a baby doll in housekeeping, he is learning about being a father. By identifying these specific actions, you will help the paraprofessional recognize what children are learning though play. Share articles in professional journals or parenting magazines that explain the importance of play and provide practical ideas to use in making props or learning centers. An aide who has gained understanding of the value of play will be able to support this important activity in the early childhood classroom.

WORKING WITH PARENTS

Play in a school setting differs from play at home. Helping parents understand the differences and how the two can complement each other can eliminate some concerns demonstrated in the phrase, "But they are just playing."

Play in the early childhood setting:

- provides a positive transition to the school environment.
- allows more opportunities for interaction with peers.
- makes available a wider variety of materials and equipment for play.
- enables adult–child interactions to facilitate and expand play.
- makes planning a central part of the play.
- provides more space for engaging in play and construction.

Home and school environments can foster different opportunities for children to learn social and cognitive skills. Play contributes to learning in both environments, and teachers can help parents understand and value the role of play in the early childhood environment (Brewer & Kieff, 1996).

NEW CHALLENGES

With a new emphasis on academic skills, especially literacy, early childhood teachers must be able to demonstrate how play provides learning opportunities. As states begin to adopt standards and guidelines in all the curriculum areas, it is

The teacher talks with parents about the importance of their child's play.

important to understand the essential role that play has in classrooms that are developmentally appropriate (Hatcher & Petty, 2004). During play, children assimilate their learning and construct knowledge. The key advantage for linking curriculum goals or standards to play is that play is inherently self-motivating. Children do not have to be made to play—it is intrinsically motivating. Johnson, Christie, and Wardle (2005) refer to the pairing of curriculum goals with play as "educational play." Perhaps this identification will help in clarifying the powerful relationship that exists between learning and play.

 ## SUMMARY

Play has been discussed and studied for hundreds of years by philosophers, theorists, and researchers. The benefits have been recognized widely by researchers and teachers who have studied children engaged in play. They conclude that play encourages communication, cognition, social competencies, and creativity. The phrases "play is the child's work" and "children learn through play" have become widely used clichés. It is essential that early childhood educators be able to explain the benefits of play to parents and community. Although research and theories are helpful, the teacher must believe in the importance of play and be able to articulate the reasons for its inclusion in early childhood environments. The teacher must be able to prepare an environment that will nurture play, select materials appropriate for the classroom, and document the learning that occurs during the activity. Without the knowledge of "why," the "hows" cannot be put into practice or supported effectively. Play is an integral part of the early childhood tradition and it must be continued in the twenty-first century. Childhood play is timeless, powerful, and essential in a changing society.

 ## KEY TERMS

associative play
autocasmic play
construction play
cooperative play
egocentric speculation
learning centers
macrosphere play
microsphere play
onlooker play
parallel play
personal experimentation
play
playfulness

pleasure principle
practice theory
preoperational play
relaxation theory
sensory exploration
sensory-motor play
social play
sociodramatic play
solitary play
surplus energy theory
Theory of the Mind (TOM)
unoccupied play
zone of proximal development (ZPD)

 ## REFLECTION

1. Explain how the interest in play has changed over time.
2. How have different theorists interpreted the important influence of play on children's development?
3. What different types of play did Piaget identify in infants and young children?
4. How do language and interactions influence play in young children?
5. Identify the different types of social play.

6. What are some of the ways the environment can be designed to nurture children's play?

7. How would you support the inclusion of play in an early childhood program?

THINKING ABOUT THE OBSERVATION OF CREATIVITY

1. How would you determine Niki's stage of cognitive development based on this creative episode?

2. What is the significance of the piece of fabric?

3. From this observation, what other play materials might be developmentally appropriate for Niki?

POSSIBILITIES FOR ADULT LEARNERS

Activity: Enriching Play

Goal: To evaluate a housekeeping center and determine how to improve the area.

Materials: These will vary, based on the needs of the specific center.

Procedure:

1. Visit an early childhood classroom that has a housekeeping center.

2. Evaluate the center as to its space, location, materials, and changing items.

3. Determine how the center could be improved.

4. Make a list of suggestions that can be shared in class.

Activity: Flexibility of Blocks

Goal: To record and analyze the language and interactions occurring in the block area.

Materials: Classroom with a well-equipped block area.

Procedure:

1. Visit a classroom that has a well-defined and well-equipped block area.

2. During block play, become an observer. Record or transcribe the children's play and language.

3. After leaving the area, review your notes and refine your observations and language annotations.

4. Bring your written documentation to class.

5. Discuss the learning that is occurring in the block area with particular focus on interactions and language used by the players.

Activity: Loose Parts Play

Goal: To experience the play that can occur with a variety of loose parts.

Materials: Cardboard boxes of different sizes and shapes, wooden blocks, hair rollers of varying sizes, pieces of plastic pipe, cardboard pieces, unusually shaped scraps of wood, milk cartons, plastic cups, twigs, and a camera (digital or instant preferred).

Procedure:

1. Divide the class into groups of three to five people.
2. Give each group a box that includes a variety of materials.
3. Provide time for each group to construct something, using the materials in the box.
4. Take a picture of each construction and display the photos with the names of the players in the group.
5. Ask the students to describe the play activity.

 ## OPEN-ENDED ACTIVITIES FOR YOUNG CHILDREN

PreK–K

Activity: Multicultural Prop Box

Goal: To provide materials that will extend the play of children by adding items from their culture or the culture of the community.

Materials: These will vary, depending on the community in which the children live.

Procedure:

1. Review the backgrounds and experiences of the young children in the classroom.
2. Determine specific toys, props, materials, or books that relate to the cultures of those represented in the classroom or the community.
3. Add selected items to the housekeeping area, dramatic play area, or other centers.
4. Observe the children's play.
5. Talk with the children about the new props that have been added to the play areas.

Primary Grades

Activity: Dramatic Center: Chinese Home (Developed by Bei Zhou)

Goals: It is useful to enrich the play opportunities of children as they learn to appreciate a culture (this center works well in a classroom where Chinese children and their families participate).

1. To promote understanding and appreciation for another culture.
2. To develop the children's language and vocabulary.
3. To expand knowledge of different foods and their preparation.
4. To experience music and art from another culture.

Vocabulary: Can be used during a discussion about the new center in the classroom.

bamboo square pillows	chopsticks
Buddah	potted landscapes
calligraphy	*zhao shang hao* (good morning)
China	pronounced: sow chien how
Chinese traditional painting	*ni hao* (hello) pronounced: knee how
dumplings	*xie xie* (thank you) pronounced: shay shay
fans	*qing* (please) pronounced: ching
Jasmine tea	*yi* (one) pronounced: e
steamed rice	*er* (two) pronounced: all
tea set	*san* (three) pronunced: san
traditional	*si* (four) pronounced; szz
vase	*wu* (five) pronounced: woo

Introduction to the Center

1. Read stories about people from China, their history, the Great Wall, panda bears, and the like.
2. Locate China on the globe and make a cutout map of the country.
3. Discuss and display pictures of China and its people.
4. Show filmstrips and videos of the land and culture.
5. Demonstrate chopsticks and add them to the center.
6. Discuss the vocabulary through experience and songs.

Teacher-Collected Props

Plates, tea set, bamboo chair set, chopsticks, square bamboo pillow, Chinese vase, traditional Chinese painting or calligraphy for the wall of the center, tape player, recordings of traditional Chinese music, and paper cuttings for window decoration.

Literacy Extensions

1. Calendar showing Chinese characters and English symbols.
2. Writing activity with Chinese characters that children can imitate.
3. Experience chart that follows a visit to a Chinese restaurant.
4. A "thank you" note to the resource person or restaurant owner who visits the classroom.
5. Collection of books about China and its people to add to the center.

Connection to the Arts in the Chinese Center

1. Tissue paper for folding and making fans or flowers.
2. Music from the Chinese culture.
3. Fans that can be made from paper and used while dancing to Chinese music.
4. Moving to Chinese music.

Field Trips and Resource People

1. Visit a Chinese restaurant.

2. Invite a parent, friend, or someone who knows about China, someone who has visited China, or someone whose family is Chinese to the classroom.

Resource Books about China

Feinstein, S., & Moore, J. (1989). *China in pictures.* Minneapolis, MN: Lerner Publications.
    Describes the topography, history, society, economy, and government of China.
Flack, M. (1933). *The story about Ping.* New York: The Viking Press.
    A little duck finds adventure on the Yangtze River when he is too late to board his master's houseboat one evening.
Haskins, J., & Hockerman, D. (1987). *Count your way through China.* Minneapolis: Carolrhoda Books.
    Presents the numbers 1 through 10 in Chinese, using each number to introduce concepts about China and Chinese culture.
Krach, M. S., & Zhang, H. (1997). *D is for Doufu: An alphabet book of Chinese culture.* Arcadia, CA: Shen's Books.
    An alphabet book that explores the beauty and richness of the Chinese culture.
Lin, G. (1999). *The ugly vegetables.* Watertown, MA: Charlesbridge.
    A little girl thinks her mother's garden is the ugliest in the neighborhood until she discovers that flowers might smell pretty but Chinese vegetable soup smells best of all. Includes a recipe.

 ## ADDITIONAL READING

Adcock, D., & Segal, M. (1983). *Play together grow together: A cooperative curriculum for teachers of young children.* White Plains, NY: The Mailman Family Press.
Casey, M. B., & Lippman, M. (1991). Learning to plan through play. *Young Children, 46*(4), 52–57.
Cecil, L. M., McPhail, G., Thornburg, K. R., & Ispa, J. (1985). Curiosity-exploration-play-creativity: The early childhood mosaic. *Early Child Development and Care, 19,* 199–217.
Chafel, J. A. (1991). The play of children: Developmental process and policy implications. *Child & Youth Care Forum, 20*(2), 115–133.
Chaille, C., & Solvern, S. B. (1996). Understanding through play. *Childhood Education, 75*(5), 274–277.
Drew, W. F. (1992). Let's play with our children! *Child Care Information Exchange, 85,* 36–40.
Eddowes, E. A. (1991). The benefits of solitary play. *Dimensions of Early Childhood, 21*(1), 31–34.
Fein, G. C. (1979). Echoes from the nursery: Piaget, Vygotsky, and the relationship between language and play. *New Directions for Child Development, 6,* 1–14.
Ferguson, C. (1999). Building literacy with child-constructed sociodramatic play centers. *Dimensions of Early Childhood, 27*(3), 23–29.
Goldhaber, J. (1994). If we call it science, then can we let children play? *Childhood Education, 71*(1), 24–28.
Jones, E., & Reynolds, G. (1992). *The play's the thing: The teacher's roles in children's play.* New York: Teachers College Press.
Klugman, E., & Smilansky, S. (Eds.). (1990). *Children's play and learning: Perspectives and policy implications.* New York: Teachers College Press.
Lewis, R. (1997). With a marble and a telescope: Searching for play. *Childhood Education, 73*(6), 346–350.
Miller, K. (1989). *The outside play and learning book: Activities for young children.* Beltsville, MD: Gryphon House.
Morrison, G. S., & Rusher, A. S. (1999). Playing to learn. *Dimensions of Early Childhood, 27*(2), 3–8.
Nowak-Fabrykowski, K. (1994). Can symbolic play prepare children for their future? *Early Childhood Development and Care, 102,* 63–69.

Owocki, G. (1999). *Literacy through play*. Portsmouth, NH: Heinemann.

Smith, D. (1995). How play influences children's development at home and school. *The Journal of Physical Education, Recreation, and Dance, 66*(8), 19–24.

Wassermann, S. (1992). Serious play in the classroom: How messing around can win you the Nobel Prize. *Childhood Education, 68*(3), 133–139.

 ## CHILDREN'S LITERATURE CONNECTION

Blos, J. W. (1984). *Martin's hats*. New York: William Morrow.
A variety of hats affords Martin many adventures. (PreK–K)

Moss, M. (1990). *Want to play?* Boston: Houghton Mifflin.
Two toddlers experience the frustrations of learning to share their toys. (PreK–K)

Rockwell, A., & Rockwell, H. (1981). *I play in my room*. Middletown, CT: Field Publications.
A young girl describes her activities and toys as she plays in her room. (PreK–K)

Russo, M. (1986). *The line up book*. New York: Greenwillow Books.
Sam lines up blocks, books, boots, cars, and other objects, all the way from his room to his mother in the kitchen. (PreK–K)

Siddals, M. M. (2000). *I'll play with you*. New York: Clarion Books.
A child asks the sun, wind, clouds, rain, stars, and moon to play. (PreK)

Thaler, M. (1974). *How far will a rubber band stretch?* New York: Parents' Magazine Press.
A little boy decides to find out how far a rubber band will stretch. (PreK–1)

Tyron, L. (1991). *Albert's alphabet*. New York: Antheneum.
Albert the duck builds the letters of the alphabet from scrap lumber. When he uses up all of his wood, he turns to other materials, such as stone, guttering, pipe, hedge, and shingles. (K–2)

Ziefert, H. (1988). *Chocolate mud cake*. New York: Harper and Row.
Molly and her little sister, Jenny, bake a make-believe cake out of mud, twigs, and berries when they spend an afternoon at their grandparents' house. (PreK–K)

 For additional resources involving creativity and the arts with young children, visit our Web site at **www.earlychilded.delmar.com**

 ## REFERENCES

Balke, E. (1997). Play and the arts: The importance of the "unimportant." *Childhood Education, 73*(6), 355–361.

Barnett, L. A. (1990). Playfulness: Definition, design and measurement. *Play and Culture, 3*, 319–336.

Bergen, D. (Spring 2002). The role of pretend play in children's cognitive development. *Early Childhood Research and Practice, 4*(1), 1–13.

Berk, L. E. (1994). Vygotsky's theory: The importance of make-believe play. *Young Children, 50*(1), 30–39.

Boyer, W. A. R. (1997). Playfulness enhancement through classroom intervention for the 21st century. *Childhood Education, 74*(2), 90–97.

Bredekamp, S., & Copple, C. (1997). *Developmentally appropriate practice in early childhood programs*. Washington, DC: National Association for the Education of Young Children.

Brewer, J. A., & Kieff, J. (1996). Fostering mutual respect for play at home and school. *Childhood Education, 73*(2), 92–97.

Brosterman, N. (1997). Child's play. *Art in America, 85*(4), 108–112.

Bruner, J. S. (1973). The nature and uses of immaturity. *American Psychologist, 27*, 686–708.

Bruner, J. S. (1992). *Acts of meaning: Four lectures on mind and culture*. Cambridge, MA: Harvard University Press.

Cherry, C. (1976). *Creative play for the developing child.* Belmont, CA: David S. Lake Publishers.

Dodge, D. T. (1988). *The creative curriculum.* Washington, DC: Teaching Strategies.

Elkind, D. (1987). *Miseducation: Preschoolers at risk.* New York: Alfred A. Knopf.

Erikson, E. (1950). *Childhood and society.* New York: Norton.

Fein, G. G. (September 1995). Infants in group care: Patterns of despair and detachment. *Early Childhood Quarterly, 10,* 261–275.

Feitelson, D. (1972). Cross-cultural studies in representational play. In B. Tizard & D. Harvey (Eds.), *Biology of play* (pp. 6–14). Philadelphia: Lippincott.

Freud, S. (1963). *A general introduction to psychoanalysis.* New York: Simon & Schuster.

Froebel, F. (2003). *Pedagogics of the kindergarten: Ideas concerning the play and playthings of the child.* Grand Rapids, MI: Froebel Foundation.

Froebel, F. (2005). *The education of man.* Mineola, NY: Dover Publications, Inc.

Frost, J. L. (June 1998). *Neuroscience, play and child development.* Paper presented at the IPA/USA Triennial National Conference, Logmont, CO.

Frost, J. L., & Kein, B. L. (1983). *Children's play and playgrounds.* Austin, TX: Playscapes International.

Gehlbach, R. D. (1991). Play, Piaget, and creativity: The promise of design. *Journal of Creative Behavior, 25*(2), 137–144.

Gross, K. (1916). *The play of man.* New York: D. Appleton.

Hatcher, B., & Petty, K. (November 2004). Visible thought in dramatic play. *Young Children, 59*(6), 79–82.

Hughes, F. P. (1999). *Children, play, and development.* Boston: Allyn and Bacon.

Isbell, R. (1995). *The complete learning center book.* Beltsville, MD: Gryphon House.

Isbell, R., & Exelby, B. (2001). *Learning environments for young children that work.* Beltsville, MD: Gryphon House.

Isbell, R. T., & Raines, S. (1991). Young children's oral language productions in three types of play centers. *Journal of Research in Childhood Education, 5*(2), 140–146.

Isbell, R., & Raines, S. (1994). *Stories: Children's literature in early education.* Clifton Park, NY: Thomson Delmar Learning.

Isenberg, J. P., & Jalongo, M. R. (2001). *Creative expression and play in early childhood* (3rd ed.). Columbus, OH: Merrill Prentice-Hall.

Iwanaga, M. (1973). Development of interpersonal play structure in three-, four-, and five-year-old children. *Journal of Research and Development in Education, 6*(3), 71–82.

Johnson, J. E., Chrisitie, J. F., & Wardle, F. (2005). *Play development and early education.* Boston, MA: Allyn and Bacon.

Johnson, J., Christie, J., & Yawkey, T. (1999). *Play and early childhood development.* New York: HarperCollins.

Kieff, J., & Casberque, R. M. (2000). *Playful learning and teaching.* Needham Heights, MA: Allyn & Bacon.

King, N. (1979). Play: The kindergartner's perspective. *Elementary School Journal, 80,* 81–87.

Leslie, A. M. (1987). Pretense and representation: The origins of "theory of mind." *Psychological Review, 94*(4), 412–426.

Lewis, H. (1974). *The relationship between sociodramatic play and cognitive performance of five year old children.* Unpublished doctoral dissertation, Ohio State University.

Lieberman, J. N. (1966). Playfulness and divergent thinking: An investigation of their relationship at the kindergarten level. *Journal of Genetic Psychology, 107,* 219–224.

Montessori, M. (1964). *The advanced Montessori method.* Cambridge, MA: R. Bentley.

Morrow, L. (1991). Preparing the classroom environment to promote literacy during play. In J. F. Chrisitie (Ed.). *Play and the early literacy development* (pp. 141–165). Albany: State University of New York Press.

Nourot, P. M., & Van Hoorn, J. L. (1991). Symbolic play in preschool and primary settings. *Young Children, 46*(6), 40–50.

Parten, M. (1932). Social participation among preschool children. *Journal of Abnormal and Social Psychology, 27*(2), 243–269.

Patrick, G. T. W. (1916). *The psychology of relaxation.* New York: Houghton Mifflin.

Pellegrini, Anthony D. (Ed.). (1988). *Psychological bases for early education.* New York: John Wiley & Sons, Inc.

Pellegrini, A. (1988). Elementary school child's rough and tumble play and social competence. *Developmental Psychology, 24*, 202–206.

Pellegrini, A. (1996). *Observing children in their natural worlds: A primer in observational methods.* Hillsdale, NJ: Lawrence Erlbaum Associates.

Pellegrini, A. D., & Boyd, B. (1993). The role of play in early childhood development and education: Issues in definition and function. In B. Spodex (Ed.), *Handbook of research on education of young children* (pp. 105–121). New York: MacMillan.

Piaget, J. (1962). *Play, dreams, and imitation in childhood.* New York: W. W. Norton.

Quinn, J. M., & Rubin, K. H. (1984). The play of handicapped children. In T. Yawkey & A. Pellegrini (Eds.), *Child's play: Developmental and applied* (pp. 63–80). Hillsdale, NJ: Lawrence Erlbaum Associates.

Rubin, K. H., & Daniels-Beirness, T. (July 1983). Concurrent and predictive correlates of sociometric status in kindergarten and grade 1 children. *Merrill-Palmer Quarterly, 29*, 337–351.

Russ, S. (1996). Development of creative process in children. *New Directions for Child Development, 72*, 31–42.

Saracho, O. N., & Spodek, B. (Eds.). (2003). *Contemporary perspectives on play in early childhood education.* Greenwich, CT: Information Age Publishing.

Shore, R. (1997). *Rethinking the brain: New insights into early development.* New York: Families and Work Institute.

Singer, J. L., & Singer, D. L. (1976). Imaginative play and pretending in early childhood. In A. Davids (Ed.), *Child personality and psychopathology* (pp. 142–169). New York: Wiley.

Sluss, D. J. (2005). *Supporting play: Birth through age eight.* Clifton Park, NY: Thomson Delmar Learning.

Smilansky, S. (1968). *The effects of sociodramatic play on disadvantaged preschool children.* New York: Wiley.

Smilansky, S. (1990). Sociodramatic play. Its relevance to behavior and achievement in school. In E. Klugman & S. Smilansky (Eds.), *Children's play and learning* (pp. 18–42). New York: Teachers College Press.

Smilansky, S., & Feldman, N. (1980). *Relationship between sociodramatic play in kindergarten and scholastic achievement in second grade.* Tel-Aviv: Tel-Aviv University, Department of Psychology.

Sparks, L. D. (1989). *Anti-bias curriculum: Tools for empowering young children.* Washington, DC: National Association for the Education of Young Children.

Spencer, H. (1896). *Principles of psychology.* New York: D. Appleton.

Sutton-Smith, B. (Ed.). (1979). *Play and learning.* New York: Gardner Press.

Vygotsky, L. S. (1967). Play and its role in the mental development of the child. *Soviet Psychology, 6*(3), 6–18.

Vygotsky, L. S. (1976). Play and its role in the mental development of the child. In A. J. Bruner, & T. S. Sylva (Eds.), *Play: Its role in development and evolution* (pp. 537–554). New York: Basic Books.

Vygotsky, L. S. (1978). The role of play in development. In M. Cole, V. John-Steiner, S. Scribner, & E. Souberman (Eds.), *Mind in society* (pp. 92–104). Cambridge, MA: Harvard University Press.

UNDERSTANDING THE VISUAL ARTS

CHAPTER 4

This chapter will provide a foundation for understanding the stages of artistic development in young children. It will include theories, explanations, and interpretations that describe how young children learn about the world of art.

After studying this chapter, you will be able to:
- **Understand why art is essential in an early childhood classroom.**
- **Describe the stages of artistic development from infancy to the primary grades.**
- **Identify artists in the community who could visit and/or work with the children.**
- **Explain the difference between a "process" and a "product."**
- **Recognize appropriate ways to introduce artists and their work to young children.**

OBSERVATION OF CREATIVITY

A project on gardening has been going on for several weeks in a multi-age K–2 classroom. One of the art activities included in the study is creating a mural about the planting and gardening the children have done. Cassandra, the teacher, has covered a large wall in the room with white paper. She has also covered the floor around the area with a clear plastic shower curtain. There are three children adding their ideas to the mural with paint and brushes. The mural already has many pictures of flowers, gourds, tomatoes, and some of the plants growing in the garden outside the classroom.

Lucas, who is not yet four years old, is painting an orange sun. He makes a circle with lines sticking out all around the form. This sun is placed as high on the paper as he can reach. Kim and Fernando, both six years old, are discussing the colors and shapes of the flowers blooming in the garden. After considerable conversation, they choose colors that match the colors of the flowers growing in the garden. Kim paints a zinnia that is red and resembles the real flower. Fredrick paints a marigold at the edge of the garden, putting great effort into making his representation like the flowers growing next to the fence.

WHAT WAS OBSERVED?

The teacher has selected a group project that is open-ended and appropriate for the developmental level of the children in her class. This activity allowed the children to select and create the items they wanted to include on the mural. The plastic on the floor was a preventive measure, to catch the dripping paint, which is sure to occur. Lucas painted a sun in a predictable way for his developmental level, while both Kim and Fredrick, who are older, are at a stage of artistic development at which they are growing more concerned that their paintings truly represent the flowers in their garden. This group project allowed the children to talk about the flowers and collaborate on what they would paint. Their drawings and words represented what they were learning about plants, as well as how to use symbols to communicate their ideas.

❋ ARTISTIC TERMS

Abstract: In visual arts, "abstract" generally refers to artwork emphasizing shapes, colors, lines, and texture over subject matter.

Color: Primary and secondary hues created by light and pigments.

Composition: Arrangement of the design and space.

Folk Art: Refers to art created by individuals who are self-taught. Their art is not developed in response to a study of art, but derives out of the experiences of their lives and the materials available that they prefer.

Form: Three-dimensional quality, which includes height, width, and depth.

Line: A mark made by using a tool across a surface (can be vertical, horizontal, diagonal, or curved).

Pattern: The repeat of design, lines, or shapes in the artwork.

Perceptual Theory: Relates to creations developed relative to how objects/subjects are seen through observation. This differs from an artist rendering things according to imaginative thoughts or ideas about how things function.

Perspective: Point of view created by techniques such as size and overlapping.

Shape: Configuration, contours, or outline.

> **"Clay was one of the first art mediums of humankind. It is exciting to see it appearing again in early childhood programs."**
> *J. B. Koster, 1999*

❋ ART IS BASIC

Art is a basic component in early childhood education. This important area must be carefully designed during the early years to enhance children's artistic development and nurture an appreciation for beauty in their world. Art is recognized as both a fundamental and distinctive way of knowing. Art is an important nonverbal

Little hands can manipulate clay.

language; a system of symbols that emerge from children's drawings. Appropriate early artistic experiences assist children in finding meaning about themselves and their world. Art enriches the lives of all children, not just a talented few. However, art should not be valued simply because of the benefits to learning. According to Fox and Diffily (2000), "Children's art has value in and of itself" (p. 5).

✺ THEORIES RELATED TO ART

There are several theories and explanations that provide insight into the artistic development of children. These theories provide understanding of how children grow artistically and identify factors that relate to this development. Although theories can assist in understanding complex phenomena, they also provide a framework for observation and reflection of the developing child.

Constructivist Theory of Art Development

The constructivist theory is drawn from the work of Jean Piaget and Lev Vygotsky. Although differences exist between these theorists, their writings have had a tremendous impact on the fields of early childhood and child psychology. This cognitive theory describes learning as a process that is influenced by children's level of thinking as they interact with the world around them. Children develop schema to organize their experiences while interacting with their environment. According to the constructivist theory, children develop through hierarchical stages and proceed in a predictable pattern. Children are recognized as powerful forces, influencing and shaping their own learning. In a constructivist environment, materials and activities are selected to encourage children's participation with little direction by the teacher. Children are encouraged to follow individual interests, make choices, and combine materials in their own way.

Vygotsky placed emphasis on the role of adults and peers in the scaffolding of children's learning experiences. He believed interactions in the zone of proximal development were helpful and assisted children in moving to higher levels of understanding. This social constructivist interpretation of the learning process could influence directly the teacher's involvement in the art program. In this environment, there is more opportunity for group and partner work. The teacher, as facilitator, poses questions, serves as a resource, and provides materials to assist the developing artist.

In the area of art, Lowenfeld and Brittain (1987) identified specific stages that occur during the artistic development of the child. These stages directly correspond to levels identified in the cognitive developmental theory. Producing art requires children to think of an experience, idea, or feeling, and construct symbols to represent or express what they know. Art is a highly symbolic activity, a form of cognitive expression (Seefeldt, 1995).

A Way of Expressing Feeling

The psychoanalytic theory describes art as a way for children to express deep feelings and emotions. Art is viewed as an emotional outlet that allows the child to release inner feelings. Proponents of this theory see children's art as an avenue for understanding their emotional workings. In times of crisis or emotional turmoil, children's drawings have been used to identify a child's true feelings about an event. Art therapists, who are highly trained professionals, use children's artwork to interpret feelings and suggest possible interventions.

Peter's picture reflects his feelings about moving and leaving his old home. (Age 4)

Children need opportunities to express their feelings and emotions. This self-expression is a healthy way of dealing with personal thoughts for an individual at his or her level of development. Children identify with their artwork and feel proud of their product, which builds their confidence. Sharing and displaying their works with others gives children another way to value what they have done.

Social Development

With art, children have the opportunity to work together in small groups. Here, children can learn to value the ideas of others as they work cooperatively on a project. They can see that other children have interesting ideas that are beneficial to the group. Learning in a social setting is enriched when children are able to use diverse materials in a variety of ways. The use of different techniques and approaches encourages children to express themselves, both individually and within the group (Drew & Rankin, 2004).

Physical Development: Large and Small Motor Development

The physical growth of children is occurring simultaneously with the other developmental domains: cognitive, social, and emotional. Art provides many opportunities to enhance large (gross) and small (fine) motor development. Small muscles develop while children are cutting, pasting, folding, and painting. Children are able to refine these skills as they use and practice them. For example, a child who is unable to cut with scissors may benefit from tearing paper or crunching newspaper. These simpler experiences help the child gain small muscle control and build her confidence before she attempts to use scissors. Art can also include activities that use large muscles. These might include painting with a roller, creating a path from stones, or creating a large mural. Art should include opportunities for children to use both large and small muscles in meaningful ways, building their body control and self-image.

Sensory Learning

Much learning for infants and young children takes place through the senses. In the passive world of watching television or working with computers, children have few opportunities to use their senses for learning about their world. Art is one of the few areas that can provide opportunities to feel the texture of fabric in a wall hanging, see colors and shapes in a painting, and smell play dough as it is squeezed and formed. Touching, seeing, hearing, smelling, and tasting involve the active involvement of the child. It is not just the presence of these senses, but rather, the interactions that occur between the child and environment. Through early art experiences, children can develop and use sensitivities that will enrich their lives (Lowenfeld & Brittain, 1987). The refinement of the senses is also related to reading and writing. A person who communicates in writing must be in touch with the environment or they will have nothing to say. The reader must be able to imagine what the words describe or there will be no comprehension. The senses feed imagination and cultivate the capacity to think (Eisner, 2003).

Visual Perception

The **perceptual theory** is based on the assumption that children draw what they see. Supporters of this view assert that children see things in wholes as the brain structures images. Perceptual theorists believe that children can improve visual discrimination if given appropriate opportunities. Using this theory as a base, perceptual theorists believe children can become better observers when guided to focus on specific features.

Left Brain–Right Brain

Recent studies on brain development have led to discussions about the operation of the left and right hemispheres of the brain. It is believed that the **left hemisphere** specializes in logical operations whereas the **right hemisphere** is the visual-spatial portion of the brain. Creative thinking and producing require the child to move out of logical operations (left hemisphere) to experiment with new ways of thinking (right hemisphere). Some believe art activities can serve as a bridge for interactions between the two hemispheres. This also can be accomplished by integrating various aspects of the curriculum to include a variety of activities requiring the child to think in different ways. Integrated curriculum, that includes both content areas and the arts is believed to provide activity for multiple portions of the brain.

Spatial Intelligence: Another Way of Knowing

Gardner (1983), in his theory of multiple intelligences, identified one of the areas as spatial intelligence. Individuals with spatial intelligence have the capacity to perceive the visual-spatial world accurately and to use this knowledge when creating. He further explained that visual intelligence involves thinking in pictures, seeing **spatial relationships,** drawing, building, designing, and creating. Such individuals are often sensitive to color, line, shape, form, space, and the relationship between each. Gardner wrote that the right hemisphere is involved in both spatial tasks and the processing of information that relates to that area. Painters, sculptors, and architects demonstrate spatial intelligence in their work and products. Art may provide some children with an avenue to be successful. This may ignite their motivation so they want to learn, explore, and create. Their art experiences allow them to follow their ideas, choose materials, and reflect on their work.

Gardner's writings have stimulated new interest in the arts and their importance in the development of children. The theory of multiple intelligences recognizes that children may be talented in specific areas and learn in different ways. For some children, art may be the way they learn best; for others, it may be a new way to experience the world. An environment that attempts to nurture all children recognizes the importance of these different dimensions of intelligence.

Use of Theories

Theories and explanations can provide new ways to understand the art of young children. However, it is important to remember that theories do not tell teachers how to develop an art education program for young children. Instead, they may help teachers learn how to recognize the factors that may be important in the artistic process. This theoretical knowledge can assist teachers, caregivers, and parents in creating art programs that are consistent with what we know about how children learn. Explanations can help teachers and parents recognize the positive benefits of art experiences and establish their relationship to other areas of the curriculum.

❈ | STAGES OF ARTISTIC DEVELOPMENT

Young children experience objects and materials in different ways as they progress through the levels of artistic development (Kellogg, 1969). Rhoda Kellogg's research has significantly increased our understanding of children's artistic development. She studied 100,000 young children's drawings produced with pencil, pen, crayon, or brush. This extensive study provided the basis for her understanding of the children's work and thinking. Kellogg was particularly interested in the scribbles of young children—work that had previously been ignored. During her work, she concluded that the scribbled art, beginning at age two, had a biological foundation. She determined that children progress from making scribbles to drawing pictures, by using a built-in, spontaneous method of self-teaching. She found that this spontaneous method continued until children were five years old (Kellogg, 1959).

From her research, Rhoda Kellogg concluded that young children throughout the world scribble in similar ways and identified 20 scribbles that were used repeatedly by many of the children in her investigation. Representations of the 20 types of scribbles are shown in Figure 4–1. Kellogg further suggested that many educators fail to recognize that young children's art, including scribbles, is innate and self-taught. It is only in the later stages of development that children's artwork can be coached and directed by an adult. She wrote that these scribbles are meaningful to a child and should be valued by the adults in their environment. Her insight helped distinguish scribbles as an art form and results in respect for very young children's efforts and artistic work (Kellogg, 1959).

> **"From the moment the child discovers what it looks like and feels like to put lines down on paper, he has found something he will never lose, he has found art."**
>
> *R. Kellogg, 1969*

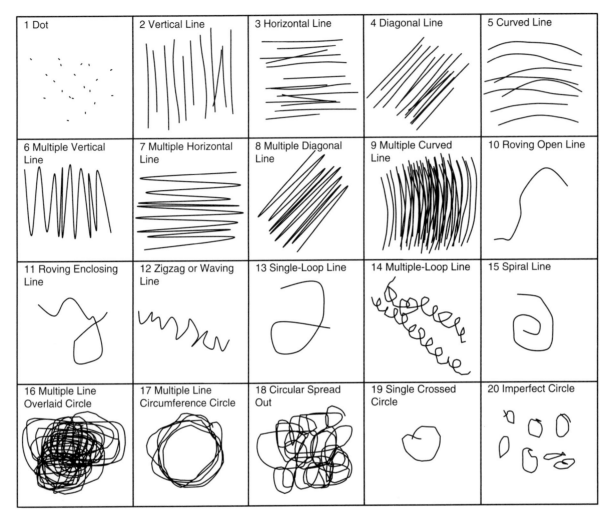

FIGURE 4–1
Representations of the 20 types of scribbles identified by Rhoda Kellogg.

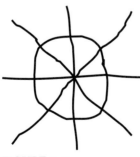

FIGURE 4–2
Mandala

Rhoda Kellogg also identified various symbols that have been drawn by children in many different cultures. For instance, the mandala design, shown in Figure 4–2, is produced by children in different parts of the world. The mandala is a simple circle or square divided by intersecting lines (Kellogg, 1959).

Kellogg explained that older children's art is produced by looking at a physical object and trying to draw a reasonable resemblance of the object, while the art of young children is not produced by looking at an object or trying to imitate a model. She found that young children move their hands to express a feeling that comes from within their bodies; they are delighted in the movement and scribbles they produce. Young children are not concerned about their artwork looking nice or resembling real things in their environment. Kellogg cautioned educators to remember that adults and children may not see the same thing in these scribbles and drawings. It is important for young children to experiment, create in their own way, and not be forced to copy models. She stated that freely created art allows the child to express the feelings and ideas that are truly integrated into each individual child's mind (Kellogg, 1973).

A description of these stages can assist teachers as they work with young children and observe them in the area of art. Although there is a predictable pattern to their development, children move through the levels in different ways and at their own pace. These stages of development provide guidelines for planning for a specific group of young children. These experiences should include open-ended opportunities so individual variations can occur.

The developmental stages of particular interest to early childhood educators are the **scribble stage, basic form stage**, and the **pictorial stage**. It is important to remember that children at each stage of development can produce art. The scribble stage is the first step in the artistic developmental process. The toddlers' scribble art is just as important as the primary-age child's drawings that may include a more complex picture. Positive support for the young child's beginning artistic efforts can provide a strong foundation for later development and enjoyment of artistic experiences. In the next section, the stages of artistic development will be discussed in further detail.

Kellogg's Developmental Stages (Kellogg & O'Dell, 1967)

Stage 1—Scribbles: These are the earliest drawings of young children. They are simple and random markings, made for the pleasure of drawing scribbles. In this stage, the young child is not trying to represent anything but rather is enjoying the process of making scribbles on the paper.

Stage 2—Lines and Shapes: In this stage, children begin to draw simple shapes. Kellogg identified several universal symbols that children use around the world. These include: mandala, sun, ladders, spirals, wavy lines, and rainbows. She wrote that these symbols were being used to communicate and were the beginnings of writing. Children in stage 2 continue to draw for pleasure.

Stage 3—Semi Representational: In this stage, **representational** drawing begins. These drawings are symbolic representations of real people or things. During this period, children use the shapes from stage 2 to represent people, houses, trees, and windows. They begin to identify their drawings, tell related stories, and expand their drawings to include new meanings.

Lowenfeld's Stages Relate to Cognitive Development

There is growing recognition that art is a cognitive event. With this understanding, art is viewed as not only using hands, but also engaging the mind. Lowenfeld's writings have been very influential in developing understanding of the relationship between learning and the artistic process. His book, *Creative and Mental Growth* (1987), now in its eighth edition, clearly describes the impact art can have on intellectual, social, and emotional development. He explains that art, for a child, is primarily a means of expression. The child is not static, but rather always changing and increasing understanding of the environment. In childhood, this process includes thinking, feeling, and perceiving, as well as responding to the environment. He stressed the importance of the process as children select, use, and evaluate their work.

Lowenfeld and Brittain (1987) identified stages that children move through as they explore art and media. These stages relate to the cognitive stages of development that Piaget described in his writings and can serve as a guide for understanding children's artistic development, with variations for the individual child.

Scribble Stage (1–2 Years of Age)

UNCONTROLLED SCRIBBLE.   During the first two years of life, most young children are in the scribble stage of artistic development. Toddlers' first marks are uncontrolled and made on paper, walls, or in sand. They use any tool that is available in their environment: crayons, markers, or sticks. They show little concern for the final product and instead are focused on making random marks. Since small motor development is not refined, motions in the scribble stage are large and often involve the entire body. They find that the materials they use are as interesting as the scribbles they produce. For example, toddlers are totally involved in sensory experiences as they feel, smell, and examine the physical properties of paint.

CONTROLLED SCRIBBLE.   As toddlers move from the **uncontrolled scribble** stage to **controlled scribbles,** they begin to establish a connection between their

Uncontrolled scribble art.
(Age 2.0 years)

actions and the marks produced on paper. They understand that they are creating an interesting scribble mark on the page. This awareness of cause and effect helps them move into using a more controlled scribble. Children begin to experiment with the different marks they can produce such as lines, zigzags, circles, and suns. This new ability—to control the scribble—is exciting to young children as they focus intently on their creations. Because their movements are still large toddlers need large blank sheets of paper and crayons or magic markers that do not restrict their motion.

Basic Forms Stage (3–4 Years of Age)

In this stage, children's drawings begin to exhibit some form and organization. As preschoolers begin to develop better eye–hand coordination, they are able to make shapes and control their placement on the page. They begin to repeat patterns, often filling a page with similar forms. Although this usually occurs during the third and fourth year of a child's life, it can vary from child to child. Young children are very pleased with the shapes they produce and enjoy the process used to obtain these designs.

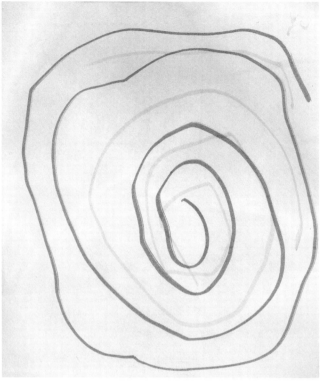

Controlled scribble art. (Age 3.4 years)

As young children gain more control of tools, they begin to produce basic forms and lines. It is important for them to have quality tools in this stage of development. Good tools support their growing artistic abilities and provide opportunities for successful experiences. Appropriate art tools for this stage include felt markers, crayons, colored chalk, paintbrushes, and tempera paint.

Some of the first forms drawn by young children are ovals and circles. They also begin to make curved lines and arches. Later, more complex forms such as rectangles and squares are added to their creations. Although the forms appear to be simple and similar among young children, they represent more refined control of their hands and the materials they are using.

Representational Art

PRESCHEMATIC STAGE (APPROXIMATELY 4–7 YEARS OF AGE). In the **preschematic stage** of development, children begin to use symbols in their work. However, these symbols may not clearly approximate the objects they represent. Their "first pictures" are seen in this stage, as children draw a variety of forms and combine them into simple compositions. They move from the totally sensory experience to using symbols to represent their world. This symbolic representation establishes a new relationship between their artwork and the ideas they wish to

These forms were drawn by a three-year-old child.

express. Being able to think about something not present and find a way to represent it is a major cognitive accomplishment (Raines & Canady, 1990).

Often, the first symbol used in the pictorial stage is a person, composed of a round head and lines for legs. Young children also combine other basic symbols from previous drawings to represent important things in their environment. For example, a tree is composed of a circle and lines. A house is a triangle with two extra lines. As children attach meaning to their symbols, they frequently name the objects included in their pictures. They can name or label their drawings, using words to describe their symbolic representation. They continue to draw as they see things from their own perspective. This is demonstrated by the drawing of their family outside their home. The picture includes all of the family members, but the largest person in the drawing is the child.

SCHEMATIC STAGE (APPROXIMATELY 7–9 YEARS OF AGE). After a great deal of experimentation with materials and tools, children move into the **schematic stage** of development. In this stage, children continue to develop symbols for their world, but the representations they use are more refined. Some children are concerned about the elements looking realistic. Their drawings are more individualized, with the development of specific symbols to consistently represent objects in a unique way. Children are beginning to understand space relationships and experiment with the placement of objects on the page.

As children's drawing becomes more representational and detailed, more refined tools are needed. These tools provide the control children need to create features and details in their work. Thinner paint brushes, wider ranges of colors, and rounded markers make creating the more detailed pictures more appropriate in the child's eye.

BEGINNING REALISM (APPROXIMATELY 9–12 YEARS OF AGE). During the primary grades, children become concerned about **realism** in their art. Many children express the desire for their drawings to look real or like a photograph. Children are interested in size, **proportion**, placement, shape, color, and perspective. In the representational drawings of early elementary-aged children, the meaning of the figures becomes specific. The development of a unique picture is now replaced by the collective understanding of what is good and right in the drawing. Gardner (1980) stated that during this period, there is a loss of freedom, individuality, and creativity once apparent in the drawings of younger children.

Variations in the artistic development of two children.

This drawing of a boy and his friends demonstrates who he views as the most important person. (Age 3.8 years)

Detailed aliens are drawn leaving their space ship.

This child's drawing of a car, with a driver and baby in car seat, is shown leaving the city and going to the mountains. (Age 9.0 years)

❖ VARIATIONS IN ARTISTIC DEVELOPMENT

It is important to remember that although there are common characteristics during the periods of artistic development, there also are individual variations. Children in the same stage of development or even the same chronological age will vary significantly in the art they produce. For example, look at the work of three five-year-old children who are in kindergarten. Notice the differences in their work and their ability to produce a picture.

"As we were walking, talking about nature, I asked a question and you threw up your hands and said I don't know, as a bird flew by."

These three pictures demonstrate the variations in artistic development. (All age 5 years)

✿ NATIONAL STANDARDS IN THE ARTS

The Consortium of National Arts Education Associations (CNAEA) has published standards. Their guidelines support the belief that for every child to be truly educated they must receive instruction in the arts. They have developed standards in dance, music, theater, and the visual arts. The standards define what a child should be able to do by the end of 12th grade.

Standards for the Visual Arts

- Understand and apply media, techniques, and process.
- Use knowledge of structure and functions.
- Understand the visual arts in relation to history and cultures.
- Reflect upon and assess the characteristics and merits of students' own work and the work of others.
- Make connections between the visual arts and other disciplines. (Consortium of National Arts Education Associations [CNAEA], 1994).

Guidelines for the Visual Arts in Early Childhood Programs

Some professionals in the field have suggested elements that should be included in an effective program for young children. These can provide useful guidelines for designing appropriate visual art experiences.

Children will explore and gain mastery over a variety of art media.
This suggests that young children should be able to explore and learn about a wide range of media, such as markers, crayons, clay, and materials used in construction.

Children will be able to use different media to express their ideas and thinking.
This supports children's need to use diverse media to represent their experiences, thoughts, and feelings. They should have opportunities to talk about the media and how it was used.

Children will recognize their own work and the work of others.
Children will need many opportunities to see their work displayed with the artwork of others. This also suggests that children should learn about artists and their work. This may include visiting artists, studying classic works, and examining illustrations from children's books.

Children should be able to talk about the visual aspects of their work and others'.
Teachers need to use the vocabulary of art, including form, shape, color, and space. When children reflect on their work, or that of others, they should be encouraged to use these terms.

These guidelines emphasize the need for the visual arts to include a variety of media, time to reflect, and opportunities to learn about the work of other artists. These standards were reviewed by the Carnegie Corporation and supported by McGraw-Hill Education (Seefeldt, 2005).

❊ PRINCIPLES OF AN ART PROGRAM FOR YOUNG CHILDREN

In the early years of a child's education, certain principles should influence the development of the art program. These important beliefs provide the foundation for creating a developmentally appropriate art curriculum during the early childhood years. Each of these concepts will be identified and discussed to provide the framework for program development.

Provide Appropriate and Varied Experiences

It is the role of the teacher to provide a variety of materials and tools that challenge children to experiment and discover ways of expression in a visual form. Variation in activities, materials, and tools encourage children to experiment and learn about the artistic possibilities available in the classroom. Diverse materials allow children to think in divergent ways, and the possibilities for combinations and creations are increased. This experimentation should be encouraged and supported at all levels of development.

Process versus Product

During the first five years of life, most children are more interested in the **process** of creation than in the **product**. At this time, the focus of art should be on participation and enjoyment of interesting art experiences. This means there may not be a product to display or take home. For example, a painting may go through many beautiful transformations as the child continues to add color, until the large paper is covered with a mass of brown paint. This is appropriate for the young child who has never worked with tempera paint or experimented with color. Children should not be bound to produce a picture to take home, a craft, or a gift. When children are asked to create a specific craft, they are often shown a model made by an adult that they should reproduce. This model limits their possibilities and communicates that the final product should look like the model. When observing in a kindergarten class, I saw a teacher show a rose to the children. She had made it from crepe paper and attached a wire stem covered with green tape. She asked the children to make a rose "just like mine" for a Mother's Day gift. This craft required the child to focus on the product. Young children should be allowed to decide what they want to create for Mother's Day. They should be able to select the materials to be used from a wide variety of choices. This allows them to be involved in the process of creating, rather than focusing on an end product that looks like the rose produced by the teacher and all the other children. Each child's creation should be different and his/her own. The creation process is far more important and essential at this stage of development than the product the child creates.

> ❝"The key is access: access to a range of working spaces, access to materials, access to other kids and other adults; these in turn give students access to their own creative processes.❞
>
> *R. S. Hubbard, 1996*

The creative process begins while exploring and playing with tools and materials. After many experiences, children move to the next step by focusing on a particular approach. Once an approach is chosen, children will use this method in the production stage. The fourth step is often stopping, evaluating, or reworking. It is difficult to pinpoint when one step ends and another begins in the visual arts. The very young child often spends more time in the exploratory step, whereas the more experienced child may spend more time at the production level. Each step is intertwined and important for the developing child.

During later periods of artistic development, or for specific in-depth projects, children may want a product that meets their expectations. This may require that they revisit and rework their creations until they meet their expectations. It is

A unique tool, a corn cob, is used for painting and printing.

important to note that it should be the child's desire to refine the product, not the teacher's. The observant teacher will recognize when the child wants to create a product that meets her expectations. When this need is recognized, a teacher should provide time and support for the child to continue the process.

Conformity or Originality

When children first use art materials, they often observe how others are using the items. For example, Ben may observe how Catherine is using the sponge to produce a print. He then tries the same sponge technique. This is an appropriate way for a child to discover how a new tool is used or to expand on what she already knows. Accepting these shared experiences as effective ways of learning allows the teacher to see beyond what may look like sameness. Vygotsky helped us understand the value of children learning from each other and the benefits of these social interactions.

During the process of artistic development, it is important to encourage, value, and display original ideas. For example, unique ways of combining materials or making things in special ways helps children venture beyond the constraints of conformity. When this occurs, children will come to understand that thinking in divergent ways is valued and accepted in this environment.

Art Belongs to the Child

Art is a personal way of communicating and provides the child with a way to express unique ideas. A respect for the personal nature of the child's artwork means the teacher does not direct the process, but allows the child to proceed and experiment in the way she deems appropriate. The child is able to create and combine materials in ways that the teacher may have never imagined. During this process, the teacher may use questions to assist the child in thinking of new possibilities or techniques.

- Have you seen the foil that was added to the art box?
- What happens when you glue the tissue paper?
- What else could you add?

A Climate of Acceptance

An environment that nurtures artistic exploration is psychologically safe. It is a classroom where the teacher supports the children's creative efforts. Children know their ideas will be respected in this environment. The teacher models acceptance as she comments on the unique way that Marian is making wavy lines using the pastry brush. These small experiences help children understand that their work is special and will be valued.

Providing Role Models

When children see adults working creatively, they begin to understand that it is an important activity that grown-up people do. They observe that it gives the artist joy and satisfaction. They can see work in different stages of progress before the finished product is achieved.

Role models can be professional artists or individuals who have hobbies that relate to art. Visitors can bring their artwork into the classroom, or the children may go to a studio or museum to watch the artist work. The most influential role model is the classroom teacher. Through the teacher's efforts, even when she is not a professional artist, children learn that art activities are worthwhile, pleasurable, and important (Dixon & Chalmers, 1990).

✿ | ART EDUCATION

In the field of **art education,** there are specific curriculum goals and standards that have been established by professional organizations. The National Art Education Association has identified these goals as creating, understanding, and appreciating. Art educators, who have specialized training related to the content of art, have provided new elements that should be examined to enrich the art program for young children.

In a National Art Education Association publication, Colbert and Taunton (1992) identified three major components of a quality, developmentally appropriate, art program for young children.

1. Young children need many opportunities to create art.
2. Young children need many opportunities to look at and talk about art.
3. Young children need to become aware of art in their everyday lives.

In the past, the primary focus of art in early childhood programs was creating. Although producing art remains a major component of the art curriculum during the early childhood years, the offerings are now being expanded to include experiences with great works of art. These experiences provide opportunities for children to develop personal preferences and share their opinion of art. Young children can recognize and appreciate artistic effort and the work of the men, women, and children who create art. Although art historians are interested in artistic categories, styles, and movements, early childhood educators focus on expanding the concepts of art and developing an appreciation of artistic form.

It is challenging for teachers to design programs that include appreciation and creativity, follow the interests of the child, and are integrated across curriculum areas. Objectives for the integration of art might include the following.

1. Construct an understanding of art as a means of community.

2. Develop a view of themselves as artists who are capable of self-expression.

3. Discover the joy of art appreciation and creation through participation in self-selected art activities (Fox & Diffily, 2000).

STUDY OF AN ARTIST: GEORGIA O'KEEFFE

This is a lesson from a series of lessons exploring the paintings of the visual artist Georgia O'Keeffe, in a PreK classroom. The series gives examples of planning that allow children to successfully construct their own understanding and build on each understanding as they progress. In this way, the children will not only explore Georgia O'Keeffe's art but will also be able to interpret and apply the concepts to their own explorations with art media and representation.

PreK Series

Goals

1. To introduce children to concepts of art perceptions
   - We can see and feel something different when we look at a painting or create an image.
   - Color, size, and shape (form) can change our perception of things.
2. To discover that art is an expression of feelings
3. To develop language skills
4. To promote inquiry in relation to visual perception and imagery
   - Children discriminate ways to identify and understand the meaning of representations.
   - Children discriminate ways to visually represent the things they see.
   - Children develop visual perception skills as they discriminate shapes (forms), line, color, composition, and meaning in representations.

Objectives

1. To experience paintings by Georgia O'Keeffe
2. To describe how the artist feels
3. To express thoughts and understandings about Georgia O'Keeffe's paintings
4. To describe, compare, and contrast paintings
5. To experience painting from content (objects) similar to Georgia O'Keeffe's
6. To choose content (objects or subjects) that can also represent the feelings attributed to Georgia O'Keeffe's paintings
   - to create images from the choices

- to discuss these images with peers: describe the thoughts, feelings, and understandings
- to compare and contrast the thoughts, feelings, and understandings of the images with those of Georgia O'Keeffe

Areas of the PreK Classroom that Support the Study of this Artist

Science

Have objects that are the subject of O'Keeffe's paintings set out for exploration

- with mirrors
- through magnifying glasses
- through manipulation of the objects
- through drawing—predicting—what they think may be inside the stem, the flower, a bud, etc.
  - In a scientific manner: open the stem, flower, and bud, to compare with predictions
- through books on flowers

Reading Area

- Biographies of Georgia O'Keeffe
- Books with images of O'Keeffe paintings
- Books that discuss ideas reflected in the paintings
- Books about color, line, or shape

Writing Center

- Tell the story of one of Georgia O'Keeffe's paintings in words.
- Tell the story of your painting in words.
- Using words, describe something by its colors.
- Using words, describe something by its lines.
- Using words, describe something by its shape.

Block Center

- Invite children to bring color into their structures.
- Invite children to discuss the meaning of their structures.
- Invite children to think about shapes of their structures.
  - Is the shape important to the meaning of the structure?
  - How is it important?
  - Why is it important?

Primary Series

Goals

1. To introduce children to concepts of art perceptions
   - Children can see and feel something different when looking at a painting or creating an image.
   - Color, size, and shape (form) can change perception of things.
2. To develop vocabulary:
   - composition
   - texture
   - color

- tone
- hue
- variation
- large scale/small scale
- representational/abstract
- landscape
- still life

3. To promote inquiry in relation to visual perception and imagery
   - Children discriminate ways to identify and understand the meaning of representations.
   - Children discriminate ways to visually represent the things they see.
   - Children develop visual perception skills as they discriminate shapes (forms), line, color, composition, and meaning in representations.
4. To learn about the life of an artist
   - relating her life historically to the time she lived
   - relating her life to the content of her paintings
   - relating the children's lives to content of the images they create
5. Introducing children to ideas about galleries and museums
   - the function for artists
   - the function for the community and the public
   - the role of galleries in the area of the school

Objectives

1. To experience paintings by Georgia O'Keeffe
2. To describe how the artist feels
3. To express thoughts and understanding about Georgia O'Keeffe's paintings
4. To describe, compare, and contrast paintings
5. To experience painting from content (objects) similar to Georgia O'Keeffe's
6. To choose content (objects or subjects) that can also represent the feelings attributed to Georgia O'Keeffe's paintings
   - create images from choices
   - discuss images with peers by describing the thoughts, feelings, and understandings related to images created by the children
   - compare and contrast the thoughts, feelings, and understandings of created images with Georgia O'Keeffe's
7. To establish a gallery in the classroom
   - represent Georgia O'Keeffe's art
   - represent the art that children create through the course of this unit
   - children consider the aesthetics involved in showing and displaying art
   - children model the roles of gallery representatives
     - in creating art
     - in establishing the gallery
     - in planning an exhibit
     - in inviting the public (parents and/or others) to the exhibit
     - in educating the public about the art represented in the gallery
       - students speak about the art

♦ students speak about the reasons for their choice of medium

♦ students speak about the influence of line, shape, color, and **scale** on the meaning of paintings

♦ students speak about the lives of the artists, in relation to the times they lived and the art they created

♦ students include information on O'Keeffe and children who created the artwork

PreK Lesson: Color, Shape, and Form

Objectives for This Lesson

1. To introduce children to Georgia O'Keeffe paintings
2. To introduce the term artist
3. To identify line, color, and shape (form) in Georgia O'Keeffe paintings
4. To relate Georgia O'Keeffe paintings to real objects, thoughts, and feelings (the latter being explored more in-depth in later lessons)

Materials

● Posters or slides of Georgia O'Keeffe paintings. Choose only O'Keeffe images that represent objects you can bring to class: *Iris* (1929), *White Trumpet Flower* (1932), *Blue Rock with Blue III* (1970), Untitled (Two Pears/1921), *Abstraction White Rose* (1927), *Petunia* (1924).

(Note: There are many online web sites available with O'Keeffe images, including: www.artcyclopedia.com/artists/okeeffe_georgia.html)

● Objects represented in the images you've chosen (e.g., iris, rock that is of a similar shape to the one in *Blue Rock with Blue III,* etc.)

  ○ Display objects in the vicinity of discussion
  ○ Create a gallery area

● Books about Georgia O'Keeffe, books with quality representations of her images, and books about her life that children can read or that teachers can read to children.

● Projector (if needed) to project slides

● Easel pad to record children's dialogue

● Tables where children can work in small groups.

  ○ Each table should have laminated copies of a number of O'Keeffe images.
  ○ Some tables will have:
    ♦ Markers matching the colors in the images
    ♦ Transparency film for children to place over the image and mark on the line and shape
  ○ Other tables will have:
    ♦ Oil pastels or pastels of the colors
    ♦ Quality drawing paper

Procedure

Be certain to allow for discussion of color, shape, and line.

1. Gather children into a circle for discussion.
2. Explain that they will look at and discuss paintings by the artist Georgia O'Keeffe.
   ● Ask if children know what the word *artist* means.
   ● Ask if children have had opportunities to look at paintings outside school.
   ● Invite children to share the circumstances of their viewings (galleries, museums, etc.).

- Ask if children have had opportunities to discuss paintings they have seen outside school.
- Explain that you brought the images to allow time to examine them.
- Talk about:
  - What the children see in the paintings.
  - What the paintings make the children think about.
  - How the paintings make the children feel.

3. Begin by looking at one O'Keeffe image at a time.
   - Ask the children what they see. Do they know what the paintings represent? Do they see something in the room that they also see in the painting?
     - Record all responses on the easel pad. Let them know that you are recording their ideas so the class can recall them later.
     - If the discussion does not generate much response, ask:
       - What colors do you see?
         - If the answer is red, ask how many reds they see and discuss the differences among the reds.
         - Do the same for other colors.
       - What shapes do you see?
         - How many?
         - Where are they?
       - Where do you see lines?
         - Can the children show you the lines?
         - How many different lines are there?

4. Review the ideas noted on the easel list.

5. Explain how to use materials at the tables.
   - Have example sets of materials from each table set up on two trays.
   - Use materials on the marker tray, to show ways the children can place the transparency film on the laminated O'Keeffe image, look through the clear film, and trace a line. Invite the children to come and find a shape or a line in the painting.
   - Use the other tray of materials, to choose a color and find which part the color matches. Ask some children to help find places in the painting where the color is represented.

6. In small groups, the children can explore the Georgia O'Keeffe images, and use the materials to locate lines, shapes, and colors. Record what the children say.

CLOSURE: Bring the children together into a small circle to share their discoveries. Take pictures of each child as she or he shares her or his work, and have someone note their comments. Later, place the images in a book or on a documentation panel with the comments printed by the images. Allow the children to revisit the ideas and examine the pictures. 🌀

Georgia O'Keeffe Books for Children:

Turner, R. M. (1993). *Georgia O'Keeffe: Portraits of women artists for children.* New York: Little, Brown.

Venezia, M. (1994). *Georgia O'Keeffe.* Danbury, CT: Grolier.

Winter, J. (1998). *My name is Georgia: A portrait.* New York: Harcourt.

Georgia O'Keeffe Books for Adults

Castro, J. G. (1995). *The art and life of Georgia O'Keeffe.* New York: Crown.

Lisle, L. (1997). *Portrait of an artist: A biography of Georgia O'Keeffe.* New York: Washington Square Press.

✿ VISITING ARTIST

Young children can learn about art by visiting local artists in their community. A field trip to a studio, shop, or gallery show provides a concrete example of the work of an artist. It is helpful if you select an artist who is interested in children and willing to let them touch and explore the materials being used. A potter who lets the children feel and mash clay will make the experience more meaningful. An artist who makes prints might allow the children to stamp a pattern or design on a large piece of cloth. These hands-on opportunities match the way children learn and provide appropriate ways to experiment with art materials.

A chair maker is demonstrating to these children how to shape spindles.

If visiting an artist in their workplace is not possible, an alternative approach is to bring the artist into the early childhood classroom. A weaver can bring a small loom so the children can see the work she is doing. Later, in the art center, some children can weave fabric strips into a simple frame. A metal sculpture could be used to show how to create a three-dimensional form in the art center, where children are able to feel the materials and bend pieces of wire. A group sculpture could be created with wire attached to a wood base and bent into shapes. The wire sculpture can then be added to and refined over several days. Photographs of the process can be included on a **documentation panel,** including the artist visit, preparation of the base, selection of the wires, and the development of the sculpture over time. Include words the children used in describing their plan, choices, and collaboration.

AESTHETICS

Aesthetics is an area of art concerned with feelings and responses to color, form, and design. There is a basic need to make sense and appreciate the world in which we live (Schirrmacher, 2006). When children have opportunities to view and explore beautiful things in their classroom, they begin to appreciate their environment. Even the very young child can recognize the special features of her environment. She will notice a new item in the room, a vase of beautiful flowers, or textured paper on the wall. Children can appreciate the shape of objects, shades of light, color, pattern, and texture. Children's responses are unique and their aesthetic observations should be valued.

According to Schirrmacher, the classroom should be an aesthetically pleasing and sensory-rich environment. For example, a light colored wall can serve as a background for beautifully displayed artwork, weavings, quilts, or photographs. A variety of textures should be used in the area, including rough, smooth, shiny, and soft. Centers related to the arts are carefully constructed and designed to be aesthetically pleasing (Isbell & Exelby, 2001).

Primary-grade children may enjoy visiting galleries and studying the techniques of specific artists (Johnson, 1997). They may want to explore different techniques and discover new possibilities for creating art. Learning about texture, color, balance, and contrast becomes real when discussing paintings viewed in an art gallery. Through guided discussion, children can develop a vocabulary about what is seen in a work of art, make comparisons, express personal responses, and make judgments about art (Cole & Schaefer, 1990).

The work of artist Georgia O'Keefe inspires a child's painting.

SUMMARY

Art has historically been viewed as a basic component in early childhood programs. Many theorists and scholars have attempted to explain how young children learn about and think about art during the process. Although they have presented differing views, most have concluded that art has a powerful influence on the cognitive, social, emotional, and physical development of young children. Some experts have used stages to explain how children progress from scribbling to drawing in realistic ways. Others have identified the same patterns found in the art of children around the world and in different cultures. More recently, art has been recognized as a way children organize their ideas and symbolically represent their thinking.

Standards and guidelines have identified the need for young children to explore a variety of materials and techniques, to be able to talk about their work and use different media to communicate their ideas. Included in these recommendations is the need for young children to learn about the work of other artists, including famous, folk, and local artists. The young child's environment should include beautiful things they can see and investigate. An aesthetically pleasing environment will nurture their appreciation of the world in which they live.

 ## KEY TERMS

abstract	pictorial stage
aesthetics	preschematic stage
art education	process
basic form stage	product
color	proportion
composition	realism
controlled scribble	representational
documentation panel	right hemisphere
folk art	scale
form	schematic stage
left hemisphere	scribble stage
line	shape
pattern	spatial relationship
perceptual theory	uncontrolled scribble
perspective	

 ## REFLECTION

1. Explain why many early childhood educators consider art "basic."
2. What theory or theories provide greater insight into the influence of art on the development of young children?
3. Describe the stages of children's artistic development. Give examples of children's artwork from each stage.
4. Art education has identified components of a quality art program. What are they, and how can they be included in the early childhood classroom?

THINKING ABOUT THE OBSERVATION OF CREATIVITY

1. How did each child respond to making the mural?
2. Describe how language supported the children's involvement in the art project.
3. What changes or additions would you make to expand the work?

POSSIBILITIES FOR ADULT LEARNERS

Activity: Vase and Faces: Drawing on the Right Side of the Brain

Goal: This activity is designed to help the teacher shift from a left-hemisphere mode (logical operations) to the right hemisphere (visual-spatial operations). This activity is adapted from Betty Edwards' (1979) book, *Drawing on the Right Side of the Brain.*

Materials: Paper and pencil.

Procedure:

1. Draw a profile of a person's head on the left side of your paper, facing toward the center. If you are left-handed, draw the profile on the right side facing toward the center. Make your own version of the profile. It seems to help if this profile comes from your own memory and creation.

2. Next, draw horizontal lines at the top and bottom of your profile, forming the top and bottom of the vase.

3. Go back over your drawing of the first profile with a pencil. As the pencil moves over each feature, name them to yourself (forehead, nose, upper lip, lower lip, chin, and neck). Repeat this step at least once. This is a left hemisphere task: naming symbolic shapes.

4. Next, start at the top and draw the profile in reverse to complete the vase. The second profile should be a reversal of the first in order for the vase to be symmetrical. Watch for the faint signals from your brain as you begin to shift modes of information processing. You may experience a moment of mental conflict while completing the second profile. You

Is it a vase or a face? (This drawing was inspired by an activity from Betty Edwards' 1979 book, *Drawing on the Right Side of the Brain.*

will find that you draw the second profile differently. Think about this and note how you solve the problem. This is a right-hemisphere mode drawing.

5. Now that you have completed the vase–faces drawing, think back on how you did it. The first profile was probably drawn rather rapidly and then, as you were instructed, redrawn while verbalizing the names of the parts as you went back over the features. This is a left-hemisphere mode of processing: drawing symbolic shapes from memory and naming them. In drawing the second profile to complete the vase, you may have experienced some confusion or conflict. To continue the drawing, you had to use a different strategy or a different process. You probably lost the sense of drawing a profile and found yourself scanning back and forth in the space between the profiles, estimating angles, curves, inward-curving and outward-curving shapes, and lengths in relation to the opposite shapes that now became unnamed and unnamable. You made constant adjustments in the line you were drawing—checking where you were and where you were going—by scanning the space between the first profile and your copy in reverse. This is using the right hemisphere to draw.

Activity:	Identifying Personal Creativity: Detective Work
Goal:	Many people are very creative but are not aware of this ability. A little sleuth work is in order to restore personal creativity. This exercise from *The Artist's Way: A Spiritual Path to Higher Creativity* by Julia Cameron (1992), you retrieve memories and misplaced fragments of your creative self.
Materials:	Paper and pencil.
Procedure:	Complete the following phrases. You may feel strong emotions as you retrieve personal memories. Allow yourself to free-associate for a sentence with each phrase.

My favorite childhood toy was . . .
My favorite childhood game was . . .
The best movie I ever saw as a child was . . .
I don't do it much, but I enjoy . . .
If I could lighten up a little, I'd let myself . . .
If it were not too late, I'd . . .
My favorite musical instrument is . . .
The traits I admire in others are . . .
The amount of money I spend on treating myself to
    entertainment each month is . . .
Taking time out for myself is . . .
If I ever wrote a book, it would be about . . .
I am afraid that if I start dreaming . . .
I secretly enjoy reading . . .
My idea of a fun weekend would include . . .
If I'd had a perfect childhood, I'd have grown up to be . . .
If it didn't sound so crazy, I'd make or write . . .
My most cheer-me-up music is . . .
My favorite way to dress is . . .

OPEN-ENDED ACTIVITIES FOR YOUNG CHILDREN
PreK–K

Activity:	Animal Paper Bags
Goal:	In African cultures, animals occupy an important place in art and folklore. People who have lived in close contact with animals see them as models with special qualities. In Africa, the spider, bird, leopard, and chameleon are animals that provide sources of power, inspiration, and guidance. This activity will allow children to select an animal they admire and create a paper bag structure to represent the chosen animal.
Materials:	Paper bags, scraps of fabric, newspaper, construction paper, glue, and scissors.

Procedure:

1. Ask the children to choose an animal they admire.
2. Provide materials for children to construct a sculpture using a paper bag as the base.
3. Stuff the paper bag with newspaper to provide structure and form.
4. Allow children to use materials to complete their animals.

PreK–K or Primary Grades

Activity:	A Rubbing
Goal:	To create a rubbing of items in the child's environment.
Materials:	Art paper, crayons, and masking tape.

Procedure:

1. Select an item that will provide an interesting texture. Possibilities include, but are not limited to:

tree trunks	textured wallpaper
shoe soles	keys
concrete	rug or carpet scraps
leaves	license plates
bricks	vents
rough stones	tombstones
tires	coins
flowers	embossed cards

2. Tape paper to or on top of the item.
3. Use crayons to rub the texture.
4. Evaluate the design, and determine if more rubbing is needed or if additional items should be rubbed.

Primary Grades

Activity: Box Painting

Goal: To create an abstract design with marbles and paint.

Materials: Cardboard box lids (should have a high rim), paper, tempera paint, marbles of different sizes, clear plastic cups, and spoons.

Procedure:

1. Select a lid that will be used for the painting.
2. Cut the paper to fit inside the lid.
3. Choose colors of paint and pour each into a plastic cup.
4. Using a spoon, put a marble into the selected color.
5. Place the marble on the paper inside the lid.
6. Roll the marble around on the paper.
7. Repeat the process with different colors and varied marbles.
8. Allow the abstract marble painting to dry in the lid before removing the creation.

Activity: Burlap Murals

Goal: Murals are an essential part of Mexican art. This activity allows children to construct a classroom mural while experimenting with a new media, burlap.

Materials: Burlap (a neutral color is preferable), tempera paint, and brushes.

Procedure:

1. Mural-making, a popular art activity in the elementary grades, can be even more exciting when burlap is used as the background. The heavy texture of the porous material absorbs the paint in a unique way.
2. Children should plan and discuss their mural as a group. This will help the mural become a composition instead of a sequence of unrelated pictures.
3. For variations, use other fabrics for painting or glue fabric to the burlap.

 ADDITIONAL READING

Creativity

Czikszentmihalyi, M. (1996). *Creativity*. New York: Basic Books.

Edwards, L. C., & Nabors, M. L. (1993). The creative arts process. *Young Children, 48*(3), 77–81.

Torrance, E. P. (1962). *Guiding creative talent*. Englewood Cliffs, NJ: Prentice-Hall.

Multicultural

Blocker, H. G. (November–December 1993). Aesthetic value in cross-cultural, multicultural art study. *Arts Education Policy Review, 95*(2), 26–29.

Bolden, T. (2004). *Wake up our souls: A celebration of Black American artists*. New York: Harry N. Abrams.

Bresler, L., & Thompson, C. M. (Eds.). (2002). *The arts in children's lives: Context, culture, and curriculum*. Dordrecht, The Netherlands: Kluwer Academic.

Brown, I. (1994). Comparing the best of both worlds: Cultures through art. *Art Education, 47*(1), 61–67.

Rohmer, H. (Ed.). (1997). *Just like me: Stories and self-portraits by fourteen artists*. San Francisco: Children's Book Press.

Research

Eisner, E. W. (1998). Does experience in the arts boost academic achievement? *Arts Education Policy Review, 100*(4), 32–39.

Hamblen, K. A. (1997). Theories and research that supports art instruction for instrumental outcomes. *Arts Education Policy Review, 98*(3), 27–33.

Potter, E. F., & Edens, K. M. (2001). *Children's motivational beliefs about art: Exploring age differences and relation to drawing behavior*. Paper presented at the Annual Meeting of the American Educational Research Association, Seattle, WA. (ERIC Document Reproduction Service No. ED452134.)

Zimmerman, E., & Zimmerman, L. (November 2000). Art education and early childhood education: The young child as creator and meaning maker within a community context. *Young Children, 55*(6), 87–92.

Visual Arts

Baker, D. W. (1991). The visual arts in early childhood education. In D. Elkind (Ed.), *Perspectives on early childhood education: Growing with young children toward the 21st century* (pp. 133–140). Washington, DC: National Education Association of the United States.

Dighe, J., Calomiris, Z., & Van Zutphen, C. (1998). Nurturing the language of art in children. *Young Children, 53*(1), 4–9.

Feeney, S., & Moravcik, E. (1987). A thing of beauty: Aesthetic development in young children. *Young Children, 43*(6), 7–15.

Gardner, H. (1982). *Art, mind, and brain*. New York: Basic Books.

CHILDREN'S LITERATURE CONNECTION

Blake, Q. (2001). *Tell me a picture*. Brookfield, CT: The Millbrook Press.
This book highlights an exhibit at the National Gallery with pictures that communicate to young children and demonstrates that children and old masters go together. Includes information about each work. (K–Primary)

dePaola, T. (1989). *The art lesson*. New York: G. P. Putnam's Sons.
Having learned to be creative by drawing pictures at home, young Tommy is dismayed when he goes to school and finds the art lesson there much more regimented. (Primary 1–3 and Teacher's Aide)

Lionni, L. (1991). *Matthew's dream*. New York: Scholastic.
Although his parents want him to become a doctor, after a trip to the art museum, Matthew dreams of becoming a painter. (K–3)

Lithgow, J., & Payne, C. F. (2002). *Micawber*. New York: Simon & Schuster Books for Young Readers.
Micawber the squirrel watches through the window of a museum as artists copy the paintings. He copies the artwork himself and displays his paintings in a museum. (K–3)

Scieszka, J., & Smith, L. (2005). *Seen Art?* New York: Viking.
A young boy looks for his friend "Art" in The Museum of Modern Art. The book includes many examples of art that are in the museum, with an index of artworks, artists, and time frames. (PreK–3)

Weitzman, J. P., & Glasser, R. P. (2002). *You can't take a balloon into the Museum of Fine Arts*. New York: Dial Books for Young Readers.
This wordless picture book shows a young girl visiting a museum with her grandparents, where her balloon escapes. They chase the balloon through the museum, passing by

paintings and sculptures. Artwork in the collection is identified at the end of the book. (K–Primary)

Williams, K. L. (1998). *Painted dreams*. New York: Lothrop, Lee & Shepard Books.
Because her Haitian family is too poor to be able to buy paints for her, eight-year-old Ti Marie finds her own way to create pictures that make the heart sing. (Primary K–3)

 For additional resources involving creativity and the arts with young children, visit our Web site at **http://www.earlychilded.delmar.com**

 REFERENCES

Cameron, J. (1992). *The artist's way: A spiritual path to higher creativity*. New York: Jeremy P. Tarcher/Putnam.

Colbert, C., & Taunton, M. (1992). *Developmentally appropriate practices for the visual art education of young children*. Reston, VA: National Art Education Association.

Cole, E., & Schaefer, C. (1990). Can young children be art critics? *Young Children, 45*(2), 33–38.

Consortium of National Arts Education Associations. (1994). *National standards for arts education: What every young American should know and be able to do in the arts*. Reston, VA: Music Educators National Conference (MENC).

Dixon, G. T., & Chalmers, F. G. (1990). The expressive arts in education. *Childhood Education, 67*(1), 12–17.

Drew, W. F., & Rankin, B. (July 2004) Promoting creativity for life using open-ended materials. *Young Children, 59*(4), 38–43.

Edwards, B. (1979). *Drawing on the right side of the brain: A course in enhancing creativity and artistic confidence*. Los Angeles: J. P. Tarcher.

Eisner, E. W. (May 2003). The arts and the creation of mind. *Language Arts, 80*(5), 340–344.

Fox, J. E., & Diffily, D. (2000). Integrating the visual arts: Building your children's knowledge, skills and confidence. *Dimensions of Early Childhood, 29*(1), 3–10.

Gardner, H. (1980). Children's art: The age of creativity. *Psychology Today, 13*(12), 84–96.

Gardner, H. (1983). *Frames of mind: The theory of multiple intelligence*. New York: Basic Books.

Hubbard, R. S. (1996). *A workshop of the possible: Nurturing children's creative development*. York, ME: Stenhouse.

Isbell, R. (1995). *The complete learning center book*. Beltsville, MD: Gryphon House.

Isbell, R., & Exelby, B. (2001). *Learning environments that work with young children*. Beltsville, MD: Gryphon House.

Johnson, M. (1997). Teaching children to value art and artist. *Phi Delta Kappan, 78*(6), 454–456.

Kellogg, R. (1959). *What children scribble and why*. Palo Alto, CA: National Press Books.

Kellogg, R. (1969). *Analyzing children's art*. Palo Alto, CA: Mayfield.

Kellogg, R. (1973). Misunderstanding children's art. *Art Education, 26*(6), 7–9.

Kellogg, R., & O'Dell, S. (1967). *The Psychology of Children's Art*. New York: CRM.

Koster, J. B. (1999). Clay for little fingers. *Young Children, 54*(2), 18–22.

Lowenfeld, V., & Brittain, W. L. (1987). *Creative and Mental Growth* (8th ed.). New York: Prentice-Hall.

Raines, S., & Canady, R. J. (1990). *The whole language kindergarten*. New York: Teachers College Press.

Schirrmacher, R. (2006). *Art & creative development for young children* (4th ed). Clifton Park, NY: Thomson Delmar Learning.

Seefeldt, C. (1995). Art—A serious work. *Young Children, 50*(3), 39–45.

Seefeldt, C. (2005). Integrating the visual arts into the curriculum. *Scholastic Early Childhood Today, 19*(5), 12.

CREATING ART

CHAPTER 5

This chapter will focus on the many opportunities young children have to create art that is uniquely theirs. It will include a discussion of art experiences that relate to both two- and three-dimensional work. Art centers and materials will be described so that the environment will inspire young artists.

After studying this chapter, you will be able to:
- **Select appropriate art activities and materials for young children.**
- **Identify two- and three-dimensional art activities.**
- **Design an art center that will nurture young artists.**
- **Collect low-cost materials to be used in the early childhood classroom.**
- **Involve children in the selection of artwork to include in their portfolio or for display.**

OBSERVATION OF CREATIVITY

Jessica goes to the art center and observes the activities that are going on in the area. She decides to work with "real" clay, the type potters use in art studios. She takes a plastic tray to the garbage pail containing a large amount of gray clay. She pulls, digs, and finally takes a plastic knife to chisel away a piece of clay the size she wants.

Jessica begins to experiment with the clay. She squeezes it with her hands, pounds it flat, and folds it into pieces. When the clay becomes dry to her touch, she goes to the sink and gets water in a small plastic bowl. She returns to the table where she adds a small amount of water to the stiff clay. She continues to experiment with the changes she creates: wet, smooth, and flexible. Next, she begins to punch holes in the clay with her fingers. She carefully adds water to each of the holes. She pulls the wet clay, full of holes, off the tray. She notices the difference in the depth of the holes and the amount of water they contain. She pounds the clay flat and punches more holes to determine their depth and the amount of water each can contain.

Now the clay becomes very wet and will not hold the shape of the holes. Jessica takes the tray and the wet clay to the container where it was stored. She returns the clay to the pail and carefully washes the tray. She goes to the table and wipes off the area where she worked.

WHAT WAS OBSERVED?

Jessica is 5.6 years of age. She worked with clay for over 45 minutes. Jessica worked independently, experimenting with the properties of clay and discovering how it responded to her actions. She was persistent and focused on the exploration for a long time. This open-ended material allowed Jessica to proceed with her ideas in personally meaningful ways, as she constructed her understanding of clay. Jessica followed a systematic plan of action, from getting clay to carefully cleaning up the area.

✿ ARTISTIC TERMS

Fiber Art: Art forms that use fibers or materials created from fibers.

Sewing: Connecting fabric or materials with thread, yarn, or ribbons.

Texture: The way an object feels or how the grain might feel when touched.

Weaving: The process of interconnecting fibers in a systematic pattern.

✿ CREATING ART

There are many different ways to create art and a wide variety of materials and tools that can be used by young children. In an early childhood classroom, many options should be provided with appropriate choices for the individual child. Stimulating art experiences, in a safe, responsive environment, provide optimal conditions for the development of creativity. The teacher demonstrates her respect for children's ways of learning when she provides open-ended materials such as clay, paint, and a variety of tools. By providing options, she nurtures the children's ability to make choices. Art does not include coloring ditto sheets or producing 20 cute pumpkins that were copied from a model. Rather, art experiences should provide the stimulus for a child to create in unique ways, use diverse materials, and have opportunities to revisit their work.

Sensory Experiences

Infants and toddlers in the sensory stage of development need experiences that support their way of learning. Older children also benefit from experiences that

> **"The power of art is discovering that each of us can learn from, appreciate, and create art."**
>
> *Gee, 2000*

The process is most important when creating with colored foam.

provide variations in sensory experiences. For example, toddlers can use colored shaving cream to create designs on tabletops. An older child would enjoy the same sensory experience extended by placing paper on the design, pressing, and producing a print of her creation.

Young children explore shells and leaves by touching, examining, and smelling. They progress to using these items in their creations and in varying combinations. Providing interesting items to be enjoyed and examined helps children become more focused on the beauty in the world around them. It helps children develop an awareness of the shades of colors, texture, shapes, and design. This sensitivity to the environment is helpful for children as they expand their experiences with art and develop representations for their thoughts.

TWO-DIMENSIONAL ART

Some of the earliest art experiences of young children are **two-dimensional** in nature. For example, toddlers often use large sheets of paper with big magic markers as they make uncontrolled scribbles on the page. A large crayon used on manila paper is a classic art activity in early childhood programs. But there are many additional possibilities for including two-dimensional art activities in the classroom.

Drawing and Sketching

Very young children draw for the joy of the movement, the response of the tool, and recognizing their ability to influence what is produced. Kindergarten children and primary-grade children become interested in drawing what they see and recognizing that they can represent their thoughts in their artwork. Children use drawing to plan, design, and represent their ideas.

An early step in this process is using lines in their drawings that provide a way to represent their thoughts with no right or wrong result. As they gain control of the lines, they can continue to focus on what they see. Questions can help them focus on

Watercolors provide a new way of painting.

aspects that may not have been identified. They can experiment with a variety of drawing materials, each with its own characteristics. For example, a pencil, a thin marker, charcoal, or chalk can be used to draw and produce very different results.

Drawing can take place outdoors as well as inside. Often, being outside allows children to be freer in their choices of subject and their interpretation of what they observe. These drawings can be quick sketches or work that they return to frequently, adding detail and more items to their work.

Painting

Paint and a brush provide another way of creating forms or expressing ideas. Tempera paint, frequently used in early childhood programs, comes in a variety of **hues** and can be used in many ways. It should be bought in liquid form, since the powdered tempera is not recommended for use by children under 12. Add a small amount of liquid dishwashing detergent to the paint. This will make the tempera paint somewhat thicker, as well as making it easier to remove from clothing and furniture. Young children can control the use of tempera paint better when it has a slightly thick consistency. Painting is an enjoyable activity that children choose to do frequently and over a number of years. It allows them to plan, choose colors, determine placement, and display their work. Children can also use water colors by adding water to blocks of color and using smaller brushes. The lighter color produced by watercolors—with a more translucent quality—provides an added way to explore the effects of painting (Schirrmacher, 2006).

WHERE TO PAINT?   There are many different places where a child can paint. Each of these locations has benefits and challenges. Therefore, it is helpful to provide different options during the year.

EASEL PAINTING.   Many early childhood classrooms provide easels for painting. This allows the child to paint with big strokes and large brushes. Paint should be placed on the tray in containers that cannot spill. However, paint does run on the paper, because of the slanted surface of the easel.

WALL PAINTING.   A section of wall in the classroom can be covered with paper for large paintings or group work. It is helpful to cover the wall and floor with plastic, before the paper is attached, for easier cleanup. A large piece of plywood can be attached to the wall for regular use for painting. When children are painting on the wall surface, they will need a place to put their paint containers and brushes.

TABLE PAINTING.   A table provides a flat surface for painting, in addition to a place to set the paints. Several children can paint at the table at the same time, thereby increasing the likelihood that they will talk to each other. Paper and paintings will be smaller because of the limited space on the table.

STANDING PAINTING.   Standing at a table to paint allows children to use larger strokes and bigger sheets of paper. The flat surface, placed at a good height for young children, will work well for this activity.

PLEXIGLAS PANEL.   Providing a standing Plexiglas surface allows children to view the work from both sides. This variation provides an interesting place to paint and to watch the progress as the painting occurs.

FLOOR PAINTING.   Children can paint while seated on the floor. This allows children to use a different position as they paint. Some children may enjoy this opportunity, which will allow them to see their work from a different perspective.

OUTDOOR PAINTING. Easels can be set up on the playground or outside the classroom. This outdoor environment provides a new place for painting. Plexiglas panels can also be securely attached to a fence and remain on the playground for an extended period. This surface can be painted and cleaned by the children.

Accessories for Painting

- Various types of paper: colored, manila, and computer paper, freezer paper, sandpaper, textured wallpaper, butcher paper, foil, and wrapping paper
- Various sizes of brushes: long handles, short handles, large brushes, and medium brushes
- Brushes used to paint houses
- Paint roller and tray
- Markers: various sizes and colors
- Dishwasher wands (paint can be put in shaft)
- Pastry brush
- Cotton swabs
- Squirt bottles (catsup, mustard, etc.)
- Liquid tempera paint (basic colors: red, green, blue, white, and black)
- No-spill paint containers with lids
- Roll of plastic sheeting (cover table, floor, or wall)
- Drying rack or clothesline
- Large sponges for cleanup
- Smocks or old shirts
- Easels
- Plexiglas sheet
- Newspaper (for covering work areas)
- Spray bottles
- Wagon (for moving art outdoors)

Print Making

A form of art that involves making a copy of something is **print making.** There are a variety of ways that young children can create prints. Many of the ways allow young children to explore the techniques as well as experience the sensory characteristics of the objects they are using.

In print making, as with other art experiences, it is important to match the activity with the physical control of the children. It is also necessary to review the experiences they have previously had with printing. Once the teacher has selected an appropriate activity, the children should be able to experiment with the paints and use the printing tools in their own way. Print making provides opportunities for young children to use their sense of touch (sensory), develop physical coordination (small motor), distinguish different objects and the patterns they make (cognition), and build their confidence as they control the paint and pattern (emotional) (Koster, 2005).

A BEGINNING EXPERIENCE WITH PRINTING. For printing, two or three young children can work standing at a low table. This allows them to move around the paper and determine where they will add prints. Be sure to cover the table with plastic or a vinyl shower curtain to make cleanup easier. Place trays with two or three colors of thick tempera paint in containers located at the center or end of the table. Place three to five printing tools on the table so the children can select the one they will use. Later, they can progress to using the others in the activity. Select easy-to-hold items with distinctive designs, such as a potato masher, cookie cutter, paper towel roll, or sponge.

Use construction paper or thicker paper, since the pressure of the child's motion and the paint will not tear it or come through. Remember that young children need time to explore the materials and pattern created before they will be interested in creating a masterpiece. Sometimes, it is helpful to demonstrate how printing works and some of the different prints that can be made with the objects available for them to use. As the children are creating, or after they have finished, talk about some of the pints they made. Perhaps they have designed a shape, an interesting texture, or a pattern of the prints. Also, pose questions about which object made the print or how the tool was moved (Koster, 2005).

Extensions of Printing

- Printing with rubber stamps: designs, letters, and shapes (use washable ink pad)
- Sponge prints: cut into shapes, designs, or use different types of sponges
- Printing with: hands, fingers, feet, or shoe
- Unique printing materials: cans of different sizes, shells, spools, toy trucks (wheels make the print), forks, corrugated cardboard, bubble wrap, or measuring cups
- Nature items: pinecones, stones, leaves, moss, flowers, or feathers

Fiber Art

Experiences with fabric and fibers provide another way for young children to create art. In these activities, children will notice the texture, line, and patterns that the materials may possess. In addition, fibers and fabrics respond to their movement, tools, and designs in a very different way. This challenges children to think in another way and to be flexible in their approach as they experiment with determining what works with new materials. The following experiences are only a few examples of the many possibilities that exist in the use of fibers and materials with young children:

YARN PICTURES. Provide a variety of yarn, with variations in color, size, and texture. Place white glue in bowls and include a container with craft sticks. Include construction paper, shelf paper, foil, cardboard pieces, and rough paper in the area. Scissors, hole-punchers, and pencils may also be displayed for use.

In circle time, the teacher may demonstrate the new art project that will be in the art center. Children who go to this area can select the yarn, paper, and tools they will use to create their yarn pictures. They may try applying the glue to the yarn with the sticks, dipping the yarn in the glue, or using their fingers to apply glue to the paper. During this experimentation, the children will determine which method they will use and move on to create a picture or design.

SEWING. Purchase four to five plastic needles with large eyes and blunt ends. Collect yarn, thread, or ribbon that will go through the eyes of the needles. For younger children, or those with less-developed small motor skills, provide needles that are already threaded with the yarn or ribbon.

Prepare cardboard pieces that are cut into different sizes and shapes. Punch holes in the pieces, varying the number of holes. The fewer the holes, the simpler the task will be. Some pieces can have holes in a circle or square, while others may have a random design. Children can select the cardboard piece and the color and thickness of the yarn or thread they will use. They can sew through the holes with different colors and thicknesses of yarn. Each child will create a unique pattern or design on the base.

WEAVING THE WIRE. Purchase a large section of chicken wire with large holes. Cut the section into smaller pieces, approximately 10" × 10" in size. Cover the rough ends with plastic electrical tape. Provide a basket of thick yarn or macramé rope. Wrap the end of the fiber with tape or dip it in white glue so the ends will not get frayed. This makes it easier for the young child to thread through the wire. Children can select the wire section they will use as well as the fiber they will weave. It is helpful to repeat the chant, "in and out, in and out, in and out the wire." The weaving can be as simple or complex as the child would like to make it. These colorful creations are interesting to hang from the ceiling or in front of a window for display.

One of the most beautiful weavings I have ever seen was in a Reggio Emilia school in Italy. On the porch of the school was a large loom created with two limbs from a tree. The entire length of the loom, from limb to limb, was strung with coarse brown twine, with no strings running across the loom that left open spaces. As children went on walks around the school, they picked up nature items and brought them back, where they would weave the leaves, feathers, grasses, and flowers into the design. I was told that this was a long-term art project that children and teachers could add to over a two-month period. What I saw was a work in progress that clearly demonstrated that young children are capable weavers and collectors of beautiful things.

Marking with Tools

Infants, as well as kindergartners, enjoy making marks. The primary medium used for creating these marks is crayons. Additional tools include markers, chalk, charcoal, colored pencils, and pastels. Young children prefer to work with tools that are easy to maneuver and produce strong colors. Older children will be interested in drawing, sketching, and shading. Pencil, charcoal, or pastels provide more possibilities for blending and shading, which the older child can appreciate.

Brushes come in many sizes and styles. They can be used to produce different types of strokes and size of lines. When a wide variety of brushes is available, children can select the tool that matches their preference for a specific activity. Sometimes young children repeat the same symbols or drawing using different types of brushes to experience the variations they produce. This experimentation encourages understanding of differences, contrast, and proportions.

UNIQUE TOOLS. Including a variety of unusual tools to be used in art activities can stimulate fluency and flexibility of thinking in the classroom. A few of the many possibilities include sponges, feathers, paint rollers, pastry brushes, dried materials, stamps, and small mops. By adding these materials to the art center, children have the opportunity to experiment with new ways of painting. And using varied tools and materials will encourage children to think of additional items that can be used in their artwork. For example, a plastic squirt bottle of paint creates a unique line, whereas a spray bottle makes a spatter design.

Surfaces for Art

Most two-dimensional art is done on paper. There are a large variety of papers appropriate for paint, crayons, and markers. Newsprint, manila, and construction paper are most frequently used in early childhood programs. Other ideas for paper include wallpaper, shelf lining, computer paper, finger-paint paper, sandpaper, wax paper, textured fabric, recycled paper, and wallboard.

Other surfaces also can work well for artistic projects. Plexiglas provides a transparent surface that allows artwork to be enjoyed from both sides. Cardboard boxes and corrugated pieces of paper can provide unique textural backgrounds for paintings. Wood, foam pieces, and clear plastic also can stimulate additional ideas when they are used for drawing or painting projects.

Photography

The addition of new technology has made photography more accessible to early childhood programs. Digital cameras have become effective tools to document children's work as they progress through the many steps of a project or unit of study. Children can assist in making photos and selecting the subjects to be used to demonstrate their learning. Disposable cameras, which are quite inexpensive, are also available to be used by the children. The pictures should be developed quickly so children can revisit, document, and adjust their techniques. With the use of printers, children are able to see the photographs being printed and make changes to the color, hue, brightness, and placement. These adjustments provide opportunities to discuss many artistic terms and to begin to develop an artist's eye for the composition of a picture.

One example of a long-term project focused on photography is an enrichment program that was located in an elementary school serving inner-city children. The program was designed to expose children to the fine arts by creating learning opportunities that emphasized each of the intelligences identified by Howard Gardner. The "Photographic Eyes" project was created to nurture the development of spatial intelligence of children. The group was composed of students in kindergarten through fourth grade with an interest in the study of photography. The teacher, who worked with the group, helped the children learn to reflect and interpret the culture of the school through the camera lens. They learned to process their own film and enlargements in a homemade darkroom in an unused room at the school. The children's work, created during the study, was displayed at the school, in town, and at the school board office. Together, the children and teacher selected and prepared the work to be displayed in an art gallery showing of their photography.

This study provided each child with a unique opportunity to develop his or her eye as an artist who can use photography to understand the visual world and communicate ideas to others. Throughout the process, the children developed their confidence as they grew in their capabilities and expanded their creative thinking. Photography was the vehicle that helped the children gain a new understanding of art.

The photographer is taking a picture of a student sharing his photograph with the principal.

This is the photograph that the student took of a plant in a window at his school.

The child and principal are talking about the picture, the design, and the developing process.

His photography is later displayed in a gallery showing at local college.

Additional Two-Dimensional Possibilities

There are many possibilities for two-dimensional art. Several examples include **rubbing**, printing, stenciling, spatter-painting, torn paper, cutting, pasting, and collage. The selection of specific experiences is determined by matching the developmental level of the children and considering their background of experience with art materials. A wonderful example for primary-age children is torn or cutout paper figures of a character from their favorite book. Encourage children to make figures with colored paper, fabric, glue, and scissors. No pencils or markers are allowed. The children must visualize the needed shapes and cut or tear the paper accordingly. This challenges children to use their spatial intelligence.

FINGER PAINT. Another medium that is fascinating to young children is finger paint. You will need slick, coated paper to work with this thick paint. Specific paper for finger painting can be purchased, or less expensive shelf lining paper can be substituted. When using finger paint, children are able to use large motions, in addition to the small muscles of their fingers. Finger painting is a perfect example of an activity in which the process is more important than the product. Observing children while they are finger painting, reveals that experimentation with the paint, watching the paint's response to their hands, and blending colors is what the children are enjoying, not what the painting will be like when they finish.

A Simple Finger-Paint Recipe

Ingredients

- 3 tablespoons of sugar
- ½ cup of cornstarch
- 2 cups of cold water

Procedure: Warm all ingredients over low heat, covered, until the mixture thickens. Cool, and add a few drops of food coloring. Refrigerate.

Variations:

- Add 1 cup of white sand

  Or

- 1 cup of sawdust, making a consistency of soft putty

  Or

- Paint on foil or Plexiglas

MURALS. Murals provide time for a small group of children to work together on an art project. The mural can be painted, drawn with crayons, or created with paper of various shapes. Often, the mural has a central theme that focuses the work for the children who are participating. For example, third-grade students may be interested in creating a representation of the town where they live. The teacher may talk with them about what makes a city. The children may suggest that a city has houses, factories, malls, and stores. Others may identify the streets, parks, and trees. If the entire class is involved in the study of the city, work on the mural could be divided into small groups that contribute specific parts, such as the residential area or the stores. As they revisit the mural, other elements that should be included are identified. What about the schools and churches? Is there a river or stream that flows through the city? This mural could be done on a large sheet of colored paper that is attached to a wall or board. Over several weeks, features are added and other aspects of the city are included. In this group work, the children collaborate, learn new language, select colors, use lines and shapes, and work with the total composition.

COLLAGES. Collage is an artistic composition of materials pasted over a surface. Artists, including Pablo Picasso and Georges Brazue, have used this technique for many years. **Collage** offers many opportunities for creating and inventing. It also provides many opportunities for change, since you add something, remove something, or cover it up with something else. The materials that can be used in a collage are very diverse. Anything that will stick with glue to a flat surface can be used. A paper collage is an easy starting point, since materials are readily available and affordable. If you want to paint the collage, use watercolors or acrylics, not oil-based paints, which will cause paper to deteriorate (Leland & Williams, 2000).

Collect these Materials
- magazines, pictures, wrapping paper, post cards, tissue paper, cardboard pieces, etc.
- scraps of construction paper, foil, paper towels, coffee filters, paper dollies, etc.
- cardboard, poster board, or art board for the base
- white glue
- variety of brushes
- markers
- scissors

A theme can be selected that interests the child or relates to current studies. Children can tear or cut the paper into various shapes, sizes, and colors. They can then arrange the pieces on the support board. After experimenting with placement and different designs, they can glue the paper to the base. This collage can be created over several days, based on the child's interest. It can also be a group project, with several children working together to create their collage. Elements of design that might be discussed with the children as they work on the collages are shape of the elements, color that is used, sizes used in the design, and pattern, which refers to texture, repeating lines, shapes, and colors.

ART WITH COMPUTERS

Today, it is possible to create art with the software currently available for computers. When selecting appropriate tools to use with art, it is important to use software that allows the child to design the art and control the creation of the pictures or illustrations. Children's creativity is limited when the software works like a workbook. This very restrictive approach is not effective in paper form or on a computer. There are, however, paint programs widely available for use on personal computers that work well for young children. Some of these are easy-to-use programs for freehand and shape drawing that allow the child to draw, create, erase, and add color to the pictures. These software programs match what we know about supporting the artistic development of young children.

Lauren Age 5

Choosing Appropriate Software for Art

The following guidelines will help in evaluating the many different computer programs available:

1. The child is able to determine what will be drawn.

2. Options are available for creating lines, forms, colors, and making changes.

3. Different drawing tools can be used to change texture, size, and the proportion of the drawing.

4. The child's name and a title/description can be added.

❀ THREE-DIMENSIONAL ART

Three-dimensional art refers to creations that have substance. They stand up instead of lying flat on the surface. This dimension will provide new ways of experiencing and creating art in an early childhood classroom. It can be used with both very young children and primary-age children, although the level of their product will vary significantly.

For many years, play dough has been widely used with young children in their homes and at school. The dough was commercially produced or made in the classroom. Each recipe produced varying textures and responsiveness. They ranged from a smooth consistency, made by cooking the mixture and using cream of tartar, to a rough texture made with a large amount of salt. Additional recipes and unusual combinations for dough are included throughout the chapter.

Real Artist Clay

This type of clay is made from the earth and often purchased in art stores or from a supply house. The clay is used by artists and can be painted or glazed and fired. It can be purchased in either powder or premixed form. This clay varies from gray to a reddish color, depending on the earth from which it was processed. Since the clay is water-based, it can be air-dried or fired in a kiln.

Young children are intrigued by the unique properties of real clay. It can be shaped, molded, and attached easily. Children can add water to the clay as they work with their hands to change its consistency and texture. Clay provides a new experience for many young children as they create sculptures and forms. If a child wants to return to refine the creation the next day, covering it with a wet cloth and plastic cover can keep the clay pliable. The clay can be stored in airtight containers and reused for several months.

Tools for working with clay include:

pizza cutters	dowel rods	metal bearings
cookie cutters	wetting brushes	pieces of tile
plastic knives	meat tenderizers	string or twine
rolling pins	bottle caps	old scissors
melon ballers	baby forks	mallet shoe horns
pastry tubes	potato mashers	toothpicks
ice scrapers	buttons	pencils
ice cream scoops	screws or bolts	

Remember that tools are added only after children have had many opportunities to explore and manipulate clay with their hands. One or two new items are all that are needed to stimulate renewed interest in clay.

Recipes

The following recipes are examples of other clay that can be used with young children. The textures of the clay are interesting and they can be stored well.

BEST PLAY DOUGH FORMULA

Ingredients

2 c. flour	2 tbsp. oil
1 c. salt	2 tsp. cream of tartar
2 c. water	food coloring

Procedure: Stir ingredients over low heat until mixture has coagulated into a nice doughy ball. Allow time for the dough to cool thoroughly. Store in a plastic container with a tight-fitting lid. This play dough has a smooth texture and will last a long time when properly stored.

Clay sculpture of birds. (Age 4.5 years)

CREATIVE PLAY CLAY

Ingredients

1 c. baking soda

½ c. cornstarch food coloring ⅔ c. warm water

Procedure: Mix baking soda and cornstarch in a saucepan. Add water and stir until smooth. Place over medium heat and bring to a boil. Stir mixture constantly until it looks like mashed potatoes. Remove saucepan from heat and pour clay onto a mixing board to cool. For color, knead food coloring into the cooled clay until well blended. This clay dries well and is perfect for painting on when dried. Makes about 1½ cups and is easily doubled. Store in an airtight container.

SAWDUST CLAY (A GREAT WAY TO RECYCLE)

Ingredients

2 c. fine sawdust

1 c. wheat paste (used for wallpaper)

½–1 c. water (to make molding consistency)

1 tsp. alum (to keep from spoiling)

Procedure: Combine ingredients and mix to the consistency of bread dough. Allow to dry slowly. Keep in plastic bag or refrigerator. This clay can be painted with tempera paint.

NO-COOK CLAY DOUGH

Ingredients

3 c. flour	3 tbsp. alum
3 c. salt	water

Procedure: Combine dry ingredients; slowly add water. Begin by mixing with a spoon; as the mixture thickens, continue mixing with your hands, until it has the consistency of clay. (Too dry—add water; too sticky—add equal parts of flour and salt.)

Three-Dimensional Constructions

❝The wider the range of possibilities we offer children, the more intense will be their motivations and the richer their experiences.❞

Malaguzzi, 1993

Wood scraps and plywood pieces can be used to create three-dimensional projects. These materials can be glued, nailed, or clamped together to make substantial structures developed over a period of time. Large boxes can provide a base for projects, and smaller boxes can be combined to create structures. Shoeboxes, gift boxes, pizza circles, and egg cartons are just a few of the possibilities that exist for making sculptures. Insulated, copper, or metal wire can be another material used to make three-dimensional representations. Wire is flexible and can be shaped into many forms or connected to other materials to create unique sculptures. Attaching the wire to a block of wood can provide a base for the creation and an attractive way to display the artwork. Foil sculptures, attached to a frame, can be pinched, folded, and crinkled to create an interesting three-dimensional shape.

Wood scraps can introduce children to how three-dimensional structures look and how they are built. Begin with three or four pieces of wood and encourage experimentation with design. Pose questions to the children that are divergent—have several possibilities with no right way to respond. Possible questions might be: How can you arrange these pieces of wood so they are interesting to look at? How can you make your structure sturdy? Can you do it another way? Then, walk around the table and look at the structure from different points and ask, How does it look from this side? Can you see it from across the room? How can you make it taller, shorter, wider, or longer? How does it look when you kneel next to the table?

After a period of exploration, add new and interestingly shaped wood scraps. Now, the children will be able to make different arrangements and designs. It is important to talk with the children about their constructions and how they are putting them together. Later, add different materials that can be combined with the wood scraps, such as pieces of fabric, metal lids, plastic tops, various pieces of foil, bubble wrap, and film cans. Throughout the experimentation, the children are developing flexible thinking as they try different options.

When children have had sufficient time exploring their options, they will be ready to construct something that interests them. At this point, they may begin to name the structure or tell you what it does: "It's a rack that the mechanic uses when he fixes your car." "This is my house and here is my bedroom." "Have you seen my tall building?" Sometimes, children have stories to tell about their constructions. When this occurs, you want to have paper and pen ready to write down what they are saying. These stories illustrate the child's thinking about the construction and why it is designed in this specific way.

Clear Plastic Cup Towers

Plastic and Styrofoam cups provide another building material. These can be lined up, stacked, nested, intertwined, or filled. Follow a sequence that is similar to that described for wood scraps.

- First, provide a few cups and allow time for investigation.
- Pose questions: What happens when you put several cups together? How can you join them together? Some possibilities may be with glue, tape, cut, string, paper clips, etc. Try one of these and see how it works. What other ways will work?
- Next, add different types of cups: smaller size, paper, colored plastic, nut cups, coffee cups, and other varieties.
- Provide tools that can be used to attach the cups together. Include some the children had identified during the previous conversation.
- When the children have completed their cup towers, take pictures of them with their construction. Place the pictures inside clear plastic cups and attach them to the display board for an unusual presentation of their work.

Storing Work in Progress

Identify a place in the classroom where children can store their incomplete work. This allows children to return to their construction again and again. By having the opportunity to revisit the structure, they will include ideas, materials that have been added, or elements that they want to change. When children are satisfied with their structure, they can be invited to draw a picture of their three-dimensional work. This drawing will represent what they have built and will also give them the opportunity to see it from a different perspective (Topal & Gandini, 1999).

Mobiles

Mobiles are three-dimensional works of art that can be described as hanging sculptures. These moving pieces provide another way to see art and construct form. The materials used for mobiles can range from pieces of cut paper to CDs strung together and hung from the ceiling. The creation of a mobile often requires the efforts of both children and teacher as they collaborate on the work. The children should be involved in the entire creative process, although they may need some adult assistance with stringing and tying.

When beginning to design mobiles, it would be interesting to look at the work of American sculptor Alexander Calder who was one of the most inventive artists of his time. In addition to his painting, creating toys, and textile work, he is most known for his mobile sculptures that twist and turn in the breeze. Studying the photographs of his work, which can be found around the world, should inspire primary-grade children to think in new ways about space and balance.

This preschooler is planning his wood and glue structure.

Teachers can collect various materials to be used in making mobiles, such as plastic coat hangers, branches, yarn, fishing line, wire, tape, glue, markers, tempera paint, old CDs, contact paper shapes, art board, foil, pine cones, sea shells, nut shells, pieces of colorful plastic, old jewelry, pipe cleaners, old puzzle pieces, etc. Children can select the item that will be used to support the pieces. For example, the tree branch (leaves or needles removed) could become the foundation for the mobile. Varying lengths of yarn, fishing line, or wire can be used to suspend small pine cones and nut shells at different points on the branch. Children can experiment with the movement that the objects make and change their selection if needed. The mobiles can be hung in the window, in the art center, or from the ceiling.

The teacher can learn about mobiles along with the children. The teacher as a learner is a wonderful model for children to observe and emulate. This cooperative learning is very exciting for both teacher and children. To learn more about Alexander Calder, read these informative books: *The Essential Alexander Calder,* written by Howard Greenfeld and Alexander Calder, and published by Harry N. Abrams, of New York in 2003; and *How to Teach Art to Children,* written by Tanya Skelton, and published by Evan-Moor Educational Publishers of Monterey, California, in 2001.

ABCs of Collected Art and Project Materials

The following items could be offered to children while they are working on projects:

A
accordion
acorns
aluminum foil

B
baby oil
bark
baskets
beads
blocks: wood, plastic, milk cartons, foam, and branches
bottle caps
bows
boxes: small, medium, and large
brads
broken jewelry
brushes: small, large, and house painting
buttons

C
cardboard pieces (all kinds and shapes, preferably without print)
carpet pieces
catalogs
cellophane
chalk
chimes: made from pipes, keys, lids, and found items
clay
coffee cans
colored pencils
colored sand
computer paper
contact paper scraps
containers (preferably white or transparent)
corks
corrugated cardboard
costume jewelry
cotton balls
cowbell
craft sticks
crayons
cymbals: juice lids or lids for pots

D
dirt: digging tools, sifters, spoons, and clear measuring cups
dowel rods
dried flowers and weeds
droppers
drums: coffee cans, buckets, and washtub

E
egg cartons: cardboard and foam
elastic pieces and thread
eyedroppers

F
fabric: varied sizes, texture, and color
feathers
felt

film canisters (empty)
fishing line
flowers/greenery in plastic, silk, and
	dried
flute: wooden and metal
foam: different sizes
foil
frames

G
glitter or sparkles
glitter glue
glue: home-made (flour and water),
	glue sticks, white, rubber cement,
	paste, and wood glue
golf balls
gourds
grocery bags

H
hand bells
hats: made from foil, wrapping
	paper, wallpaper, crepe paper,
	and fabric
hose: pieces and strips

I
Indigo: blue paint, paper, pens,
	crayons, and markers

J
jugs
juice lids

K
keyboard
keys: metal, plastic, and varied sizes

L
lace
leather remnants
lids
lumber: scraps, woodturnings, and
	plywood

M
machines (small) that don't work
	(i.e., watches, clocks, etc.)
macramé rope
magazines
marker lids (from dried-out markers)
markers

masking tape: different colors and
	widths
matting board
metal tubing
milk jugs
mirrors (small)

N
nails
newspaper

O
orange socks, paper, paint, and beads

P
packing materials
paint (finger, watercolor, acrylic,
	tempera, and fabric)
paint roller
paper plates and cups
paper (of different weights, textures,
	and colors)
paper: butcher, manila, shelf lining,
	newsprint, and construction
paper clips
pastels
pinecones
pipe cleaners: varied color and texture
plastic sock holders
play dough
pom-poms
postcards and greeting cards

Q
quilt pieces

R
ribbon: different widths and colors
rocks
rubber bands
rulers

S
salt (epsom and rock)
scissors
screws
sea shells
seed pods (small)
sheets: white and colored
shiny paper and fabric
sponges
spools

spray bottles
squirt bottles: catsup, mustard, and
    frosting
stamps and stamp pads
stapler (to be used with supervision)
straws
string
Styrofoam trays: varied sizes

T
tape: masking, colored, electrical,
    clear, and double-faced
textured tools: cookie cutters and
    potato masher
tile scraps
tissue paper
toothpicks
tree twigs, leaves, and bark
trim: tassels, lace, border, pom poms,
    and fringe
tubes: paper rolls, toilet rolls, carpet,
    and wrapping paper

U
unique tools: kitchen items, cleaning
    items, combs, and turkey baster

V
volume: different-sized plastic contain-
    ers, measuring spoons, and cups

W
wallpaper
wire: electrical, copper, and metal in
    various lengths and colors
wood and plywood scraps
wrapping paper: gift, brown, and
    butcher

X
X rays for doctor's office or hospital
    center
xylophone

Y
yarn: different colors, thickness, and
    texture
yellow fabric, plastic food, paper, and
    markers

Z
zither

✾ GROUP PROJECTS

Some art is created by an individual child while working on a specific item in her own way. But some of the most interesting art projects can be done by a group of children working together on **group projects**. These creations provide opportunities to plan, discuss, and create a work of art that is very different from those produced by individuals. During the early childhood years, children are learning to work together, to share materials, and to discuss their work. Group work provides important and meaningful experiences as children create together. These collaborative efforts provide opportunities for children of varying abilities to work together and create a masterpiece.

A collage is composed of different elements, and can be either two- or three-dimensional. For example, a group of young children can work together to make a collage of found nature items or favorite foods cut from magazines or advertisements. Another idea may consist of prints made by kitchen utensils. During this process, children can plan what utensils they will include, discuss where the prints will be located, and critique the elements that are needed to complete the picture.

Project work, a focused study on specific topics of children's interest, also can lead to a group art experience. For example, children who are working on a project related to their garden might draw how the area looks in the spring when the seeds have been planted. Later, they can draw pictures of the plants growing during the summer. The garden can be revisited in the fall when the harvest of vegetables is completed. The children's drawings can be displayed in sequence to demonstrate the changes that have occurred in the garden over time. Both artwork and

A toddler is making a collage with tissue paper and paint.

photographs can provide documentation of group projects focused on the garden. The children's language, recorded during the project, can provide additional insight into the creative thinking and should be included on documentation panels.

GROUP ACTIVITIES

As young children become more experienced with art, the elements, and materials, they can begin to work on group projects. Projects provide opportunities for them to work cooperatively, learn from others, and collaborate on ideas. Before children begin to create work together, talk with them about their responsibilities and some guidelines for being a contributing member of the group.

Some Simple Guidelines Might Include:

- Respect the work of group members.
- Share ideas and tools.
- Work up to another person's work but not over it.
- Evaluate every member's contribution to the artwork.

Some excellent group projects include murals and posters to illustrate a theme or project. Children can design works of art that represent a children's book or an author's techniques. Collages provide another way to work together and use diverse materials in creative ways.

Guide children in identifying the positive elements of working together in a group. Encourage them to critique ways they can improve their group project, with an emphasis on the collaborative effort: "We might add more color" or "We need more work in this area of the painting." This conversation builds positive feelings of being a contributing member of a team working together successfully. When the masterpiece is completed, list all the artists who worked on the project. This supports the idea that this was a group project (Gee, 2000).

✿ ART CENTER

One of the traditional centers included in early childhood programs is the **art center.** This specific area of the classroom is designed to serve as the hub for artistic creations. In this space, art supplies and tools are stored to provide children with easy access while selecting materials. The environment is designed to support a variety of activities as children work together or individually.

Some important physical features of the art center are washable surfaces, a water source, and materials that are well-organized, visible, and accessible. Art activities can be messy. Children need to be able to work without concern for keeping the area clean during the creating process. Of course, one of the responsibilities of working in the art center is participating in cleaning up when the creative process is over.

The art center should contain a wide range of materials and tools that support budding artists while challenging them to try new approaches. These materials include basic art supplies such as a variety of paper, paint, tape, staplers, glue, scissors, and clay. Unique items should be rotated into the area as well. Textured wallpaper, pieces of sandpaper, or rough fabric, for example, could generate an interest in the effect of tempera paint on different surfaces. Natural materials can add a new dimension to the art area as children paint with pine branches or a pinecone. A box of collected "junk" materials should be available for the children when they

Art materials attractively displayed and accessible to children.

Clear plastic containers make contents seen and artistically displayed.

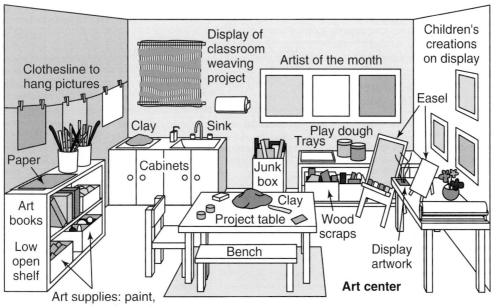

An art center.

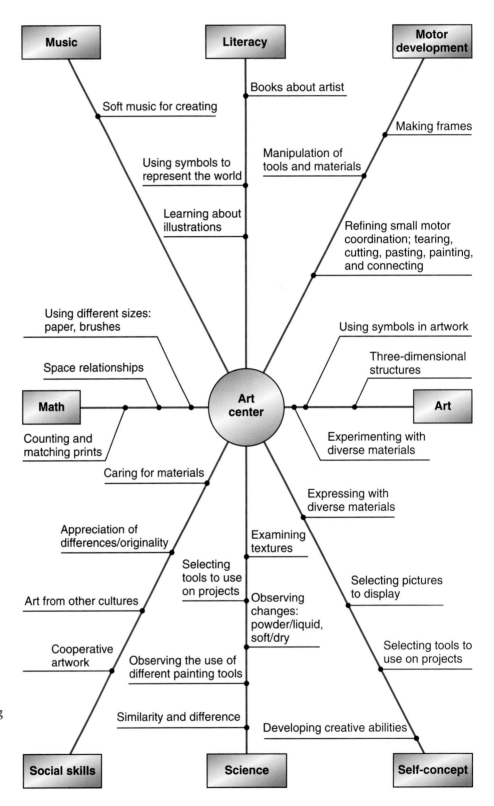

FIGURE 5–1
Web of integrated learning in the art center. (From Isbell, R. [1995]. *The complete learning center book*. Beltsville, MD: Gryphon House)

need to find items to complete their ideas or projects. Fabric, decorative trims, pieces of foil, cardboard scraps, wire, wrapping paper, pom-poms, craft sticks, wood, and sandpaper inspire elaboration of ideas. The box also can include scraps left over from previous art projects. This reuse can help children learn to conserve materials in their environment.

The art area is used during center time when children choose to work on art activities. The art center also can be used throughout the day when children need a place to work or use art supplies. The additional use of this space expands the possibilities for children as they create illustrations for books or build something that relates to a project. Art and the art center provide many opportunities for integrated learning including science, math, social skills, and motor development. A web of some of the learning that can occur in this area is demonstrated visually in Figure 5–1 (Isbell, 1995, p. 58).

PICASSO MUSEUM: THE LIFE AND ARTWORK OF PABLO PICASSO (AGE GROUP: PREK–2)

Objectives for the Picasso Museum Art Center

The American Council for the Arts in Education states that:

> learning *in* the arts is of unique educational value . . . learning *about* the arts is learning about the rich world of sensation, emotion, and personal expression surrounding us each day . . . learning *through* the arts has the potential to enhance one's general motivation to learn to develop one's respect for a disciplined approach to learning (Lasky & Mukerji, 1980).

The visual arts have long been an acknowledged foundation of early childhood learning. The focus has been mainly on fostering creativity as a way to support development of the young child's cognitive, fine-motor, and socioemotional skills. Along with this focus, art educators describe four components of a complete art program that early childhood educators need to apply in developmentally appropriate ways.

1. Art education involves the development of an aesthetic sense—learning to see the world and appreciate its beauty.

2. Art education involves having the opportunity to create artistic products using a variety of materials.

3. Art education includes learning about artists and art history.

4. Art education programs teach students to respond to artwork in an informed way, to learn the elements of design, and to evaluate the principles of art.

The components of art education may be developed through study in an art center that has been transformed into a "Museum" focusing on Pablo Picasso, which exposes children to his paintings, his life story, and introduces several different techniques, media, principles, and elements of design.

A Five-Phase Process

The process allows the teacher to adapt the art center five times to cover five different aspects of Picasso and his art. These are:

1. The Life and Work of Picasso—Introduce the artist to the children in a broad way. In preparation for studying some aspects of his art in more depth, allow children to explore a variety of his paintings, talk about

them, and learn vocabulary. This gives the children an opportunity to get visually acquainted with Picasso's imagery and discuss what they see and feel in relation to his work.

2. The Blue Period
3. The Rose Period
4. Cubism
5. Collage

In each phase, the children will view paintings of the period and have opportunities to discuss, explore, and create their own artwork in response to Picasso's work. The section found here shows how to plan for the Blue Period phase of the study. Learn how to plan for the other phases, by visiting the Thomson Delmar Learning Online Companion at: www.earlychilded.delmar.com.

Adapting the Art Center to the Picasso Museum

Adapt the art center for this project. Figure 5–2 shows a diagram of a basic setup for the art center.

SOME THINGS NEEDED FOR THE MODIFICATION
- A floor-to-ceiling arrangement of Picasso's artwork in real frames on more than one wall, to represent the way a museum actually looks
- A display of the children's framed artwork, to look like a real museum
- A rug in the museum area, to give children a focal point for viewing and discussing the work of the artist
- An area to display books about the artist and his medium
- A table and easels, to allow for creative explorations in response to the study
- A supply of art materials, replacing those that are less conceptually related to each phase with materials that can extend thinking specific to the current phase (see Table 5–1)

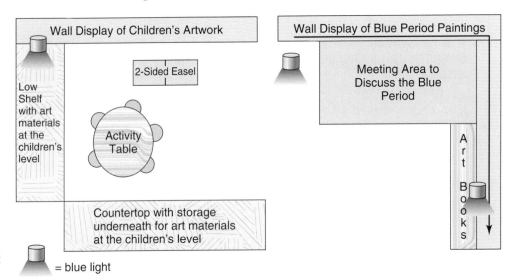

FIGURE 5–2
Picasso Museum Art Center

TABLE 5–1 Materials for Painting Explorations

• Limit paint to large containers of blue paint and smaller containers of primary and secondary colors. This visual distinction helps guide the child's thinking visually, without words	• Paintbrushes • Jars for mixing paints • Large jar of water (for rinsing)
• Blue tempera paint	
• A variety of tempera paint in small amounts	
• Large white paper (provide a variety of quality artist's papers)	

The Blue Period–Additions to the Art Center

- Prints of Picasso's paintings:
  ○ *Child with a Dove*
  ○ *The Old Guitarist*
  ○ *Poor People on the Seashore*
- Blue lights scattered around the art center, or a string of blue lights
- Blue sheer and opaque fabrics that can be used for observing the effect of changes in light and color
- A light table with access to a variety of blue materials on a nearby shelf that are sorted by color and texture

Objective of the Blue Period Phase

(Remember that the Blue Period is the second phase of this study. Teachers would initially want to present information on the Life of Picasso to familiarize children with the artist's name and discuss what it means to be an artist.)

The objective of this phase is to introduce children to several examples of Picasso's work during the Blue Period so they can examine the color form, design, styles, techniques of each, and feelings that the paintings evoke. The children will respond to the paintings in many ways that include discussion about Picasso's artworks, painting, exploring with other materials in the center, and discussions about their work in relation to Picasso's.

Introducing the Picasso Museum Art Center

Gather children in the center where several examples of Picasso's Blue Period work are displayed. Use open-ended questions to facilitate discussion and generate children's ideas about the artwork.

- What do you think about this painting by Picasso?
- How does it make you feel?
- What is the main color that you see?
- Can you name some objects that are blue?
- What do you think of when you see the color blue?
- How does blue make you feel?

Children can be encouraged to share answers to these questions while the teacher writes the answers down. The purpose of the questions and discussion is to explore the feelings that the color blue evokes in the children before sharing Picasso's feelings. After the children have been given ample time to respond, the teacher may explain Picasso's feelings of sadness and loneliness at the death of his friend, which are his reasons for using the color blue in these paintings. Children can be encouraged to share things that make them sad or lonely, or explore the other feelings they mention.

PROCEDURE

1. Blue paint will be the main color and theme of the artwork.
2. Pour approximately four ounces of blue paint in several jars, and add a few drops of a different color to each jar, to slightly alter the blue paint to a new shade. (For example, add white to become a powder blue or add green to become an aqua. The idea is to provide the color blue in varying shades.)
3. When a selection of blues has been mixed, it is time to paint.
4. Instruct the children to paint a picture using shades of blue.

QUESTIONS THAT MAY BE ASKED DURING THE ACTIVITY

- What color do you think would be good to show happiness? Anger? Peacefulness? Silliness? Etc.
- How does your painting make you feel?

HOW TO EVALUATE.   Observing children at work and play is an effective way to learn what they think and know. During discussions, note their ideas and use your notes to develop ideas about new materials to add to your center that support their thinking. For example, if children are interested in the faces in Picasso's paintings, bring a small mirror into the art center to look into and create portraits.

Observe, to learn what words children use to describe the paintings, the ways children work together to create, and the ways children solve problems like mixing a color. Use the observations to prepare new ideas, such as to propose collaborations like murals or puzzles made with blue media.

EXTENDING THE ACTIVITY

- Allow children to continue their explorations at each phase until their interest wanes.
- Visit a museum or art gallery.
- Have local artists visit and discuss their artwork.
- Have an art exhibit for other classes, parents, and the community, with a reception for the artists and announcements in the local newspaper.

Vocabulary

art criticism	artist model	color meaning	pose/posing
art exhibit	artist's period/blue	composition	professional artist
art gallery	period	design	shade
art museum	background	figure	shape
art reception	brush strokes	form	theme
art studio	color interpretation	line	tone

Picasso Resources

Bauer, D. (2000). Picasso Comes to PreK/K. *Focus on PreK & K, 12,* 4–5.

Kohl, M. F., & Solga, K. (1996). *Discovering great artists: Hands-on art for children in styles of the great masters.* Bellingham, WA: Bright Ring.

Lasky, L., & Mukerji, R. (1980). *Art: Basic for young children.* Washington, DC: National Association for the Education of Young Children.

"Mr. Picassohead" Website: www.mrpicassohead.com.

In addition to this Picasso Museum adaptation, you will find additional resources, including an adaptation of the art center to make a Children's Museum of Clay, by visiting the Thomson Delmar Learning Online Companion

 at: www.earlychilded.delmar.com.

✿ ❙ ILLUSTRATOR'S CORNER

Illustrations in picture books are often young children's first exposure to art. These illustrations include many different techniques that can be used to introduce children to an artist and art approach. The study of an illustrator can help children see and learn about the artist. Picture books communicate to young children, by combining art and text. As children read books and study the illustrations, they experience how art is used to communicate ideas, stories, and happenings. Illustrations make the text more understandable for them and add information not included in the text. For example, Eric Carle's story of *The Very Hungry Caterpillar* demonstrates the powerful effect of illustrations. These wonderful illustrations help the child understand the different foods that caterpillars eat and their amazing transformation into a butterfly. The illustrations are an essential part of the story and as important as the words (Prudhoe, 2003). Art techniques that are used in children's books can inspire young artists.

Some illustrators and books that work well with young children include:

- Eric Carle—Printmaking: *The Tiny Seed*
- Ezra Jack Keats—Photo-montage: *Jennie's Hat*
- Leo Lionni—Torn Paper: *Frederick*
- Lois Ehlert—Cut Paper: *Waiting for Wings*
- Bryan Collier—Watercolor and Photography: *Uptown*
- Jeannie Baker—Texture Collage: *The Hidden Forest*
- Robert McCloskey—Drawing: *Make Way for Ducklings*
- Audrey Wood—Painting: *The Napping House*
- Chris Van Allsburg—Pastel: *The Polar Express*
- Judith Viorst—Pen and Ink: *Alexander and the Terrible, Horrible, No Good, Very Bad Day*
- Tomie de Paola—Sculpture: *Giorgio's Village*
- Frank Asch—Watercolor: *Water*
- Omar S. Castaneda—Weaving: *Abuela's Weave*

After reading and discussing the work of an artist, provide children with similar materials to use. They can create their own illustrations using torn paper, photographs, fabrics, pastels, or natural materials (Cornett, 1998).

ART IN THEME STUDY

Recently, a concerted effort has been made to integrate the arts into the early childhood curriculum through **thematic units.** There are a number of different strategies for using themes in the classroom. In the past, early childhood teachers might have selected and implemented a unit on color that included color stories, color math, and color combining science. In this thematic unit, art is included to support the teaching of color. It might include placing the three primary colors of tempera paint in the art center, dying fabric with food coloring, or placing layers of colored sand in a bottle. In the emerging curriculum, a theme study or project may be developed from a child's interest. For example, several children are observed experimenting with materials that are rough and smooth. They are interested in the variation of textures they have found. The teacher's observation of the children's interest in rough and smooth can become the focus of a project or investigation of variations in texture.

FOLK ART

Many people participate in some kind of **folk art** such as needlework, whittling, creating birdhouses, or making sculptures from recycled materials. Folk artists rarely have formal training but have learned their craft from elders or peers in their family or the community. The aesthetics and techniques of their folk art are an expression of their individual creativity, as well as their cultural heritage.

Examples of folk artists include Sidney Slovack, who uses fiber and seeds to weave symmetrical webs; Edith Hikaman, who weaves Finnish rag rugs using a big wave pattern; and Jeremy Huddleston, who creates bird carvings from cider wood. These folk artists create artwork that is both unique and individually special (March, 1990).

A classroom quilt created by combining a piece of each child's favorite fabric.

Most communities have folk artists who use different materials and techniques. These artists can provide young children with another way of viewing art. In the southern Appalachian area, quilters are an example of folk artists in the community. Quilters compose designs with complex patterns, color schemes, and intricate edges. Young children in this region would enjoy having a quilter visit their classroom and have the opportunity to sew fabric pieces together into a pattern. In addition, most quilts have wonderful stories that the quilters can share with children. Through this experience, they are able to see a folk artist at work and begin to identify art in the world around them. For younger children, it would be more appropriate to use colored shapes of paper or to glue fabric pieces to a cardboard form.

✿ | THE REGGIO EMILIA APPROACH

The Reggio Emilia schools in Northern Italy have received international recognition because of their excellent early childhood program. The environment in Reggio Emilia schools is different from many programs for young children. Here, children are seen as capable learners, able to think and create in ways never before thought possible. In these schools, children are focused intensely on long-term projects that follow their interest. Together, children and teachers question and learn about their world as they develop plans, create, and revisit their work, time and again. The Reggio Emilia approach views art as a language children use to think and express their ideas.

In Reggio, each school has an **atelierista,** or art specialist, who provides the catalyst for artistic expression. The atelierista works with the children and teachers as they create, experiment, and explore new avenues of expression. In each school, there is an **atelier,** or art studio. In addition, there is a smaller atelier attached to each classroom. These art areas contain an enormous array of natural materials, art supplies, and tools children can use while working on projects and creations. The materials in these spaces are beautifully displayed, sometimes grouped by color, texture, or function. Children's projects are displayed or stored for future work and refinement. The Reggio environment is visually attractive and intellectually challenging.

Visual Arts: Central to the Early Childhood Classroom

The visual arts center can be considered central to the early childhood classroom when teachers rely on using this area to expand on or extend the ideas expressed in other areas. Here, children can develop inquiries that lead to critical thinking and reflection about learning. The schools in Reggio Emilia, Italy, provide a good resource for an understanding of how best to use the art center. A key to their approach is the notion that children are invited to represent an idea and re-represent it in a new medium (material). They continue to revisit the creative work, expanding on their understanding with more elaboration or further representations in a new media. This challenges children to learn more deeply about the concepts at the heart of their representations (Cadwell, 1997).

Drawing to Learn

Take, for example, a group of children who are representing their understanding of cats as they pretend to be cats in the dramatic play center. When they are asked to draw their stories of cats, the stories particular to their play, they construct relationships among their ideas about the play, their knowledge of cats, and their ideas and knowledge about drawing. The drawing medium allows them to elaborate on the ideas of their play because they can draw cat houses with details that are not apparent in their dramatic play center. What is described here is an example of expanding or extending play from another center of the room through elaboration afforded by drawing.

Multiple Representations

Now that a new representation of the ideas that emerge from children's play exists, it has the potential to serve as a map for inquiry to extend the ideas of the children. The child can verbalize the story of the drawing, and, as the teacher notes the relationship between the child's words and the image, the child can begin to ask related questions. For example, the child may say, "This is Babe the cat, who plays and then goes inside to play with me." The teacher can respond, "I can see the cat and the house, but I can't see how the cat plays. Can you show me how the cat plays outside?" A number of other questions may arise from this conversation:

- Can you show how the cat plays inside?
- Can you show why the cat climbs that tree? (as generated by the drawing of another child in the group)
- Can you show the inside of the house, so we can see:
  - where the cat sleeps?
  - how the cat plays with you inside?

Many of these questions rely on actions that are more easily represented in words and play than with drawings, so it may be appropriate, at this point, to move to another mode. To provide an idea of how to proceed, we continue to look at this particular group of children.

Invite the children to draw their cats on cardstock paper, to create stand-up paper-doll figures that they can play with, and answer the questions that challenge and interest them. During the process, details about the size and proportion of cats, in relation to people and houses, are discussed, and the children may decide they want the figures to align realistically with one another and the houses they draw. Ideas about differences between the back and front of the cutout figures may emerge as children realize they can see the back of the figures as they play.

Teachers Facilitate Children's Inquiry with Many Media

Note that the children do not initially think of drawing on the back of their figures. Instead, they could be invited by teachers to consider the idea. These gradual challenges, posed in a way that provokes curiosity and wonder—inquiry—can effectively stimulate children to continue to elaborate through critical reflection. It feels like play because it is directly related to the core ideas within the children's play activity. The process may continue with the group as the children construct a three-dimensional house to contain the play, a process presenting new questions and lessons along the way. These new concerns deepen the children's understanding of cats, in relation to people, play, and houses, allowing the three-dimensional house to find its way to another part of the classroom where dramatic play can progress.

Visual Arts Bridge the Learning from One Center to Many

A multimedia approach bridges the dramatic play center to the art center and back again. Consider many possible ways to integrate the visual arts into other centers to expand and extend the children's play in those areas:

- Creating props for dramatic play helps children think about the purpose of the props in relation to the content of their play.
- Making instruments helps children question the relationships between materials and sound.
- Recording musical patterns helps children use color to differentiate sounds and create songs.
- Developing illustrations for a classroom connects to the library center.
- Designing clothing for specific centers extends children's thinking into these areas.

Learning from this Artistically Focused Program

Young children learn about aesthetics by living in an environment that includes beautiful items. How can we create classrooms that are more attractive and visually interesting? Begin by including natural materials that can be explored and enjoyed by young children, such as a bouquet of spring flowers, a collection of interesting stones, or clear tubes of varying sizes that can add visual interest to the classroom space.

The next step is thinking about how children's work should be displayed. If their artwork is framed or arranged in an interesting pattern, it will be more impressive. The children have opportunities to appreciate the visual impact of the collage or group project when it is attractively displayed. It clearly demonstrates

Teachers collaborate on a project that focuses on "rocks."

that artwork is valued. In addition, displaying children's art provides opportunities for children to revisit their work throughout the year.

Art materials and tools should be expanded to include many new possibilities that traditionally were not part of early childhood programs. Do not limit choices for young children; instead, think about unique materials that allow children to be creative. Three-dimensional materials can be added to provide opportunities for looking at things in a new way. Using sketching pads and charcoal pencils can provide a way of planning and thinking about what will be created by the children.

Begin to include long-term projects that can be reworked and revisited by the children. These in-depth experiences can replace the short-time, one-shot art activity that has dominated early childhood classrooms. Projects expand and continue explorations while allowing children to create, refine, and evaluate their work in ways not possible in a shorter time frame. By collaborating with their peers and teachers, young children will build confidence in their artistic abilities, and art will become an integrated component of the early childhood curriculum.

✿ CHILDREN AS ART CRITICS

Children should be encouraged to evaluate their own artwork and group projects. For example, a child can select a painting she wants to display from the three produced that week. This selection process allows the child to critique her paintings and offers an opportunity for aesthetic decisions. A gallery in the classroom or adjoining area can provide an opportunity for children to select the picture they would like to frame and exhibit. Photos of art work or group projects provide another way to document the progress. These photographs can serve to show the art history of the classroom and the artists that work there. As new art is completed, children can determine which works should be added to the growing display and which items should be removed or placed in another area. Opportunities to evaluate, display, and document work can help children learn to value art and appreciate the work of others.

✿ DISPLAY OF THE CHILDREN'S WORK

Children's artwork should be displayed so that all may appreciate the efforts of the child. Making a frame for a picture, choosing a textured background, or putting a clay sculpture on a wooden box can make the display more interesting. These special efforts demonstrate that the artwork of the children is valued in this classroom.

Displaying art allows children to view their work from a different perspective. When it is attractively arranged, it communicates to children that we respect their work and value their accomplishments. While making selections for art displays, it is important to talk with the children about their work and help them build a sense of pride in their work. The words and stories of the children can be included in the display. The art and accompanying language helps us gain understanding of what learning has occurred and how the children's language was used. This combination provides an avenue for clearer communication with children, teachers, and parents.

Art displays in the classroom and school invite parents to look at the work of their own children as well as the work of other children. The children's creations, photographs, and dialog help parents understand what they are learning and creating.

A grapevine tree is an interesting place to display crepe paper flowers created by children.

A wooden corner cabinet can be use to attractively display children's artwork.

These displays are another way to build a sense of community. In this place it is evident that we appreciate the work of many children and the different ways each child approaches the experiences.

Art and Portfolios

Teachers are observers, documenters, and evaluators. The art center and group artwork can provide an appropriate place for children to be observed as they are involved in active learning. **Documentation** of what is seen and what is happening helps retain the information that is needed for analysis used in informal evaluation. These techniques help the teacher determine the progress children make and determine if the environment matches their level of development. These observations help the teacher understand the individual child's special interest and identify any problem areas.

Early childhood teachers often collect artwork to include in each child's portfolio. It is important to begin collecting this work at the beginning of the year, since significant changes occur between September and June. Be sure to include the child's name and the date when the work was produced. Art provides a way of examining children's progress in representation, use of tools, language descriptions, and interest in materials. Group work can demonstrate the child's social skills and ability to cooperate on a project. Since several children are involved in the creation of collaborative work, you may need to take photographs of the work to include in the portfolios of all the children involved.

Professional artists develop portfolios that contain a collection of their work. Their portfolio represents what they can do with different art media. They also include photographs of their work. This process works for children as you build a portfolio to show what they have learned and have done. Children should be involved in the selection of the work that will be included in their portfolio. This allows them to evaluate their own work and determine what they like best (Genishi, 1993).

QUESTIONS TO HELP CHILDREN SELECT WORK FOR THEIR PORTFOLIO

- Which is your favorite piece?
- What do you like about it?
- Why do you want to include this particular piece?
- Explain how you created this effect. (Point to a special feature.)
- What do you remember about doing this?
- Which would you like to share with your parents?
- Of these three, which one do you want to include?

Artwork provides a "safe" place to start a discussion with parents about their child, by identifying the work, techniques used, and developing skills that you have observed. This helps a parent begin to understand their child's development and interests. Teachers should help parents recognize the contribution that art makes to cognitive, social/emotional, and physical development.

 SUMMARY

Art in early childhood programs should provide opportunities for children to explore a variety of materials, choose techniques, and begin to see themselves as capable artists. The environment should provide opportunities for young children to experience the artistic elements of line, color, shape, form, pattern, and texture. Art helps children learn to appreciate and use these elements in their work. The early childhood teacher is both a facilitator and guide, as she asks questions, poses problems, and provides materials and experiences needed by the children. In early childhood programs, the teacher is often the art specialist who needs to know about art and artists, while providing developmentally appropriate activities that match the child's level of development and personal interest.

 RECIPES FOR THE ARTS

When children learn to mix and make their own materials, many avenues of creative expression open up to them. This is a collection of quality clay and play dough recipes that offer a variety of textures, ingredients, and uses. Most of the materials used in these recipes are inexpensive and found in the home. A few items must be purchased at a grocery store. In either case, the finished media will be less expensive than the ready-made products and certainly more rewarding. It is recommended that children be supervised during activities.

Helpful Hints Before You Begin

Use an electric skillet whenever possible to keep heat low. Provide plenty of cooling time for clay or play dough that has been cooked. Use more drops of food coloring to create bright and intense colors. To prevent sticky fingers while kneading cooled clay or dough, spray hands with cooking oil. Provide steady tables with enough space for children to explore the media. For easy cleanup, place sheets of heavy plastic on top of the working surface. Store finished product in an airtight container in a cool place.

Clay Recipes

CORNSTARCH CLAY

Ingredients

1 c. cornstarch   1⅓ c. water
2 c. salt

Procedure: Put salt and 2/3 c. water in pan; bring to a boil. Combine cornstarch and 2/3 c. cold water. Mix well. Carefully blend the two mixtures together; knead into clay. In order to set, the clay must be heated as it is blended. Recipe makes 3 c.; store unused clay in airtight container in the refrigerator. Clay can be painted when dry.

PLAY CLAY

Ingredients

½ c. salt   ¼ c. cold water
½ c. hot water   ½ c. cornstarch

Procedure: In a saucepan, mix salt and hot water. Bring mixture to a boil. In a small bowl, stir cold water into cornstarch until well blended. Add cornstarch mixture to boiling saltwater. Stir vigorously to break up lumps. Cook over low heat, and let cool on breadboard. When cooled, knead until smooth; store in an airtight container. This clay has a unique and wonderful texture. *Optional:* Food coloring can be added after adding cornstarch to boiling saltwater.

SALT MODELING CLAY

Ingredients

1 c. all-purpose flour (do not substitute)   ⅓ to ½ c. water
½ c. salt   food coloring (optional)
1 tbsp. powdered alum

Procedure: Combine flour, salt, and alum in a bowl. Add water, a little at a time, and stir until it is like pie dough. Knead until dough is thoroughly mixed. Add food coloring and knead until blended well; store in an airtight container. This clay has a grainy texture and dries well. This is a good recipe for projects that require painting dried clay.

Dough Recipes

CLASSIC PLAY DOUGH

Ingredients

1 c. flour	1 tbsp. vegetable oil
1 c. warm water	¼ c. salt
2 tsp. cream of tartar	food coloring

Procedure: Combine all ingredients; add food coloring last. Stir, over medium heat, until smooth and dough pulls away from pan. Remove dough from pan and knead until completely blended. After cooling, place in plastic bag or airtight container.

Alternative Ingredient List:

1 c. all-purpose flour	1 tbsp. vegetable oil
1 c. warm water	½ c. salt
½-1 tsp. cream of tartar	food coloring

Alternative Ingredient List:

2 c. flour	2 tbsp. vegetable oil
1 c. hot water	1 c. salt
4 tsp. cream of tartar	food coloring

Suggestion: For an interesting effect, add glitter to the dough until it sparkles.

USED COFFEE GROUND DOUGH (A GREAT WAY TO RECYCLE)

Ingredients

2 c. used, dry, coffee grounds	1½ c. cornmeal
½ c. salt	warm water

Procedure: Combine dry ingredients, and add enough warm water to moisten; store in an airtight container. The dough has a unique texture, and is good to roll, pat, and pound.

Bubble Recipes

SIMPLE BUBBLE SOLUTION

Ingredients

2 tbsp. dishwashing liquid	½ c. water

Procedure: Gently mix the dishwashing liquid and water together. Makes about ½ c.

SUPER-SIZED BUBBLE SOLUTION (ISBELL & RAINES, 2003)

Ingredients

1¾ c. dishwashing liquid	14 c. water

Procedure: Mix the dishwashing liquid and water together. Makes about 1 gal.

THE BEST BUBBLE BREW (ISBELL & RAINES, 2003)

Ingredients

1 qt. water	measuring cup
1 clean 2-qt. bottle with a tight lid	3 tbsp. glycerin (also called glycerol)
4 oz. dishwashing liquid	bowl

Procedure: Place the water into the bowl. Add the soap. Swish the liquids together and pour them into the empty bottle. Add the glycerin. Cap the bottle tightly and shake the liquids together.

COLORFUL BUBBLE SOLUTION

Ingredients

2 c. liquid detergent	6 c. water
¾ c. sugar	food coloring

Procedure: Combine all ingredients; add food coloring last. Before using, allow to stand at room temperature for four hours.

Suggestion: Use wire coat hangers to blow large bubbles.

Paint Recipes
PUFF PAINT

Ingredients

1 c. flour	tempera paint
1 c. salt	plastic squeeze bottles
1 c. water	

Procedure: Combine flour, salt, paint, and water. Pour mixture into plastic squeeze bottles. Squeeze mixture out; as it dries, paint will puff out.

FINGER PAINT

Ingredients

1 c. liquid laundry starch	½ to 1 c. water
¾ c. dry laundry detergent	food coloring or liquid tempera paint

Procedure: Gradually, combine the starch and detergent, stirring until smooth. Add water, as needed for appropriate consistency.

Suggestion: Provide food coloring or liquid tempera paint to be added to each mixture until desired color is reached.

CLOWN PAINT

Ingredients

⅛ c. baby lotion
¼ tsp. liquid tempera paint
1 squirt liquid dishwashing soap

Procedure: Mix ingredients together. This paint can be easily removed by soap and water. Before applying, it should be tested on the child's skin for possible reactions.

Miscellaneous "Recipes"
COLORFUL PASTA SHAPES

Ingredients

¼ c. rubbing alcohol	2 c. pasta in various shapes
food coloring	newspaper or paper grocery bags
1-qt. zipper-close bags	

Procedure: Combine alcohol and food coloring in plastic zipper-close bag. Seal bag, and shake to mix. Open bag and add pasta. Seal bag and rotate, to coat the pasta evenly. Allow to "soak" for about an hour, turning after 30 minutes. Empty colorful pasta onto paper and allow to dry overnight. Children can do some of this on their own. An adult should handle the alcohol and allow the children to choose the color and the pasta to put in their bags. Make sure all bags are sealed before handling.

Then, an adult should pour the pasta out to dry. Various shapes of pasta can be used; rigatoni makes good necklace beads.

CRAZY PUTTY

Ingredients

white glue (Elmer's)   Sta-Flo Liquid Starch

Procedure: Combine two parts white glue with one part starch. (*Note:* Elmer's School glue does not bounce or pick up pictures; be sure to use the regular white glue.)

GOOP

Ingredients

1 c. cornstarch   plastic bowl
¼ to ⅓ c. water

Procedure: Pour cornstarch into plastic bowl. Add water, and mix well. Allow to stand until mixture solidifies. When you handle the goop, it turns back into liquid. Cover the table and floor, as this can get very messy.

PASTE

Ingredients

⅓ c. all-purpose wheat flour   1 c. water
2 tbsp. sugar   ¼ tsp. oil of cinnamon

Procedure: Combine flour and sugar in a saucepan. Gradually add water, stirring to break up lumps. Cook over low heat until clear, stirring constantly. Remove from heat, add oil of cinnamon, and stir until well blended. Spread paste with a brush or tongue depressor. Paste has a good spreading consistency, and can be stored in a sealed jar for several weeks without refrigeration.

RAINBOW SAND/SALT

Ingredients

1 box salt   zipper-close bags
food coloring: red, blue, green, and yellow

Procedure: Combine salt and a couple of drops of food coloring into the plastic bag (deeper colors require more drops). Seal bag and mix with your fingers. Shake the sand around in the bag, to ensure all the sand gets colored.

 | **KEY TERMS**

art center	print making
atelier	rubbing
atelierista	sewing
collage	texture
documentation	thematic unit
fiber art	three-dimensional
folk art	two-dimensional
group projects	weaving
hue	

REFLECTION

1. Identify some of the different ways art can be created by young children.
2. What insights can be gained from the Reggio Emilia schools that have a strong artistic component?

THINKING ABOUT THE OBSERVATION OF CREATIVITY

1. Describe the ways Jessica explores the properties of clay.
2. Why did Jessica work with clay for such a long period of time?
3. How was the environment designed to encourage Jessica's independence?

POSSIBILITIES FOR ADULT LEARNERS

Activity: The Power of Clay

Goal: This activity is designed to help the student explore the characteristics of clay, a three-dimensional art material.

Materials: Several mounds of potter's clay or homemade clay. Sheets of plastic or shower curtains, paper towels, plastic plates or trays, small bowls containing water, and plastic knives. Other materials that could be added are sponges, a rolling pin, a pizza cutter, etc. Informational books about farm, zoo, or domestic animals serve as resources for the students.

Potter's clay is used extensively by children in the Reggio Emilia schools. Clay is valued because of the responsiveness to the child, the inspiration for thinking in a three-dimensional way, and providing another avenue for communicating. The sculptures they create are revised again and again, over an extended period of time as the child refines his/her work. Information books and references are used when children want to research their design or gain specific knowledge related to the sculpture. Later, the sculptures are painted, fired, and beautifully displayed.

Procedure:

1. Cover classroom tables with plastic or shower curtains. Each table should have a bowl of water and a collection of tools.
2. Each student pulls or cuts a piece of clay from the mound that is the size he or she wants to use.
3. Give students time to explore the clay—how it feels, how it moves, how it can be shaped, and other qualities of the substance. This time should be unstructured—an opportunity to explore.
4. A question can be asked: How can you change the texture of the clay? Provide time for students to pose possibilities and experiment with the tools.
5. Another question could be posed: How can you attach pieces of clay together? Allow students time to explore, experiment with techniques, and share ideas with each other.

6. Ask students to create an animal with their clay.

7. While working, some students may discuss characteristics of the animal. Others may want to look at books or pictures to gain insight. Both of these approaches are acceptable ways to gain information needed in the construction of the sculpture.

8. At the end of class, cover the creations with wet paper towels and plastic so the sculptures will remain moist and can be revisited during the next class period.

9. During the next class, each sculpture is evaluated by the artist and refinements are made by that person.

OPEN-ENDED ACTIVITIES FOR YOUNG CHILDREN

PreK–K

Activity:	Building a Landscape (contributed by J. Broderick)
Goal:	To use natural materials to create a landscape. This process encourages children to see things in their environment and to recognize how they can be used in art projects. This activity helps children experience constructing three-dimensional art from natural materials
Materials:	Bag for each child, items collected from a nature walk, 1 pound bag of wheat paste (wallpaper paste), cardboard pieces (for base), newsprint (can be cut, torn, or crumpled), paper towels, brushes, markers, tempera paint, masking tape, thin wire, plastic bowl, and water.

Procedure:

1. Give each child a bag before going on a nature walk. Encourage children to collect leaves, sticks, stones, grasses, and other interesting nature items.

2. Mix the wheat paste in the plastic bowl, using warm water. Stir the mixture until it is the consistency of cream.

3. Place newsprint, paste mixture, and collected nature items on a low table.

4. Children can select a piece of cardboard to use as a base for the landscape.

5. Children can wet pieces of newsprint in the paste to wrap around the nature items and attach to the base. In addition, children can use wire and/or tape to attach branches, rocks, moss, etc. to the base.

6. Talk with the children while they are working. Questions may include: How are you getting the stick to stand up? What shapes are you making? Where did you find that item on our walk? How does that feel?

7. Assist children who have difficulty or seem frustrated by the materials.

8. When completed, allow one to two days for the landscapes to dry. Revisit the landscapes and encourage the children to add other items to their creations.

9. Display the landscapes in the classroom with names of the children who contributed materials and/or ideas.

Activity: Recycled Paper Collage

Goal: To learn that recycled paper can be used to create beautiful art.

Materials: Large pieces of cardboard (for base); glue; brushes; materials to cover the frame; and paper collected from the playground, school, or on a walk (*Note:* Make sure the paper does not contain food or other unsanitary substances—e.g., newspaper, candy wrappers, scrap paper, gum wrappers, magazines, envelopes, junk mail, wrapping paper, wallpaper, etc.)

Procedure:

1. Collect paper on the playground, at school, or on a walk (*Note:* Make sure the paper does not contain food or other unsanitary substances). Discuss what kind of paper has been collected and how it was originally used.

2. Children can select a large piece of cardboard to use as a base for the collage.

3. Children can select pieces of paper to glue on the base. Assist children in planning where they will attach their paper, and remind them that they may want to tear the paper into a size to fit their design.

4. This work in progress can remain in the art center with additions made over several days.

5. When completed, create a large cardboard frame to go around the art-work. Children can cover the frame with foil, tissue paper, contact paper, or other available materials.

6. Display the collage in the classroom with names of the children who contributed paper and/or ideas.

PreK–K or Primary Grades

Activity: Painting Without a Brush

Goal: To discover that many different items can be used for painting. To investigate what designs, patterns, and textures can be created with various "brushes."

Materials: Various colors of thick tempera paint; aluminum pie pans (to hold paint); and items to use for painting (e.g., tree branches, empty roll-on deodorant bottles, cotton swabs, cardboard pieces, dishwashing wand, feathers, small rubber tire, craft sticks, gloves, plastic bottles with hole in lids, squirt bottles, etc.)

Procedure:

1. State the problem: We don't have any paintbrushes, but we want to paint. Ask parents and children to collect items that can be used for painting instead of using a brush.

2. Protect a low table by covering with paper; tape the edges down. Place paint, pans, and items where they can be accessed.

3. Children can select the item and paint they will use for their creation.

4. Encourage experimentation with a variety of items and colors.

5. When completed, label the items they used on the painting.

6. Display the paintings in the classroom with names of the children who contributed.

Primary Grades

Activity: A Wall of Prints (contributed by J. Broderick)

Goal: To raise visual awareness of items in the environment that can make prints. This activity also provides an opportunity for children to collaborate with others in creating a printed masterpiece.

Materials: Various colors of tempera paint, three to four containers (for paint storage), aluminum pie pans (to hold paint during print-making), collection of teacher-provided items, plastic sheet (to cover wall and floor), and a large piece of paper (at least 3 feet long).

Procedure:

1. Cover a wall and floor with the plastic sheet and attach the paper for printing to the plastic.
2. Allow groups of four or five children to place items in the paint of their choice and make imprints on the paper. Encourage them to print several times on the paper with different colors and at varied heights.
3. Have the groups of children take turns adding their prints to the masterpiece. When all children have taken their turn, allow them to make additions of more prints individually.
4. Discuss the creation using art terms such as line, color, space, texture, composition, etc. Try to guess which items created each print on the paper.
5. Display the creation in the classroom with names of the children who contributed to the masterpiece.

Activity: A Swinging Mobile

Goal: To design and construct artwork that moves.

Materials: Plastic coat hangers; yarn, twine, or plastic fishing line; and discarded household items (e.g., plastic utensils, coffee filter, bottle tops, old CDs, juice lids, disposable cups, large nails, sponges, silk flowers, old keys, etc.)

Procedure:

1. Discuss what a mobile is and how it moves.
2. Provide a box of discarded household items.
3. Children can select a plastic coat hanger and items to use in making their mobile. Encourage each child to experiment with the different materials and ways to attach the items to the coat hanger.
4. Children can create a mobile that moves from the materials provided, and test its mobility by placing it in the window, over a vent, or in front of a fan.
5. Allow children to redesign or make additions to their mobile.
6. Display the mobiles in the classroom with names of the children who contributed.

✸ ADDITIONAL READING

Art Methods

Hart, K. (1994). *I can paint!* Portsmouth, NH: Heinemann.

Honigman, J. J., & Bhaunagri, N. P. (1998). Painting with scissors: Art education beyond production. *Childhood Education, 74*(4), 205–213.

Skelton, T. (2001). *How to teach art to children.* Monterey, CA: Evan-Moor Educational Publishers.

Wolf, A. D. (1990). Art postcards—another aspect of your aesthetics program? *Young Children, 45*(2), 39–43.

Creativity

Jalongo, M. (1995). Awakening a sense of artistry within young children. *Dimensions of Early Childhood, 23*(4), 8–14.

Multicultural

Heintz, J. R. (1991). Inspired by African art. *School Arts, 90*(6), 16–19.

Curriculum

Aylward, K., Hartley, S., Field, T., Greer, J., & Vega-Lahr, N. (1993). An art appreciation curriculum for preschool children. *Early Child Development and Care, 96*(1), 35–48.

Colbert, C. (1997). Visual arts in developmentally appropriate integrated curriculum. In C. H. Hart, D. C. Burts, & R. Charlesworth (Eds.), *Integrated curriculum and developmentally appropriate practice: Birth to eight* (pp. 171–200). Albany: State University of New York Press.

Schiller, M. (1995). An emergent art curriculum that fosters understanding. *Young Children, 50*(3), 33–38.

Wright, S. (1997). Learning how to learn: The arts as core in an emergent curriculum. *Childhood Education, 73*(60), 361–366.

Integration

Bresler, L. (1998). "Child art," "fine art," and "art for children:" The shaping of school practice and implications for change. *Arts Education Policy Review, 100*, 3–10.

Clemens, S. G. (1991). Art in the classroom: Making every day special. *Young Children, 46*(2), 4–11.

Szyba, C. M. (1999). Why do some teachers resist offering appropriate, open-ended art activities for young children? *Young Children, 54*(1), 16–19.

Photography

Ewald, W., & Lightfoot, A. (2002). *I wanna take me a picture: Teaching photography and writing to children.* Boston: Beacon Press.

Friedman, D., & Kurisu, J. (2003). *Picture this: Fun photography and crafts.* Toronto, ON: Kids Can Press.

Gibbons, G. (1997). *Click!: A book about cameras and taking pictures.* Boston: Little, Brown.

Johnson, N. L. (2001). *Photography guide for kids.* Washington, DC: National Geographic.

Van Gorp, L. (2001). *Digital photography in the classroom.* Westminster, CA: Teacher Created Materials.

Research

Althouse, R., Johnson, M. H., & Mitchell, S. T. (2003). *Colors of learning: Integrating the visual arts into the early childhood curriculum.* New York: Teachers College Press. (ERIC Document Reproduction Service No. ED472509)

Teacher Resources

Cadwell, Louise B. (2003). *Bringing learning to life: A Reggio approach to early childhood education (Early Childhood Education, 86)*. New York: Teachers College Press.

Forman, G., Langley, J., Oh, M., & Wrisley, L. (1998). The city in snow: Applying the multisymbolic approach in Massachusetts. In C. Edwards, L. Gandini, & G. Forman (Eds.). *The Hundred Languages of Children: The Reggio Emilia Approach—Advanced Reflections* (2nd ed.). Stamford, CT: Ablex.

Formaro, A. (2001). *9 Easy to make musical instruments for kids*. [Online] Retrieved January 11, 2005. http://www.thefamilycorner.com/family/kids/crafts/9_musical_instruments.shtml.

Greenfeld, H., & Calder, A. (2003). *The essential Alexander Calder*. New York: Harry N. Abrams.

Group 23 Solutions. (2005). *Idea box: Craft recipe*. [Online] Retrieved January 11, 2005. http://www.theideabox.com/ideas.nsf/craft+recipe.

Khatena, J., & Khatena, N. (1999). *Developing creative talent in art: A guide for parents and teachers (Publications in creativity research)*. Stamford, CT: Ablex.

Kolbe, U. (2001). *Repunzel's supermarket: All about young children and their art*. Paddington, Australia: Peppinot Press.

Merenda, R. C., & White-Williams, S. (2002, Spring). Recipes that foster creative arts and crafts (Classroom idea-sparkers). *Childhood Education, 78*(3), 160–162.

Project Zero & Reggio Children. (2001). *Making learning visible, children as individual and group learners*. Reggio Emilia, Italy: Reggio Children SRL.

Shiney, L. (2005). *Play dough options: Recipe index*. [Online] Retrieved March 17, 2005. http://www.teachnet.com/lesson/art/playdough061699.html.

Smith, D., & Goldhaber, J. (2004). *Poking, pinching & pretending: Documenting toddlers' explorations with clay*. St. Paul: Redleaf Press.

Topal, C. W. (1992). *Children and painting*. New York: Sterling.

Vecchi, V., & Giudici, C. (Eds.). (2004). *Children, art, artists: The expressive languages of children, the artistic language of Alberto Burri*. Reggio Emilia, Italy: Reggio Children SRL.

Visual Arts

Hafeli, M. (1997). Connecting ideas through materials: Visual arts learning in the primary classroom. *Primary Voices K-6, 5*(2), 18–24.

Sylwester, R. (1998). Art for the brain's sake. *Educational Leadership, 56*(3), 31–35.

Topal, C. W., Gandini, L., & Golding, C. M. (1999). *Beautiful stuff: Learning with found materials*. Worcester, MA: Davis.

Warash, B. G., & Saab, J. F. (1999). Exploring the visual arts with young children. *Dimensions of Early Childhood, 27*(1), 11–15.

Videos

Jed Draws His Bicycle: A Case of Drawing to Learn. Commentary by George Forman. VHS video, 13 minutes. (A Reggio Emilia–inspired resource that can be purchased at www.learningmaterialswork.com.) Learn about how children can reflect on their own thinking and learn to ask themselves better questions through the process of drawing, in this 13-minute video of a seven-year-old boy who uses drawing to find out how his bicycle works. A booklet supplements the video and presents detailed notes on Jed's work.

The Long Jump: A Video Analysis of Early Education in Reggio Emilia, Italy. Narrated by George Forman. VHS video, 120 minutes (second edition). (A Reggio Emilia–inspired resource that can be purchased at www.learningmaterialswork.com.) Learn about how symbol-making and communication can help young children construct their knowledge. In this long-term project, children construct an understanding of a complex event (an Olympic-style athletic event for four- to six-year-olds) through the use of their bodies, invented symbols, and conversations with their peers.

Thinking Big: Extending Emergent Curriculum Projects. Video, 26 minutes. (A production of Harvest Resources that can be purchased at www.hilltopcc.com.) Preschool teachers Ann Pelo and Sarah Felstiner expand their view of children as capable learners and extend emergent curriculum projects into the community as they represent and re-represent their ideas with different art media. Filmed at Hilltop Children's Center, Seattle, Washington.

Arthur, a favorite book character, is represented in a preschooler's drawing.

CHILDREN'S LITERATURE CONNECTION

Crum, S., Beder, J. (ill.) (2004). *Click!* Toronto, ON: Fitzhenry & Whiteside, Limited.
　　This book tells about the adventures of a polar bear cub and a young photographer. Infants and children in preschool will enjoy the realistic watercolors and pictorial story line. (Infant–PreK)

dePaola, T. (1988). *The legend of the Indian paintbrush.* New York: Scholastic.
　　Little Gopher, an Indian boy, learns to paint with the brilliance of the evening sky and becomes known as He-Who-Brought-the-Sunset-to-the-Earth. This is a story about the beautiful flower, the Indian Paintbrush. (K–3)

Gibbons, G. (1987). *The pottery place.* San Diego: Harcourt Brace Jovanovich.
　　Describes the history and process of pottery making by following a potter through a day of work. (PreK–2)

Gibbons, G. (1998). *The art box.* New York: Holiday House.
　　Describes the many different kinds of tools and supplies that artists use to produce their work. (PreK–3)

Hurd, T. (1996). *Art dog.* New York: Harper Collins.
　　When the Mona Woofa is stolen from the Dogopolis Museum of art, a mysterious character, who calls himself Art Dog, tracks down and captures the thieves. (K–3)

Lionni, L. (1959). *Little blue and little yellow.* New York: Scholastic.
　　Little blue and little yellow are best friends. When they hug each other, something special happens! (Primary 1–3)

McClintock, B. (1996). *The fantastic drawings of Danielle*. Boston: Houghton Mifflin.
　　Even though her photographer father urges her to try a more practical form of art, a young artist in turn-of-the century Paris finds that her talent for drawing can be useful. (Primary 1–3)

McPhail, D. (1988). *Something special*. Boston: Little, Brown.
　　Surrounded by parents and siblings with remarkable talents, Sam yearns to be good at something and finds his own special talent when he discovers the pleasures of painting. (PreK–1)

Mallat, K. (1997). *The picture that mom drew*. New York: Walker.
　　Introduces the seven basic elements of art by using colored pencils to add colors, lines, shapes, forms, shades, patterns, and textures, one at a time, to a piece of paper. (K–3)

Markun, P. M. (1993). *The little painter of Sabana Grande*. New York: Bradbury Press.
　　Lacking paper, a young Panamanian artist paints the outside of his adobe home. (K–3)

Moon, N. (1995). *Lucy's picture*. New York: Dial Books for Young Readers.
　　A young girl creates a special picture that her grandfather, who is blind, can "see" with his hands. (PreK–3)

Reynolds, P. H. (2004). *ish*. Cambridge, MA: Candlewick Press.
　　Drawing makes Ramon happy. A reckless remark turns Ramon's art into joyless struggles, until his sister sees the world differently and opens his eyes to something far more valuable. (K–3)

Rylant, C. (1988). *All I see*. New York: Orchard Books.
　　A child paints with an artist friend who sees and paints only whales. (K–3)

Thomas, A. (1994). *Pearl paints*. New York: Henry Holt.
　　When Pearl receives a set of watercolors for her birthday, all she wants to do is paint. As Pearl explores her new paints, the author highlights the painting styles of several well-known artists. (K–3 and Teacher's Aide)

Walsh, E. S. (1989). *Mouse paint*. New York: Scholastic.
　　Three white mice discover the properties of color as they use paint to hide from a cat. (PreK–K)

 For additional resources involving creativity and the arts with young children, visit our Web site at **www.earlychilded.delmar.com**

 REFERENCES

Cadwell, L. B. B. (1997). *Bringing Reggio Emilia Home: An Innovative Approach to Early Childhood Education*. New York: Teachers College Press.

Cornett, C. E. (1998). *The arts as meaning makers: Integrating literature and the arts throughout the curriculum*. Upper Saddle River, NJ: Merrill.

Gee, K. (2000). *Visual Arts as a Way of Knowing*. York, ME: Stenhouse.

Genishi, C. (1993). Art, portfolios, and assessment. *Scholastic Early Childhood Today, 67*.

Isbell, R. (1995). *The complete learning center book*. Beltsville, MD: Gryphon House.

Koster, J. B. (2005). *Growing artists: Teaching art to young children* (3rd ed.). Clifton Park, NY: Thomson Delmar Learning.

Lasky, L., & Mukerji, R. (1980). *Art: Basic for young children*. Washington, DC: National Association for the Education of Young Children.

Leland, N, & Williams, V. L. (2000). *Creative collage techniques*. Cincinnati: F & W Publications.

Malaguzzi, L. (1993). History, ideas, and basic philosophy. In C. Edwards, L. Gandini, and G. Forman (Eds.). *The hundred languages of children: The Reggio Emilia approach to early childhood education* (pp. 41–89). Norwood, NJ: Ablex.

March, R. (1990). Close to home and close to heart. Exploring folk arts in education. *Spectrum, Journal of Wisconsin Art Education, 2*(1), 29–34.

Prudhoe, C. M. (2003). Picture books and the art of collage. *Childhood Education, 80*(1), 6–11.

Schirrmacher, R. (2006). *Art & creative development in young children* (4th ed.). Clifton Park, NY: Thomson Delmar Learning.

Topal, C. W., & Gandini, L. (1999). *Beautiful stuff: Learning with found materials*. Worcester, MA: Davis Publications.

MUSIC, MUSIC, MUSIC

CHAPTER 6

New studies on brain development indicate that music is an essential experience for young children. This chapter will explore the many ways music can be included in early childhood programs. Four aspects of music are included: listening to music, singing, making music, and moving to music.

After studying this chapter, you will be able to:
- **Understand how musical abilities are developed during the early years.**
- **Identify the four components of music that should be included in early childhood programs.**
- **Select songs and recordings that work well for young children.**
- **Determine appropriate musical instruments for children to play.**
- **Design a music center that inspires musical participation.**
- **Identify how music can be used in routines, transitioning, and building a source of community.**

OBSERVATION OF CREATIVITY

A tiny five-month-old infant is lying in his crib. He is just beginning to focus his vision on toy farm animals that are hanging from the mobile on the side of his bed. When he sees his father enter the room, his arms and legs begin to move rapidly. He recognizes the voice of his father as he enters the room, and, as his father approaches the bed, he sings his son's name in a simple rhythmic pattern: Ja-mal, Ja-mal, Ja-mal. The baby's arms and legs move even faster, as he listens to the musical phrase. He smiles, demonstrating his enjoyment of the sounds and the anticipation of being held by his father.

WHAT WAS OBSERVED?

Jamal and his father are connecting through music. The sounds and interactions bring enjoyment to both the father and baby. This beginning musical experience will nurture Jamal's development by providing a secure base for future cognitive and emotional development. A positive beginning for Jamal's budding interest in musical sounds will help him learn about the world.

"The children should manipulate and play with sounds, musical and environment, as a means of ordering and organizing their musical world."

B. Andress, 1980

Today, there is great excitement about the use of music in the early years of children's lives. Almost weekly, there is an article or research study that identifies the positive benefits of listening to or playing music. Many authors have concluded that music can enhance the intellectual development of children, stimulate brain function, and produce gains in test scores (Rauscher, 1995). Current media coverage has brought a surge of interest in music for young children to the public, administrators, and even governors.

Although media attention has created renewed interest in the field of music, it has always been an integral part of the lives of young children. Throughout history, singing, playing, and dancing have been important for children and adults across cultural and socioeconomic levels. Music provides opportunities for children and families to interact, develop understanding of their heritage, and enjoy shared experiences. Music has been a powerful thread that has woven many families and children together and provided them with a special identity.

For many years, music has been considered an important component in early childhood programs. Music is valued because of its potential intellectual benefits and for the enjoyment that it provides to children. Nurturing music in early childhood should be considered essential because of the richness it brings to young children's lives (Feierabend, 1990). Music can draw diverse groups of children together, often reaching the most distant child. Songs move children smoothly from activity to activity during potentially difficult transition times. Musical recordings can quiet the active child for a period of relaxation. Music provides children with opportunities to actively participate during circle times. When music is an integral part of the early childhood classroom, it expands the learning experiences of children and broadens their world to include the creative arts. It has been suggested that an environment that includes music supports the development of the whole child (Blackburn, 1998).

Musical Terms

Dynamics: The volume of sounds; soft or loud.

Harmony: The blending of sounds. This may be produced by two sounds performed at the same time.

Melody: The tune of music. The pattern of sounds that make up the musical composition.

Pitch: The highs and lows of musical sound patterns.

Rhythm: The beat of music. This includes tempo and meter.

Timbre: The tone of sound; for example, the uniquely different qualities produced by a log drum or steel drum.

MUSICAL DEVELOPMENT ACROSS THE EARLY CHILDHOOD YEARS (BIRTH THROUGH EIGHT)

The development of most children follows a pattern that can provide helpful guidelines for planning an appropriate environment. Understanding the unique characteristics of young children during specific developmental periods can provide a framework for developing a responsive curriculum. An appropriate match can ensure that children are successful and challenged as they participate in meaningful musical activities. Although many similarities exist during each stage of development, there are individual variations as well. These individual differences may influence the pace, attitudes, and behaviors that make each child unique. In a developmentally appropriate classroom, group and individual needs must be considered in designing the music curriculum.

Intertwined with the developmental characteristics of children are specific abilities that have an impact on musical development. An understanding of these developing musical skills ensures that expectations are congruent with children's capabilities. It is helpful to realize that adjustments must be made for the special needs and unique talents of the children within each classroom.

Infancy

During the first months of life, an infant is receptive to music. He responds to the sounds in his environment by moving his arms and legs or turning his head toward the source. Later, more active listening occurs as he moves or makes sounds that seem to respond to the music.

Infants produce sounds that often have musical qualities. Their cooing and babbling have rhythm and pitch. The infant will find pleasure in his voice and can be heard playing with sounds, patterns, and pitches when alone in the crib. If a caregiver echoes the cooing and babbling sounds, an interaction may occur. The infant will learn from these exchanges that the sounds he makes are important. He discovers that repeating these sounds draws the caregiver's attention to him.

As infants begin to gain some control of their bodies, they reach out to grasp, hold, and move toys. During these early months, they are particularly interested in toys that have musical sounds. For example, a mobile will be hit again and again to activate the bell sound. He will experiment with the different sounds that are produced when the mobile is hit with his foot, arm, or another toy. A wrist toy with sound is first randomly shaken. When the connection is made between the movement and the sound, the infant will increase his hand motion to produce additional musical sounds. He will begin to clap his hands along with music or hit a drum to produce a sound. These new skills bring him great joy and are repeated again and again.

Toward the end of the first year, infants demonstrate their recognition of a song or **finger play** by moving or laughing in anticipation. Individual interest begins to surface as infants show a preference for specific songs, books, or finger plays. For example, the following finger play (Totline Publications, 1994) will have children anticipating the arrival of the bees and laughing with glee.

An infant and teacher clap to the rhythm of music.

> ### The Beehive (Traditional)
>
> Here is the beehive. (Make a fist.)
> Where are the bees? (Tilt head to one side.)
> Hidden inside where nobody sees.
> Watch, and you'll see them come out of the hive.
> Here they come buzzing out of the hive. (Slowly begin to open fist.)
> One, two, three, four, and five! (Raise fingers one at a time.)
> Zzzzzz, zzzzzz! (Slowly move your hand toward the baby.)

With gestures or sounds, infants indicate when they want to hear the song or story again. When they tire of the activity, they conclude their involvement by simply turning away or crying in an irritated way. It is important to learn to read these infant messages so that adult interactions can follow their interest and pace.

Toddlers

In this period of development, the first true words begin to appear. These words identify important people and meaningful objects in their world. Toddlers are interested in echoing words and phrases used by caregivers. This indicates their focus on these sounds and patterns. If a word is needed that is not in their vocabulary, toddlers will create a new label to identify the object. This practice clearly demonstrates the creative nature of the very young child. Toddlers are fascinated by the words and phrases that are repeated in songs, finger plays, and poems. They can be heard chanting unique sound patterns and interesting words to their caregiver or to themselves throughout the day.

Toddlers are gaining more control of their bodies as they become mobile and move around their space. They are able to hold and manipulate objects to carefully examine materials. They experiment with hitting and tapping on a variety of objects to discover the sounds they can produce. They can play simple **percussion instruments** with a mallet or striker in a rhythmic pattern. Toddlers enjoy listening and often dance to accompany the sounds.

Toddlers try to establish their autonomy and become more independent. This can be observed when the toddler chooses to join one activity or refuses to participate in another. During a song, the toddler may wander off to participate in another part of the

An attentive toddler is trying to imitate a finger play.

room. Later, he may be heard singing a familiar phrase of the song from across the space. Toddlers can continue an activity or song long after the adult has stopped, indicating an enjoyment of the activity and the desire to continue. Their creativity is demonstrated as they develop new actions or sound effects to accompany familiar songs or finger plays.

Preschoolers

Three- and four-year-olds gain competencies in many different areas. Preschoolers' language becomes more refined, and their communication is clearer. Songs and finger plays are of great interest to them as they repeat and sing familiar melodies. Preschoolers enjoy singing together as they begin to build their repertoire of songs. During this period, the group may sing around the melody while some children will sing in tune. Preschoolers use songs and music to accompany their activity throughout the day. They can be heard in the bathroom creating a song: "wash, wash, wash your hands—squirt, squirt, squirt the soap—wash, wash, wash it off." Preschoolers are using music to express themselves, and they are improvising and playing with musical sounds (Kenney, 1997).

Small motor coordination of preschoolers improves as they gain better control of their bodies. They can jump, walk, and clap to music. When an adult demonstrates and continues to play the pattern with them, preschoolers can keep a steady beat. Their movement to music becomes more consistent with the mood and rhythm of the recording. Some preschoolers will be comfortable participating in movement activities in a group, whereas others will be self-conscious and only move when no one is watching.

Many opportunities to listen to and discriminate sounds should be provided in this developmental stage. Preschoolers can recognize melodies they have experienced previously. They can substitute new words for familiar songs. Preschoolers enjoy different types of music, varied instruments, and the sounds they produce. They can suggest different ways to accompany music with **rhythm instruments.** Some children are able to create simple songs and repeat the composition for others to enjoy.

Kindergartners

The kindergarten year is a time for refining abilities that were begun during the early years. Language skills are well developed in many children. Kindergartners can express their ideas and make plans for future projects. They are able to work cooperatively, as they adjust their roles and use language in their play. Classroom learning centers, including a music center, provide expanded opportunities for them to make choices, use their language, and work in areas of interest. Kindergartners are growing in self-confidence as they understand their capabilities by successfully participating in classroom activities.

Literacy becomes increasingly important as kindergarten children become more interested in symbols, print, and writing. Visual symbols are recognized and can be used to direct participation in group activities. Books and tapes that include print are particularly interesting to children during this period. They can be observed "reading" these materials to themselves and others. Books that include sound effects capitalize on this interest and provide additional opportunities for experiences with music. Flip charts that contain the words of favorite songs are used in kindergarten classrooms for group singing and making another connection

The sounds of a zither and recorder are explored and then played together.

with print. These sing-alongs can provide a successful and enjoyable experience for children of varying levels of singing ability.

During this stage, children continue to investigate the use of tools and materials. They want to know how things work and how they can be combined in new ways. This interest can be nurtured through the use of musical instruments such as the **guitar, keyboard,** and **Autoharp.** Chording instruments provide a pleasant accompaniment for their developing singing voices. Their increased physical competencies and growing musical skills will allow kindergartners to produce more complex rhythm patterns with instruments. They also can begin to experiment with melody instruments.

Primary Grades

Children in the primary grades are moving into a new educational environment, where there are many challenges. In this new setting, the development of skills and abilities is often the focus. Primary-grade children are emerging readers and writers. Their abilities in these areas vary significantly during the early years. Understanding and respecting their different levels of development is essential as children progress through this complex process. Some children will be able to read words of a song from a book or flip chart. They will be able to write new words for a song or develop a symbolic representation of a rhythm pattern on paper. But there also will be children who are trying to figure out how books and writing work. Providing varied opportunities for participation in musical activities will support literacy development, as well as enhancing different levels of interest in words, patterns, and print.

Primary children become more logical in their thinking, although most are still bound to concrete experiences. They continue to need opportunities to explore, examine, and reflect. Meaningful experiences that integrate learning and the arts can provide new avenues for the development of thinking. Primary-grade children are able to keep written records of their thoughts and gain additional understanding through reading. They can develop charts or graphs that indicate their musical preferences, participation, and interest. They can discuss how they feel about the music, the artist, or give an interpretation of the composition.

Musical instruments were created from PVC pipes, elbows, and joints for a class band.

Children in the primary years continue to develop their **social competencies.** They are very concerned about rules and fairness. They enjoy singing games, playing instruments, and participating in musical groups. They can work well in large groups but most often prefer small ones. If interested in an area or project, they can work independently for long periods and return to refine the product at a later time.

For some children, the primary grades are the period when they begin lessons in piano, dance, or instruments. During this time, a music teacher with a specialization in this area often handles the music program in the school. It is important to realize that music should be included in both the special setting and the regular classroom where children spend the major portion of their day. In the best situation, the classroom teacher and the music specialist collaborate to meet the needs and interests of specific children in the group. Together, they support projects and themes with music, instruments, and movement that can be used in both places.

> **"Music hath charms to soothe a savage breast, to soften rocks, or bend a knotted oak."**
> *W. Congreve*
> *(in Fitzhenry, 1993)*

GOALS FOR MUSIC IN EARLY CHILDHOOD

The children will:

- enjoy participating in musical activities.
- express themselves using music, both vocally and instrumentally.
- experience a variety of types of music through listening, singing, playing music, and movement.
- understand and experience basic musical concepts appropriate for their level of development.

THE EARLY CHILDHOOD TEACHER

A teacher's interest in music is highly contagious. She does not have to be a great singer or musician to enjoy music with young children. The teacher must, however, understand the importance of including appropriate musical experiences in the early childhood classroom. She will plan opportunities for musical development while encouraging the spontaneous music that children produce each day. A vast number of music recordings and available instruments makes the integration of music possible for all early childhood teachers, even those who feel uncomfortable singing. It is important to note, however, that young children are not music critics concerned with pitch or tone. Young children enjoy a teacher who joyfully participates in making music with them.

Early childhood teachers can compose a song or chant to accompany activities in the classroom. If you don't feel comfortable creating the song, you can use the tune from a familiar one and write new words. For example, the tune to "Here We Go Round the Mulberry Bush" is simple and easy to use in varied ways. "This is the way we wash our hands," or "This is way we clean the table."

There are a number of tunes that can be used in this way and adapted to many situations. "Where is Thumbkin?" can become "Where is Jason?" for a circle song that names children in the circle. "If you're happy, and you know it" can become "If you want to go outside, get your coat." Combining music with an activity strengthens the responsiveness of the children and makes the work or request more pleasant.

Teachers can encourage the wonder and exploration that accompanies young children's interest in music. In the early years, it is important for the focus to be on divergent thinking that allows for many musical responses. The early childhood teacher, interested in creative development, may encourage the child to find different ways to play the xylophone instead of suggesting only one way.

Children can teach us how music develops when we listen and follow their interest. Young children are innately responsive to music when the environment is designed to nurture this interest. The teacher is not a performer: he is the facilitator who plans appropriate opportunities using elements of music. He plans for musical variety that exposes young children to many different kinds of music and diverse performers. Both the teacher and the children will benefit from a classroom filled with music.

A teacher who participates in music encourages other to join in.

The teacher plays the key role of facilitator and guide in music environments. One of her important tasks is describing and labeling what the children are doing in group, individual, or center activity. Using musical vocabulary with children helps them learn how to describe their music making. After chanting "Hickory, Dickory, Dock," the teacher, as facilitator of music, might encourage the children to make clock sounds, tick-tock, tick-tock. After their participation, she might explain that they are ticking with a steady beat. Children could use rhythm sticks to sound like a tiny travel clock, or a giant grandfather clock. The travel clock might be soft, while the grandfather clock ticks loudly.

Early childhood teachers should not strive for musical perfection or rehearse until the children's singing is totally accurate. Teachers should understand that children's musical abilities develop at different rates and vary from child to child. The teacher's goals for children during the early years should be to develop a love for music while joyfully participating in the process.

❁ COMPONENTS OF MUSIC

Music is composed of elements that include listening, singing, and making music with instruments and movement.

Musical Behaviors

Musical experiences should include learning about the basic components of music (melody, rhythm, timbre, and form) through musical behaviors (singing, listening, playing instruments, movement, and creating). These aspects are interrelated, and each influences the other, while all are essential to the musical process. Some appropriate musical experiences can be planned, but many opportunities will be spontaneous and built on the observed interest of each child. Both planned and responsive musical experiences are important in an effective environment for young children.

Listening

The ability to hear is present in most infants at birth. During the first years of life, very young children begin to refine their ability to listen to sounds in their world. This focus on the sounds they hear, and their ability to respond to them, provide the basis for active listening that is important in musical development.

Listening is defined on several levels. **Auditory awareness** is simply attending to the sound and recognizing its presence. Recognizing the voice of his father and the siren of the fire truck are examples of the young child's auditory awareness.

Auditory discrimination is the ability to distinguish between sounds that are heard. Many early childhood educators recognize the importance of auditory discrimination because of its relationship to beginning reading. However, they often are unaware that auditory discrimination is essential to the development of musical ability. When the toddler can distinguish the opening of the refrigerator door from the opening of the house door, he demonstrates his ability to discriminate between two sounds. We know he can distinguish the difference when he calls out for "milk," when the refrigerator is opened.

Auditory sequencing is the ability to remember the order of sounds heard. This ability is demonstrated when a young child echoes a pattern on the rhythm sticks or repeats the verses of a song in order (Haines & Gerber, 1999). Auditory memory assists young children in many areas, including reading, singing, and playing instruments.

Another level that has been identified is listening for **appreciation.** This refers to the listener enjoying the sounds of music that they hear. This directly relates to young children developing an appreciation for music and a preference for specific selections.

During the early years, young children need many opportunities to hear sounds and focus their attention on them. Listening and active participation in musical experiences are avenues that can enhance this ability. Infants demonstrate their need to combine listening and activity as they move their bodies in response to music. The continuation of this active listening is appropriate throughout the first eight years of children's lives.

Listening to Music

Focused listening helps young children attend to specific sounds or words that give direction. This listening is considered by many experts to be the basis for all musical learning (Bayless & Ramsey, 1986). Listening to a variety of music is important in the development of auditory abilities. Variety provides opportunities for children to determine the music they like and to make new connections with sounds they have never heard before. Young children enjoy hearing different kinds of music and examining new sounds. They also like to hear familiar music that connects with their background and previous experiences. Playing music from families of children in the classroom throughout the day can provide new opportunities for listening that will expand the offerings. It is important to include both familiar and new selections in planning musical listening experiences for young children.

Active listening opportunities can include singing games that give directions in the words. Music that consists of periods of moving and stopping encourages children to listen and respond. Records that have sound clues require children to listen closely and respond with clapping, movements, or repeated phrases. Playing instruments with specific passages of music requires focused attention to sound patterns. These are examples of the many opportunities to refine the listening abilities of young children.

Listening for enjoyment and appreciation is an important part of musical learning in early childhood. Experiencing a variety of music expands the opportunities for children to appreciate different types of music. Musical selections that can be used in early childhood classrooms include classical, jazz, folk, Native American, Cajun, African, marches, and polkas. Some popular music can be appropriate and connect to the children's current interests. Listening to these many variations encourages young children to enjoy a variety of music.

Music can produce strong emotional reactions or provide a calming effect. For this reason, soft and slow music often has been used to encourage children to relax during rest time. Listening to soothing music allows children to relax at their own pace and in their own way. Music also can excite children and encourage them to participate. Marching music can move children from place to place without demanding their attention. A variety in mood and tempo should be considered in planning listening experiences for young children.

Music can be performed in many different ways. Some possibilities include solo vocal, chorus, duet, orchestra, band, guitar, drums, piano, harp, or flute. Recordings

Soft music can help an active child relax at rest time.

of each of these are available and can be enjoyed by children. It is not necessary for these recordings to be specifically for children, but it should be a high-quality recording that will provide good listening possibilities for young listeners.

Listening to live performers is particularly motivating for young children. The performance should, however, be appropriate for the developmental level of the children. A high school band member playing the trumpet in the kindergarten classroom is very exciting for the children. Going to a choral rehearsal instead of attending a long performance will be enjoyed by young children and remembered fondly. Children will admire a parent who plays bluegrass on the guitar in an informal performance in the classroom. These live musical performances connect with children in a way not possible when using a recording or a CD.

Musical stories provide another way to listen to music. There are a number of books with text that comes from songs. Some books include musical phrases, while others might benefit from having music added. Some musical stories include musical notation in the back of the book as in, *Today is Monday* (Carle, 2001) or *The Wheels on the Bus* (Kovalski, 1990). These provide an opportunity to look at the musical score and discuss the different ways of writing a melody.

Some stories that are good for telling have a musical phrase or musical sound that can be repeated during storytelling. This encourages children to listen to the story and participate in singing the musical phrase. The story, *The Fisherman and*

His Wife (Isbell & Raines, 2000), has a phrase that is used to call the fish from the water, "Magic fish, magic fish, we have a wish." The fisherman uses this musical pattern to call the fish, when he has another wish. The children who are listening will quickly join in the singing to call the fish. The pattern is repeated six times in the story. (The complete story can be found in Appendix C) *Chicka Chicka Boom Boom* (Martin, Archambault, & Ehlert, 1991) is a popular book that is not a song but has a unique rhythmic pattern that can be accompanied by a drum (Achilles, 1999). Combining books and storytelling with music enriches the experience and makes it more appealing for children with diverse ways of learning.

Singing

> **"Music is the favorite passion of my soul."**
> *Thomas Jefferson (in May, 1970)*

The development of singing seems to follow a predictable pattern during the early years (Wolf, 1994). These steps provide insight to the parent or teacher who wants to encourage children to use their voices in song. The first step in the process is listening. Long before young children sing, they listen to songs. During this time, they are storing the melody, pattern, and rhythm for future use. These listening experiences provide the basis for singing and participating in musical activities during the early years. Songs can be recorded music or an adult singing to an infant. Although both can be beneficial, music sung by a caring adult can be especially effective. Toddlers who have been exposed to songs on a regular basis, will begin to tag on to familiar tunes. They will repeat "round and round" when hearing

Singing together builds a sense of community in an early childhood classroom.

"The wheels on the bus" or clap their hands when they recognize the song. They will take the tune with them when participating in other activities. Toddlers may sing, "Wash, wash, wash your hands" as they play in the housekeeping sink or in water outside.

In the preschool years, children continue to listen and tag on, but most join along with the singing. During this period, singing in groups and learning new songs becomes very important. Children often have favorite songs that they want to sing again and again. Although it is important to expand their repertoire of songs, the familiar favorites should be sung on a regular basis. These comfortable singing experiences are filled with joy and provide opportunities for successful participation.

Singing independently usually appears during kindergarten. Many children are able to sing a song with some accuracy. The development of singing independently varies, as some children reach this independent stage earlier or later than others. Singing alone should never be pushed and should be encouraged only when the child indicates an interest.

In the primary grades, children can participate in broader singing experiences such as **duets,** small groups, or **rounds.** Songs of their heritage and personal favorites should remain the foundation for building new interests and abilities. These familiar songs can be varied, reworded, or accompanied in new ways while building from a secure musical base.

Selecting Songs for Singing

For many years, several categories of songs were used in early childhood programs. These continue to be widely used, although many new types of songs are being included as our understanding of cultures and the musical world is extended.

NURSERY RHYME SONGS. The melodies of nursery rhyme songs are simple and easily remembered. Some children have heard these and others have been exposed to variations that have been used in the media or in modern books. Examples of these songs include "London Bridge Is Falling Down" and "Baa Baa Black Sheep." These songs are a part of the culture of childhood and should be included in early childhood programs. Songbooks that include collections of nursery rhyme songs, several traditional children's songs and musical instruments that you can make are included at the end of the chapter.

LULLABIES. Lullabies are often soft and slow. They create a soothing mood that children enjoy and find calming. Some children have heard lullabies and use them to rock themselves or baby dolls to sleep. Well-known lullabies include "Lullaby

A rhythm pattern is used while rocking a baby.

and Goodnight" and "All the Pretty Horses." There are many collections of lullabies that can provide songs appropriate to use in early childhood classrooms. Recordings of lullabies also can be used at rest time as children quietly sing along with the music or relax their bodies.

FOLK AND TRADITIONAL SONGS. These catchy tunes are part of our heritage and have been sung by young children for hundreds of years. Some examples are "Where Have You Gone, Billy Boy?" and "This Land Is Your Land." Children enjoy singing their favorites over and over. Although the teacher may tire of singing these songs, the children find them comfortable and exciting. Young children often use the melodies as they create their first variations on a theme or accompany their activities with song. There are many traditional songs to choose from and the collection at the end of the chapter identifies some that will be helpful.

CHANTS. In the early years, children begin to **chant** phrases or directions. These **chants** are easy and very rhythmic in nature; they are often described as half-singing and half-talking. Since they are such a natural part of children's singing development, it is important to include them in the early childhood classroom. Some chants are spontaneously created by the child, and can be repeated by the teacher or shared in a group. Others come from stories and poetry they hear, and can be repeated in unison. Children use their voices to make the messages in chants come alive. Chants can be traditional singsong or developed to match the words in a poem. Young children enjoy experimenting with the rhythm and words of chants to find a way to respond to language (Buchoff, 1994).

A number of recording artists have used chants to draw children into participation with music. Ella Jenkins has many African chants that young children love and can quickly begin to repeat. The patterns are easy to learn and magnetic in quality. These chants can provide successful experiences for many beginning singers. Drums and rhythm instruments can be used very effectively with children singing chants.

Miss Mary Mack (Traditional)

Oh Mary Mack, Mack, Mack
All dressed in black, black, black
With silver buttons, buttons, buttons
All down her back, back, back
She asked her mother, mother, mother
For fifteen cents, cents, cents
To see the elephant, elephant, elephant
Jump the fence, fence, fence
He jumped so high, high, high
He reached the sky, sky, sky
And never came down, down, down
Till the fourth of July, ly, ly . . . (Bronner, 1988, p. 65)

FINGER PLAYS AND ACTION SONGS. **Action songs** combine melody with movement. This is a wonderful combination for active young children. When a new song is introduced, many children will participate only in the movement that they can replicate easily. As they become more familiar with the song, they will sing and use the movement together. Action songs are great favorites for young children because of the repetition of the phrases and the combination of movements. Young children can extend these songs as they add new verses with appropriate actions. Creating extensions provides opportunities for children to develop their flexibility and originality.

Some rhymes are played as a game. Child number one speaks first, then child number two speaks those lines marked with a two, as shown in the following example (Johnson & Sayers, 1959).

1. I went up a pair of stairs.

2. Just like me.

1. I went up two pairs of stairs.

2. Just like me.

1. I went to the room.

2. Just like me.

1. I looked out the window.

2. Just like me.

1. And there I saw a monkey.

2. Just like me.

Additional rhymes and finger plays can be found in Appendix B.

JUMP ROPE RHYMES AND STREET CHANTS. Primary-grade children are interested in street chants and jump rope rhymes because they invite them to interact orally and be active physically. These verses are part of the oral tradition that links rhyme, rhythm, and humor, and are meant to be shared aloud in a social setting.

Street chants originated in diverse cultures and provide a valuable contribution to what might be unique for one group or familiar to all society. *Street Rhymes Around the World* (Yolen, 1992) includes rhymes from different countries and is illustrated by artists from the areas represented. These chants help children recognize that rhymes can come from different parts of the world and can be enjoyed internationally.

Many folk rhymes are sung or recited. They provide interesting sound patterns and humor that give children pleasure and a mechanism for all bouncing, handclapping, and rope-jumping (Buchoff, 1995).

Primary children enjoy participating in hand jives.

Handclapping rhymes are popular with primary children. An example is the
following (Bronner, 1988).

> Playmate, come out and play with me
> And bring your dollies three
> Climb up my apple tree
> Slide down my rain barrel
> Climb down my cellar door
> And we'll be jolly friends
> Forevermore. (p. 61)

Some sources for rhymes and chants include these publications.

Boardman, B., & Boardman, D. (1993). *Red hot peppers: The Skookum book of jump rope games, rhymes and fancy foot work*. Seattle, WA: Sasquatch.

Cole J. (1989). *Anna Banana: 101 jump rope rhymes*. New York: Morrow.

Cole, J., & Calmenson, S. (1990). *Miss Mary Mack and other children's street rhymes*. New York: Morrow.

Schwartz, A. (1992). *And the green grass grew all around*. New York: HarperCollins.

Withers, C. (1988). *A rocket in my pocket: The rhymes and chants of young Americans*. New York: Henry Holt.

Yolen, J. (1992). *Street rhymes around the world*. Honesdale, PA: Wordsong.

✿ PLAYING MUSIC

Music is an aural language that uses the basic elements of pitch, rhythm, timbre, and form. Countless combinations of these elements have given rise to a remarkable variety of music found throughout the world. Howard Gardner (1983) concludes that people who have frequent experience with music can use the elements in musical activities, including playing with instruments and composing. The foundation for this interest can be laid in the early childhood classroom by providing many opportunities for children to play and create with musical instruments.

Playing music can provide involvement with many different materials and instruments. For playing to be effective in developing discriminating taste, the musical materials should be of good quality. The sounds produced by the instrument or materials should be pleasant to the ear and easily manipulated by small hands. There are many possibilities for playing music in the early childhood classroom. The following suggestions are only a beginning list of the possibilities for the development of a music curriculum that includes making music and participating in the playing of instruments.

Rhythm instruments can accompany musical recordings or singing.

Instruments Played by the Children

Children can use their bodies to create rhythm or instruments to produce patterns of accompaniment.

PHYSICAL ACCOMPANIMENTS. Children, using parts of their bodies, can produce many sounds and rhythms. Toddlers demonstrate this ability very early as they clap to the music they hear. The possibilities for producing these body sounds are almost limitless. Some of the most frequently used with young children are handclapping, tapping thighs, rubbing hands together, stomping feet, and tapping head. Older children will be able to snap fingers and clap hands with partners. Using these accompaniments with listening and singing provides another combination of sounds for developing young children.

PERCUSSION INSTRUMENTS. One of the most popular instruments with young children is the drum. A drum should be easily accessible in every early childhood classroom so it can be used with songs and recordings during the day. Drums should be selected that produce a good sound and can be played with either

The Ashiko African drum introduces a child to the sounds of another part of the world.

hand or mallet. Providing several sizes and types of drums will encourage children to experiment with the variations of sounds they produce. This encourages both auditory discrimination and creative problem-solving. Bongo drums (two drum heads) and larger African drums provide sounds that encourage different ways of playing and producing rhythm patterns. Children also use drums to experiment with loud and soft sounds. Using the hand to produce sounds helps establish an understanding of the relationship of force to volume. Making different kinds of mallets can encourage further experimentation with sounds. A sponge mallet will produce a very different sound from a mallet made of hard rubber. Young children discover these differences as they explore and manipulate the percussion instrument.

RHYTHM INSTRUMENTS. Keeping the beat or creating a rhythm pattern is a very important ability to nurture during the early years. Beat competency reflects the ability to keep time with, or feel the pulse of, music (McDonald, 1979). For many years, rhythm instruments were the only musical instruments used in early childhood programs. Although they remain important, they are only one type of instrument that should be available in a classroom designed to enrich the arts.

Primary-grade children are using instruments to accompany specific segments of a classical recording.

Some of the rhythm instruments that should be included in the classroom are:
- shakers
- bells on elastic
- rhythm sticks (of varying length and thickness)
- triangle
- wood blocks
- maracas
- bells on sticks
- cymbals (use one side with a mallet)
- tambourine
- hand drums

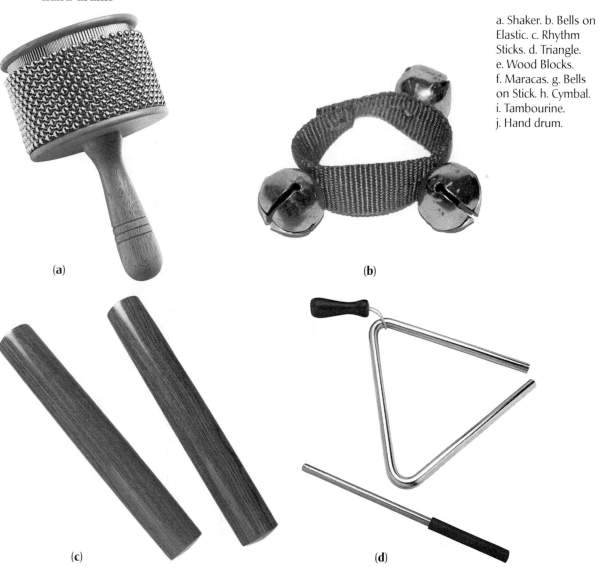

a. Shaker. b. Bells on Elastic. c. Rhythm Sticks. d. Triangle. e. Wood Blocks. f. Maracas. g. Bells on Stick. h. Cymbal. i. Tambourine. j. Hand drum.

(a)

(b)

(c)

(d)

(e)

(f)

(g)

(h)

(i)

(j)

These rhythm instruments can be used by individual children or in small groups. They can accompany listening, singing, and movement activities. Remember that children will need to explore the sounds of these instruments before they are able to play at specific times or in certain patterns. Kindergarten and primary-grade children will be able to use rhythm instruments in more complex ways and develop charts with symbols for their playing.

Instruments Played by Teacher and Children

Some musical instruments can be played by the teacher to accompany songs or used to support the children's beginning efforts with specific instruments.

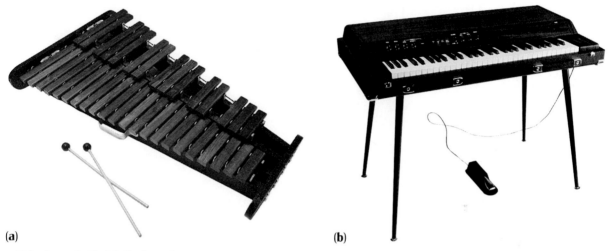

(a) **(b)**

a. Xylophone. b. Electric Keyboard.

MELODY INSTRUMENTS

Recorder. This melody instrument can be used to introduce or accompany children's songs and singing. It is generally played by the teacher, since most children do not learn to play the recorder until the fourth or fifth grade. An older child who plays the recorder would be an interesting classroom guest.

Step Bells (xylophone).   This set of bells contains metal bars on a frame that provide a C major octave. It has a stair-step design with the lowest tone on the bottom step and the highest tone on the top step. This allows children to connect the visual representation with the sound they hear. These bells are played with a mallet and produce a clear tone. Early experiences with the xylophone are simply exploring the sounds produced. Later in the development of musical skills, some children will be able to play simple patterns and melodies.

Resonator Bells.   On a set of **resonator bells,** each bar is attached to an individual wooden sound box that provides a resonance to the sound. The bars can be separated and played individually, or specific notes can be grouped together to accompany a specific song. A set for an early childhood classroom should contain a scale from middle C to C in the octave above. The beautiful tone of the resonator bells makes them appropriate for inclusion in the early childhood classroom since young children are very sensitive to sound during this period.

Keyboard (piano or electronic). A piano or keyboard provides new opportunities to hear and play simple melodies. The children will enjoy teachers who can play simple melodies on the keyboard. Melody instruments help them establish the tune of a song. Children can experiment with the keyboard, recognize tonal effects, and improvise melodies.

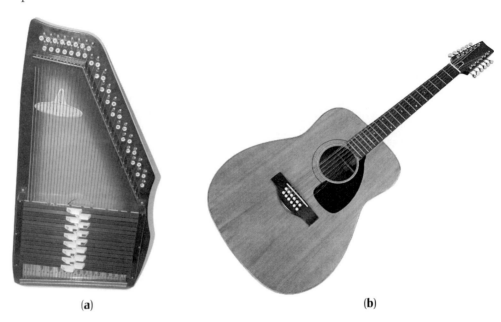

a. Autoharp. b. Guitar. (**a**) (**b**)

CHORDING INSTRUMENTS

Autoharp or Omni Chord (electronic). This simple chording instrument is an effective accompaniment for young children's voices. The teacher simply presses a button and strums. This activates the strings of a specific chord to accompany the song. These chords add richness to singing and opportunities for children to experience tones in harmony. Many songbooks include the chords the teacher can use with an Autoharp or guitar.

The More We Get Together
     D   A7   D
The more we get together, together, together,
                                   A7   D
The more we get together, the happier we'll be.
A7   D   A7   D
Your friends are my friends, and my friends are your friends,
                        E   A7   D
The more we get together, the happier we'll be.

(The more we sing together . . . For your song is my song . . .)

(Glazer, 1973, pp. 48–49)

Guitar. The guitar can be used to accompany songs that young children enjoy singing in the early childhood classroom. Many of these songs are in the key of C or F, and require only three or four chords to support the children's singing. The guitar is a very popular instrument that children have seen many times. They are very interested in hearing and playing the guitar. When selecting a guitar for an early childhood classroom, be sure it produces a good sound and can be strummed by the children.

A visiting musician uses a guitar to accompany her singing.

Teacher- or Child-Made Musical Instruments

Many early childhood teachers do not have sufficient funds to support the purchase of all the musical materials they would like to have in their classroom. There are many ways to design, make, and use musical instruments with young children. No matter whether the instrument is purchased or made, it should produce a beautiful sound, rather than a thud. When selecting the instruments to be made, always evaluate the quality of the music that it will produce. If it creates a sound that is pleasant, clear, and can be controlled by the child, it may be worth the effort spent in creating the instrument.

An example of an appropriate instrument for a primary classroom is a teacher- or child-made rain pipe. This is created by using several 12- to 15-inch pieces of PVC pipe. The diameter of these pieces can vary, so they can be held comfortably in the children's hands. After collecting scrap pieces or cutting the PVC, purchase end covers that fit the PVC pipe being used. Shape heavy-duty aluminum foil into rolls and form it into a spiral that will fit inside the pipe. This provides additional surfaces to create the "rain" sound.

Provide stones, beans, small bells, coins, metal nuts, or other interesting items, to create the sounds inside the pipe. Children can make the foil spirals and select the materials that they wish to place inside their pipe. End pieces can be taped on, so the children can change the contents, to produce different sounds. Encourage the children to experiment with the sounds they make, by using various items. The musical rain pipes can be decorated with acrylic paint or exterior latex paint or covered with contact paper.

These rain pipes produce a pleasant sound and can be used to accompany songs and recordings. This musical instrument originated in South America, where it was traditionally made by using the dried wood of a cactus. The hollow wood was filled with pebbles, and the ends were closed with small pieces of wood. This instrument imitates the sound of the rain. The end of the chapter contains additional ideas for instruments that teachers and children can make to produce music.

✺ MOVING TO MUSIC

Music and movement are interconnected for young children (Jalongo, 1996). The importance of movement in the early childhood years will be discussed extensively in Chapter 7.

A unique addition to the music center is the inside workings of a piano. Children can experiment with the sounds the strings produce.

✺ MUSIC CENTER

Every preschool and kindergarten should have a music center where children can explore sounds. The primary goal of an effective music center is to attract the children to the area and stimulate their music-making. A carefully designed center provides many opportunities for children to manipulate, compare, contrast, and create with a variety of musical materials. Some items that should be in the center on a regular basis are a good tape recorder with a variety of tapes, a collection of instruments, and songbooks. An interesting grouping of instruments for the center could include a drum, rhythm sticks, triangles, resonator, and step xylophone. These provide variations in sound to encourage rhythmic experimentation in the center. Other items should be rotated into the center to provide changes that will stimulate new exploration with sounds. A collection of African instruments encourages children to create new sound patterns and chants, chording instruments provide multiple sounds to examine, and melody instruments produce clear tones.

The center provides a music environment that is based on free-choice participation, allowing for exploration based on the needs, interest, and ability of the child. Here, children direct their own activity, decide how much time to spend in the area, and how they will use the materials (Achilles, 1992). Child-centered learning is very important in an early childhood classroom. These experiences are guided by children's natural curiosity and their desire to learn about the world. Center time is an example of child-centered learning. In this allotted time, the child is able to choose from a wide variety of activities that are developmentally appropriate and personally meaningful. The music center provides time to choose what to listen to, what to play, or what instrument to use. Engaging in the child-centered music center allows children opportunities to make music in their own way. Through play in the center, they are able to construct their understanding of music, develop skills, and enjoy the process. A music center is a wonderful addition to the early childhood classroom. It is also recommended for music rooms where music educators are directing specific educational activities (Turner, 1999). In a special edition of the *Music Educators Journal—Special Focus: Interdisciplinary Curriculum* (Snyder, 2001), the music specialist is encouraged to allow time for children to participate in a music center, since play is an important tool in children's learning.

The teacher is responsible for setting up an effective music center and changing the materials in the area to maintain interest. But his most important role is to observe the children as they learn about music. This center provides many opportunities for the teacher to observe children's interest, abilities, and expressive techniques. The children can experiment with music, follow their interest, and work at their own pace. They are able to play with music without being tied to a specific song or group activity. This open-ended center provides a safe place for children to explore musical elements freely. Although the teacher can pose questions about the sound of the drum being played in the center, most frequently he is not involved in

The Music Center. Reprinted from *Early Learning Environments that Work* (page 51), with permission from Gryphon House, Inc. www.ghbooks.com.

A stage and a microphone inspire children to sing and dance.

the musical play. The teacher is a model for the enjoyment of music during the day but it is the child who is creating the music for himself in the music center (Isbell, 1995; Kenney, 1995).

Other options for the music center include extending the songs children are learning in the large group circle time to the music center. The addition of songs to the center will give children an opportunity to recall and practice the melody. Recordings of the children singing the songs can invite using instruments or creating new words to the familiar tune. Charts can be placed on the wall of the center that include words, motions, or pictures of a familiar song to stimulate musical interest. These symbols help children remember the words and make the connection with music.

Literacy in the music center should include books that have been read to the whole class and then placed in the area. For example, *The Wheels on the Bus* (Kovalski, 1990) might be read during circle time, and later, a child may sing the words as she turns the pages of the book and uses the illustrations as clues. A songbook of class favorites can also be included in the center, making another connection between literacy and music.

The exploration of instruments can provide another way to discover the variety of sounds that can be produced. A used guitar or a chime mobile are examples of materials that will stimulate interest in the music center.

ITEMS NEEDED FOR THE MUSIC CENTER

- listening station with earphones
- tape player and/or CD player
- keyboard
- rhythm instruments
- large box to house the recording studio
- pictures of bands, orchestras, or choirs
- sheets of music or songbooks
- CDs and tapes of a variety of music: solos, choirs, bands, children, and world music
- music stand
- conductor's baton
- xylophone or resonator bells
- collection of drums
- a stage: raised area built from wooden pallets
- microphone
- pillows, carpet pieces, and sound boards to absorb sound

The sounds of children in the music center demonstrate that young musicians are actively engaged in discovering the joy of making music. Providing this time for child-center musical activities, which follow personal interests, is a necessary and essential part of the early childhood classroom. As children play, they gain understanding and appreciation of the joy that music can bring.

EXPLORING MUSIC FROM MANY CULTURES

Music provides insight into the people of the world. All cultures have music they sing and instruments they play. Begin with the music and instruments from your region and country. This could range from bluegrass music and instruments to Western ballads. Expand the children's world, by providing music and instruments from cultures other than their own. You might ask families to share instruments or invite them to play for the children. Encourage them to share children's songs from their culture. Include photographs and maps (if developmentally appropriate) showing the origin of the instruments. Help children handle instruments and recordings with respect. Add new instruments or recordings to the music center, so that children can explore and try out these tools of music. Be sure to include diverse music for children during rest time and in the music center.

COMPOSING MUSIC

Children have a natural propensity for making music. They can help guide us toward what they want to know, what they need to know, and what skills they need to successfully accomplish their wishes. What begins as listening and imitating leads to organizing and creating. Young children need many musical experiences, before they are ready to compose music. A great way to support the budding composer is to record the children while they are improvising in the music center. For example, when a couple of children are experimenting with different drum patterns on an African drum, this is the ideal time to record the children's rhythms. It is helpful for the children to hear their patterns soon after they were created. These can be shared with the other children or their parents. A recording studio can be made out of a large box and placed in the music center. In this studio, children will be able to record and listen to songs, patterns, or stories that they have created. These tapes can be labeled and placed in an open storage area so that children may listen to their own tapes or the tapes of their classmates. Later, they may begin using music symbols and notation and understand that these are written symbols that communicate a melody and/or rhythm (Ohman-Rodriquez, 2004).

Children's books can help inspire music and songs. Jazz musicians use improvisation as they create and change melodies, as depicted in *Charlie Parker Played Be Bop* (Raschka, 2004). Raschka uses pictures, history, and words, to explore jazz music and musicians. This book may provide an inspiration for children to experiment with composing. Primary-grade children enjoy learning about "real" composers and listening to their music. Many of the biographies of composers include notation in the musician's own hand.

Music provides many opportunities to move beyond the repeating of a song to the creation of musical compositions. The early childhood teacher provides varied experiences that are the basis for the children's musical development. The teacher surrounds the children with music by weaving it throughout the day and across the curriculum (Hildebrandt, 1998). The songs of childhood, listening to the classics, playing instruments, and moving to music are the foundation for musical understanding and enjoyment in young children. These are essential components for all children to experience during the early years. Musical experiences that match the developmental characteristics of young children will provide pleasure and satisfaction. Early experiences in listening, singing, playing, and movement provide a secure foundation for creating music in their own individual way. From this base, established early, children will move on to create new words for songs, expand verses, develop variations of melody, improvise with voice, and use instruments in new ways.

 ## SUMMARY

Music has long been valued in early childhood programs because it provides enjoyment, opportunities for participation, and relaxation for the weary child. Today, we are more aware of the potential for music to nurture not only the souls of children but also their intellects. Music has a magnetic quality that draws all children into the sounds, rhythms, and patterns it produces. Music provides opportunities to understand different cultures, appreciate musical preferences, and identify similarities and differences.

When music is an integral part of the early childhood program, it includes listening, singing, making music, and movement. It is interwoven throughout the day and included in theme studies or projects. Young children enjoy participating in all aspects of music and are not concerned about obtaining perfection during the process. A classroom filled with music inspires young children to be musicians, singers, and composers while providing a positive experiential base for extending their budding musical interest.

 ## KEY TERMS

action songs
active listening
appreciation
auditory awareness
auditory discrimination
auditory sequencing
Autoharp
chant
duets
dynamics
finger play
guitar

harmony
keyboard
melody
percussion instruments
pitch
resonator bells
rhythm
rhythm instruments
rounds
small motor coordination
social competencies
timbre

 ## REFLECTION

1. Describe how musical abilities develop from infancy through the primary years.
2. What are some appropriate goals for music in early childhood?
3. How can an early childhood teacher demonstrate an interest in music?
4. What are the major elements of music that should be included in the early childhood classroom?
5. Identify the different types of songs and music that can be used with young children.
6. What instruments can young children play to accompany their singing or recordings?

THINKING ABOUT THE OBSERVATION OF CREATIVITY

1. How can you determine that Jamal is attending to the musical chant?
2. Is this interaction important to Jamal and his father? Why?
3. In what musical ways can the father share his heritage with his son?

POSSIBILITIES FOR ADULT LEARNERS

Activity: Music Appreciation

Goal: To listen to different types of music and appreciate the preferences of others.

Materials: A CD player and recordings of at least three different kinds of music (jazz, marching bands, Native American, pop, classical, or bluegrass).

Procedure:

1. The teacher selects three recordings and plays them for the students without comment or critique.
2. Ask students to listen to all the recordings and select their favorite from these.
3. After listening, take a poll to learn each person's favorite selection and discuss their preference.
4. Discuss the different preferences and the reasons for the selection.
5. Can these selections be used with young children?

Activity: Expanding Your Repertoire

Goal: To discover some of the recordings that are on the market today specifically for use with young children.

Materials: A CD player or tape player, and a collection of some of the musical recordings used in early childhood programs.

Procedure:

1. Ask the students to identify recordings they have heard.
2. Play some recordings from musicians they have not heard to expand their repertoire.
3. Lead a discussion with young children about using a variety of music that includes popular favorites as well as other music.

OPEN-ENDED ACTIVITIES FOR YOUNG CHILDREN

PreK–K

Activity: On Stage

Goal: To encourage children to use their singing voice.

Materials: Microphone (this can be made from a paper tube with a round ball attached to the end) and tape player or recorder.

Procedure:

1. Add the microphone to the music center or drama area. Some children will immediately begin to sing and perform. Others will watch the performance and add their own voice later.

2. The tape recorder will encourage the children to tape their recreations and listen to how the music sounds.

3. If they wish, the children can share their musical recordings with their classmates.

PreK or Primary Grades

Activity:	Making Instruments
Goal:	To create musical instruments and use them to make music.
Materials:	Pieces of wood dowel rods of varying thickness and lengths, sandpaper, several colors of latex paint, and brushes.

Procedure:

1. Children can select two pieces of dowel rods that they would like to use.

2. Have them sand the rough edges with sandpaper and paint in the colors they prefer.

3. After the paint dries, the children can use the rhythm sticks to accompany a musical recording or their singing.

Primary Grades

Activity:	Our Musical Composition
Goal:	Children will create their own musical composition.
Materials:	Chart paper and markers.

Procedure:

1. Divide the class into groups of two or three children.

2. Ask each group to create a musical phrase, and write the rhythm or notes on chart paper. (The phrase can be sung, clapped, or created in another way.)

3. Bring the children back together and let each group share their musical phrase.

4. Allow the entire class to determine the order in which the phrases will be used in the composition.

5. Place the chart papers in order of the composition. Group members can stand in front of their phrase.

6. Play the entire composition with each group performing its phrase.

7. Discuss the sounds, patterns, and sequence.

8. Allow the class to try the composition in a different order and evaluate again.

9. Keep the musical phrases and return to this project at a later point.

✸ TRADITIONAL CHILDREN'S SONGS FOR GUITAR AND AUTOHARP

The chording for guitar and Autoharp has been added by Rebecca Isbell.

The Bear Went over the Mountain

G   D7   G
Oh, the bear went over the mountain, the bear went over the mountain,
                      C   D7   G
The bear went over the mountain, to see what he could see.
          C   C   C   G
To see what he could see, to see what he could see.
                              D7   G
Oh, the bear went over the mountain, the bear went over the mountain,
                      C   D7
The bear went over the mountain, to see what he could see.

(Glazer, 1973, p. 12)

Old Mac Donald

G   C   G   D7 G
Old MacDonald had a farm, E-I-E-I-O.
                        C   G   D7 G
And on that farm he had a duck, E-I-E-I-O.
          G   G
With a quack-quack here, and a quack-quack there,
Here a quack, there a quack; Everywhere a quack-quack.
                  C   G   D7 G
Old MacDonald had a farm, E-I-E-I-O.
(Old MacDonald had a dog, cat, horse, cow, chicken, pig, sheep, etc.)

(Glazer, 1973, pp. 56–57)

Johnny Works With One Hammer

C   G7   C
Johnny works with one hammer, one hammer, one hammer,
(Beat right fist on right knee.)
                                 G7   C
Johnny works with one hammer, then he works with two.
  C   G7   C
Johnny works with two hammers, two hammers, two hammers,
(Beat left fist on left knee.)
                                G7   C
Johnny works with two hammers, then he works with three.
  C   G7   C
Johnny works with three hammers, three hammers, three hammers,
(Tap right foot on floor.)
                                G7   C
Johnny works with three hammers, then he works with four.
  C   G7   C
Johnny works with four hammers, four hammers, four hammers,
(Tap left foot on floor.)

G7   C
Johnny works with four hammers, then he works with five.
C   G7   C
Johnny works with five hammers, five hammers, five hammers,
(Move head back and forth.)
              G7   C
Johnny works with five hammers, then he goes to sleep.

(Glazer, 1973, p. 61)

This Old Man

F
This old man, he played one,
      C7 F C7 F C7
He played nick-nack on my thumb (tap thumb).
F
Nick nack, paddy-wack, give a dog a bone,
C7   F C7 F
This old man came roll-ing home.

Next verses, each followed by the chorus: **two**-shoe; **three**-knee; **four**-door (*fore-head*); **five**-hive (*shoo bees away*); **six**-sticks (*tap two fingers together*); **seven**-up in heaven (*fly*); **eight**-pate; **nine**-spine; **ten**-once again. Finish chorus with "Now we'll all go running home."

(Glazer, 1973, pp. 82–83)

If You're Happy!

     C   G7
If you're happy and you know it, clap your hands,
                    C
If you're happy and you know it, clap your hands,
    F   C
If you're happy and you know it, then your face will surely show it,
    G7   C
If you're happy and you know it, clap your hands.

Other ideas: tap your toe, nod your head, snap your fingers, scratch your head, blink your eyes, and click your teeth.

(Fowke, 1969, pp. 44–45)

The Farmer in the Dell (English Folk Song)

  G
The farmer in the dell!
  G
The farmer in the dell,
Hi-ho, the derry oh!
  D7   G
The farmer in the dell!

Where, Oh Where Is Dear Little Mary? (American Folk Song)

  G
Where, oh where is dear little Mary?

D7
Where, oh where is dear little Mary?
G
Where, oh where is dear little Mary?
D7   **G**
Way down yonder in the paw-paw patch.

 ## MUSICAL INSTRUMENTS YOU CAN MAKE

Chimes

Materials:

ruler, stick, or coat hanger

washers, nuts, or nails

string or fishing line

wooden spoon

Procedure: Use pieces of string or fishing line to hang the washers, nuts, and nails from the ruler, stick, or clothes hanger. Strike the washers with the wooden spoon to play.

Coffee Can Drum

Materials:

empty coffee can with lid

yarn or cord

foil

contact paper

heavy fabric or vinyl

markers

Procedure: Decorate the coffee can with contact paper, yarn, foil, and markers. Cover top with heavy fabric or vinyl, and glue to the top of the can. Secure the edges with yarn or cord. Beat to play.

Comb Buzzer (Formaro, 2001)

Materials:

pocket comb

tissue paper

Procedure: Fold a piece of tissue paper over the tooth edge of a comb. To play, hum through the tissue paper.

Hummer

Materials:

paper towel roll

waxed paper

rubber band

pen or pencil

Procedure: Cover one end of the paper towel roll with waxed paper and secure it with a rubber band. Punch a row of holes along one side of the roll with the tip of a pen or pencil. To play, hum a tune into the open end of the instrument.

Kitchen Cymbals

Materials:

two matching pot covers

wooden or metal spoon

yarn or ribbon

Procedure: Tie the ribbon or yarn around the handles of the pot covers. To play, strike together. One top can be played by hitting with a spoon.

Shoebox Guitar

Materials:

shoebox

scissors

several thick rubber bands

short pencil or dowel

Procedure: The teacher should cut an oval-shaped hole in the top of a shoebox. Stretch thick rubber bands around the box, to cover the oval hole. Place a pencil under one end of the rubber bands. Children can experiment with different size rubber bands and the sounds each produces.

Stick Bells

Materials:

2 paper towel rolls

hole punch

jingle bells

string or yarn

Procedure: Punch several holes along each end of the paper towel rolls. Tie jingle bells to each of the paper towel rolls by running string or yarn through the holes. Shake to play.

Tambourine

Materials:

2 foil pie plates

stapler or glue

jingle bells

markers

Procedure: Place two or three bells between the plates. Staple or glue the foil pie plates together, facing each other. Decorate the outside with markers. Shake to play.

Twig Rattle

Materials:

Y-shaped twig

yarn or ribbon

scissors

tape or glue

decorative materials

beads, buttons, and washers

Procedure: Completely cover a Y-shaped twig by winding yarn or ribbon over the branches. Add decorative materials in with the yarn or ribbon, as you cover the twig. Secure ends of the yarn or ribbon with a knot, tape, or glue. Attach a piece of yarn or ribbon to one arm of the twig's Y, and thread it through several beads, buttons, and washers. Secure the yarn or ribbon to the other arm. Shake to play.

 ## MUSIC RESOURCES

There are a number of different types of resources that can be used to enrich the music program for young children. Some of the most helpful are songbooks with collections of appropriate songs and books that follow a musical theme.

Books

Bennett, P. D., & Bartholomew, D. R. (1996). *Songworks I: Singing in the education of children.* Belmont, CA: Wadsworth.
  Teachers often lack the confidence to present music to their students because they have little formal training in this area. This book emphasizes singing as the means to teaching music in the classroom.
Raschka, C. (2004). *Charlie Parker played be bop.* New York: Scholastic.
  A book about musicians and musical improvisation for children ages 3–6. Regardless of whether they've heard of jazz or Charlie Parker, young readers will bop to the pulsating beat of this picture book.

Songbooks

There are many collections of children's songs that are available to help early childhood educator, build their musical repertoire. Listed below are some sources for songs that young children will enjoy singing.

Glazer, T. (1980). *Do your ears hang low?: Fifty more musical fingerplays.* New York: Doubleday.
  This book presents words and music to 50 songs with directions for accompanying finger plays.

Guthrie, W., & Guthrie, M. (1992). *Woody's 20 grow big songs*. New York: HarperCollins.
> This is a replication of an unpublished songbook, lost for over 40 years. It was written in the late 1940s by the legendary songwriter and folksinger Woody Guthrie and his wife Marjorie Mazia, a modern dancer. Inspired by their own young daughter, the Guthries wrote these songs to perform and share with children.

Hudson, W., & Hudson, C. (1995). *How sweet the sound: African-American songs for children*. New York: Scholastic.
> *How Sweet the Sound* gives readers a glimpse at the history of African Americans through their music. Key periods are spotlighted by a variety of songs from Africa, spirituals, work songs, gospels, jazz, blues, play songs, chants, soul, and popular music of our time. Includes music and bibliographic references.

Kidd, R. (1992). *On top of old smoky: A collection of songs and stories from Appalachia*. Nashville, TN: Ideals Children's Books.
> A collection of eleven traditional songs and three folk tales from Appalachia, including "The Frog He Went A'Courting," "I Gave My Love a Cherry," and "Jack and the Bean Tree."

Langstaff, N., & Langstaff, J. (1986). *Sally go round the moon*. Boston: Nimrod Press.
> These traditional songs form an extraordinary body of beautiful tunes—catchy, rhythmic, and fun—many of which contain a small child's first introduction to poetry and verse.

Manning, J. (1998). *My first songs*. New York: Harper Festival.
> For toddlers who love to sing and dance, this collection contains ten favorite, easy-to-sing songs. (Infant–Toddler)

Orozco, J. (1994). *De colores and other Latin-American folk songs for children*. New York: Dutton Children's Books.
> This rich collection of children's music from the Spanish-speaking world represents the contributions of many people from cultures in Europe, Africa, and the Americas who have handed down songs from one generation to the next such as songs for special occasions and for every day, songs for learning, songs for singing in a family or group, and songs just for fun.

Raffi. (1993). *Raffi: Children's favorites*. New York: Amsco.
> Over 50 songs written or adapted by Raffi for the delight of children everywhere. In easy-to-play, full-sounding arrangements with complete lyrics and guitar chord boxes.

Raffi. (1996). *Raffi's top 10 songs to read*. New York: Crown.
> Includes lyrics, music, illustrations, and a suggested activity for each of the ten children's songs. (PreK–2)

Musical Instruments

Several books include directions for making musical instruments and others have a theme that relates to the playing of an instrument. Both of these resources can provide another way to create music and appreciate the process.

Doney, M. (1995). *Musical instruments*. New York: Franklin Watts.
> Provides step-by-step instructions for making a variety of musical instruments from around the world including Mexican rhythm sticks, Ethiopian bells, and a paper prayer drum from India. (Primary)

Dunleavy, D., & Phillips, L. (2001). *The jumbo book of music*. Tonawanda, NY: Kids Can Press.
> This book is all about making music—with homemade instruments, with your voice, your hands, your feet, and lots of other body parts.

Hausherr, R. (1992). *What instrument is this?* New York: Scholastic.
> Identifies an array of popular musical instruments, and discusses how they are made, how they sound, and the styles of music for which they are best suited. (Primary K–3)

Martin, B., Jr. (1994). *The maestro plays*. New York: Henry Holt.
> A colorful book that shows the maestro playing a variety of musical instruments. (PreK–K)

Moss, L. (1995). *Zin! Zin! Zin! A violin*. New York: Simon & Schuster Books for Young Readers.
> Ten instruments take their parts, one by one, in a musical performance. (PreK–K)

Oates, E. H. (1995). *Making music: Six instruments you can create*. New York: HarperCollins.
> Includes instructions for making a variety of simple musical instruments from ordinary household items. (PreK–3)

Schaff, P. (1980). *A violin close up.* New York: Four Winds Press.
  A close-up look at the violin: naming and illustrating its parts, and describing how it makes music. (PreK–1)
VanKampen, V., & Eugen, I. C. (1989). *Orchestranimals.* New York: Scholastic.
  A band of animal musicians introduces the symphony orchestra. (PreK–1)

Selected Musical Recordings

Collections of Various Artists:

Putumayo World Music. (2004). *Putumayo kids presents: Caribbean playground* [sound recording]. New York: Putumayo World Music.
  This music is for all ages and includes rhythms and sounds of the Caribbean, which shine through all the tracks. It contains interesting information about the people and cultures represented in the songs. The artists are, almost without exception, standouts in their fields, resulting in music of high quality.
Verve Music Group. (2004). *Jazz for kids: Sing clap, wiggle and shake* [sound recording]. Santa Monica, CA: Universal Music Group.
  This recording, for ages 4–7, is a wonderful introduction to jazz, with a collection of kid-friendly novelty tunes by some of the biggest names in jazz. Fun, funny, and breezy, the collection will have both kids and parents dancing, singing, clapping, wiggling, and shaking.
Smithsonian folkways children's music collection: This collection of 26 songs, play-party games, and poems was selected from over 200 outstanding recordings of music performed for and by young children.
  Collection. (1998). *Smithsonian folkways children's music collection* [sound recording]. Washington, DC: Smithsonian Folkways Recordings.
A fish that's a song: Songs and stories for children: Nineteen culturally diverse songs by legendary performers to delight young children.
  Collection. (1993). *A fish that's a song: Songs and stories for children* [sound recording]. Washington, DC: Smithsonian Folkways Recordings.

Ella Jenkins:

You'll sing a song and I'll sing a song: This lively recording invites children to sing, play rhythm instruments, whistle, hum, clap, and chant.
  Jenkins, E. (1992). *You'll sing a song and I'll sing a song* [sound recording]. Washington, DC: Smithsonian Folkways Recordings.
Multicultural children's songs: Ella introduces young children to the chants, songs, and rhythms of a variety of cultures with this collection of 23 songs.
  Jenkins, E. (1995). *Multicultural children's songs* [sound recording]. Washington, DC: Smithsonian Folkways Recordings.
African American folk rhythms: This compilation of songs celebrates the musical heritage of African Americans.
  Jenkins, E. (1998). *African American folk rhythms* [sound recording]. Washington, DC: Smithsonian Folkways Recordings.
Songs and rhythms from near and far: Ella and her friends take listeners on a journey to many lands. They treat us to songs and dances and a variety of musical instruments and textures.
  Jenkins, E. (1997). *Songs and rhythms from near and far* [sound recording]. Washington, DC: Smithsonian Folkways Recordings.

Greg & Steve:

We all live together: Greg Scelsa and Steve Millang present music that will invite young children to participate.
  Scelsa, G., & Millang, S. (1995). *We all live together* [sound recording]. Huntington Beach, CA: Young Heart Music.
Kids in motion: Songs for creative movement: Fifteen spirited songs that invite children to get up and move to the music.
  Scelsa, G., & Millang, S. (1995). *Kids in motion: songs for creative movement* [sound recording]. Huntington Beach, CA: Young Heart Music.

Pete Seeger:

Birds, beasts, bugs, and fishes (little and big): These songs create an irresistible collection of songs to sing along with, draw pictures about, play hand games to, and be enjoyed and learned by the entire family.
Seeger, P. (1998). *Birds, beasts, bugs, and fishes (little and big)* [sound recording]. Washington, DC: Smithsonian Folkways Recordings.

American folk, game, and activity songs for children: A compilation of two previously released albums, this collection includes 22 classic folk and activity songs for children of all ages.
Seeger, P. (2000). *American folk, game, and activity songs for children* [sound recording]. Washington, DC: Smithsonian Folkways Recordings.

Raffi:

Singable songs for the very young: Raffi fascinates children and encourages self-respect and appreciation for diversity.
Raffi. (1996). *Singable songs for the very young* [sound recording]. Cambridge, MA: Rounder Records Corp.

Rise and shine: Cheerful songs let kids get into the act with fun-to-do sound effects and simple body movements.
Raffi. (1996). *Rise and shine* [sound recording]. Cambridge, MA: Rounder Records Corp.

Thomas Moore:

I am special just because I'm me: This recording combines active music exploration, while emphasizing positive self-images and demonstrating vital early childhood concepts.
Moore, T. (1986). *I am special just because I'm me* [sound recording]. Charlotte, NC: Thomas Moore Records.

Singing, moving and learning: Thomas and the children sing about the bus driver, the doctor, the opera singer, and waiter. This recording also includes a rock-and-roll version of "Itsy Bitsy Spider" and reinforces geometric shapes with "Moving Hands."
Moore, T. (1989). *Singing, moving and learning* [sound recording]. Charlotte, NC: Thomas Moore Records.

Songs Children Love to Sing: Including many of the traditional songs that are sung with young children. Instrumentals of all songs are included on this recording.
Moore, T. (2000). *Songs children love to sing* [sound recording]. Charlotte, NC: Thomas Moore Records.

Woody Guthrie:

Nursery Days: Woody Guthrie combines delicious-sounding words from down to earth imagery and flavors it all with humor.
Guthrie, W. (1992). *Nursery days* [sound recording]. Washington, DC: Smithsonian Folkways Recordings.

 ## ADDITIONAL READING

Achilles, E. (1999). Creating music environments in early childhood programs. *Young Children, 54*(1), 21–26.

Andress, B. L., & Walker, L. M. (Eds.). (1992). *Readings in early childhood music education.* Reston, VA: National Association for Music Education.

Beaton, P. (1995). The importance of music in the early childhood language curriculum. *International Schools Journal, 15*(1), 28–38.

Campbell, L., Campbell, B., & Dickinson, D. (1996). *Teaching and learning through multiple intelligences.* Needlam Heights, MA: Allyn & Bacon.

Gharavi, G. J. (1993). Music skills for preschool teachers: Needs and solutions. *Arts Education Policy Review, 94*(3), 27–30.

Lang, S. S. (1999). Music: Good for not only the soul, but the brain. *Human Ecology Forum, 27*(2), 24.

Merrion, M., & Rubin, J. E. (1996). *Creative approaches to elementary curriculum.* Portsmouth, NH: Heinemann.

Nantais, K. M., & Schellenberg, E. G. (1999). The Mozart effect: An artifact of preference. *Psychological Science, 10*(4), 370–374.

Nichols, B. L., & Honig, A. S. (1997). Music teaches children about themselves and others. *Early Childhood Education Journal, 24*(4), 213–217.

Peery, J. G. (1993). Music in early childhood education. In B. Spodex (Ed.), *Handbook of research on the education of young children* (pp. 207–223). New York: Macmillan.

Silberg, J. (1998). *The I can't sing book: For grown-ups who can't carry a tune in a paper bag but want to do music with young children.* Beltsville, MD: Gryphon House.

Snyder, S. (1996). Early childhood music lessons from "Mr. Holland's Opus." *Early Childhood Education Journal, 24*(2), 103–105.

Tarnowski, S. M. (1999). Musical play and young children. *Music Educators Journal, 86*(1), 26–29.

Webster, P. R., & Richardson, C. (1993). Asking children to think about music. *Arts Education Policy Review, 94*(3), 7–11.

CHILDREN'S LITERATURE CONNECTION

Bramhall, W. (2004). *Hepcat.* New York: Philomel Books.
> This story is about a piano-playing "Hepcat" who gets scared before a performance and loses his groove. He searches for his groove and finds inspiration from the Beatles, Elvis, and Little Richard, so that, when he performs, he's the coolest cat around. (PreK–3)

Conover, C. (2004). *Over the hills & far away.* New York: Farrar Straus Giroux.
> Tom the otter plays only one song as he travels the countryside playing his pipe. Includes the musical score and song lyrics. (Infant–K)

Cox, J., & Brown, E. (2003). *My family plays music.* New York: Holiday House.
> This cut-art picture book is about a very musical family in which each member plays a different instrument. The main character is a young girl who plays the tambourine, triangle, cymbals, cowbell, woodblock, maracas, rhythm sticks, and handbell. So, Daddy calls her a "percussionist." Everything from jazz to polkas is discussed. (K–3)

Crozon, Alain. (2004). *What am I? Music!* Paris, France: Editions du Seuil.
> This book contains interactive learning concepts and ideas that come to light in an interactive format. (Infants–PreK)

Degan, B. (1983). *Jamberry.* New York: Harper & Row.
> A little boy, walking in the forest, meets a big lovable bear that takes him on a delicious berry-picking adventure in the magical world of Berryland. (PreK–1)

Dewan, Ted. (2005). *Bing: Make music.* New York: Random House Children's Books.
> This book uses everyday materials to make instruments, as well as music.

Gollub, M., & Hanke, K. (2000). *The jazz fly.* Santa Rosa, CA: Tortuga Press.
> This book and CD tell the tale of a musician fly who is inspired by animals he meets on his way to a performance. (PreK–1)

Greenfield, E. (1991). *I make music.* New York: Black Butterfly Children's Books.
> A young girl experiences music with the help of her mother and father. (Infant)

Harter, D. (1997). *Walking through the jungle.* New York: Mulberry.
> A young explorer discovers the different animals and terrains of the world before arriving home, safe and sound, for supper. (PreK–1)

Hurd, T. (1984). *Mama don't allow.* New York: HarperCollins.
> Miles and the Swamp Band have the time of their lives playing at the Alligator ball until they discover the menu includes Swamp Band Soup. (Primary K–2)

Johnston, T. (1991). *Grandpa's song.* New York: Dial Books for Young Readers.
> When a young girl's beloved, exuberant, grandfather becomes forgetful, she helps him by singing their favorite song. (Primary K–3)

Koscielniak, Bruce. (2000). *Story of the incredible orchestra: An introduction to musical instruments and the symphony orchestra.* Boston: Houghton Mifflin.
> This book takes a lively look at the orchestra's history and the instruments in it. (Primary)

Kraus, R. (1990). *Musical Max.* New York: Simon & Schuster Books for Young Readers.
> The peace and quiet following Max's decision to put his instruments away drives the neighbors just as crazy as his constant practicing. (Primary K–3)

Krementz, J. (1991). *A very young musician.* New York: Simon & Schuster Books for Young Readers.
> Text and photographs feature a boy who is learning to play the trumpet. (Primary 1–3)

Krull, Kathleen. (2003). *M is for music*. San Diego: Harcourt Children's Books.
  An alphabet book that introduces musical terms, from allegro to zarzuela. (Ages 5–8)
Kuskin, K. (1986). *The philharmonic gets dressed*. New York: HarperCollins.
  The 105 members of the orchestra are shown showering, dressing, traveling, and setting
  themselves up on stage for an evening's concert. (Primary 1–3)
McDermott, G. (1997). *Musicians of the sun*. New York: Simon & Schuster.
  In this retelling of an Aztec myth, Lord of the Night sends Wind to free four musicians that
  the Sun is holding prisoner, so they can bring joy to the world. (Primary 1–3)
Rowe, J., & Perham, M. (1993). *Making sounds*. Chicago: Children's Press.
  The book describes different sounds, how they are made, and how they travel. (Primary 1–3)
Sage, J. (1991). *The little band*. New York: Margaret K. McElderry Books.
  A little band marches through town, delighting everyone with its beautiful music. (PreK)
Schuch, S. (1999). *A symphony of whales*. San Diego: Harcourt Brace & Company.
  Young Glashka's dream of the singing of whales, accompanied by a special kind of music,
  leads to the rescue of thousands of whales stranded in a freezing Siberian bay. This book is
  based on a true story. (Primary K–3)
Sturges, P., & Wolff, A. (2004). *She'll be comin' round the mountain*. Boston: Little, Brown.
  This southwest adaptation of the classic folk song includes animals awaiting the arrival of
  a mysterious guest, who turns up in a bookmobile. (PreK–1)
Weatherford, C. B. (2000). *The sound that jazz makes*. New York: Walker.
  An illustrated history of the origins and influences of jazz from Africa to contemporary
  America. (Primary K–3)
Williams, V. (1983). *Something special for me*. New York: Greenwillow Books.
  Rosa has difficulty choosing a special birthday present to buy with the coins her mother
  and grandmother have saved, until she hears a man playing music on an accordion.
  (Primary K–2)
Williams, V. (1984). *Music, music for everyone*. New York: Mulberry.
  Rosa plays her accordion with her friends in the Oak Street Band and earns money to help
  her mother with expenses while her grandmother is sick. (Primary K–3)

 For additional resources involving creativity and the arts with young children,
visit our Web site at **www.earlychilded.delmar.com**

 REFERENCES

Achilles, D. (January 1999). Creating music environments in early childhood programs. *Young
  Children, 54*(1), 21–26.
Achilles, E. (1992). Current perspectives on young children's thinking. In B. Andress (Ed.),
  Readings in early childhood education (pp. 67–74). Reston, VA: Music Educators'
  National Conference.
Andress, B. (1980). *Music experiences in early childhood*. New York: Holt, Rinehart & Winston.
Bayless, K., & Ramsey, M. (1986). *Music, a way of life for the young child*. Columbus, OH:
  Merrill.
Blackburn, L. (1998). *Whole music: A whole language approach to teaching music*. Portsmouth,
  NH: Heinemann.
Bronner, S. J. (Ed.). (1988). *American children's folklore*. Little Rock, AR: August House
  Publishers.
Buchoff, R. (1994). Joyful voices: Facilitating language growth through rhythmic response to
  chants. *Young Children, 49*(4), 26–30.
Buchoff, R. (Spring 1995). Jump rope rhymes in the classroom? *Childhood Education, 71*(3), 149.
Carle, E. (2001). *Today is Monday*. New York: Philomel.
Feierabend, J. (1990). Music in early childhood. *Design for Arts in Education, 91*(6), 15–20.

Fitzhenry, R. I. (Ed.) (1993). *The Harper book of quotations* (3rd ed.). New York: HarperCollins Books.

Formaro, A. (2001). *9 Easy to make musical instruments for kids.* [Online] Retrieved January 11, 2005. http://www.thefamilycorner.com/family/kids/crafts/9_musical_instruments.shtml.

Fowke, E. (Ed.). (1969). *Sally go round the sun.* Garden City, NY: Doubleday.

Gardner, H. (1983). *Frames of mind: The theory of multiple intelligences.* New York: Basic Books.

Glazer, T. (Ed.). (1973). *Eye winker Tom tinker chin chopper.* Garden City, NY: Doubleday.

Haines, J. E., & Gerber, L. L. (1999). *Leading young children to music.* Upper Saddle River, NJ: Prentice Hall.

Hildebrandt, C. (1998). Creativity in music and early childhood. *Young Children, 53*(6), 68–74.

Isbell, R. (1995). *The complete learning centers book.* Beltsville, MD: Gryphon House.

Isbell, R., & Raines, S. C. (2000). *Tell it again! 2: Easy-to-tell stories with activities for young children.* Beltsville, MD: Gryphon House.

Jalongo, M. R. (1996). Using recorded music with young children: A guide for non-musicians. *Young Children, 51*(5), 6–14.

Johnson, E. S., & Sayers, F. C. (1959). *Anthology of children's literature.* Boston: Houghton Mifflin.

Kenney, S. (1995). The voice within. *Teaching Music, 2*(5), 36–37.

Kenney, S. (1997). Music in developmentally appropriate integrated curriculum. In C. H. Hart, D. C. Burts, & R. Charlesworth (Eds.), *Integrated curriculum and developmentally appropriate practice: Birth to eight* (pp. 103–144). Albany, NY: State University of New York Press.

Kovalski, M. (1990). *The wheels on the bus: An adaptation of the traditional song.* New York: Little, Brown & Company.

Martin, Jr., B., Archambault, J., & Ehlert, L. (1991). *Chicka chicka boom boom.* New York: Simon & Schuster.

May, B. (1970). *Jefferson himself: The personal narration of a many-sided American.* Charlottesville, VA: University Press of Virginia.

McDonald, D. (1979). *Music in our lives: The early years.* Washington, DC: National Association for the Education of Young Children.

Ohman-Rodriguez, J. (2004). Music from inside out: Promoting emergent composition with young children. *Young Children 59*(4), 50–55.

Raschka, C. (2004). *Charlie Parker Played Be Bop.* New York: Scholastic.

Rauscher, F. (1995). Does music make you smarter? *PTA Today, 20*(5), 8–9.

Snyder, S. (March 2001). Connection, correlation, and integration. *Music Educators Journal— Special Focus: Interdisciplinary Curriculum, 87*(5), 32–39, 70.

Totline Publications (Eds.). (1994). *1001 rhymes & fingerplays for working with young children.* Torrance, CA: Totline Publications.

Turner, M. E. (1999). Child-centered learning and music programs. *Music Educators Journal, 86*(1), 30–51.

Wolf, J. (1994). Let's sing it again: Creating music with young children. *Young Children, 47*(2), 56–61.

Yolen, J. (1992). *Street rhymes around the world.* Honesdale, PA: Wordsong.

CREATIVE MOVEMENT: MORE THAN THE HOKEY POKEY

CHAPTER 7

During the first eight years of development, children are gaining control of their bodies. A major goal for early childhood teachers is to enhance **motor development** through creative experiences. Using **creative movement** allows young children to respond to open-ended activities in unique ways. Designing movement experiences with creativity in mind provides an opportunity for all young children to experience success and build confidence in their physical and expressive capabilities.

> **After studying this chapter, you will be able to:**
> * **Recognize the different theories that explain the importance of movement.**
> * **Identify the sequence and direction of the development of movement in young children.**
> * **Plan appropriate movement activities for children from birth through the primary grades.**
> * **Understand how movement can be integrated into the curriculum.**
> * **Support the necessity of outdoor play for children.**

OBSERVATION OF CREATIVITY

Connor was a joy to watch as a four-year-old. He enjoyed racing through his grandmother's house, making sputtering sounds like a race car or playing hide and seek with his grandfather. When Bethany, his seven-year-old sister, asked her aunt to hold the limbo stick, it was evident from Connor's expression that he did not know how to do the limbo. With her aunt holding a long broom handle level to the floor, Bethany tried bending backward low enough to get under. Connor simply jumped over the top until Bethany explained the dance. Then Mary Kate, the two-year-old, joined in and crawled under the broom instead of bending under like her sister. This activity persisted for over thirty minutes, with each child making variations on the theme of getting under or over the limbo broom. Eventually, they each adopted the others' methods. Bethany and Kate tried jumping over the broom like their brother. Connor and Bethany crawled under, in Mary Kate's style. Finally, all three children tried bending backward low enough to get under the broom. The only people who were tired at the end of the thirty minutes were the adults holding the limbo broom.

WHAT WAS OBSERVED?

Each child approached the activity at their developmental level. Bethany, seven years old, knew the rules of the game. Conner, four, jumped over the stick. Mary Kate, two, climbed under the stick. Each child was actively involved in the movement. Since the activity was open-ended, many different variations were used.

Movement Terms

Dynamic Balance. Balance maintained while moving through space, including hopping.

Energy. The force that is used to show intentions. This can include smooth or sharp, and sudden or sustained.

General Space. The shared space in which children move. Indoors, it is usually limited by floors, walls, and ceilings.

Kinesthetics. The use of the body to learn about physical capabilities, develop body awareness, and gain understanding of the world.

Locomotor Skills. These involve movement through space that includes walking, marching, jumping, and skipping.

Manipulative Skills. Any gross motor skills in which an object is usually involved (manipulated), including throwing, catching, striking, and kicking.

Nonlocomotor Skills. Stationary actions that include stretching, bending, swaying, and shaking.

Personal Space. The personal or shared area that is used by the body during movement. This includes the levels of high and low, and directions such as forward, backward, up, and down.

Static Balance. Balance maintained while remaining in place, including standing on one foot.

Time. This includes rhythm, speed, emphasis, and duration of the movement.

Movement is fun for children. When they play on their own, invent new games, and want to liven up what is happening, they move. The physical development demonstrated by two-year-old Mary Kate, four-year-old Connor, and seven-year-old Bethany is appropriate for their age and stage of development. They move like healthy, active children. Play experiences provide evidence of children's neuromuscular development, movement skills, cognitive interpretations, communications, and personal-social abilities. Their development was further enhanced by the lively impromptu play at grandmother's house, designed by the seven-year-old to entertain herself and joined by the other children in her family.

Movement for movement's sake is significant because children who learn to use their bodies well and move with confidence, feel more self-assured, enjoy themselves, and develop a physical awareness that enhances their ability to explore on their own. The child's innate desire to move is appreciated by educators who provide unstructured time for movement and who incorporate movement, and activity into the daily schedule.

Sometimes, early childhood educators and physical educators stress different movement approaches. Early childhood educators tend to focus on creative movement as a part of play and the curriculum. Physical educators stress learning to move in structured and prescribed ways. Today's educators combine the two. Certainly, early childhood educators value play and the child's own interpretation of movement, as in Connor's racing through the house, revving up his engine while starting and stopping like a race car driver. Learning to play limbo prompted a different type of motoric movement and control that was a response to a structured activity learned in a physical education class. The early childhood classroom teacher will incorporate both, while providing a significant amount of open-ended activities that allow the individual child to interpret movement and to express her own individuality.

> **"Creative rhythmic movement is the individual's interpretation of thoughts and feelings expressed through the use of the body."**
> *G. Andrews, 1954*

A colorful sheet responds to the toddlers' movement.

❀ THEORIES RELATED TO MOVEMENT AND CREATIVITY

Rudolph Laban's perspective on young children and movement provides a theory that both early childhood educators and physical education teachers can embrace. Laban (1963) recommends that children develop **body awareness, space awareness,** and an understanding of how movements can be varied. Generally considered the father of movement education, Laban developed a system of analyzing movement through what he termed the elements of time, weight, space, and flow. Educators can use his work to promote both motor skill development and creativity by keeping these elements in mind as the children move.

As children are exploring the locomotor skill of walking, for example, teachers can ask them to try it in different directions, along varying pathways, and at different levels in space (the element of space). They can challenge them to walk both quickly and slowly (time), lightly and strongly (weight), and with and without pauses (flow). Laban also determined that experimentation was a valuable learning tool. His work is the origin of the teaching styles described in this chapter as guided discovery and exploration, both of which enhance creative-thinking skills.

Also pertinent to the use of the body in the development of both critical- and creative-thinking skills is Howard Gardner's (1983) theories of multiple intelligences. Gardner describes bodily-kinesthetic intelligence as the ability to unite the body and mind in physical performance. Beginning with control of automatic and voluntary movements, kinesthetic intelligence progresses to using the body in highly differentiated and skilled ways. All talented performances require an acute sense of timing and the transformation of intention into action. Highly developed kinesthetic intelligence is discerned easily when observing actors, athletes, or dancers. It also is evident in inventors, jewelers, mechanics, and others who work skillfully with their hands or objects. According to Campbell, Campbell, and Dickinson (1996), "bodily-kinesthetic intelligence is the foundation of human knowing, since it is through our sensory-motor experiences that we experience life" (p. 67). Drama, dance, and musical expression involve active problem solving that challenges children to use their physical learning system (Given, 2000).

✿ PRINCIPLES OF PHYSICAL DEVELOPMENT

Very young infants move in random ways. Their movements become more coordinated and purposeful as they develop into toddlers. As they repeat actions and interact with adults, they gain greater control. Young children enjoy practicing their growing collection of movements and skills. As they learn to use their bodies, there are several interactive components at work: **sensory development** (seeing, hearing, touching, tasting, and smelling) and motor development (large and small muscles). Sensory experiences provide a foundation for the curriculum of young children. Through the senses, young children learn about the world and explore the properties of objects around them. It is valuable for young children to gather information through their senses and to have opportunities to develop these abilities during the early years.

Motor development, the ability to use and control the body, is often broken down into two distinct categories: **gross motor skills** (large muscles like those in the arms, legs, and trunk) and **fine motor skills** (small muscles like those in the hands and fingers). Many educators have consolidated motor skills and sensory skills into a single phrase that they term **sensori-motor development.** Maxim (1997) summarizes a number of developmental principles that can assist early childhood educators in understanding the progression of motor development.

> **"Knowledge is tied to actions. It is through children's exploration and discovery among their actions that the first structures of the mind are formed."**
>
> *J. Piaget, 1973 (in John-Steiner, 1985)*

Directional Growth

It is expected that physical growth progresses from the head down to the toes **(cephalocaudal),** and from the center of the body outward **(proximodistal).** The muscles closest to the head are the first the child is able to control. For example, an infant will be able to lift her head first, and later, be able to raise her body from the floor and crawl. First, the infant will use her shoulder muscles to swat at an object. During the first year, she will be able to pick up a tiny piece of fuzz with her fingers, using a pincer grip.

General to Specific

Physical development progresses from large muscle to small muscle control. The random movements of the infant progress to the specific movements of drawing and cutting observed in preschool. During this differentiation, the child gains control over specific parts of the body and refines their use.

Individual Variations

Growth rates vary from child to child, and each child has his own timetable. In the area

An infant is using her pincer grip to pull leaves from a flower.

An observant teacher can provide assistance to a child who is fearful of walking on a raised balance beam.

of motor development, these individual differences are very observable. There is, however, an orderly sequence of development. Most children crawl before they walk or run. Both heredity and the environment can influence this development as the child gains coordination and control of his body through use and experimentation.

STAGES OF DEVELOPMENT

Developmental specialists describe movement in terms of **locomotor skills** such as walking, running, jumping, hopping, galloping, and skipping. **Nonlocomotor skills** are movements that can be performed while remaining in one place; they include bending, stretching, twisting, and turning the body. **Manipulative skills** are those typically involving the manipulation of an object, such as throwing, catching, and kicking. **Static balance** means staying balanced when still. **Dynamic balance** is maintaining equilibrium while moving.

Each of these motor skills and abilities has milestones to help the observer determine if the child is in the range of normalcy. While there are overlapping stages of development, the child is expected to refine her movements along a continuum, gaining more control with age and experience. Authors on the subject of developmental movement have described ranges of locomotor skills in months, years, and levels of refinement.

Developmental movement is evaluated in general terms:

walking (13 to 25 months)

running (18 months to 5 years)

jumping (18 months to 6 years)

galloping (3 to 6 years)

hopping (4 to 6 years)

skipping (4 to 6 years) (Gallahue & Ozmun, 1995; Hoffman et al., 1981)

Manipulative abilities include:

reaching, grasping, and releasing (2–4 months to 14–18 months)

throwing (2–3 years to 6 years)

catching (2 to 6 years)

kicking (18 months to 6 years)

striking (2–3 years to 6–7 years)

Movement patterns include:

static balance (10 months to 6 years)

dynamic balance (3 to 7 years)

nonlocomotor movements (2 months to 6 years)

An important point for the early childhood educator to remember is that these stages are determined by biological timing, experiences, and environment. Developmentally, children are biologically expected to start walking by their first birthday; however, some will walk at nine months and some at 15 months and still be considered in the range of normalcy. Some children can balance on a low balance beam or walking board by the time they are three, whereas others may not be proficient until they are four, but still should be considered in the range of normalcy. Young children can strike a ball at the age of three if it is stationary, but many will not perform this skill until they are five (both children would be considered in the range of normal development). Developmental milestones provide information used to identify children who do not seem to be progressing at the expected rate. Additional evaluation by specialists such as physical and occupational therapists may identify issues of development that need to be addressed during the early years.

PLANNING FOR MOVEMENT ACTIVITIES

Movement programs for young children should be conducted in a noncompetitive environment, with an emphasis on the child receiving individual satisfaction and enjoying the company of others instead of competing with them. Contemporary specialists in children's physical education agree that body-management activities, fundamental motor skills, and manipulation opportunities with equipment should be in the framework of a curriculum for young children (Carson, 1994).

To help educators plan effectively for movement activities, Hoffman et al. (1981) refined six developmental themes that reflect Laban's earlier work.

1. **Becoming aware.** Learning about and establishing basic movement capabilities.
2. **Becoming independent.** Increasing self-reliance and confidence in moving.
3. **Accepting and expressing feelings and ideas.** Communicating through movement.
4. **Accepting responsibilities and working cooperatively.** Sharing the movement environment, and respecting and interacting productively with others.
5. **Improving quality of response.** Refining and elaborating movement capabilities for a purpose.
6. **Drawing relationships.** Comprehending the significance of movement in one's lifestyle.

Rae Pica (2004) described three methods of including movement in early childhood programs. These different approaches provide options for early childhood educators as they plan experiences that encourage motor development and creative movement.

Direct Approach

Some motor activities are best taught through direct instruction. Through demonstration, modeling, and imitation, young children can learn about moving their bodies in specific ways. For example, doing a forward roll can be demonstrated and imitated by young children who have never participated in this activity.

A toddler echoes the clapping pattern of his teacher.

While the direct approach is efficient and helps children learn to follow directions, it does not promote creativity, as all of the children are expected to respond in one way only.

Guided Discovery

This child-centered approach allows experimentation and inventiveness as the teacher guides children through the process. Questions can be posed as the children discover ways to use their bodies to complete an activity. For example, rather than teaching the forward roll through demonstration and imitation, teachers can ask children to first show an upside-down position. They then follow up with such challenges as: "Show me an upside-down position that uses the hands and feet, with the tummy facing the floor." "Can you look at the ceiling from that position?" "Look at even more of the ceiling, and show me you can roll from that position."

When using guided discovery, it is important to accept all responses—even those considered "incorrect." The children can then be given more time to "find another way," or the teacher can continue, asking even more specific questions, until the desired outcome is achieved. This method is most appropriate for older preschoolers and primary-grade students.

Exploration

A divergent problem-solving approach should be used as frequently as possible. This approach matches how young children learn and allows them to determine ideas for themselves. When children are given open-ended possibilities, they can produce a variety of responses. This allows the child to develop creative thinking as well as different movements. For example, if children are asked to move two parts of their bodies at the same time, numerous combinations are possible. When teachers validate all of the responses they see and encourage children to continue finding new responses, children become more confident with their creative abilities.

According to Pica (2004):

> Exploration allows *every* child to participate and succeed at her or his level of development and ability. In addition to the self-confidence and poise continual success brings, this process promotes independence, helps develop patience with oneself and one's peers, and allows the acceptance of others' ideas. Perhaps most important for young children, exploration leads them to the discovery of the richness of possibilities involved in the field of human movement. (p. 241)

✿ BECOMING AWARE OF BODIES IN SPACE AND MOVEMENT

The first stage is becoming aware of one's own body: the space that it occupies and its capability of movement. For example, a two-year-old might look in the mirror as a parent or caregiver sings, "Head, shoulders, knees, and toes." The child will move in response to the song. Then, if the child points to a body part, the adult simply incorporates that into the song: "head, chin, tummy, and shin."

A four-year-old developing body awareness might travel through an obstacle course, with the teacher asking the children to crawl under the table, jump over the blocks, go around the chair, and hide under the blanket. Then, a child can take a turn giving directions to others, using the directional words that help children develop awareness of what they are asking their bodies to do. After the children have experience with obstacle courses, they can design their own, with the teacher following their suggestions.

Seven-year-olds can enjoy more sophisticated movements such as curling up like a sleeping caterpillar, stretching arms out like the wings of a bird awakening in the morning, diving like a pelican, or yawning like a waking parent. Then, the children can think of other movements they want to describe and others can follow their lead. A variation on this theme would be to have the children pantomime or demonstrate a movement, and let others guess what they are doing.

These children are experimenting with jumping on foam blocks.

✿ MUSIC AND MOVEMENT

Young children can experience music and movement together. Their innate responses and rhythmic motions feel appropriate to them. The infant, lying on her back, responds to fast music by quickly kicking her feet. Later, she is soothed and relaxes when slow music with wind instruments plays in the background. Toddlers often bounce up and down in response to lively music. Preschoolers play simple rhythm instruments and march in response to the beats they create, especially responding to the tempo. Kindergartners, who have more muscle control, enjoy twirling around and interpreting the sounds of music ranging from classical to jazz, or Latin to rock and roll. Primary-grade children enjoy dance movements, interpreting the feelings of a piece of music, or responding with exaggerated frantic movements when they hear maracas and kettledrums. They may use light floating movements with music that is played by flutes and recorders.

> **"The truest expression of a people is in its dance and its music."**
>
> *A. de Mille, 1952*
> *(in Partnow, 2001)*

Another way to integrate movement and music into the early childhood classroom is through the use of centers designed and equipped to encourage active involvement in the music process. When creating a music and/or movement center in the classroom, plan to store materials for both individual and small group activities. Tape and CD players, rhythm instruments, hoops, scarves, ribbons, and crepe paper streamers are a few of the necessities. Perhaps, the most important ingredient for the music and movement center is space.

Children with special needs benefit from these kinds of movement opportunities. For example, Erica is five years old and has spastic cerebral palsy. She uses a wheelchair for mobility. When some children are moving to music, Erica is partnered with Adam who is very sensitive to her needs. He holds Erica's hands, and helps her move her arms in rhythm to the music. The teacher comments that each child is moving in different ways. Erica's unique way of moving is appreciated by the teacher and the other children.

Children naturally respond to music by moving. An interesting movement experience is to darken the room, play slow classical music, and let the children hold flashlights in their hands as they move around the room. The movement of the light responds to the actions of the child and the music provides a catalyst for the activity.

Responding to rhythm takes practice for some children, whereas others seem to grasp it quickly. Help youngsters hear the rhythms by echoing the patterns or counting for emphasis. Using drums, which allow the teacher to emphasize the rhythm pattern, often helps movement in response to the rhythm. Always provide opportunities for the children to make up their own rhythms and let others imitate them. This encourages creative responses. Linking Jennifer's rhythm to Jeff's rhythm is a way to expand the rhythm and repeated pattern.

For many cultures, frozen statues is a popular childhood game. Add music to the game and let the children move as they please to the music. When the music

Music can be moved outdoors to stimulate larger movements by children.

ends, the children must stop and "freeze" in place. Using partners to move together and then freeze can extend the game and the enjoyment. Copeland's Grand Canyon Suite includes the composition Rodeo. This music provides a great deal of variation of tempo that encourages children to move slowly in certain sections and to explode into vigorous movement in other parts of the piece. Asking children to freeze when the music is stopped provides another opportunity to respond to the music.

According to Pica (1999), "When a child tiptoes to soft music, stamps her feet to loud music, moves in slow motion to Bach's *Air on the G String* then rapidly to Rimsky-Korsakov's *Flight of the Bumblebee,* sways to a ¾ meter and skips to a piece in ⅝ time, she is experiencing music on many levels. Not only is she listening, but also she is using her body, mind, and spirit to express and create. Because she is using a multimodal approach, what she learns will make a lasting impression" (p. 113).

DANCE

Excellent early childhood teachers engage children in movement in response to music and incorporate music and movement throughout the curriculum. Another professional who uses music and movement is the dance teacher. Numerous dance classes and dance academies are available for young children. Dance teachers may use the more creative and free flowing activities that early childhood teachers promote. However, they may suggest that imitation and learning choreographed movements can help children become aware of their bodies and learn to control their movements.

The issues of what constitutes quality dance education for young children have been debated for decades. The concept of "creative dance as guided exploration" has many similarities to our descriptions of appropriate movement for young children. Blythe Hinitz (1980) reviewed the literature for dance in early childhood education. Hinitz states, "Creative dance is the guided exploration of movement concepts, designed to increase the child's awareness and understanding of his own range of movement and that of others. It is offered as a pre-dance, pre-sport movement experience, one in which the child is the center, and creative involvement and challenge are part of each experience" (p. 1).

> **"Nothing is more revealing than movement."**
> *M. Graham, 1935*
> *(in Partnow, 2001)*

For many dance instructors, meeting the parents' expectations of choreographed dance movements, complete with costumes, forces more of an emphasis on performance than early childhood educators would advocate. Yet the concept of imitation is valued by early childhood educators as a form of learning, provided there is room for the child to use what has been learned through imitation and creatively design movements for herself. Some dancers argue that through imitation, they become aware of their bodies and their movements, then they use the movements in their own expressions. The aesthetics of dance are rooted in movements that express feelings, emotions, and actions. Certainly, the great ballets are stories and interpretations of events with highly choreographed movements. However, highly trained adults perform these ballets. The freedom of interpretive dance is more in tune with the life of the young child and with the promotion of creativity.

Mary Ann Lee (1993) suggested that children use interpretive dance with *The Tale of Peter Rabbit* by Beatrix Potter (1976). Lee uses an approach of "springboards of activity" rather than choreographed movement. Each child is able to interpret the movements throughout the story in her own way. For example, in the beginning of the story, when the little bunnies are waking up, the children can pretend to wake. Then pretend to get dressed. The springboard for the movement is what is implied in the story. They simply act it out with movement in their own way. Later in the story, when Peter is squeezing under the gate of Mr. McGregor's garden, the children use the idea as a springboard to interpret the movement as they lie on their tummies and wiggle under the imaginary gate. The instructor does not tell them what to do; she allows for individual interpretation. This approach allows children to move in their own way using the motor skills they currently have available. They experience the joy of using the body instead of developing feelings of inadequacy that might occur if they were unable to perform a choreographed pattern.

✺ CURRICULUM ACTIVITIES THAT INCORPORATE MOVEMENT

Mirror activities are fun for children. One child can move in a certain way, a right hand on her head, while the other child faces her and places a left hand (mirror image) on her head. By adding more complicated and more exaggerated movements, the children mirror each other. They can take turns creating the images for their partners to mirror. Very young children enjoy mirroring in a real mirror to observe their movement.

Adding a rake to the sand area outdoors encourages movement that produces a design.

Folktales are easily remembered stories from many cultures. Interpretations of folktales are excellent movement devices for storytelling and movement experiences. Start with short tales the children know well such as *Goldilocks and the Three Bears* or *Henny Penny*. At first, the children can play all of the parts and simply move in ways that interpret what the teacher is telling or reading. Later, several children in the class can play parts of the story. For example, three children might be Goldilocks, three children the Papa Bear, and so on. Longer and more complicated tales can be introduced as the children become comfortable in their movements.

Movement activities also can be used to interpret knowledge from the curriculum. For example, the water evaporation cycle may begin by becoming a vapor from a lake, moving to a cloud, and returning to earth as a raindrop. This cycle can be interpreted through movement. Similarly, the butterfly's life span of egg, larvae, caterpillar, and butterfly can be demonstrated in movement. Movement to weather such as storm clouds gathering to a great thunderstorm crashing can be interpreted by children moving in response to music, the teacher's direction, or flashing lights to simulate the lightning. Learning experiences through movement provide another way of understanding a concept or process, and match some children's style of knowing.

❧ OUTDOOR PLAY

Most outdoor play involves movement. Young children tend to move with great ease in an outdoor environment, using their large muscles. Playground equipment can be arranged to encourage movement practice. For example, a low balance beam with boards securely nailed and raised off the ground a few inches, provides an excellent way to practice balance. Railroad ties embedded in the ground or a white line painted on the tricycle track also can be walked for balance.

Tricycles, three-wheelers, and other wheeled toys are great fun for children as they engage in dramatic, imaginative play. Setting up an obstacle course for the wheeled toys can benefit the young child learning to follow directions. Safety courses that teach children to obey the safety signals and yield to pedestrians crossing also are helpful for the wheeled toy riders.

Various sizes of balls, hoops, beanbags, and lengths of rope are excellent items to add to the playground. Children often will invent their own games and ways of moving. Bouncing, rolling, and catching balls is excellent for eye–hand coordination. A variety of sizes and textures encourage different skill levels.

A piece of fabric inspires partners to move simultaneously.

❧ SUMMARY

Early childhood educators stress the need for young children to have opportunities to develop in all domains, including cognitive, social–emotional, and physical. Although this view often is expressed in the area of physical development, it is neglected frequently or left to chance occurrence during outdoor play only. Gardner's and others' work with kinesthetic intelligence and the study of different learning styles combined with the recognition of today's inactive child, have led to new interest in the inclusion of motor activities in early childhood programs.

Movement activities—directed, guided, and creative—provide unique opportunities for young children. These motoric experiences help children gain control of their bodies and discover their physical capabilities as they move through space. They also provide another way for children to make connections that unite the mind and body.

Creative movement combines the benefits of motor activities and divergent thinking. It provides children the opportunity to respond in personal ways, learn in different styles, and explore the use of their bodies. As young children discover their growing abilities in the use of their bodies and creative thinking, they build their self-esteem and generate a positive view of themselves.

Music inspires children to activate their bodies, respond to rhythm, and experiment with body movements. The combination of music and movement provides another avenue for adding motor experiences into the early childhood program that is dedicated to the development of the whole child, which certainly includes movement.

KEY TERMS

body awareness	manipulative skills
cephalocaudal	motor development
creative movement	nonlocomotor skills
dynamic balance	personal space
energy	proximodistal
fine motor skills	sensorimotor development
general space	sensory development
gross motor skills	space awareness
kinesthetics	static balance
locomotor skills	time

 REFLECTION

1. In the past, early childhood educators and physical educators did not always agree on movement instruction. Today, however, their views are more alike. Discuss the two perspectives.

2. Describe good movement activities for a two-year-old, a four-year-old, and a seven-year-old.

3. Imagine yourself as an early childhood educator who enjoys movement activities and is committed to involving children in creative movement and learning to move effectively. Describe three movement activities that are open-ended and promote creative responses while helping children increase their motor proficiency.

4. Body awareness activities begin in infancy and continue through a child's development. Select an age that interests you and design an activity that encourages body awareness.

5. Discuss the pros and cons of dance education for preschoolers. Define dance education as you know it and the ways it may differ from the discussion in this book.

THINKING ABOUT THE OBSERVATION OF CREATIVITY

1. What typical activities did Connor, the four-year-old, demonstrate?

2. In this episode, children of different levels were participating in the limbo. What were the benefits of this multi-age collaboration?

3. Explain how each child moved in a way that matched his or her level of motor development.

POSSIBILITIES FOR ADULT LEARNERS

Activity:	A Trip Down Memory Lane
Goal:	For students to remember favorite activities of their childhood.
Materials:	Paper and chart board or dry-erase board.

Procedure:

1. Ask each student to take a sheet of paper and write, on a separate line, five of their favorite activities when they were children, before they started school. For example, the list may include playing hide and seek, coloring, racing my big brother, playing in the sandbox in our backyard, or building a pretend fort or house with blankets and chairs.

2. Ask students to write down five of their favorite activities to do when not in school but during the primary grades. Examples may include riding my bicycle, jumping rope, learning cheers, playing with dolls, or playing ball.

3. On the board, categorize the activities. Ask your students to share their favorite activities and categorize them by gross motor, fine motor, independent, or small group. For example, riding a three-wheeler is gross motor whereas drawing is fine motor. Jumping rope is usually independent while one is learning, but it can become a small group activity in the primary grades as children learn to jump to chants and rhymes.

4. Continue the exercise and decide what other major area of development was involved in each activity. For example, playing hide and seek is social development because it involves playing by the rules, and is mathematical because children learn to count by waiting until the counter reaches ten, twenty, or one hundred.

Activity: Personal Space

Goal: To discover ways to help children and adults understand the concept of personal space.

Materials: Sheets of newspaper, hula-hoop, or long pieces of rope.

Procedure:

1. Explain the concept of personal space as it relates to movement activities.

2. Ask each student to place the newspaper, hula-hoop, or rope on the floor.

3. Have them stand inside the hoop or rope formed into a circle.

4. Ask the students to move inside the boundaries as many different ways as they can. Suggest that the hoop or paper provides them with concrete identification of their space.

5. Make suggestions for movements such as bending, stretching, shaking, or moving specific parts of their bodies; and vary the use of space (high, low, and in the middle).

6. After the activity is concluded, discuss the different ways they moved and how the materials help them understand personal space.

OPEN-ENDED ACTIVITIES FOR YOUNG CHILDREN

PreK–K

Activity: Let's Move

Goal: To identify the movement required using an object.

Materials: A collection of items from home or the classroom (for example, a broom, clothes brush, eggbeater, towel, or dust cloth).

Procedure:

1. Let the children choose one item and ask them to show how to move when using this object. For example, a broom is used for sweeping, an eggbeater is used for beating eggs, and a towel is used to dry things.

2. Let the children invent a new way to use the object. Possibilities include riding the broom like a horse; turning the eggbeater up on end and pretending it is a space ship while rotating the beaters with the blast; or swinging the towel overhead like a helicopter.

3. Invite the children to collect other objects and think of ways they can use them to move in a new direction or pretend to be something else.

Activity: Scarves and Music

Goal: To experience using a material that responds to movement.

Materials: A colorful collection of scarves of varying sizes.

Procedure:

1. Let the children who are interested select a scarf.

2. Ask the children to experiment with the scarves: see how they float, swerve, and respond to fast movements.

3. Play different types of music such as classical, rock, jazz, or hip-hop, and let the children move however they feel, using their scarves to interpret the music.

4. Other materials, such as crepe paper streamers, pieces of fabric, or netting, could be used.

A group works together to help all members stand from a seated position.

PreK–K or Primary Grades

Activity: Obstacle Course

Goal: To use the body effectively while moving through obstacles.

Materials: Large cardboard boxes, tubes, blanket or sheet, chairs, sturdy table, blocks, and directional arrows or written signs and symbols.

Procedure for PreK–K:

1. Set up a simple obstacle course using a box, chairs covered with a sheet, table, and other items.
2. Place footprints or directional arrows that show children how to move through the obstacle course.
3. The children can rearrange the materials and directions, repeating the movement through the course.

Procedure for Primary Grades:

1. Construct a more complex obstacle course and include signs with written directions. These could include *over, under, around, stop,* and so forth.
2. Music could be added to encourage movement that matches the tempo of the recordings.

Extension: A course can be set up outdoors using different materials such as barrels, spools, collapsible tunnels, tumbling mats, and landscape timbers.

Primary Grades

Activity: Copy Cat

Goal: To develop body awareness by imitating the movements of others.

Materials: Can be done with a musical recording.

Procedure:

1. Form a circle of children.
2. One person in the group starts to move and the others imitate the movement. The same motion is repeated around the entire circle.
3. The next person in the group creates a different movement that is repeated around the circle.
4. Questions can guide the children to try various movements such as "How do feet move when walking on hot sand?" "How would you catch a gigantic snowball?" "What two parts of your body can move at the same time?"

Kindergarten

Activity: Personal Space Game

Goal: To develop understanding of the term personal space.

Materials: Hula-hoops, carpet squares, or newspapers.

Procedure:

1. Explain the concept of personal space before beginning the movement activities.
2. Give each child a hula-hoop, carpet square, or newspaper.
3. Ask each child to place the object on the floor and stand inside her personal space.

4. Ask the children to move as many different ways as they can while remaining in their personal space. The hula-hoop, carpet square, or newspaper will give them a concrete way to identify the boundaries of this space.

5. Make suggestions for movements such as moving a specific part of the body or the use of space (high, low, or in the middle).

6. After the activity is concluded, discuss the different ways the children moved while staying in their personal space. Later, the same activity can be repeated without the physical boundaries of the hula-hoop, carpet square, or newspaper.

ADDITIONAL READING

Achilles, E. R. (1996). Musical awareness through creative movement. *General Music Today, 9*(3), 5–8.

Andrews, A. G. (1996). Developing spatial sense: A moving experience! *Teaching Children Mathematics, 2*(5), 290–294.

Bagheri, H. (1990). Dance as a multicultural education for young children. In W. J. Stinson (Ed.), *Moving and learning for the young child* (pp. 189–199). Reston, VA: American Alliance for Health, Physical Education, Recreation, and Dance.

Bond, K., & Deans, J. (1997). Eagles, reptiles and beyond: A co-creative journey in dance. *Childhood Education, 73*(6), 366–372.

Bucek, L. E. (1992). Constructing a child-centered dance curriculum. *Journal of Physical Education, Recreation & Dance, 63*(9), 39–42.

Clements, R. L., & Oosten, M. (1995). Creating and implementing preschool movement narratives. *Journal of Physical Education, Recreation & Dance, 66*(3), 24–30.

Diem, L. (1991). *The important early years: Intelligence through movement experience.* Reston, VA: American Alliance for Health, Physical Education, Recreation and Dance.

Downey, V. W. (1995). Expressing ideas through gesture, time, and space. *Journal of Physical Education, Recreation & Dance, 66*(9), 18–22.

Dyer, S. M., & Schiller, W. (1993). Not wilting flowers again! Problem finding and problem solving in movement and performance. *Early Child Development and Care, 90*(1), 47–54.

Eastman, W. (1997). Active living: Physical activities for infants, toddlers and preschoolers. *Early Childhood Education Journal, 24*(3), 161–164.

Friedlander, J. L. (1992). Creating dances and dance instruction: An integrated-arts approach. *Journal of Physical Education, Recreation & Dance, 63*(9), 49–54.

Gillbert, A. G. (1992). A conceptual approach to studio dance, preK-12. *Journal of Physical Education, Recreation & Dance, 63*(9), 43–49.

Griss, S. (1994). Creative movement: A language for learning. *Educational Leadership, 51*(5), 78–81.

Griss, S., & Merecki, V. (2000). *Minds in motion: A kinesthetic approach to teaching elementary curriculum.* Portsmouth, NH: Heinemann.

Ignico, A. (1994). Early childhood physical education: Providing the foundation. *Journal of Physical Education & Dance, 69*(9), 33–38.

Koff, S. R. (2000). Toward a definition of dance education. *Childhood Education, 77*(1), 27–31.

Marxen, C. E. (1995). Push, pull, toss, tilt, swing: Physics for young children. *Childhood Education, 71*(4), 212–217.

Rodger, L. (1996). Adding movement throughout the day. *Young Children, 51*(3), 4–6.

Sanders, S. (1998). Challenging movement experiences for young children. *Dimensions of Early Childhood, 26*(1), 9–17.

Schoon, S. (1998). Using dance experience and drama in the classroom. *Childhood Education, 74*(2), 78–83.

Schwartz, P. (1993). Creativity and dance: Implications for pedagogy and policy. *Arts Education Policy Review, 95*(1), 8–16.

Stevens, D. A. (1994). Movement concepts: Stimulating cognitive development in elementary students. *Journal of Physical Education, Recreation & Dance, 65*(8), 16–24.

Stinson, S. (1988). *Dance for young children: Finding the magic in movement.* Reston, VA: American Alliance for Health, Physical Education, Recreation, and Dance.

Stinson, S. W. (1990). Dance education in early childhood. *Design for Arts Education, 91*(6), 34–41.

Swaim, S. (1997). Dancing a story: Myth and movement for children. *Early Childhood Education Journal, 25*(2), 127–131.

Weikart, P. (1987). *Key experiences in movement for children ages 3 to 5: Round the circle.* Ypsilanti, MI: High Scope Press.

Werner, P., Sweeting, T., Woods, A., & Jones, L. (1992). Developmentally appropriate dance for children. *Journal of Physical Education, Recreation & Dance, 63*(6), 40–45.

Werner, P. (1994). Whole physical education. *Journal of Physical Education, Recreation & Dance, 65*(6), 40–44.

CHILDREN'S LITERATURE CONNECTION

Ackerman, K. (1988). *Song and dance man.* New York: Alfred A. Knopf.
Grandpa demonstrates for his visiting grandchildren some of the songs, dances, and jokes he performed when he was a vaudeville entertainer. (K–3)

Bassett, Carol. (2003). *Walk like a bear, stand like a tree, run like the wind: Cool yoga, stretching and aerobic activities for cool kids.* Nubod Concepts.
This book includes many fun ways to get your kids moving. (Infants–PreK)

Boyton, Sandra. (1993). *Barnyard dance.* New York: Workman Publishing.
This book tells a story of square-dancing farm animals. Each page also includes dance instructions that children can follow along with as you read. (Infants–PreK)

Carle, E. (1997). *From head to toe.* New York: HarperCollins.
Twelve animals invite children to imitate them as they stomp, wriggle, thump, and clap across the pages. (PreK)

Cauley, L. B. (1992). *Clap your hands.* New York: G. P. Putnam's Sons.
Rhyming text instructs the listener to find something yellow, roar like a lion, give a kiss, tell a secret, spin a circle, and perform other playful activities. (PreK)

Dillon, L., & Dillon, D. (2002). *Rap a tap tap: Here's Bojangles—Think of that!* New York: The Blue Sky Press.
In toe-tapping verse and joyful paintings, this book celebrates the legendary dancing spirit of Mr. Bojangles, with the repetitive phrase, "Rap a tap tap—think of that!" and illustrations of him dancing in the streets, in fancy clothes, with bands, and with rhythm. Includes biographical information about Mr. Bojangles. (Infant–PreK)

Geras, A., & McNicholas, S. (2003). *Time for ballet.* New York: Dial Books for Young Readers.
This is the adventure of a little girl who is taking ballet lessons. It illustrates learning some of the ballet poses and preparation for a recital where she plays a cat.

Harter, D. (1997). *Walking through the jungle.* New York: Orchard Books.
A young explorer discovers different animals and terrains of the world before arriving home, safe and sound, for supper. This is a wonderful chant-like story. (PreK)

Helldorfer, M. C., & Nakata, H. (2004). *Got to dance.* New York: Random House Children's Books.
This is the story of a young girl with nothing to do in the summer. She decides to dance. She dances barefoot, at the zoo, under the bus seat, in sneakers, and in shoes with wings. Dancing chases away her summertime blues. (K–2)

Hoff, S. (1994). *Duncan the dancing duck.* New York: Scholastic.
All Duncan wants to do is dance. He becomes so famous that he gets a big show-business award. (PreK–K)

Hoffman, M. (1993). *Amazing Grace.* New York: Scholastic.
Although a classmate says that she cannot play Peter Pan in the school play because she is black, Grace discovers that she can do anything she sets her mind to do, with the encouragement of her grandmother. (K–3)

Holabird, K. (1983). *Angelina ballerina.* New York: Clarksin N. Potter.
A pretty mouse wants to become a ballerina more than anything in the world. (PreK–1)

Landy, Joanne M., & Burridge, Keith R. (2000). *Ready to Use Fundamental Motor Skills and Movement Activities for Young Children.* Canada: The Center for Applied Research in Education.

This book contains fundamental motor skills and movement activities for young children. (PreK–3)

Martin, B., & Archambault, J. (1985). *Here are my hands*. New York: Henry Holt and Company.
The owner of a human body celebrates it by pointing out various parts and mentioning their function, from "hands for catching and throwing" to the "skin that bundles me in." (K–3)

Marzallo, J. (1990). *Pretend you're a cat*. New York: Trumpet Club.
Rhyming verses ask the reader to purr like a cat, scratch like a dog, leap like a squirrel, and bark like a seal. (PreK–K)

Newcome, Zita. (2002). *Head, shoulders, knees, and toes: And other action counting rhymes*. Cambridge, MA: Candlewick Press.
This book contains more than 50 verses, with energetic illustrations that get kids moving. (Infant–PreK)

Pica, Rae. (2003). *Teachable transitions: 190 activities to move from morning circle to the end of the day*. Beltsville, MD: Gryphon House.
This book makes everyday transitions fun and valuable learning experiences. (PreK–3)

For additional resources involving creativity and the arts with young children, visit our Web site at **www.earlychilded.delmar.com**

 REFERENCES

Andrews, G. (1954). *Creative rhythmic movement for children*. Englewood Cliffs, NJ: Prentice Hall.

Campbell, L., Campbell, B., & Dickinson, D. (1996). *Teaching and learning through multiple intelligences*. Needlam Heights, MA: Allyn & Bacon.

Carson, L. M. (1994). Preschool physical education: Expanding the role of teacher preparation. *Journal of Physical Education, Recreation & Dance, 65*(6), 50–53.

Gallahue, D. L., & Ozmun, J. C. (1995). *Understanding motor development: Infants, children, adolescents, adults*. Madison, WI: Brown & Benchmark.

Gardner, H. (1983). *Frames of mind: The theory of multiple intelligences*. New York: Basic Books.

Given, B. K. (2000). Theaters of the mind. *Educational Leadership, 58*(3), 72–75.

Hinitz, B. F. (1980, November). *History of dance in early childhood education*. Paper presented at the Annual Meeting of the National Association for the Education of Young Children, San Francisco, CA.

Hoffman, H. A., Young, J., & Klesius, S. E. (1981). *Meaningful movement for children: A developmental theme approach to physical education*. Dubuque, IA: Kendall/Hunt.

John-Steiner, V. (1985). *Notebooks of the mind: Explorations of thinking*. Albuquerque, NM: University of New Mexico Press.

Laban, R. (1963). *Modern educational dance*. London: MacDonald and Evans.

Lee, M. (1993). Learning through the arts. *The Journal of Physical Education, Recreation & Dance, 64*(5), 42–47.

Maxim, C. W. (1997). *Sensory motor skills in the very young: Guiding children from infancy through the early years*. Upper Saddle River, NJ: Merrill.

Partnow, E. (2001). *The quotable woman, the first 5,000 years*. New York: Checkmark Books.

Pica, R. (2004). *Experiences in movement: Birth to age 8* (3rd ed.). Clifton Park, NY: Thomson Delmar Learning.

Pica, R. (1999). *Moving and learning across the curriculum*. Clifton Park, NY: Thomson Delmar Learning.

Potter, B. (1976). *The tale of Peter Rabbit*. New York: Frederick Warne and Company.

CREATIVE DRAMA

CHAPTER 8

Creative drama is an appropriate avenue for young children
to express and improvise their ideas. Several types of creative drama will be examined in
this chapter, including sociodramatic play, pantomime, group drama, puppets, literature
enactment, and conflict resolution. In each area of the dramatic arts, children create their
own action, dialog, sound effects, and props. The focus is not on performance but on the
nurturing of children's ability to express their ideas in a supportive environment.

After studying this chapter, you will be able to:
- **Explain the relationship between drama and how young children learn.**
- **Identify the benefits of including creative drama in early childhood classrooms.**
- **Discuss the different types of drama that can be used with young children.**
- **Determine the fundamental elements in creative drama and play making.**
- **Use readers' theater effectively with primary children.**

OBSERVATION OF CREATIVITY

A group of young children listen intently to their teacher telling
a folk tale, *The Turnip*. Every child is focused on the teller, as she
describes how the seed was planted, who cared for it, and how
many different people tried to pull the enormous turnip out of
the ground. At the end of the story, she explains that a tiny blue
bird added the pull that released the turnip. After the telling, the
teacher poses several questions about the happenings in the story.
Why did the turnip get so big? How many people tried to pull the
turnip up? How big was the gigantic turnip? Which character would
you like to be? As the characters are named, the teacher writes them
on a large flip chart. She talks with the children about "acting out"
the story. Next, each child is able to choose what character she or
he would like to play. Mary Ann chose to be the little girl who
pulled behind her mother. Jessie wants to be the father, because he
is very strong. Dedra wants to be the grandma. Camisha wants to
be the tiny bird that helped the others pull the turnip out of the
ground.

The teacher and children talk about the story and the important happenings that occurred. Informally, the children begin to
dramatize the story. Although they follow the sequence of the story,
they use their own words to describe the events. They did, however,

WHAT WAS OBSERVED?

The young children were active
participants as they reenacted the folk
tale. Each child was able to choose the
part they were comfortable playing
and could perform successfully. The
young actors worked cooperatively,
while extemporaneously adjusting
their lines, as they interacted with the
other characters. They demonstrated
their interest and enjoyment, when
they exclaimed, "Let's do it again!"

retain the repetitive sentence that was used throughout the story, "They pulled, and pulled, and pulled, but the turnip would not come up." When the little bird pulls the imaginary turnip out of the ground, all the children cheer, "We did it, we did it!" After a brief pause, they add, "Let's do it again!"

✿ CREATIVE DRAMATICS

Creative drama is a powerful learning medium that emerges from the spontaneous play of young children. In sociodramatic play, the highest level of symbolic play, children create their own happenings based on their experiences. In this pretend play, they develop roles and language that follow the interest of the children who are working cooperatively around a chosen theme, center, or event. Sociodramatic play engages young children and provides the bridge to dramatizations. Children have a natural interest in play and enjoy "acting out" events (Toye & Prendiville, 2000).

A kindergartener is thinking about her role, as she selects an outfit to wear.

Creative drama uses the art of theater to build and enhance participants' artistic sensitivity and develop dramatic imagination. It allows participants to imagine and reflect on experiences, real or imagined. The dramatic process is practical, immediate, and engages both the emotions and the intellect. Children are asked to step out of real situations and project themselves into imagined ones and roles. Individual and group drama experiences enhance the participant's ability to communicate ideas, images, and feelings through action (Pinciotti, 1993).

It is important to make a distinction between sociodramatic play and creative dramatics (theme fantasy play). Sociodramatic play involves pretend activities such as setting a table, putting a doll to bed, or cooking dinner. Creative dramatics, also referred to as thematic-fantasy play, consists of imaginary scenarios and fictional narrative. During this fantasy play, children create an imaginary world based on the plots of stories they have heard or from their own imagination (Hendy & Toon, 2001). Bruner described these two forms as "paradigmatic mode" and "narrative mode." He further explained that paradigmatic thought is involved with experiences, sequence, and analytical thinking. Role-playing of familiar people is an example of a sociodramatic activity. Narrative thinking requires the construction of real or imagined events. This fantasy play is a more complex activity and requires interactive story making (Bruner, 1986).

Creative drama is more structured than sociodramatic play. It makes use of a story that has a beginning and ending. It is an improvised drama in which the characters create the dialog. The words are not written down or memorized, but often become more detailed each time the drama is repeated by the children. The story can be a classic that has been read or an original created by the children. Few props and costumes are used in creative drama. It is not prepared for an audience but rather is designed to enhance children's expression and artistic development (McCaslin, 1990).

Drama Terms

Characters. The people who carry out the story and action. Often, the characters use dialog as they communicate with each other.

Children's theater. This indicates a formal dramatic production that is directed, for which dialog is memorized, and that is performed for an audience.

Cooperative work. The ability to work with a group and adjust personal ideas during the process.

Creative drama. An informal technique that includes spontaneous acting without rehearsals and props.

Drama in Education (DIE). The use of drama as a way of teaching other subjects in school. It can be used to study a specific topic and learn more about the area.

Focus. Concentrating on the drama and staying involved in the process.

Plot. The sequence of events in the drama that creates the meaning; setting the place where the action occurs.

Sociodramatic play. Children imitate the actions and people that they have experienced in their play. They repeat, solve problems, and relive these experiences.

Use of body. The coordination of the body in drama to communicate with the use of gestures, facial expressions, and movement.

Verbal expression. Speaking clearly and effectively using volume, tone, pitch, and pauses. It includes the ability to improvise dialog.

✿ DRAMA MATCHES HOW YOUNG CHILDREN LEARN

According to the theories of cognitive learning, most child development theorists and researchers agree that young children learn through play and experiences within their environment. Piaget (1963) explained that gesture and mime are language in motion. They are the real social language of children. Drama provides a connection between language and movement, bridging the spoken word and the real thing.

Drama begins with the concept of meaningful communication, and provides many opportunities for social interaction and feedback. These interactions offer the support Vygotsky (1978) deemed necessary for the internalization of new knowledge. For example, Talley is pretending to be the troll who lives under the bridge that scares the three Billy Goats Gruff. While practicing the role, a classmate reminds him, "The troll is scary, but not too, too, scary." As a result of this interaction, Talley uses a low voice and big gestures, but he tries not to make the sounds "too scary."

> "The essential value of drama lies in drama's unique power to stir human emotions through its sensory-aesthetic qualities."
>
> *G. B. Siks, 1983*

"I hear and I forget. I see and I remember. I do and I understand."

Chinese Proverb
(in Fitzhenry, 1993)

MULTISENSORY LEARNING

Drama is well-suited to the way young children learn because it is **multisensory.** The dramatic arts involve three of Gardner's (1983) multiple intelligences: bodily-kinesthetic, spatial, and linguistic. In drama, action and visual elements support verbal language, creating multiple connections in the brain. During the enactment of *The Turnip,* the little girl determined where the seed was planted (spatial intelligence) and how hard she would pull (bodily-kinesthetic intelligence). She used her language (linguistic intelligence) to ask for help when unable to get the turnip out of the ground. This drama required that she use three types of intelligences, which made connections between different parts of her brain and integrated thinking.

Social-Emotional Development

Social skills can be developed in drama. Working together, children and adults determine the conclusion, overcome difficulties, and solve problems that arise in the story to be dramatized. During the dramatic process, they interact and cooperate in an active partnership. Children also experience working with peers as they negotiate plans and implement the drama. In these interactions, children begin to understand how to work together while having an impact on their creation. These collaborative efforts are effective in fostering a community of learners in which there is mutual respect for diverse ideas and approaches.

The addition of a bouquet of flowers to the home living center inspires a pretend wedding.

BACKGROUND OF CREATIVE DRAMA FOR YOUNG CHILDREN

With respect to young children, the field of drama has had an impact on policy decisions, for which commitments can be seen at two levels. On the preschool level, there has been increased interest in the importance of drama. This has been developed through the reexamination of play and physical activity as essential for social and cognitive growth during the early years. In addition, developmentally appropriate models have used dramatic play to integrate learning into the curriculum. At the primary school level, new regulations for states have embraced the arts as an essential component of the curriculum. They have included drama as equal to other forms of art. For the first time, the language of dramatic learning is being incorporated into early childhood programs.

STAGES OF DRAMA DEVELOPMENT

The artistic and developmental roots of creative drama are seen as a learning continuum that extends from the beginning of spontaneous imaginative play in the very young child to the creative activity and production of a theater performance. Creative drama provides the medium that elaborates and extends young children's dramatic play. It develops into an understanding and respect for the process, and later the product, of theater. Early experiences begin with imitation and expand into new areas. The child is able to make a connection between imagination and action. Although both creative drama and imaginative play use many of the same dramatic learning strategies, creative drama is a more structured and complex learning activity. Both involve communication, movement, gesture, and dialog about imagined objects, events, or characters.

Imaginative play requires unstructured time, a place for things to happen, and props to support the activity. It is the process that is most meaningful. In creative drama, there is a leader who encourages and stimulates dramatic learning. This person sets the goals, introduces the experiences, and assists in dramatic production. The group may work together to create the **story line,** events, and conclusion.

Children become aware of drama's purpose and power as they are better able to transform self, objects, and place to create a shared reality. This ability to transform begins early, as the toddler uses a toy telephone to represent the real thing. As ability progresses, the preschooler may use a block to represent a bulldozer. In later childhood, a child places an imaginary crown on the king's head, demonstrating that he has an internal symbol for the object.

Creative drama activities allow children to experiment, rehearse, and recreate actions and words in a social setting. As children get older, they develop an understanding of setting, mood, conflict, plot, time, relationships, and theater. They begin to explore the roles of actor, writer, director, designer, and audience member. These expanded abilities provide an avenue for complex discussion of story and roles.

Creative drama is not **junior theater.** Creative drama is not performed for a paying audience and does not include endless rehearsals. The emphasis is on the educational and artistic benefits for the participants, not on the quality of the final production.

Improvised drama can be begun at the age of five or six, although it can be used with students into high school, where it is often referred to as "improvisation." Creative drama is centered on participation of the children rather than on sharing. In this activity, the children in the group who are not actors are observers of the drama rather than an audience. Frequently, the drama is replayed with different children in the roles and previous actors becoming observers. This provides many opportunities to discuss the actions, roles, thinking process, and conclusion.

Drama in Education (DIE) is begun during the elementary years. The object is to develop understanding of an event, historical period, or topic being studied.

Rather than dramatizing a story, the children imagine themselves in the moment, time, or place. Although a play may result, the ultimate goal is to learn more about the topic through the dramatization.

❧ | BENEFITS OF CREATIVE DRAMA

Creative drama activities require children to recall personal, sensory-rich experiences and select dramatic actions to express these images. In *The House of Make-Believe,* Dorothy and Jerome Singer (1990) discuss the benefits of imagery and imagination. As children grow older, drama becomes the extension of their imaginary play. The connections between imagination and action, begun as a young child, become more flexible and fluent with experience.

Language Development

Oral language is used and expanded in drama. During this critical period of language learning, young children need many opportunities to talk, expand their vocabulary, and listen to the words of others. Research indicates that children who attend programs with a creative dramatics component, have advanced language and are able to communicate their ideas verbally. In a summary of research studies investigating the relationship between drama and oral language, 21 studies showed significant improvement in oral language or reading skills (Vitz, 1983). Similar results were found in both kindergarten and primary-grade children.

Oral language is an essential element in cognitive development during the first eight years of life, and provides the basis for literacy development, including reading and writing. Drama is an effective tool—it has a positive impact on the oral language development of young children.

Extemporaneous Speaking

Creative drama focuses on the extemporaneous use of language. Although the children are aware of the story elements, they select the words, gestures, and voices that they will use as the drama is occurring. These spontaneous interactions require the child to listen to the other characters and quickly determine how they will respond. This is a useful skill that will be needed in drama and life experiences. Seldom do children and adults present a prepared speech. But, they are frequently asked to give their ideas and opinions and to participate in discussions.

Social and Emotional Development

One of the strengths of creative drama is the opportunity for small group work. In drama, children interact and communicate to create a community of ideas, images, and actions. As they adjust their action in response to the group, children gain skills in negotiating and collaborating. Through improvisational activities, young children begin to adjust to the responses of the group. They develop the ability to reflect and think on their feet. Working in a group continually requires the child to participate in cognitive, social, and emotional exchanges. Drama facilitates social development because it requires interaction, negotiation, and cooperation. Emotional development is also enhanced as children are encouraged to express and explore their feelings.

Experiences in creative drama promote response acquisitions through teacher instructions and modeling. The teacher guides the students in teamwork and cooperation. Rules are kept simple, with guidelines such as listening when others speak and giving space to others. Children gain emotional skills as they deal with conflict, frustration, and problem-solving. They gain the perspective of others as they discuss actions and experience different roles. Teachers should encourage evaluation of the drama by analyzing the story, timing, and teamwork, rather than specific actions of each child. The goal is to improve the drama, not to criticize what went wrong (Freeman, Sullivan, & Fulton, 2003).

Developing Imagination

To work creatively, a person must be able to use his or her imagination. It is necessary to move beyond today's experiences and project into another situation and a different person. Creative dramatics and play making provide the avenues to develop imagination as children move into make-believe, problem-solving, and responding spontaneously. Through drama, the imagination can be stimulated and pleasure can be found by participating. Although young children learn through experiences, drama provides a way to vicariously explore feelings, roles, response, and creative approaches (McCaslin, 1990).

✿ | PROCESS OR PRODUCT

Most drama professionals believe that young children should participate in drama that is process-oriented without a focus on the product. Young children learn by participating in the drama without unnecessary demands that relate to an effective performance (Brown, 1990). Informal drama allows children to respond extemporaneously and to adapt to the situation in a flexible way. The focus is on learning with participation throughout the creative process.

In the art center, children create props to be used in their play.

Empowering Children

In modern society, older and more powerful human beings govern young children's lives. Yet learning to control one's life is a crucial developmental task. It is important for early childhood educators to provide safe and appropriate ways for the child to explore his independence. Drama provides an excellent vehicle for children to make choices or decisions and solve problems. The teacher–learner partnership in drama provides a forum for cooperative undertaking in which children are able to negotiate and work with others toward a satisfying goal (Warren, 1993).

The long-term benefits of creative drama include:

- independent thinking
- problem-solving
- collaboration skills
- empathy for others
- putting creative ideas into action
- development of imagination
- expanding oral language
- developing moral and spiritual values
- understanding of self
- learning to make decisions and choices

✿ TYPES OF DRAMA FOR YOUNG CHILDREN

There is a large variety of drama activities appropriate to use with young children. Their developmental level and background experiences, as well as their interests and needs, should be considered when determining what drama experiences are appropriate for a specific group of children. The range of possibilities provides options for early childhood educators designing a program to nurture the arts, including drama.

Dramatic Play and Sociodramatic Play

Sociodramatic play is the imaginative play that occurs during the early years of a child's life. During this play, children explore familiar experiences as they take on roles, develop sequence, and use language in the activity. Dramatic play helps young children move from egocentric thinking to becoming more capable of adapting and adjusting to others (Smilansky, 1990). It allows them to practice roles and experiences as they try to understand how the world works.

When a center is designed appropriately, children are able to play for an extended period of time. The teacher is free to observe and record what is happening in the area. These observations provide the teacher an opportunity to determine the effectiveness of the center and document skills the children use when involved in meaningful activities. These annotations provide a tool for assessing the development of young children who are using the center.

Thematic centers provide a focus for children's play that encourages related roles and use of selected materials. In classrooms where there is limited space prop boxes can be prepared to store and retrieve materials that will be included in the changing thematic centers. For example, a prop box for a fitness center could contain an appointment book, movement tapes, exercise clothes, small balls, jump ropes, and other related materials. It is helpful to label the prop box with the dates when the center was used and props that are needed for future use.

Prop Boxes

An effective way to organize play materials to be rotated into the early childhood classroom is by using prop boxes. A large clear plastic container can be used to collect and store props that can be used to encourage play around a specific theme. A beauty salon prop box could contain a blow dryer (plug removed), combs, brushes, empty spray bottles, hair magazines, appointment book, cape, and a hand-held mirror. This box can be labeled and stored in the classroom until the beauty salon center is set up. Once the prop box is created, the teacher and parents can add items throughout the year—extending the collection and potential play opportunities.

Suggestions for the Classroom

Play in learning centers provides an appropriate environment to encourage sociodramatic play. Open-ended centers such as blocks and housekeeping allow children to choose their roles and construct an understanding of the world during their play. In the pretend roles, they are able to communicate in meaningful ways and develop social skills. Thematic centers establish the setting and direct the play that occurs in the area. For example, a greenhouse center will encourage roles and activities that focus on growing plants, arranging a display, and selling the flowers.

It is helpful to plan centers by establishing learning objectives, selecting props, making a plan for the space, and evaluating the effectiveness of the center. Observations of the learning centers and the activities of the children using the areas allow the teacher to add props as needed, make adjustments, and close the center when interest is dwindling. An example of a creative center for the classroom is found in Figure 8–1. Figure 8–2 illustrates the web of integrated learning in the flea market/garage sale center.

Pantomime

Pantomime is the use of movement and gestures to express ideas or feelings. Communication is obtained through action, not words (Salisbury, 1986). Pantomime can be an effective beginning drama experience for young children because it does not require language or dialog. Therefore, pantomime can provide both a safe and successful initial experience with drama. It is easier for young children to begin pantomiming familiar activities such as walking in snow or sand. More advanced pantomimes ask the child to express a mood or feeling. For example, a child could walk as though he had just found out that his best friend could not come home with him. Later, children can begin to work with characterizations: the funny shoe salesman, the clumsy pizza maker, or the fisherman who can't catch a fish.

FIGURE 8–1
A Creative Center
for the Classroom:
Flea Market–
Garage Sale (Isbell,
1995).

Flea Market/Garage Sale Center

Learning Objectives of the Center

1. To collect and produce items that can be sold to others.
2. To experience the buying and selling of products.
3. To expand language by communicating with others.
4. To learn that some items can be recycled instead of thrown away.
5. To collaborate with others in managing the sale.

Vocabulary Enrichment

Some new words that might be included in the flea market are:

- display
- useful
- cost
- money
- products
- mark down
- change
- booths
- recycle
- sale
- receipt
- barter
- treasure
- purchase
- haggle
- free
- names of specific items that will be sold

Teacher-Collected Props

1. Several low tables, sheets of fabric, or canopies to cover some displays.
2. Items for selling, such as old clothing, small appliances, car accessories, used books, old children's toys, and kitchen tools. The choices are unlimited.
3. Money box with play money and receipts.
4. Labels, markers, and plastic bags (in which to put purchases).

Child-Made Props

1. Advertisements for the sale.
2. Items that could be sold, such as original paintings, clay sculptures, plants they have started (spider plants, piggyback plants, and ferns), and flower bouquets they have made.
3. Refreshments that could be sold, such as popcorn, cookies, lemonade, hot chocolate, fruit, and trail mix.

Adding a Spark

When interest in the center is fading, have a sale. Mark down all the items in the center and sell out. Children can create new price tags, regroup items, or change displays to encourage selling.

Evaluation of the Flea Market Center

1. Are children making items to sell in the flea market center?
2. Are children talking about reusing items, creating products, and setting up appealing displays?
3. Are children using "money" as they buy and sell in the market?
4. Is creativity enhanced as they think about new products and displays?
5. Are children working cooperatively to set up and maintain the flea market?

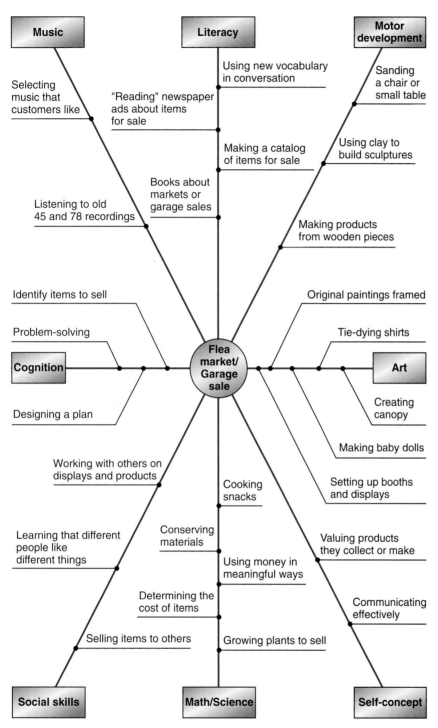

FIGURE 8–2
Web of integrated learning in the flea market/garage sale center.

Suggestions for the Classroom

Pantomime

Preschool to Kindergarten:

- eating an ice cream cone, a hot dog, or Popsicle
- walking a big dog, tiny dog, or several dogs
- mopping the floor
- getting dressed in the morning for cold weather or a heat wave
- climbing on a play structure
- playing with a baby
- soothing a crying baby
- playing in mud, snow, pebbles, and water

Primary Grades:

- eating different foods, such as spaghetti, sour pickle, hot cereal, pizza, or a gigantic taco
- visiting the grocery store, discount store, hair salon, shoe store, shopping mall, post office, restaurant, or other local spot
- a sequence of events, such as playing soccer, taking a ballet class, eating lunch, and playing in a baseball game
- visiting an aquarium or museum, or other field trip
- playing a drum or trombone, or being drum major in a parade
- swimming in a pool
- walking on hot sand, snow, or a steep trail
- feeding a pet
- riding on a crowded school bus

More Complicated Pantomimes (Situations):

- You are getting ready for your birthday party. You and your sister are going to decorate the table. What decorations are needed? Will there be presents? What about the cake?
- You get up on Saturday morning and it is snowing very hard. The lights and television go off in your house. What will you do? Is it cold? What can you fix for breakfast?
- Your friends are going to get a pizza with the team coach. You don't have any money, but you really want to go. What would you do? How could you get some pizza?

With each positive experience in drama, children build their confidence. They become more willing to take risks, try out roles, and make suggestions for improvement. Pantomime shapes perception and stimulates imagination as children remember actions, objects, and feelings.

Participation Stories

Another simple way to involve children in nonthreatening drama experiences is using participation stories. Stories that have chants, sound effects, and repeated phrases invite children to participate. As the story is read or told, the children participate in the presentation by listening attentively and providing the play elements. For example, the well-known folk tale, *The Little Red Hen* has a cast of characters who reply, "Not I." And ultimately say, "I will help you eat the bread." By inviting the children into the story, they have a safe beginning experience of saying a line, following the story, and repeating the final sentence with others. Aesop's fable of *The Tortoise and the Hare* can have participation segments including, "I'm the fastest rabbit in the town," or the turtle that says, "Slow and steady wins the race." Sound effects can draw children into the story as the car races down the street or the children cheer (Stotter, 2000). For a shy child or a child unsure of her capabilities, these group responses provide a safe way to participate and build confidence.

Creative Dramatics and Play Making

Children can participate in drama by improvising dialog and action. For young children, the goal is the personal development of the players instead of a professional performance. Creative drama is often guided by the teacher or leader, but seldom includes any scenery or costumes.

> "The unique thing about creative dramatics is that it is always improvised. It is never fixed by being written and memorized, but is different at each playing."
>
> W. Ward, 1952

Geraldine Siks, a leading authority on children's drama, believes that young children (up to the age of eleven) should participate only in informal drama. Children should have many opportunities to create their own dialog before they move into reciting memorized lines. According to Siks and Dunnington (1967), in creative dramatics, the child is an active participant who shapes the happenings. This is an important step in the development of dramatic ability. With each playing of the story, it becomes more organized and detailed, yet it remains extemporaneous and is not designed for the audience (McCaslin, 1990). If teachers are to assist children in their playmaking, they need to understand the structure and fundamental elements.

Characters. The people, animals, or imaginary characters deliver the story. They must be believable and be appropriate for the drama.

Theme. The underlying thought or basic idea of the story.

Plot. The plot is the story—what happens between the beginning and ending. The plot can be simple or complex, but it must interest the children.

Dialog. What is said by the characters in the story. Their words and lines carry the message of the story.

Mood. Created by the sound effects and music, which can produce feelings and a dramatic element to the story.

Climax. The final conclusion to the story.

Story Dramatization

Story dramatization involves creating an improvised play based on a story or piece of literature. A leader guides the development and possibilities that can occur during the creative process. The children act out the play using improvised dialog and action. There are many different ways literature can inspire drama, such as providing content for puppet shows, sequence for pantomime, and characters for shadow plays. Several stories to dramatize with young children are included in Appendix C.

Suggestions for the Classroom

Read or tell the story. Discuss the storyline, characters, and plot. Let children select their roles. If the group is large, have a small number of children participate in the dramatization, while the others become observers. Then reverse the groups. After the dramatization, talk with the children about their thoughts, feelings, and reactions to the process.

Steps in Story Dramatization

1. Presentation of the story: read or told
2. Organization of characters, scene, space, and material
3. Improvisation of story
4. Evaluation: talking about the happenings
5. Replay: do it again

Child-Created Plays

Children can be inspired to create their own plays after an interesting experience or field trip. Plays created by children can also be the culmination of a study or project. Most of these plays are developed over a period of time. The children will determine if they need simple scenery and costumes. They create the lines or dialog, but they are not memorized. The children know the story line and plot because they created the drama. Sometimes, primary-grade children will cooperatively write a play and the dialog to be used. In this instance, their script is used as they rehearse the story. The writing, performing, and evaluating of the play makes an excellent literacy activity. It is also a group effort that will develop social skills and build confidence in dramatic capabilities.

For example, within a primary classroom, children have been studying medieval times. From their research came a play that was written by several children to perform for other members of the class. It was an inspiring experience, and other members of the class wanted to present the play again and again. Each time, the original cast assisted the other children in their production. This play provided the children with an avenue to put their research into action and enriched their understanding of the medieval period of history.

Puppetry

"Puppets offer children two ways to express creativity: 1) making the puppet and 2) making the puppet come to life."

M. Mayesky, 1998

Storytelling and **puppetry** are ancient forms of oral expression that developed historically in similar ways. The oral story was passed down from generation to generation. These stories were a binding link for families and cultures. The puppeteer often augmented the storytelling by providing visualization and surprise elements to the story presentation. The design and use of puppets has been influenced greatly by the culture and society of the puppeteer. A diverse cultural influence can be seen in ornate Chinese shadow puppets and in the pure geometric form of African rod puppets. From these historical roots of oral language and cultural transmission, a new view of puppets has emerged.

Currently, a new variety of puppets are appearing that are personally expressive and appeal to wider audiences. These changes have moved puppets from being

A simple stage encourages a child to use a puppet to tell a story.

used exclusively for entertainment to tools that can be used in education, therapy, and communication. Jim Henson's Sesame Street Muppets have had a powerful influence on this transformation. His popular use of large, expressive Muppets has led to an increased interest in puppets and the role they can play in education (Raines & Isbell, 1994).

Young children are drawn to puppets. This magnetic quality can provide a powerful experience in drama for young children. A puppet becomes a tool for children to use in expressing ideas and personal views. Some shy children may become quite verbal when the puppet does the talking. Young children believe the puppet is real, whereas primary-grade children pretend that the puppet is alive. Both age groups enjoy listening to a wonderful story presented by the teacher/puppeteer or use puppets to tell the story themselves.

Suggestions for the Classroom

Provide a collection of puppets in the dramatic area. Select animals that could be used in the enactment of a number of stories. For example, a group of farm animal puppets can be used in many different stories and experiences. These will provide the stimulus for a puppet show.

Storytelling

Stories told orally, without the use of written text, provide children with opportunities to visualize characters and events. The storyteller uses words, gestures, and sometimes props to convey the meaning of the story. Storytellers often use folktales that have a long history of being shared orally and continue to be effective with

Puppet possibilities.

Rolled paper tubes

Some simple puppets

Posterboard figure

Hamburger box puppet

Finger puppets

Old glove

Holes for fingers

Paper cup

Hollow rubber ball

Slit

Small cream box

Paper bag puppets

Sock puppet

today's children. The teller selects and adapts the story to match the developmental level of the children in the audience. The teller creatively weaves his story and captures the imagination of the children as they enjoy both the teller and the story.

Recent research on how the mind develops supports what many storytellers have long believed. Stories help children organize their thinking, reflect on the content, remember the sequence, and gain understanding of other people. Research of people throughout the world also demonstrates that storytelling is a way to preserve traditions and transmit cultural beliefs (Jalongo, 2003).

Toddlers and preschoolers particularly enjoy stories that have:

- predictable patterns that include repetitive phrases
- characters that are understandable
- a setting they can visualize
- a moral that gives meaning to the story
- sounds or gestures that accompany the telling

It is important to select appropriate stories for each age group. Examples of stories appropriate for preschool and primary children can be found in *Tell It Again* (1999) by Raines and Isbell, and *Tell It Again 2* (2000) by Isbell and Raines. Stories for telling preschoolers include "Three Billy Goats Gruff" (1999), "Teeny Tiny" (1999), "The Little Red Hen" (2000), and "Johnny Cake" (1999). Primary-grade children enjoy stories that are more complex in nature. The stories should be selected to match the specific group of children and their interests. Examples of stories to tell primary children include "The Four Musicians" (1999), "The Story of the Ugly Duckling" (1999), "The Lost Mitten with Tiny, Shiny Beads" (1999), "The Boy Who Cried Wolf" (2000), and some of *Aesop's Fables*. Less familiar stories as well as personal stories, can add spice to storytelling experiences.

Children as Tellers

Children who have experience listening to stories begin to tell their own stories. Their first tellings often will be very close to the stories they have heard. Later, they will change characters and elements of the story as they tell it again. When they have gained confidence in their storytelling ability, they will begin to create original stories. These will include elements of story understanding such as a beginning, "Once upon a time"; and an ending, "That's the end of my story"; and a narrative, "The donkey said hee-haw, hee-haw all the way home." These demonstrate a "sense of story" described by Applebee (1978) in his studies of young children. Research has identified specific benefits of storytelling to young children. When children listen to stories told, they increase their comprehension of the story, identify more elements of the sequence, and are more fluent in their retellings. Hearing a storyteller use voices, gestures, and sounds inspires children to use these techniques in their stories (Isbell, Sobol, Lindauer, & Lowrance, 2004). Young children are drawn to narrative. This interest helps them gain skills and knowledge when the story is told. Storytelling enhances children's imagination, supports social development, and enhances cognitive skills (Phillips, 2000). Teachers who tell stories inspire children to tell their own stories, providing them with opportunities to develop more sophisticated listening and speaking abilities.

Stories that are told by the teacher or a visiting teller can serve as a stimulus for creative drama. Hearing stories told aloud allows children to internalize the images and characters that will assist them as they begin to dramatize a story. Every

Suggestions for the Primary Classroom

Tell Rudyard Kipling's story of *The Elephant's Child* (Kipling & Cauley, 1983) who can't stop asking questions. Talk with the children about the questions the elephant's child asked and the responses he received. Then pose the question, "How did the elephant get the long trunk?" Encourage the children to retell or create their own version of this classic story and record it for the library area. The children will enjoy hearing it again, looking at the book, and appreciating the recorded retellings of their classmates.

child can become a storyteller if provided a supportive environment with appropriate opportunities (Hamilton & Weiss, 1990).

- Experience Stories: This is simply relating experiences that are personally meaningful—First day of school, things that make us laugh, a time when we were lost, the best birthday present.
- Jokes and Rhymes: Children enjoy humor and relating funny happenings or silly jingles.
- Retelling Stories: Familiar stories provide a safe way to begin telling stories.
- Transforming a Story: Taking a familiar story and making it different. *The Three Little Pigs* become *The Three Little Rabbits*.
- Writing an Original Story: Telling it.

Presentation or Performance

It is helpful to make a distinction between presentations and performances. Presentations come from children's work that was created in small groups. These dramatizations, which are shared in the safe classroom environment, are enjoyable experiences. The main purpose of these presentations is to communicate the children's ideas to others. Opportunities for sharing these dramas can include group time or presenting to other groups, another class, or a parent meeting. These experiences give children the opportunity to develop their skills at speaking and dramatizing, and to learn about audiences' responses. The drama is shared and enjoyed by both the participants and the audience.

Children who have had successful experiences with presentations over a period of time may be ready to make the transition from classroom drama to performing. Performances are more focused on a rehearsed production that appeals to the audience (Hendy & Toon, 2001).

Readers' Theater

Readers' theater is a relatively new concept in the creative arts. It is particularly appropriate for older children who are able to read fluently. Readers' theater is a way of enjoying good literature through an oral presentation using a written script. There are many different ways to implement a readers' theater, ranging from sitting in a chair to including movement that coincides with the text. Stories also can be partially narrative, with readers assuming the roles of specific characters during the presentation. Readers' theater does not require an audience beyond the members of the classroom. Some of the values of this technique are obtained through the selection process, the oral interpretation of the literature, and the practice in reading aloud. A readers' theater lesson plan is presented in Figure 8–3.

Goals

1. Students will work in small groups to create and perform a mystery Readers' Theater production.
2. Students will practice social and personal skills while working with a group of peers.
3. Students will engage in a meaningful literacy activity.

Objectives

The students will be able to:

- interact easily with peers when working cooperatively.
- use discussion and compromise to resolve conflicts.
- make independent choices of materials, activities, and work.
- sustain attention to work over a long period of time.
- follow directions that involve a multistep sequence of actions.
- understand and interpret a story.
- read text fluently, independently, and for varied purposes.
- personally assess their involvement with the use of a rubric.

Materials

The following materials will be needed to conduct this project:

- Readers' Theater checklist
- Readers' Theater rubric
- Director's job list
- Six copies of three plays
- Folders (for the children to store their checklists, rubrics, and scripts)
- Highlighters, pencils, paper, copy machine, tape recorder, audiotape, and video recorder

Introduction

The teacher will enlarge a copy of the Reader's Theater checklist and tape it to the Plan of Action board. Step one of the day's Plan of Action will ask students to read the checklist to become familiar with the steps of this project. During Morning Meeting, the students will discuss the following question: "How can we be responsible while working on our Readers' Theater performance?" The students' responses will be recorded on the board.

Procedure

1. During project time, the teacher will begin the discussion by handing out a rubric for the readers' theater. The rubric will be discussed, and the teacher will role-play instances of specific behavior and ask the students what evaluation they would receive if they did these things. For example, if I really got upset and decided I didn't want to play a specific role and stopped practicing and listening to the director, what evaluation would I receive?

FIGURE 8–3
Implementation of Readers' Theater Lesson Plan: Primary Grades.

FIGURE 8–3
(*continued*)

Readers' Theater Checklist

Name: _____

You will be working with your group to perform a Readers' Theater mystery production. This is not a play, but more like listening to an old-time radio show. Use this checklist to complete the daily activity requirements. Check off the requirements as you complete each one.

Monday

_____ Watch *The Ice Cream Caper*

Tuesday

_____ Review the grading rubric and checklist

_____ Break up into your assigned groups and read the play

_____ Pick someone to be the director

_____ Assign roles and complete the following questions:

My play is: _____

My role is: _____

The director is: _____

Wednesday

_____ Highlight your lines

_____ The director will begin the first reading of the play with everyone reading his or her lines

_____ Pick a prop (one prop per person)

Thursday

_____ Run through the play with everyone reading their lines and using/wearing a prop

_____ Write the program and give it to the teacher to copy (The program should include the title of the play, the director's name, a list of characters and the actors' names, and an illustration)

Friday

_____ Perform your Readers' Theater for the third grade

Readers' Theater Checklist (Courtesy of Stacy Larsen)

2. After the rubric is discussed, the teacher will hand out the Readers' Theater Checklist. This checklist will be used by students to complete daily requirements as they work toward performing their show. The teacher will discuss each step listed on the checklist and highlight the requirements for today (review the rubric and checklist, break into groups, individually read the play, assign a director and roles, and complete three questions).

3. The next step is to break students into three groups (teacher can assign groups or let the students decide who should be in each group). Each group will meet in a designated area of the classroom. The students will follow

the order of requirements found on the checklist. The teacher will walk around to facilitate discussion and model appropriate group behavior. When roles have been assigned, the director will make a list to turn in to the teacher. This list will be enlarged and displayed on the project board. This activity time will be followed by a question-and-answer session.

FIGURE 8–3
(*continued*)

4. This project will take one to two weeks to complete, and the teacher will facilitate the students' work during daily project time. The activity will wrap up with a performance by each group that the teacher will audiotape and videotape. The teacher will make duplicate copies available to the students and their families. Each group has the additional option to present its mystery Readers' Theater performance to other classrooms in the school.

5. Following the performances, students will review their rubric and evaluate their work throughout the project. The teacher will have a conference with each student individually to assess his or her work together.

Readers' Theater Rubric

Name: _____

3
_____ Worked well with the group
_____ Didn't goof off during practice
_____ Presented best effort during performance
_____ Completed all items in the checklist book
_____ Used self-control
_____ Listened to the director
_____ Did not misuse props

2
_____ Used most of the practice time
_____ Performed with so-so effort
_____ Completed most of the checklist book
_____ Participated in the performance
_____ Didn't misuse his or her prop
_____ Usually worked will with the group
_____ Listened to the director

1
_____ Did not work well with the group
_____ Goofed off during practice and rehearsal
_____ Completed less than half of the checklist book
_____ Did not listen to the director
_____ Had trouble using self-control
_____ Misused props
_____ Poor effort during performance

After reading this rubric, I believe I should receive a grade of _____

Readers' Theater Rubric. (Courtesy of Stacy Larsen)

FIGURE 8–3
(*concluded*)

The Director's Job

❏ Help everyone pick a role

❏ Help everyone read their lines correctly

❏ Help people pick a prop

❏ Do the final check of the program and make sure it is given to the teacher to make copies

❏ Hand out the programs

❏ Introduce the play and actors

❏ Help everyone in the group work well together

Remember, you can always ask the teacher for help if you need it.

GOOD LUCK!

The Director's Job (Courtesty of Stacy Larsen)

Evaluation

1. How did each student interact within his or her group?
2. Did the students use discussion and compromise to resolve problems in the group?
3. Were students able to make independent choices for props, roles, and work?
4. How well did students sustain attention to their work throughout the week?
5. Were students able to follow multistep directions when completing the checklist? Did most students complete the checklist appropriately?
6. How well did students interpret their mystery story? Did they convey the meaning appropriately in the performance?
7. How did the students feel about their performances? Did they enjoy the project?

Extension

Provide students the opportunity to write and produce their own mystery story.

✿ DEALING WITH CLASSROOM ISSUES

Sometimes, drama provides an avenue for dealing with class issues. The situation is set, roles selected, and the action occurs spontaneously. This **group process** or playing out of problems allows children to resolve issues and observe the effects of their behavior on others. Children are able to see the situation from another perspective and respond in appropriate ways. For example, the teacher observes Roberta having a difficult time getting into block play. A group of boys seems to be controlling the people who can play in the area. During group time, the teacher leads a discussion about block play. As a class, they brainstorm the different kinds of structures that can be built in the block center. Then the teacher presents a problem: a child wants to play with blocks but is having trouble getting into the area. How can the children playing in this area help this new child join in block play? One of the boys in the block group is given the role of the new child trying to play with blocks. They act out the situation and discover ways to invite the new child into their play. After the dramatization, the children's solutions are discussed and extended. Practicing appropriate responses provides new options for the children and helps them become more aware of the importance of involving everyone in block play. Supporters of the process of creative drama identify the benefit of building personal confidence gained through work in a nonthreatening environment. Success in these activities leads to enhanced self-efficacy, learned appropriate behavior, and reduction of defensive behavior (Freeman, Sullivan, & Fulton, 2003).

✿ PLANNING DRAMA

As with most learning experiences, careful planning by the teacher is essential. But at the same time, the experience must be designed so it allows input from the children. The early childhood educator who is planning drama experiences needs to decide the objectives for the activity, the stimulus for the drama (story, experience, and the like), the focus or problems to be presented, and ideas for possible roles in the drama.

The details of the story line and the actions of the characters in the drama will be left for the children to decide as the drama progresses. Planning for the drama occurs spontaneously as the activity progresses in response to the children's ideas and suggestions. It is important for the children to see their own ideas included and functioning effectively. An appropriate drama experience is one in which the children's ideas are respected and the teacher provides guidance. The teacher must be able to ask questions that will help draw on the children's knowledge and extend their understanding in new ways. Bruner and Haste (1988) and Vygotsky (1986) use the term *scaffolding* to describe the teacher's important role of extending and developing children's knowledge of the world. This approach works effectively in the dramatic arts as the teacher uses the story and the children's dialog to extend their play making.

It often is necessary for the beginning teacher to work closely with a plan. With more experience in drama, the teacher will be able to move to a more skeletal plan that allows the children to have more say in determining their part. The most child-centered drama begins with children's interests and takes direction from the ideas they offer (Brown & Pleydell, 1999). The following is an example of a plan to implement drama in the classroom.

1. *Introduction*

   Before beginning any creative dramatics activity involving imagination, the class must be prepared. The children need to understand what they

This teacher is reading a story that will be dramatized by the children in the group.

are going to do and how the activity works. It may involve reading a story, imagining a place, or revisiting personal experiences. The purpose is to engage the attention of the children and help them relate their own experiences to the idea, story, or poem that will be used in the drama. This preparation period helps young children understand the boundaries and feel more comfortable with the activity.

2. *Presentation of the Story or Situation*
   A story can be told or read. Telling the story allows the children to imagine the happenings in their head without binding them to the illustrations in the book. The reader, or teller, uses his voice to make the story interesting and to emphasize specific parts. Young children should be invited to join in when phrases are repeated throughout the story.

3. *Plan of Action*
   After listening to the story, the teacher and children make a plan of action to act out the story. First, talk about the story or situation with the children; then, review the sequence of events. Let the children volunteer for parts in the drama. Some children will want to have the starring role whereas others are ready to be the tree. It is important for children to decide which part to play; only they can determine their comfort level. As children gain more experience in drama and when their involvement is valued, they will increase their level of participation.

4. *The Teacher's Role*
   Teachers have at least three roles to choose from during drama experiences. One is the side coach, where the teacher gives suggestions from the sideline without stopping the action. A second possibility is to participate in the drama to help the children keep the action going. Sometimes it is

helpful for the teacher to have a role with authority so questions can be asked and action encouraged. With more experienced children, the teacher may assume a minor role that does not shape the drama. The third option is often the best: to be a member of the appreciative audience.

5. *Dramatization*
Try to keep the playful spirit of the drama. Allow children to follow their intuitions and create responsive dialog. Remember to keep the process enjoyable and to be supportive of the children's efforts.

6. *Closing and Evaluation*
Evaluation is an important part of the dramatic process. The children will want to talk about their experience and reflect on the performance. The teacher may ask questions related to the objectives and evaluation of the activity. This often is a forgotten step in creative dramatics, but it is very important. Bringing closure to the activity helps children return to reality and brings them back home.

7. *Plan and Replay*
Repeat the process of planning, acting, and evaluating. Another part of the story could be used or the same story can be repeated with different children playing the roles. The replay allows different children to have parts or change the dialog to revisit the story.

CHILDREN AS AN AUDIENCE

Creative dramatics often are performed in small working groups. The children who are not performing become the audience. After one presentation, these groups may change places—the original actors become the audience and the audience becomes the players. In drama activities, children develop listening skills on two levels. The first level consists of basic listening skills that are required in order for the dramatization to continue, such as listening for clues. The second level involves the evaluative listening skills that develop when children serve as audience members, such as considering how the action is progressing and what they would do differently (McMaster, 1998).

Young children enjoy learning about the role of the audience and their participation in this part of the dramatic production. Children begin to understand that the audience will need to see and hear what is happening in the drama. They learn to listen and watch carefully during the play. Being an audience member is important to the drama because the audience laughs at the appropriate time, cheers for the hero, and shows their appreciation by clapping at the end of the show.

CONVENTIONS OF THE THEATER

Before attending a live theater event, it is helpful for children to understand some of the experiences that are part of this event. Before a performance begins, the lights in the lobby may blink. This tells the audience to take their seats because the performance is about to begin. The performance begins when the lights are dimmed. The curtain closing indicates the act or performance is over. After the performance is over, actors come back on stage to bow while the audience applauds. This is a "curtain call." Young children who have never been to a play or musical production will not understand these signals. It is helpful to talk about the special ways audiences communicate before attending a production. Kindergarten and primary-grade children will enjoy including these conventions in their dramatic play.

❊ THEATER FOR CHILDREN: LIVE PERFORMANCES

Primary-grade children may enjoy attending live performances, if they are carefully selected. Theater productions for children should be filled with action—showing, rather than telling. The story must be meaningful to the children, with characters that are believable. The production should not be too long, and should provide breaks between scenes. Many children's productions include music and dance, which will add to the interest.

Drama expert Nellie McCaslin (1990) identified the basic elements of a play for children:

- a worthwhile theme
- a story that holds interest
- characters that are believable and active
- appropriate scenery and costumes
- music or dance is included

❊ APPRECIATING THEATER

Children can enjoy attending plays, puppet shows, or other performances if the selection is appropriate for their level of development. Productions should be chosen that would be enjoyable for young children to attend. This should not be a stressful experience that requires active children to be quiet and still for a long period of time. Also important in the selection process is the location of the performance. If it requires a one-hour ride on the bus before a two-hour performance, it is probably inappropriate for preschoolers. It would be much more appropriate to attend the rehearsal of a play that is being performed at a closer location.

One of the best ways for young children to enjoy a production is to attend a **rehearsal**. In this less formal setting, young children can be active and curious without distracting the actors or audience. Often, there may be a time when the children can talk with the actors or go on the stage to see the scenery. Primary-grade children may be able to cope with longer programs, but they also need the opportunity to take breaks. Remember that attending a performance is designed to encourage children's interest and nurture an appreciation of drama. It should not be so demanding that it would turn young children off to attending future performances.

Attending live performances also can provide inspiration for reenactment of the play when children return to the classroom. After attending a performance of *Pinocchio,* a marionette could be added to the library area. The performance and the addition of this puppet can provide the stimulus for recreating the story. The observant teacher will be able to determine the children's comprehension of the production by observing their language and play.

❊ GROUPING FOR DRAMA

Another consideration when planning drama is how children will be grouped for the experience. Should the children work individually, in pairs, in small groups, or in one large group? Pairs and small groups provide more opportunity for children to use language and provide further opportunities for more complex dialog. When using a large group, there is more waiting, less sharing, and a smaller audience. These aspects, as well as the drama and form, will be used to determine the grouping for specific activities. As in all areas of art and creativity, it is important to provide variety. Grouping is one of the components that can provide further variation.

Children in Theater

In the children's theater type of drama, a play is written by a playwright and presented by actors in front of an audience. Actors can be adults and/or children who are selected for the parts through audition. Lines are memorized, action is directed, and scenery and costumes are used. This is a formal presentation with the primary purpose of providing entertainment. This formal type of drama is inappropriate for young children because there is a strong focus on practice and performance. Informal drama is more effective where young children develop their abilities in relaxed drama experiences. Some children in third or fourth grade may be interested in participating in community theater or local productions. These experiences should be selected and supervised carefully, to ensure that they are appropriate for the child and his or her developmental level.

CHILDREN WORKING AS A COMMUNITY

Drama is a tool for development of children's social skills. In these positive experiences, children learn how drama works and how a community can collaborate to make things happen. The children become a part of a system that accepts order, takes turns, problem-solves, and respects the ideas of others. In drama, children work together as a unit, and help each other function effectively. Children who have difficulty working with a

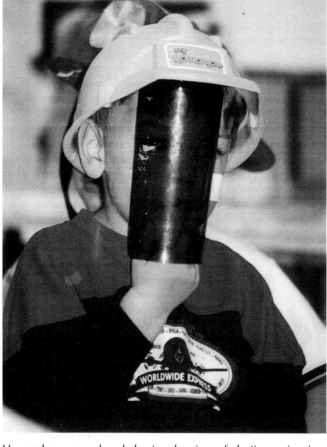

Unusual props, such as helmet and a piece of plastic, can inspire dramatic play.

number of peers may begin working with others as a partner or member of a small group.

All members of the drama community should:

- be respected
- listen carefully to others
- be able to contribute ideas
- help others who are having difficulty
- solve problems collaboratively
- be fair
- operate by democratic values
- care about other's feelings

Drama provides a different way of understanding social and community values. It fosters connections between concrete situations and affective modes. The experience encourages thinking responsibly, thinking creatively, and showing empathy (Toye & Prendiville, 2000). These examples of interpersonal intelligence are described by Gardner (1983) in his theory of multiple intelligences. They are able to discern and respond to needs and desires of other people. In drama, children communicate by sending and receiving messages, as well as trying to understand another person's point of view.

During this process of give and take, children begin to understand themselves—their thoughts, feeling, and emotions. This intrapersonal intelligence is related to the child's ability to detect and symbolize feelings (Gardner, 1983). It also includes knowledge of one's personal strengths and weaknesses. Creative drama, storytelling, pantomime, and story dramatization all provide an avenue to gain understanding of self, while discovering how to work with others in appropriate ways.

 ## SUMMARY

The foundation for the theater arts is built with young children through the use of creative drama. Dramatizations can be developed from improvised stories based on literature, personal experiences, or children's imaginations. All children can be involved in drama as they experience success, learn to listen, contribute ideas, collaborate with others, and support their classmates' creative endeavors. At times, children may want to share their drama with others outside the classroom, but entertaining an audience is not the goal. Rather, the goal is the personal growth of individual children as they actively participate in shaping the creative drama.

It is important that dramatic learning does not stop at the housekeeping center or the block area. Creative drama is indeed a unique art that is appropriate for use with young children in an early childhood classroom. It has the potential for communicating to young children in their own language, the language of make-believe. The physical, visual, and verbal elements of drama make it a multisensory learning experience that is very powerful with young learners (Brown, 1990).

 ## KEY TERMS

characters	plot
children's theater	puppetry
cooperative work	readers' theater
creative drama	rehearsal
Drama in Education (DIE)	social skills
focus	sociodramatic play
group process	story dramatization
junior theater	story line
multisensory	storytelling
oral language	use of body
pantomime	verbal expression

 ## REFLECTION

1. How does creative drama match the developmental level and learning styles of young children?

2. Discuss the similarities and differences of sociodramatic play and creative dramatics.

3. What are some of the benefits of using drama with PreK–K and primary-grade children?

4. Identify and describe some types of drama that are appropriate to use in early childhood classrooms.

5. What are the steps in planning an interesting dramatic experience for a group of young children?

6. What stories or literature would you use to inspire children to participate in drama and reenactment?

THINKING ABOUT THE OBSERVATION OF CREATIVITY

1. How was the story used to encourage the development of a drama?

2. Why is it important for children to select the part they will play?

3. In the production, some lines are repeated as in the book, while the characters create others. Why is this important?

4. What were the benefits of the story dramatization for the children?

POSSIBILITIES FOR ADULT LEARNERS

Activity: Mirror Images

Goal: This activity allows learners to experience drama through a pantomime activity.

Materials: None needed.

Procedure:

1. Pair the students so two people are working together.

2. In the pantomime experience, one person faces the other with hands touching. One person is the mime and the other is the mirror reflecting the action. Allow a few minutes for them to experiment with the leading and following experience.

3. Next, ask the mime to use facial expressions that communicate feelings of happiness, upset, anger, and mischief. Give time between each direction to let the mirror image respond.

4. Now, have the pair reverse roles. This time, ask the mime to communicate without words: very hungry, feeling ill, being upset, and acting silly.

5. Talk about the process and how each person felt in the different roles. Ask them to brainstorm other emotions, actions, or experiences that could be used in this activity.

Activity: Fractured Stories

Goal: This activity will demonstrate the use of connecting drama and literature.

Materials: None needed.

Procedure:

1. Divide the class into groups of five to six students.

2. Ask each group to select a familiar children's story that they can dramatize.

3. After they have determined the story they will use, give them about 10 minutes to choose the roles, the events, and the way they will change the story. If they wish, they can rehearse some parts, but the focus is on the roles and story line. Remind the groups that they can re-create the story in their own way.

4. Each group will share its story and experience, extemporaneously creating the dialog.

OPEN-ENDED ACTIVITIES FOR YOUNG CHILDREN

PreK–K

Activity:	Mask-Making
Goal:	To encourage the development of language and role-playing though the use of masks.
Materials:	Paper plates, yarn, pieces of fabric, metallic paper, hole punch, pipe cleaners, colored paper, and other collected items.
Caution:	Masks may frighten some young children and some cultures may find them offensive.

Procedure:

1. Masks can be an extension of creative drama. The mask can be simple, elaborate, or grotesque, but it is not realistic. A paper plate can serve as a base for a simple mask.

2. Children can experiment with materials to create a three-dimensional quality and make each mask unique. Holes for eyes, mouth, and nose can be cut in the appropriate places with the teacher's assistance, if needed.

3. The children play out a drama while their faces remain hidden behind the created mask. The children can dramatize a story they have heard or create one that uses masked characters.

Primary Grades

Activity:	Making and Using Shadow Puppets
Goal:	To create a puppet than can be used in a different way: shadow play.
Materials:	Sheet, lamp, cardboard, art board, poster paper, scissors, masking and duck tape, dowel rods, and rulers.

Procedure:

1. Flat puppets or rod puppets can be created and used in shadow shows by primary children. Placing a lamp behind a sheet enables the child to make shadows on the sheet.

2. When flat puppets are moved between the light and the sheet, they create silhouettes. These puppets can be cut out of light-weight cardboard or art board, and glued to tongue depressors or sticks.

3. Each child can create a unique puppet of his own design, or a group of children can decide on a play and make specific characters for the drama.

4. Some children may want to create moveable parts for the puppets by using brads in the connecting joints. When attached to a long stick, these puppets can be moved to make body motions.

5. Music and dialog can be added to the shadow show to create additional interest.

Extension: In Asian theater, where shadow plays originated, puppets were made of wood or hide and decorated with elaborate openwork patterns.

RESOURCES FOR MASKS AND PUPPETS

Doney, M. (1995). *Masks.* New York: Franklin Watts.

Fleming, C. S. (1983). Puppets put learning center stage. *Learning, 11*(9), 94–98.

Hunt, T. (1984). *Pocketful of puppets: Never pick a python for a pet and other animal poems.* Austin, TX: Nancy Renfro Studios.

Lynch-Watson, J. (1980). *The shadow puppet book.* New York: Sterling.

Renfro, N., & Armstrong, B. (1979). *Make amazing puppets.* New York: The Learning Works.

PUPPET JUNK BOX

cardboard tubes and boxes	pencils
paper plates	tape
paper bags (various sizes)	paint
cups (various sizes)	stapler
yarn	dowels
string	craft sticks
lace	rubber bands
ribbon	paper clips
wallpaper scraps	egg cartons
plastic bottles	buttons
lids	pom-poms
scraps of cloth	corks
felt	envelopes
cardboard	socks
aluminum foil	sewing machine
paper	pipe cleaners
markers	old jewelry
glue	cotton balls
scissors	tape recorder
crayons	blank tapes
cartons	flashlights (for lighting)

Simple puppet stages.

Some simple puppet stages

Felt story apron

Blanket over chair

Bush or hedge

Box

Behind table

Window

Hinged plywood

Blanket across doorway

Shoe box for finger puppets

Box top

Refrigerator box

Turn upside down for marionettes

PUPPET STAGES

windows

a table turned on its side

a card table or piece of cloth across a doorway

a broomstick and blanket between two chairs

a table top

a big box with a hole in it

PVC pipe

behind a sofa

 ADDITIONAL READING

Boutte, G. S., VanScoy, I., & Hendley, S. (1996). Multicultural and nonsexist prop boxes. *Young Children, 52*(1), 34–39.

Einarsdottir, J. (1996). Dramatic play and print. *Childhood Education, 73*(1), 352–358.

Howell, J., & Corbey-Schullen, L. (1997). Out of the housekeeping corner and onto the stage: Extending dramatic play. *Young Children, 52*(6), 82–88.

Johnson, A. P. (1998). How to use creative dramatics in the classroom. *Childhood Education, 75*(1), 2–5.

Kelner, L. B. (1993). *The creative classroom: A guide for using creative drama in the classroom, K–6.* Portsmouth, NH: Heinemann.

Maguire, J. (1985). *Creative storytelling: Choosing, inventing and sharing tales for children.* Cambridge, MA: Yellow Moon Press.

Martinez, M., Rosner, N. L., & Strecker, S. (1999). "I never thought I could be a star": A readers' theater ticket of fluency. *The Reading Teacher, 52*(4), 326–334.

Mellou, E. (1994). A theoretical perspective on the relationship between dramatic play and creativity. *Early Childhood Development and Care, 100*(1), 77–92.

Merrefield, G. E. (1997). Three billy goats and Gardner. *Educational Leadership, 55*(1), 58–61.

Naumer, K. (1999). The magic drum: Making drama emergent. *Stage of the Art, 11*(1), 14–21.

Pigott, I. (1990). Drama in the classroom. *The Gifted Child Today, 13*(1), 2–5.

Siks, G. B. (1977). *Drama with children.* New York: Harper & Row.

Straub, C., & Straub, M. (1984). *Mime: Basics for beginners.* Boston: Plays.

Wagner, B. J. (1979). Using drama to create an environment for language development. *Language Arts, 56*(3), 268–274.

Warash, B. G., & Workman, M. (1993). All life's a stage: Children dictate and reenact personal experiences. *Dimensions of Early Childhood, 21*(4), 9–12.

Williamson, P. A. (1993). Encouraging social competence and story comprehension through fantasy play. *Dimensions of Early Childhood, 21*(4), 17–20.

 CHILDREN'S LITERATURE CONNECTION

Bany-Winters, Lisa. (2000). *Show time! Music, dance, and drama activities for kids.* Chicago: Chicago Review Press.
    Containing over 80 activities for kids that focus on developing skills in three areas of drama, this book also includes a play glossary. (Primary)

Brandenberg, F. (1984). *Aunt Nina's visit.* New York: Greenwillow Press.
    Aunt Nina's six kittens disrupt a puppet show given by her nieces and nephews. (PreK–K)

Brown, M. (1985). *Hand rhymes.* New York: E. P. Dutton.
    A collection of nursery rhymes with diagrams for accompanying finger plays. (PreK–1)

Cleeland, Holly. (2004). *Glue and go costumes for kids: Super-duper designs with everyday materials.* New York: Sterling.
    A guide to making costumes with ordinary materials and supplies. (Primary)

Cohen, M. (1985). *Starring first grade*. New York: Greenwillow Books.

> Even though he doesn't like his part in the first grade play, Jim saves the performance when one of the key players gets stage fright. (PreK–1)

Dunleavy, D., & Kurisu, J. (2004). *The jumbo book of drama*. Tonawanda, NY: Kids Can Press.

> Drama takes you into the wonderful world of make-believe, where anything is possible. This book is full of drama activities and ideas. (Primary)

Ehrlich, F. (1992). *A class play with Ms. Vanilla*. New York: Viking.

> When Ms. Vanilla's class puts on a play of *Little Red Riding Hood*, the wolf is played by Ms. Vanilla. (PreK–K)

Haley, Gail E. (2002). *Costumes for plays and playing*. Boone, NC: Parkway.

> A guide to making costumes for plays, Halloween, parties, or make-believe. (Primary)

Harley, B. (1996). *Sarah's story*. Berkeley, CA: Tricycle Press.

> Sarah cannot think of a story to tell in class for her homework assignment, but on her way to school, she gets help from some unexpected sources. (Primary)

Kohl, Mary Ann F. (1999). *Making make-believe: Fun props, costumes and creative play ideas*. Beltsville, MD: Gryphon House.

> Explore the world of make-believe, with fun and easy-to-make props and costumes. There are over 125 ideas for activities and projects in this book. (K–3)

Krementz, J. (1991). *A very young actress*. New York: Alfred A. Knopf.

> A ten-year-old girl who starred in a workshop production of *Annie 2* describes her experiences on- and offstage, from audition through rehearsals to opening night. (Primary)

Loxton, H. (1989). *Theater*. Austin, TX: Steck-Vaughn.

> An overview of theater as an art form with emphasis on the English-speaking theater. Includes information on the history of the theater, acting methods, staging, putting on a play, and theater careers. (Primary)

Mason, J. (1994). *Now hiring: Theater*. New York: Crestwood House.

> A good reference book full of information and descriptions of jobs available in the theater. (Primary)

Ormerod, J. (1996). *Ms. MacDonald has a class*. New York: Clarion Books.

> After visiting the farm, the children in Ms. MacDonald's class learn to move and look and sound very different while preparing to present the performance of a lifetime. (PreK–1)

Tryon, L. (1992). *Albert's play*. New York: Atheneum.

> Albert helps the children of Pleasant Valley School stage a play. (PreK–1)

 For additional resources involving creativity and the arts with young children, visit our Web site at **www.earlychilded.delmar.com**

 REFERENCES

Applebee, A. (1978). *The child's concept of story*. Chicago: University of Chicago Press.

Brown, V. (1990). Drama as an integral part of the early childhood curriculum. *Design for Arts in Education, 91*(6), 26–33.

Brown, V., & Pleydell, S. (1999). *The dramatic difference: Drama in the preschool and kindergarten classroom*. Portsmouth, NH: Heinemann.

Bruner, J. (1986). *Actual minds, possible worlds*. Cambridge, MA: Harvard University Press.

Bruner, J. S., & Haste, H. (Eds.). (1988). *Making sense: The child's construction of the world*. New York: Routledge.

Fitzhenry, R. I. (Ed.) (1993). *The Harper book of quotations* (3rd ed.). New York: HarperCollins.

Freeman, G. D., Sullivan, K., & Fulton, C. R. (January–February 2003). Effects of creative drama on self-concept, social skills, and problem behavior. *The Journal of Educational Research, 96*(3), 131–139.

Gardner, H. (1983). *Frames of mind: The theory of multiple intelligences*. New York: Basic Books.

Hamilton, M., & Weiss, M. (1990). *Children tell stories: A teaching guide*. Katonah, NY: Richard C. Owen.

Hendy, L., & Toon, L. (2001). *Supporting drama and imaginative play in the early years.* Buckingham, U.K.: Open University Press.

Isbell, R. (1995). *The complete learning center book.* Beltsville, MD: Gryphon House.

Isbell, R. T., & Raines, S. C. (2000). *Tell it again 2: Easy-to-tell stories with activities for young children.* Beltsville, MD: Gryphon House.

Isbell, R., Sobol, J., Lindauer, L., & Lowrance, A. (2004). The effects of storytelling and story reading on the oral language complexity and story comprehension of young children. *Early Childhood Education Journal, 32*(3), 157–163.

Jalongo, M. R. (2003). *Early Childhood Language Arts* (3rd ed.). Upper Saddle River, NJ: Pearson Education.

Kipling, R., & Cauley, L. B., ILL (1983). *The elephant's child.* San Diego: Harcourt Brace Jovanovich.

Mayesky, M. (1998). *Creative activities for young children* (6th ed.). Clifton Park, NY: Delmar Learning.

McCaslin, N. (1990). *Creative drama in the classroom* (5th ed.). New York: Longman.

McMaster, J. C. (1998). Doing literature: Using drama to build literacy. *The Reading Teacher, 51*(7), 574–584.

Piaget, J. (1963). *The origins of intelligence in children.* New York: Norton.

Phillips, L. (September 2000). Storytelling: The seeds of children's creativity (critical essay). *Australian Journal of Early Childhood, 25*(3), 1.

Pinciotti, P. (1993). Creative drama and young children: The dramatic learning connection. *Arts Education Policy Review, 94*(6), 24–29.

Raines, S., & Isbell, R. (1994). *Stories: Children's literature in early education.* Clifton Park, NY: Thomson Delmar Learning.

Raines, S. C., & Isbell, R. T. (1999). *Tell it again: Easy-to-tell stories with activities for young children.* Beltsville, MD: Gryphon House.

Salisbury, B. T. (1986). *Theatre arts in the elementary classroom: Kindergarten through grade three.* New Orleans: Anchorage Press.

Siks, G. B. (1983). *Drama with children* (2nd ed.). New York: Harper & Row Publishers.

Siks, G. B., & Dunnington, H. B. (Eds.). (1967). *Children's theatre and creative dramatics.* Seattle: University of Washington Press.

Singer, D. G., & Singer, J. L. (1990). *The house of make-believe.* Cambridge, MA: Harvard University Press.

Smilansky, S. (1990). Sociodramatic play: Its relevance to behavior and achievement in school. In E. Klugman & S. Smilansky (Eds.), *Children's play and learning* (pp. 18–42). New York: Teachers College Press.

Stotter, R. (September–October 2000). Creative dramatics: Beginnings workshop: Starting with a story. *Child Care Information Exchange, 135,* 45–60.

Toye, N., & Prendiville, F. (2000). *Drama and traditional story for the early years.* London: Taylor and Francis.

Vitz, K. (1983). A review of empirical research in drama and language. *Children's Theatre Review, 32*(4), 17–25.

Vygotsky, L. S. (1978). The role of play in development. In M. Cole, V. John-Steiner, S. Scribner, & E Souberman (Eds.), *Mind in society* (pp. 92–104). Cambridge, MA: Harvard University Press.

Vygotsky, L. S. (1986). *Thought and language.* Cambridge, MA: MIT Press.

Ward, W. (1952). *Stories to dramatize.* Anchorage, KY: Children's Theatre Press.

Warren, K. (1993). Empowering children through drama. *Early Child Development and Care, 90*(1), 83–97.

CREATIVITY ACROSS THE CURRICULUM

Creativity can be nurtured in all areas of the early childhood curriculum and classroom. Opportunities for creativity are enhanced by giving children choices, allowing them to follow their interests, stimulating new ways of thinking, and encouraging creative expression. Creativity and the arts will be discussed as we examine ways the curriculum can be organized through **themes**, units, and projects.

After studying this chapter, you will be able to:
- **Describe how young children learn in a holistic way.**
- **Demonstrate how the arts can be integrated into the early childhood curriculum.**
- **Discuss how projects can be developed from the interests of children.**
- **Explain the role of art in the Reggio Emilia Schools.**
- **Compare and contrast direct instruction, thematic units, and projects.**

OBSERVATION OF CREATIVITY

Darren, a seven-year-old, wanted to be the photographer for a class project that focused on caring for the environment. After the group had researched the topic, several children began to notice all the litter in the creek near their school. They suggested that the creek should be cleaned up. When the children, teacher, and parents went to the site, Darren took his camera and clicked posed pictures of the children. While the cleanup was in progress, he saw one of the mothers taking pictures of the refuse the children were collecting in their garbage bags. Inquisitive, Darren asked the mother about her digital camera and what she was photographing. She explained that she was taking pictures to show the kinds of trash and the litter that was found in the stream. She showed him the pictures she had taken of old tires, soft drink containers, and Styrofoam cups. She also invited Darren to look in the camera's viewfinder, to see what other pictures might be taken. For some shots, she crouched low in the weeds. For others, she stretched out, propping up on her elbows and holding the camera steady, to take a picture of tossed candy wrappers.

Darren imitated a few of the mother's postures and tried different angles. Next, he began taking pictures, while the children were collecting the trash. Then he included the children in the picture, as well as the litter they had removed from the creek. He even crouched on the ground, to get a picture of a friend's muddy shoes and the aluminum cans near his feet.

WHAT WAS OBSERVED?

Darren and his classmates were involved in a study built on their curiosity, which led to new understanding about their environment. Darren experimented with taking pictures and gained knowledge through his interactions with the mother who served as his mentor. He gained confidence in his abilities, as he shared information about photography with his peers and saw his work attractively displayed. Darren was engaged in meaningful learning, which led to a deeper understanding of his environment.

Later, the children and teacher looked at the photographs and selected the ones that would help tell their story. During the selection process, they revisited their experiences, talked about the methods they used and the trash they collected. The selected photos were attractively displayed on a panel in the classroom so children and parents could see the trash that had been collected and the process they went though to retrieve the items. Darren proudly shared his photography tips with his friends. Later, the children decided to construct a three-dimensional "Trash Monster" from the items they had collected at the creek. This focused study grew and was extended, based on the interests of Darren and his classmates. During the continuing project, their teacher was actively involved, posing provocations, identifying resources, and helping the children find answers to their questions.

Introduction

Collecting trash from the creek near the school was part of a larger environmental education unit in this second-grade classroom. One might wonder if a science project, focusing on the need to keep our environment clean, also could provide opportunities for creative expression. As the creative episode demonstrates, it certainly does. Included are examples that illustrate the children's creative representations of what they learned while studying the environment.

In this school-wide project, each classroom bulletin board displayed children's posters illustrating slogans about cleaning up the environment. Some slogans included, "Don't be a trashy person," with a collage-person made from pieces of trash collected at the site. "Fill up your stomach; don't fill up the field" was depicted with fast-food wrappers. "Toss it in" was shown with wire mesh stapled to poster board to represent a wastebasket where gum wrappers and bits of paper were tossed in.

At the front door of the school, representatives from each of the classrooms created another large exhibit. The representatives painted a huge blue stream onto a white sheet and hung it from a rod to illustrate the South Elkhorn Creek. They stacked old tires at the bottom of the painted creek. A sign read, "I'm the creek, and I'm tired of tires." The exhibit was at the front door where those who passed were told to take their old tires to the recycling center. The center's address was given in bold print.

Children's representation of new knowledge was interpreted in their poster displays and the message exhibited at the front door. The significance of their learning was clear from the children's posters, Darren's photos, and a whole array of activities that touched each content area of the curriculum. The curriculum unit was evident at different times throughout the day, used different children's interests, and provided opportunities for them to choose their own ways of expression.

❀ DEFINITIONS OF CURRICULUM DEVELOPMENT

The "Cleaning Up Our Creek" unit is an example of a science project that integrates all areas of the curriculum. There are many ways to organize curricula, depending on personal perspectives of child development, knowledge of various disciplines, and curriculum content. Ways of organizing units of study are numerous. However, their perspectives on child growth and development influence teachers by knowledge in various disciplines and by the content of the curriculum. Each influence casts shadows on the early childhood practitioners' views. Yet the basic questions are, "What is to be learned?" and "How, when, and why?" (Bredekamp & Rosegrant, 1995). Theorists, from as early as Rousseau in the 1700s, Pestalozzi and Froebel in the 1800s, and Dewey in the early 1900s, have influenced the answers to these questions on curriculum development (Ornstein & Hunkins, 1988; Raines & Canady, 1990).

The term **Developmentally Appropriate Practices (DAP),** as referred to by the **National Association for the Education of Young Children (NAEYC),** has influenced the current thinking of early childhood educators. In discussions of developmentally appropriate practices, some educators talk about them as if they were the curriculum. Instead, developmentally appropriate practices refer to the way the teacher carries out the curriculum, the organization of the learning environment, the materials, and the children's interactions with each other and the teacher. According to Bredekamp & Rosegrant (1992), "Curriculum is an organized framework that delineates the content that children are to learn, the processes through which children achieve the identified curricular goals, what teachers do to help children achieve these goals, and the context in which teaching and learning occur. The early childhood profession defines curriculum in its broadest sense, encompassing prevailing theories, approaches, and models" (p. 10).

According to the Association for Childhood Education International (ACEI), the thematic unit, "embraces the teaching of all content areas, presented as integrated experiences that develop and extend concepts, strengthen skills, and provide a solid foundation for learning in language, literacy, math, science, health, art and music" (Moyer, Egertson, & Isenberg, 1987, p. 23). Jarolimek and Foster (1989) define curriculum as a "coordinated series of learning activities planned around a broad topic that will involve the whole class in a comprehensive study" (p. 54).

The questions of the quality of the experiences—breadth versus depth of the curriculum—and the element of time cause us to examine our curriculum plans. In many discussions on the definition of early childhood curriculum, questions are raised about the nature of the experiences planned as part of a quality curriculum. When considering the quality of the experience, quality can be judged by whether the experience leads to "meaning-making" by children (Raines, 1997). Given that the teacher and the children plan the curriculum around a topic or theme that fits into larger curriculum units and disciplines, the need for concept development is based on the quality of the experience that promotes children making sense of their experiences. How one makes sense of the experiences is explained by learning theory in which constructing concepts is the creative endeavor of the mind. How the learner represents what he or she has learned is an opportunity for creative expression.

Issues of time and breadth versus depth are serious in early childhood classrooms. The most common complaint of teachers is that they do not have time to devote to all the topics they want to cover, which infers a breadth approach (Jalongo & Isenberg, 2000). The depth viewpoint is not how many different topics or themes are covered but what children gain from an in-depth study of a topic, including the learning processes, information-gathering strategies, and the quality and meaningfulness of the experiences. In-depth studies provide opportunities for children to build on their knowledge and increase their understanding of a selected topic. These extended experiences that continue over a period of weeks

"Tell me and I'll forget. Show me, and I may not remember. Involve me, and I'll understand."

Native American saying

(in Fitzhenry, 1993)

allow children to explore, plan, implement, revisit, reflect, and expand their learning. They can provide an important way to add depth to the curriculum and allow children to connect their experiences. Children can become "experts" who are able to share their knowledge and information with teachers, parents, and others.

PLANNING FOR A CREATIVE AND INTEGRATED CURRICULUM

The way a teacher organizes the curriculum allows children to express what they have learned, gain competence at representing what they have learned, and use their own creativity. Themes, units, and the **project approach** provide ways of organizing the curriculum to promote creative thinking and expressions.

Early childhood educators value child-centered, experience-centered, and knowledge-centered approaches to curriculum planning. Themes, units, and project approaches to curriculum planning provide possibilities for the integration of information, learning processes, and creative expression. Many preschool and kindergarten teachers organize units around themes from social studies or science. Topics chosen often include families, neighborhoods, simple machines, and gardening. Some examples of projects include: How to care for a class pet, Creating a classroom museum, and Who are the people in our community? Primary teachers frequently select topics that are related to and support their curriculum or standards that are adopted by states, school systems, or professional associations. Primary teachers also include topics that match the needs and interests of the children in their classroom, music of the community, or children's authors in the area.

A child's interest in collecting pinecones can lead to a project about trees.

There is renewed interest in the integrated or multidisciplinary curriculum. This has been sparked by writings of theorists and research on brain development. Gardner's Theory of Multiple Intelligences has supported the multidisciplinary curriculum, since he identified eight different ways of learning, which include music, movement (kinesthetic), and visual imagery. These ways of knowing are considered to be equally as important as linguistic and mathematical understanding. His work indicated that all intelligences are necessary for children to develop and communicate. With this understanding, all intelligences, including the arts, should be a part of the early childhood curriculum. Research on brain development and Jan Healy's (1990) book, *Endangered Minds: Why Children Don't Think and What We Can Do About It*, stress the importance of the early years and the inclusion of music and the arts in an effective learning environment.

During this same period, curriculum specialists were suggesting that the explosion of information had made learning facts no longer appropriate. Based on these theories, research and curriculum designers began to challenge the traditional model of curriculum and suggested a different approach. With these influences, many concluded that education should develop understanding, generalize concepts, and increase critical and creative thinking rather than memorization of information.

Current interest in testing and accountability has also had an impact on curricula, since educators must now be able to demonstrate children's learning in the classroom no matter what curriculum design they are using. Teachers can, with careful planning and observation, identify and document what young children are learning in an integrated curriculum that includes themes, projects, and learning centers. Through systematic observation of children involved in all aspects of the integrated curriculum, the teacher will be able to demonstrate and identify the learning that occurs by the individual child as well as by the group. He will be able to understand and plan for future learning in all areas of the curriculum and classroom.

✿ BELIEFS ABOUT HOW CHILDREN LEARN

Themes, units, and projects provide the mechanism for organizing activities that often are referred to as integrated learning. This way of designing curricula is based on the beliefs that early childhood educators have about how children learn:

Young children learn best when exploring what interests them.

Being able to make choices motivates children.

Young children learn best as active participants in firsthand experiences.

When firsthand experiences are not available, connections must be made between the known and the unknown.

Active, expressive, engaged learning fosters a child's social, emotional, cognitive, language, and physical development.

The curriculum operates through learning environments inside the classroom, the outside physical setting, and interactions between the teacher and child. The curriculum also operates through a plan that the teacher has about opportunities to learn, including concepts and skills, the child can retain long after the unit, theme, or project is finished. Children may recall what they experienced, whereas the teacher recalls what was learned and how the children changed in their creative expressions, behaviors, skills, and interpretations of what was learned.

A major influence in curriculum design and implementation is derived from the laboratory schools of the John Dewey era. The curricula were planned around **human impulses** (Dewey, 1902; Raines & Canady, 1990). Smith, Stanley, and Shores (1957) simplified Dewey's impulses to include:

- socializing
- constructing
- inquiring

- questioning
- experimenting
- expressing or creating artistically

Dewey's human impulse view of curriculum planning has a place in this century because over time, we have come to realize that Dewey's descriptions are accurate. The desire to socialize, inquire, question, experiment, and express and create artistically are the processes and learning styles that also are expressed in many of Gardner's (1993) descriptions of multiple intelligences.

Well-developed themes, units, and projects meet the needs of Dewey's human impulses. For example, teachers provide opportunities for children to socialize because of the belief that children need to learn how to get along with each other. Children also learn from social engagements with each other and with adults in their environment. Early childhood educators believe that when children construct representations of what they have learned to express their gained knowledge, they also gain experience in construction and are motivated by being able to choose what they will construct.

Children are inquisitive, curious learners who enjoy inquiry and want to know more. Children's questions should be taken seriously and used as points for directing classroom inquiry, whether individually or collectively. Experimentation leads to discoveries and simple experiments that often are the foundation of more complex constructs of knowledge. Support of children's individual and collective expressions occurs

An ongoing project related to gardening.

by promoting creative and artistic choices. Creative expression helps children learn at deeper levels, provides enjoyment, and leads to problem-solving. Allowing children to be inventive and use their own ingenuity shows respect for them as children and as individuals.

Curriculum planners may question whether child-centered, experience-centered, and knowledge-centered methods of planning can coexist. Certainly, teachers and program models follow along a continuum. Some programs for young children base the entire day on children's choices. In other settings, the daily focus follows a theme, broadening the children's experiences with weekly field trips and firsthand involvement. There are programs, concentrating on direct instruction, that are focused on learning facts, skills, and knowledge with drills, lists of information to be learned, and demonstration of abilities. Curriculum planners who follow the interests of children are at the extreme when looking along a curriculum continuum. However, many early childhood educators propose a balance of child-centered

Binoculars provide a way to take a closer look at a bird's nest and birds.

choices with teacher-directed activities. For example, teachers may offer periods of time with choices or time set aside to observe the skills acquired. Teachers may balance inside play in a controlled environment with outside time in a more active mode. Directed lessons are balanced with choices of activities to express what has been learned, as well as opportunities to express oneself artistically for the sake of the art and for the enjoyment of play and self-expression.

DEVELOPMENTALLY APPROPRIATE PRACTICES

Early childhood educators often use the term *developmentally appropriate practices* to govern the choices teachers make to plan and carry out the curriculum. Developmental appropriateness refers to what is known about human growth and development for the age of the child, and the stage of individual development. According to Bredekamp & Copple (1997), "two dimensions, age appropriateness and individual appropriateness are cornerstones of the teacher's thinking when planning the curriculum" (p. 2).

Developmental appropriateness refers to the universal, predictable sequences of growth and change, and the individual appropriateness of each child's timing of growth, individual personality, learning styles, and family background. What is developmentally appropriate for three-year-olds may not be challenging enough for most seven-year-olds. What is appropriate for some may not be appropriate for all because of who they are as individuals. For example, insisting that the shy, hesitant, child perform alone in front of others is not developmentally appropriate, although she might enjoy moving to music with a group of children.

Children's development is also shaped by the social context in which they live. There is a need for early childhood educators to understand the influence of the social–cultural context on learning, and to respect children's different ways of expressing their ideas, feelings, and achievements (Bredekamp & Copple).

Taking into account our beliefs about how children learn, developmentally appropriate practices, and social and cultural context, early childhood educators are left with the questions of what they should include in the curriculum, and how they should organize their time, space, and resources to maximize children's opportunities to learn.

The position reflected in the Developmentally Appropriate Practices documents, from the National Association for the Education of Young Children (NAEYC), is that as children become adults they will need to be able to analyze situations, make judgments, and solve emerging problems. They will have to learn new approaches, skills, and knowledge in a changing environment. In music and the visual arts, children will need a body of new knowledge and skills. High-quality early childhood programs provide safe and nurturing environments that promote the physical, social, emotional, aesthetic, intellectual, and language development of each child (NAEYC, 1997).

How does paint work when used on a tree limb? A three-year-old paints a limb outside.

✿ CHILDREN WITH SPECIAL NEEDS

Young children with special needs can benefit from participating in the arts. These open-ended activities allow every child to work at his or her individual level and feel successful. All children, whatever their physical, cognitive, or emotional level of development, have individual interests and special capabilities. The arts provide experiences that will enrich their lives and provide another avenue for finding their special interest. The arts encourage manipulating objects, problem-solving, using symbols, exploring materials, and interacting with peers. These opportunities encourage children with special needs to participate in the creative process, while working alone or with others. Most activities in the arts can be adapted to the educational needs of individual children. The following suggestions provide a beginning point in making adaptations for children with special needs. It is important to remember that every child is different and progresses at his or her own pace.

Categories

Disabilities and the special needs of children can be organized into several categories:

- physical challenges
- speech and language problems
- autism spectrum disorder
- developmental and/or cognitive delays
- behavioral challenges
- visual challenges
- gifted and/or talented

PHYSICAL CHALLENGES. Children in this category have a condition that influences their motor development and the use of their body.

Adaptations. Children with physical challenges may benefit from adapted positioning that provides support for them to work on small motor activities. A healthcare professional may suggest positioning devices such as chair inserts, or standing aids. Sometimes, children with physical issues will benefit from working at a taller table or from kneeling on the floor. A child in a wheelchair will need an area that is the appropriate height to be comfortable when working with materials. When doing movement experiences with other children, it is important to find ways for the physically challenged child to participate. For instance, a shaker or streamers can help them feel a part of the activity, as the others move around the room to music.

SPEECH AND LANGUAGE PROBLEMS. This is one of the most common diagnoses found in the early childhood special education population. A child with speech and language issues has problems with oral language and/or lacks an understanding or use of language.

Adaptations. Children with speech and language issues will benefit from working with other children and adults who will enrich their language. It will be beneficial for the children to talk about their artwork and share ideas with peers. This provides additional opportunities for the child to hear new vocabulary that relates to the arts and what they are doing. Playing in learning centers such as art, housekeeping, and blocks will encourage language interactions in a meaningful context. Puppets are also useful for children who are hesitant to share their ideas verbally. Puppets provide a safe way to express their thoughts and relieve fear of talking in front of others. Language and new vocabulary can be inspired by participating in interesting activities related to art, music, and movement.

AUTISM SPECTRUM DISORDER. Children in this category manifest delays in social skills and language. Some children in this category also have cognitive delays. They may resist change in their environment and have limited play skills. Some children with autism spectrum disorder may be very sensitive to sounds, light, and touch.

Adaptations. Children whose diagnosis falls within the autism spectrum may need guidance in working with others. They learn best from participation in sensory activities that include visual and tactile experiences such as art. Learning centers can be used to help them learn about playing and interacting with others, although they often will play independently. When using music, observe their level of sensitivity to the sounds and adjust the level so it is comfortable for them. Often these children will need a quiet place where they can remove themselves from classroom activities if they become overwhelmed. This can be a private place in a section of the classroom or a three-sided box with large holes and filled with soft pillows.

DEVELOPMENTAL AND/OR COGNITIVE DELAYS. Children with delays often learn skills more slowly than other children. Some children in this category may have mental retardation. Later, these children may be identified as having learning disabilities.

Adaptations. Children with delays benefit from having peers or adults model an activity. It helps for them to see how things work and how they are to be done. Breaking down the activity into simple steps will also help them succeed and progress at their own pace. If a child is having difficulty with an activity, it may be helpful to provide fewer choices of materials and clearer directions. Sometimes, other children participating in the activity can demonstrate and help the child with delays. This benefits both children, as they learn from each other and build caring relationships. Music, art, and movement provide many ways to participate with adjustments for children with delays. These areas may provide the child the best opportunity to feel successful and be a participating member of the group.

BEHAVIORAL CHALLENGES. This category identifies children who have behavioral difficulties. The most common diagnoses in this category are attention deficit disorder and attention deficit/hyperactivity disorder. Children with these diagnoses appear to be in constant movement and have difficulty staying with a task to completion.

Adaptations. Children who are behaviorally challenged need to have activities that allow movement. Moving to music, standing when working on art, or building with blocks invites active participation and allows their movement. Use simple and consistent instructions when explaining any activity. Encourage them in positive ways when they are working on a project in an appropriate way. Observe the child to determine when she or he is becoming frustrated with an activity so that preventive measures can be used. This might include offering assistance, changing the activity, or providing a break from the involvement.

VISUAL CHALLENGES. This includes children who have problems with vision. Some children may have visual acuity problems that require corrective lenses. Their vision often varies with lighting, time of day, or even the weather. Many children with visual challenges are overly sensitive to touch and sound.

Adaptations. Be sure the activity areas and learning centers have adequate light. High-contrast materials are also easier for children with visual challenges to see, such as black, white, red, and yellow. They will benefit from art activities that encourage touch and manipulation. Music provides another area for enjoyment and involvement.

GIFTED AND/OR TALENTED. Children who are very bright or talented in specific areas need to be challenged to try new things and work creatively. These children can be academically gifted or have exceptional abilities in specific areas, such as music, art, movement, creative thinking, or drama. A variety of combinations of these strengths and abilities are possible. However, few children are exceptional in all areas.

Adaptations. Provide materials that are new and have not been used before to challenge the gifted child's thinking. Open-ended activities are very effective, since all levels of work are possible and the child may want to develop more complex ideas. Include books and references that allow these children to expand their knowledge and work at their own pace. Often, these children like to read and learn about artists, inventors, or famous thinkers, and investigate their work. They may also try the techniques or materials of the person they are studying. Children who have special abilities in art, music, or movement can share their talents for the other children to enjoy.

The creative child often has unusual ideas that may be ridiculed by other children. Help all children respect and value the unique ideas of others. This acceptance will help talented children feel more comfortable with their abilities. Most importantly, do not underestimate their capabilities or hold them back by making them do things the same way as other children. Requiring that everyone make the same art project is not beneficial for any child. But it is particularly detrimental to gifted children. It does not allow them to reach the potential of which they are capable.

Evaluate the child with specials needs as he or she participates in activities. Ask these questions:

- Is the child using the materials effectively?
- Is the child participating with the other children?
- Is the child making choices related to the activity?
- Is the child being appropriately challenged?
- Is language being used that relates to the arts and participation?
- Is the child enjoying or appreciating the experience?
- Do you need to make additional adjustments for the child?

All children like to have their work admired and displayed. When children with special needs create pictures, build structures, or illustrate books, they are demonstrating what they are learning and their involvement in the process. Display and label their artistic work in the classroom, art center, and school. Digital cameras can be used to document what they are doing, the steps in the process, and the final project. Talk with children about their work, the displays, and future extensions. The arts may be where some children with special needs do their best work and find the most satisfaction.

DECIDING THE TOPIC OF THE THEME OR UNIT OF STUDY

Choosing appropriate themes or topics for study is based on the teacher's view of the child as a learner. Some themes are chosen from social studies or science and are used to support art, music, literature, mathematics, play, and learning centers as a way to distribute opportunities to learn throughout the curriculum and classroom. The social studies curriculum typically places the child at the center, and units relate to topics

Projects encourage cooperative work on topics that interest several children.

that have a degree of immediacy to the child's social environment. For example, families, friends, neighborhoods, community workers, feelings, and celebrations are viewed from the child's perspective. The "lived social studies curriculum" of the classroom is how the child learns to get along with others and be a productive member of the group while retaining her own identity.

Themes and topics in preschool and kindergarten are based on children's interests and the physical environment in which they live. The child's ability to experience the theme immediately drives the early childhood curriculum choices. Appropriate science themes might include food sources, nature, health, and caring for pets, birds, and animals native to the region.

The experience-based curriculum does not mean that teachers cannot expose children to other cultures, physical environments, or literature from another time and place. It does mean that the teacher begins with the children's own experiences and builds connections and comparisons between what the children already know and what they are attempting to understand. Relating the unknown to the known builds a bridge to understanding from the experienced to the inexperienced. However, enough connections must be present for the child to build and retain new concepts. An example of a creative primary unit can be found in Appendix D.

In the primary grades, the theme is sometimes selected based on the potential to support the curriculum and/or standards that are to be met. Children's interest should also influence the studies as they pose questions, share their knowledge, and select ways to be involved. It is important to remember that the theme will be more meaningful if the students are involved in the decision-making process. Curriculum and standards can provide the basis for planning, while they are enriched and expanded to match the children in a specific classroom. It is still essential that primary-grade children have concrete experiences, opportunities for personal choices, and possibilities for digging deeper into a topic or study. The creative arts can provide a way to learn in different ways, to enrich learning, and to make the experiences more joyful. Questions the teacher should continue to ask include, "Is this important for my students to know?" "Why?" (Snyder, 2001) "How can the project be meaningful?" and "How can the students demonstrate what they have learned?"

HIGH/SCOPE APPROACH

The **High/Scope** approach to curriculum planning, formerly known as the cognitive curriculum and the cognitive-oriented curriculum, provides a framework for teachers to organize around the content of creative representation, language and literacy, initiative and social relations, movement, music, classification, seriation, number, space, and time. Lessons or interactions are staged in the "plan–do–review" format, for teachers to assist children in organizing their thoughts. Key experiences are identified and serve as a guide for planning and evaluation. They are embedded in activities that can be extended with language and nonverbal representation. Active learning, choices, and child-initiated and adult-initiated sequences are recommended (Hohmann & Weikart, 1995).

The structure is derived from the planning of the space, the requirements of the curriculum, and the ways of organizing the children's thinking and responses (Bredekamp, 1996). The teacher's role is to instigate problem-solving by providing a variety of materials and activities, asking children to plan what they are going to do, and asking questions and making suggestions that stimulate children's thinking.

While the High/Scope curriculum is more structured than the project approach and the Reggio Emilia approach, there is room for children's choices, following their interests, and creative responses to what is being learned. The program also includes music, movement, and arts as important elements in the curriculum.

There is an ongoing longitudinal research study that is investigating the effects of High/Scope on low-income children who attended the program. The study has been conducted for over thirty years, as the children have become adults and are now in their forties. When High/Scope students are compared with a control group, some interesting findings emerge. High/Scope participants stayed in school longer, were more likely to have graduated from high school, more likely to be employed, less likely to be involved in crime, and less likely to be on welfare. This research and the findings are frequently used to demonstrate the importance of early childhood programs and the long-term benefits for children who attend high-quality programs. The newest report indicates that high-quality preschool programs can have positive effects for many years (Schweinhart, Montie, Xiang, Barnett, Belfield, & Nores, 2004).

TIME AND SCHEDULING FOR THE INTEGRATION OF CURRICULAR THEMES

The thematic unit is most apparent during circle or group time with book selections in the classroom library, in the choice of special projects and activities, and in the addition of special centers. Major ideas or theme concepts are revisited several times during the day when children are scheduled for circle time, library and read-aloud, special projects and activities, and special centers.

Thematic units include:

- circle or group time
- classroom library
- special projects and activities
- centers

This complex block structure was built over a period of days.

TABLE 9–1 Kindergarten Schedule

8:50	Arrival, greeting, group time
9:25	Centers and work time
10:45	Whole-group sharing and debriefing
11:00	Gross motor activity (indoors or out)
11:30	Lunch
12:00	Whole-group story and discussion
12:30	Integrated language arts, science, or mathematics
2:30	Group share, story, and music
3:00	Preparation for home

Reprinted by permission of the publisher from Raines, S. C. (1995). *Whole language across the curriculum: Grades 1, 2, 3.* New York: Teachers College Press, p. 37. © 1995 by Teachers College Columbia University. All rights reserved.

Young children need blocks of time to work at their own pace, to experience activities, use materials, and engage with other learners. This schedule design uses less teacher-directed time and greater child-choice time. Jalongo and Isenberg propose a kindergarten schedule that meets the requirements of larger blocks of time for child-choice activities related to a theme, and interactions with the teacher in a whole-class setting or small groups. Table 9–1, adapted from Raines (1995), contains a schedule taken from a kindergarten classroom. It reflects a respect for the young child's need for time and choice of activities. Variations on this schedule are appropriate, but teachers must protect the need for larger blocks of time that promote child-choice and in-depth work.

Steps in Planning the Thematic Unit

After teachers have selected a topic for the thematic unit, several organizing devices help with planning. Teachers need to consider major concepts they want to promote throughout the study, such as activities, materials, use of space, and time. Themes can be project-, question-, problem-, or issue-driven, such as cleaning up our creek. They can be topic-driven, such as families or neighborhoods, or literature-based, such as tall tales or poetry.

Step one in planning any thematic unit is to decide on the theme. The teacher selects the thematic unit and the project develops from children's interest. The second step is to list the major concepts associated with this theme and the supporting ideas, which the teacher will highlight throughout the study. For proponents of integrating literature throughout the curriculum, the third step is to select between five and ten books that capture the major concepts of the theme. The fourth step is to brainstorm as many activities as possible that will support the development of these concepts. And the fifth step is to select the activities and make plans on a daily basis. In the following section, each step will be discussed in greater detail.

STEP ONE.   The first step in planning a thematic unit is selecting a topic. Once the topic is determined, list the major concepts and supporting ideas. Begin your web design by drawing a circle with the topic inside (Figure 9–1).

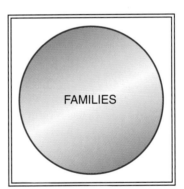

FIGURE 9–1
Unit theme—"families."

STEP TWO.   Decide on the major concepts to be gained from this unit of study and the supporting ideas. For example, see the concept web in Figure 9–2 for the unit on families. Two of the major concepts are listed below.

1. There are many definitions of family.
   - Not all families are alike.
   - Families have different members.
   - There are adopted families and foster families.
   - Family names are used to identify families.
2. We learn values from our families.
   - Right and wrong.
   - Working together and cooperating helps our family members get more done.
   - Respect for others is learned in families.

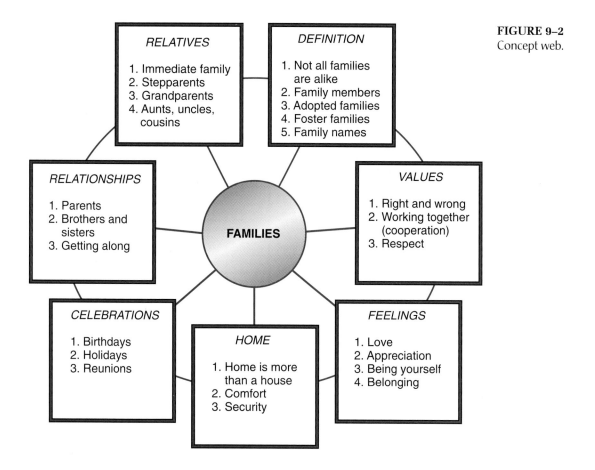

FIGURE 9–2
Concept web.

Other major concepts that the teacher hopes the children will build and retain long after the study is complete relate to the distinctiveness of home, family celebrations, relationships within families, and who our relatives are. For the purpose of the web, these concepts have been shortened to single words: definition, values, feelings, home, celebrations, relationships, and relatives.

STEP THREE.   Select feature books that have the same theme and concepts are shown in Figure 9–3. For example, Norma Simon's (1976) *All Kinds of Families* is an excellent book to illustrate the major concept that there are many different definitions of a family. Ann Morris' (1990) *Loving* provides beautiful photographs of families in loving embraces and with loving expressions on their faces or in their actions. Russell Hoban's (1964) *A Baby Sister for Frances* is one of a large number of books that tackles the situation of a new child joining the family.

STEP FOUR.   Brainstorm ideas for different areas of the classroom. Preschool, kindergarten, and child care teachers may choose to think of different centers in the classroom, as illustrated in the eight-cell planning sheet (Figure 9–4). Some

FIGURE 9–3
Concept web with books.

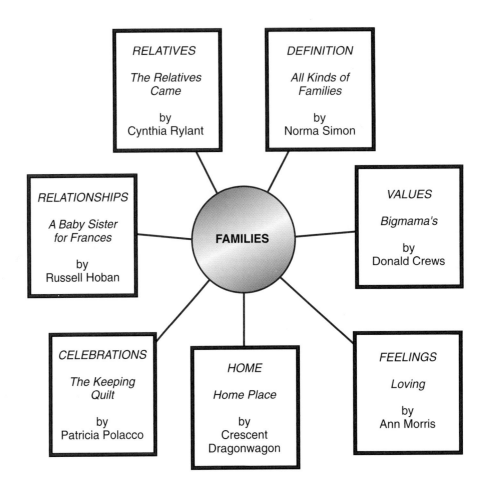

primary-grade teachers may choose to use a tool that reflects their classroom areas or subject areas.

STEP FIVE. Use brainstorming ideas to select activities and place them on the web with the major concepts and featured book selections. Deciding which activities to select will vary with materials, investment of time, and interests of the children. These theme-supporting activities are ones available to children but they are not required of every child. Open-ended activities of the art, music, sociodramatic, blocks, and construction centers will remain available to children. Special activities created by Raines and Canady (1989, 1991, 1992), indicated as story s-t-r-e-t-c-h-e-r-s, are selected to support the concept development associated with the theme topic. The relationship to focus books helps reinforce the concepts around which the unit is built.

From the story s-t-r-e-t-c-h-e-r web (Figure 9–5), it is clear that there are numerous opportunities for creative responses. Some examples include drawing my family who lives with me, dramatizing special family moments, storytelling on a front porch, writing "thank-you" notes on cards of one's own design, singing lullabies, and devising ways to show the geography of a car trip to visit relatives.

Group Time/Story Time	Library/Literature/ Writing Center
Art/Displays	Music/Movement
Creative Dramatics/ Housekeeping	Blocks (Small & Large) and Math/Manipulatives
Science/Nature	Sand/Water/Carpentry/ Special Projects/Events

FIGURE 9–4
Eight-cell planning sheet.

✣ INTEGRATED CURRICULUM AND THE SUBJECT AREA DISCIPLINES

Many primary teachers say they enjoy thematic teaching but are compelled to teach more discreet lessons to be sure their students are learning to read well, write well, compute, think scientifically, and know the basics of geography and historical facts. Concerns over learning the basics of a discipline or **subject area** are valid issues. In fact, the skills and basics of subject areas such as reading, writing, and mathematics are often emphasized more than the fundamentals of social studies, science, and the arts.

In thematic teaching, the unit of study often concerns social studies or science. The expression of what one has learned is frequently represented artistically. Teachers wonder if reading, writing, and mathematics instruction will suffer when using thematic approaches to the curriculum. Certainly, if the teacher does not plan for adequate instruction, practice of skills, and application of the fundamentals of a discipline, the basics will suffer. However, the advantage of the thematic teaching approach is that it gives the child some interesting ways to apply what she is learning as a reader, writer, and mathematician. The skills are used in meaningful activity and relate to a topic of interest instead of being presented in isolation.

Using the example of the "Families Thematic Unit" (Figures 9–1, 9–2, 9–3, and 9–5), the teacher can apply reading, writing, and mathematics instruction while thinking about families. For example, from the scheduled read-aloud, circle, or group time, the teacher can present a reading lesson. When the teacher reads Norma Simon's book, *All Kinds of Families,* the lesson likely will begin with a discussion of what the word *families* means. The teacher may ask young children to

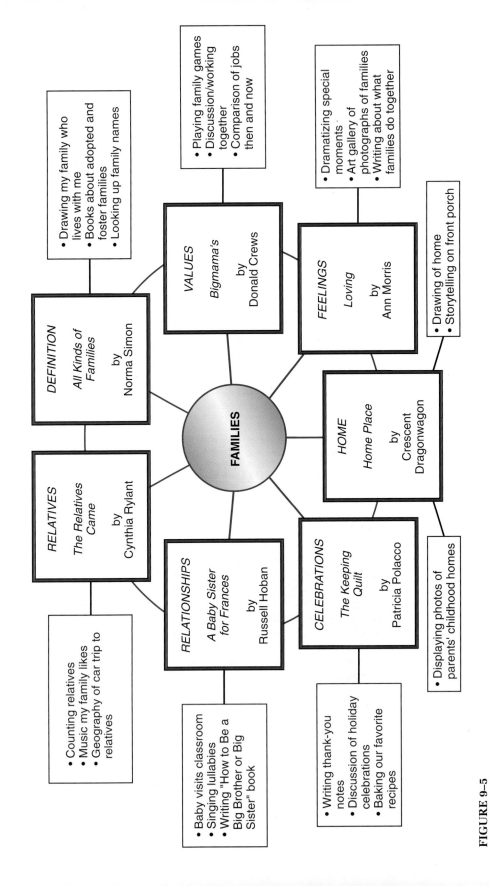

FIGURE 9–5

Story s–t–r–e–t–c–h–e–r web for family unit.

identify the letters that make up this word and note the children in the classroom who have names starting with the various letters of the word. In addition, the teacher might write a sentence or two that the children dictate about families. For example, on a chart tablet, the teacher may print:

"Aaron said, 'My *family* is my mother, father, grandmother, and baby sister.'"

"Michael said, 'My *family* is daddy, Aunt Susan, and my big brother.'"

"Leah said, 'My *family* is my mother and my brother.'"

"Simone said, 'I have two *families*. I live with a foster *family* and my other *family* is my mother and my little brother.'"

"Norma Simon, the author, wrote, 'There are all kinds of *families*.'"

From the emphasis on the word family and families, a reading lesson is constructed and the concept of a family is developed. After the circle, group time, or read-aloud time in the schedule, children are free to choose activities. There also may be some required activities. The teacher may ask that the children complete one of the tabletop activities before progressing to selecting a center. At the tabletop activities, children may be asked to draw, paint, use colored chalk or markers, or use clay to create an image of their family and to label their artistic rendering with the word *family* or *families*.

During mathematics instruction time, the children can count the number of members in their family and the teacher can emphasize for younger children the numeral that represents the number of family members. For older children, after reading the book *All Kinds of Families*, the children can identify the number of different types of families from the book, then graph the number of different family members represented in the class. Addition and subtraction can be illustrated with story problems of Michael's family visiting Leah's family to determine the number of parents, children, babies, and so forth. Having a school event and preparing for those who will attend can represent the problem of larger numbers.

Social studies are taught throughout the unit because of the nature of the families theme while teaching the fundamentals of geography by stretching the content of Cynthia Rylant's (1985) *The Relatives Came*. In the story, the relatives travel from Virginia. The teacher can illustrate where they might be going by helping the children locate Virginia on a map and discussing how people talk about where they are going such as "down to Grandmother's in Atlanta," "over to my cousin's in Roanoke," or "up from Virginia." Younger children may focus on the concept of where they live, whereas older children can construct comparisons of where they live versus where their relatives live. The concept focuses on relatives as part of a study of families so an application can be made in the social studies and geography contexts.

✺ CLEANING UP OUR CREEK

In the thematic unit on "Cleaning Up Our Creek," opportunities were abundant for using the basics of reading, writing, and mathematics. For example, after visiting the South Elkhorn Creek, the children read the book *Come Back, Salmon* by Molly Cone (1991). The children wrote a class letter asking the local Sierra Club for additional environmental materials. Reading the brochures provided a wonderful opportunity for the teacher to illustrate that reading is for different purposes, a basic understanding in reading instruction.

While focusing on the main concept of our responsibility to take care of the physical environment, children browsed the Sierra Club materials for facts about the cost of littering and stream pollution. Their writing portfolios included accounts of what was learned at different times throughout the study. In mathematics, children weighed the amount of refuse they collected, measured the distance between various points on the South Elkhorn Creek and the Kentucky River on a geological survey map, and calculated the cost of their class effort to clean up the creek if they had been paid $5 an hour.

As the creek unit demonstrates, learning the basic and practicing skills can be done in a thematic unit. The significance of unit thematic curricular organization is that skills are applied to interesting subjects and the need to know the skills is meaningful. Thematic unit teaching does not preclude the need for some students to have additional practice, one-on-one instruction with the teacher, and dedicated time to focus on skills. The difference is that the teacher, in the thematically organized unit of instruction, will make certain that children are applying skills in interesting ways that help them internalize and retain what has been practiced, in isolation from the content.

✿ INITIATING ACTIVITIES, K-W-L CHARTS, AND CULMINATING ACTIVITIES

Many teachers and curriculum planners begin units with **initiating activities** that focus the children's attention on the topic to be studied. K-W-L charts are useful for keeping track of the inquiries that drive the child's investigations and as a way to document what has been learned. Culminating activities are designed for reflecting on what has been learned, consolidating understanding, and affirming one's role in learning.

The initiating activity might be as simple as reading the book *All Kinds of Families* or as exciting as asking parents to bring a new baby to class. The objective of the initiating activity is to focus children's attention on the topic, stimulate questions, and include children in the planning. Exhibits of family photographs may start a family unit that culminates in a special photography day for families to come to the school and have their pictures taken.

The initiating activity for the "Cleaning Up Our Creek" unit was a walk to the creek from school. Children observed the creek and the debris, then made guesses about the source of the pollution. They also discussed their concerns for the fish, wildlife, and plants affected by the pollution, and their need for a fresh water supply.

To help teachers and children keep track of what they are learning during a unit of study, teachers can use K-W-L charts. K stands for what is known. W is what we want to know. And L indicates what has been learned. Some teachers construct K-W-L charts to begin the questioning and inquiry that motivates children to find answers. Some use the charts on a daily basis, whereas others construct the charts at intervals to investigate the children's understanding. Figure 9–6 is an example of a K-W-L chart developed by a multi-aged primary classroom during their study of "Cleaning Up Our Creek."

The last statement in the K-W-L chart is an important one. Often, the chart will be revised and dated to list new questions so that every few days, a new chart is constructed. As the children learn more, the new K is based on the L from the previous days, and new questions become the new W, or what we want to know. The children's notation that they did not know the names of all the fish in their creek became one of the points for the new W. The **culminating activity** was planned to be a cleanup day at the creek. However, after the actual cleanup day, the children wanted to "do something," and their public awareness campaign for the entire school and

K-W-L Chart for Cleaning Up Our Creek	
K	**What we know about our creek**
	It is the closest creek to our school.
	There are other creeks with names similar to our creek.
	It is not straight; it twist, and turns.
	It is at different levels at different times of the year.
	Heavy rains cause it to flood in places.
W	**What we want to know about our creek**
	Where does our creek end?
	How does the trash get into the creek?
	What animals live on the banks?
	Are there any fish, frogs, or turtles living in the creek?
	Who owns the creek?
L	**What we have learned about our creek**
	Our creek flows into the Kentucky River, which flows into the Mississippi River, which flows to the Gulf of Mexico.
	Trash gets into the creek because people throw it into the creek or the water picks up trash on the banks when it floods over into parks, roads, and fields.
	We could hear the creek and the animals and insects when we stood very still and listened.
	There are many animals that live in the creek or along the banks.
	Some people who live near the creek have seen animals such as raccoons, opossums, muskrats, beavers, squirrels, and chipmunks.
	Ducks, crows, cranes, kingfishers, cardinals, blue jays, finches, hummingbirds, buzzards, and geese have been seen floating on, bathing in, and flying around the creek.
	Frogs, toads, and turtles live in the creek or on the banks.
	Thousands of insects, mosquitoes, gnats, spiders, and butterflies have been seen and heard near the creek.
	Minnows and small catfish have been seen in the creek. We don't know the names of all the fish.

FIGURE 9–6
K-W-L Chart for Cleaning Up Our Creek.

community began. It resulted in slogans, bulletin boards of artwork and photographs, a large display at the entrance to the school, newspaper accounts of the children's cleanup efforts, and a broadcast on the school's closed-circuit television station.

❀ CREATIVE EXPRESSION IN THE K-W-L CHART ON "CLEANING UP OUR CREEK"

In addition to the creative expressions of the slogans, bulletin boards, and large displays, there were numerous other opportunities for the children to be creative. A wood duck with a beautiful green head floating in the creek inspired several paintings. The twists and turns of the creek were modeled in the sand and water table, with packed mud added to simulate the banks. The litter patrol made up a

TABLE 9–2 Comparison of Systematic Instruction, Thematic Unit and Project Work

Systematic Instruction	Thematic Unit	Project Work
Teacher determines curriculum, skills, and instruction	Theme is selected by teacher	Children's interest guides the study
Child works for teacher and rewards	Objectives for the learning are stated by teacher	Child determines the direction of the work
Teacher selects activities and materials	Specific Lessons and activities are planned	Child selects activities that support the work
Teacher evaluates, using formal or informal measures	Content areas and arts are integrated into the study	Children and teacher determine questions, plans, and work
	Time frame is determined by teacher	Project may continue for a long time
	Books, centers, and activities focus on the theme	Books, centers, and experiences grow from the children's inquiry and interest
	Evaluation is based on the learning objectives for the thematic study	Observations and documentation are used to determine child's learning and interest

song to accompany their walk along the banks of the creek. And an audiotape of a gurgling creek inspired a story about children camping out but not being able to sleep because of the unfamiliar night noises.

Project work has many different interpretations, depending on the place, teachers, and children. In this book, we refer to a "project" as a part of the curriculum that encourages children to use their emerging skills in informal and open-ended activities. The project is an in-depth study that focuses on a specific topic that is of interest to the children and evolves as they investigate the topic. Work of the project can take place over a two-week period or a two-month period, based on the interest of the children who are involved.

❈ THE PROJECT APPROACH

In their book *Engaging Children's Minds: The Project Approach*, Lilian G. Katz and Sylvia C. Chard (2000) use many of the same descriptors discussed in this chapter. Katz and Chard state, "In some countries, project work is referred to as theme or topic work. Others refer to a project as a unit. Some teachers combine project work with a learning-center approach" (p. xii). A project is an in-depth study of a particular topic that one or more children undertake that emerges from the child's interest. Often, thematic teaching in the United States refers to the entire class of children studying a topic or children working in smaller groups. For example, in a unit on pets, different children may choose to learn individually about their own pets whereas the whole class will be involved in the group activities related to pets. A project idea might evolve from an individual, a group, or the whole class. Projects involve the children in planning and require their sustained interest in the topic.

Katz and Chard also describe projects on going shopping, including setting up a classroom shop or market. This approach is much like the one described by Isbell (1995) in the Grocery Store Center. Many primary-grade children study the weather as part of the recommended science curriculum. Katz and Chard's description of weather projects includes temperature studies, wind, shade and shadow, rain, animals, climate, and sayings and myths.

The project approach begins with the children's emerging interest and may last for several weeks to months. Through planning, the teacher and children discuss what already is known about a topic and decide how to learn more. Then, while the project is ongoing, the teacher expands the learning with visitors to the classroom, special investigations, or connecting to other areas of the children's interests. Finally, the children reflect on what they have learned, and make representations and engage in play related to the topic. For example, children might make a book or build a car after making careful observations, sketches, measurements, and taking photographs. The newly built car can be used for dramatic play to extend the learning until the children's interest wanes.

In the preschool classroom, projects may be used in conjunction with learning centers, circle time, or other traditional elements. Appropriate early childhood activities, such as story reading, music, and art, are often included in the plan or in addition to project work. Young children usually work in small groups, as they research and participate in the project. In the primary classroom, projects can be included in combination with systematic instruction. This project work provides children an opportunity to apply the skills they are learning in meaningful activities. Projects that are of interest to children will engage their minds and make the learning of skills more

> **"Project work relies on intrinsic motivation. It capitalizes on the child's own interest in the work . . . and a much wider range of possible activities."**
>
> *L. Katz & S. Chard, 2000*

> **"Well developed projects engage children's minds and become adventures that teacher and children embark on together."**
>
> *J. H. Helm & L. G. Katz, 2000*

An interest in space leads to the construction of a spaceship made from foil and wood.

likely to occur. Primary children can work on projects as an individual, in small groups, or with the entire class (Katz & Chard, 2000; Katz & Helm, 2001).

The project approach emphasizes children's active participation and teachers who provide guidance and assistance during the study. Children are encouraged to question, wonder, gain knowledge, and learn about the world around them. Project work is emergent and constantly changing, as children investigate, collect information, and record what they learn. Since projects are emerging, they provide a less structured time and more active learning in a program. Project work often comes from questions that children pose about their environment and things they have experienced. For example, preschoolers in an urban area might be fascinated by ways to make their community playground more interesting. A project that might develop from the interests of kindergarten children living in a rural area could be, "What is grown on a local farm?" And, primary children may wonder about the insects they find on the playground. These investigations are built on the children's questions, the place they live, and the experiences they have had.

Why Use Projects?

The practices that are part of the project approach are not new to early childhood education; the same practices were originally suggested by Dewey (2001) and Kilpatrick (1925). The project approach can also be recognized in programs from England in the 1920s and the British Infant Schools. The "Plowden Report" suggested that learning is more effective if it grows out of the interests of the children rather than the teacher (Silberman, 1970). More recently, the project approach resembles the program offered and developed at the Bank Street College of Education in New York.

Katz and Chard (2000) conclude that research on children's development and the way they learn supports the inclusion of the project approach in early childhood programs. They explain that project work can stimulate and expand children's intellectual and social development. Project work is of interest to the children. Therefore, it is intrinsically motivating.

Since project work is more informal and emerging, it allows children to work on their level, while choosing the activities and research tools they will use. This provides balance to a program that may include some teacher-directed aspects as well as traditional components of high-quality early childhood programs.

The Teacher's Role in Project Work

In the project approach, the teacher assumes new roles as researcher and learner. As a researcher, he or she finds experts, resources, or references that might contribute to the studies and poses questions that may capture the children's attention or be left for future investigation. The teacher provides provocations that challenge children to extend their thinking and observes the children as they develop plans; he or she may also suggest that they draw or web the possibilities. In project work, the teacher is not the person who lectures or gives information to the group. Rather, the teacher's role is to guide discussions, collect materials, and learn alongside the children. The teacher is a model of a learner who is curious, excited about learning, and venturing into new areas of study. The teacher is also involved in the documentation of the project, as he or she works with children to determine the information and photographs that should be included on a panel. During this process, the teacher can help children discover ways to effectively demonstrate learning, being an artist, creating a drama, designing a museum for display, or writing a song.

EMERGING CURRICULUM AND THE REGGIO EMILIA APPROACH

The term **emerging curriculum** is used to differentiate between structured, pre-planned lessons, and those that emerge from the child's interests and exploration of a topic. Susan Wright (1997) described the Reggio Emilia preschools to illustrate how children may choose their topics and become engaged in them through a variety of activities that continue over days, weeks, or sometimes months. Ideas emerge from the children's desire to know rather than from special objectives for the lessons or experiences predetermined by the teacher. Instead, the teachers create a learning environment, rich with materials for construction, artistic expression, and general exploration. Then, when a topic of study is selected, teachers and children plan together, collect additional materials, and work on ways to learn about the

> "We think of a school for young children as an integrated living organism, as a place of shared lives and relationships among many adults and very many children."
>
> *L. Malaguzzi, 1993*

Organizing art materials makes selection easier.

topic. Parents can be included by informing them of the topics children are exploring and requesting their input of possibilities for expanding the study. The curriculum emerges without the designation ahead of time of what will be learned and what will be achieved (Rinaldi, 1993).

Some of the ingenuity of the Reggio Emilia approach and the emergent curriculum is that the teachers listen to the children, follow their curiosity, and find ways to support exploration. For example, in a discussion of the emerging curriculum, Rinaldi described teachers who discussed summer vacations with their children and observed that the children frequently mentioned "the crowd." From the children's interest in and perceptions of being in a crowd, a rich study emerged. The children observed crowds, drew themselves and others in crowds, dramatized their feelings in crowds, photographed crowds, counted people, and researched what drew crowds. The project emerged from the teachers' careful observation of the children while listening to their ideas.

In the Reggio Emilia approach, young children become immersed in learning. Instead of moving children through a schedule, preschoolers spend great expanses of time focused on a project. The teacher or facilitator helps with vocabulary, possibilities for representing what is learned, and provides materials that support research in order to nurture learning, language, and the arts.

Rinaldi described a long jump project in which the children generated 22 different activities from looking at pictures of Olympic long jumpers. The children set up rules for a long jump contest, designed discreet measurements during the contest, and planned the ceremony for winners. In Reggio Emilia classrooms, children express, represent, and extend what they are learning. Teachers are highly observant and spend a great deal of time documenting what they see. They provide provocation for the children's learning by adding materials to the learning environment. In the Reggio classroom, the curriculum comes from the children and leads

Clay is first explored and later used to represent ideas.

to in-depth study. The work of the children is focused and intense. Their language (including drawing, sculptures, and dramatic productions) often demonstrates their learning.

 ## SUMMARY

Creativity and the arts can be woven throughout the early childhood program. The curriculum can be planned to meet children's developmental needs, individual needs, or provide avenues for expression, including the need for self and artistic expression. Some of the techniques that can be used include systematic instruction, integrated curriculum, thematic units, emerging curriculum, and the project approach. Most early childhood programs include a combination of these different approaches because they provide varied learning opportunities and provide a connection to children's interests. They often include a component that assesses the children's learning either formally or informally. These observations and skill identification provide the teacher with information that can be used to develop the curriculum and select activities that will nurture children's development intellectually, social/emotionally, and physically. Experts have repeatedly identified the need to include the arts, since they lead to the development of the "whole child." Themes, projects, and developmentally appropriate activities provide ways for children to learn to identify their interests and express their ideas in different types of language.

The classroom environment, including the organization of the centers, displays of materials, and documentation, also has an impact on the curriculum. Thematic units and projects provide a way to integrate content areas and the arts into a comprehensive curriculum that provides opportunities to build sustaining interest, while engaging children in personally meaningful learning. The curriculum can include K-W-L charts that help identify what children know, what they want to know, and reflect on what was learned. A culminating activity can help children synthesize the information, while creatively demonstrating their learning. The emerging curriculum provides opportunities for children and teachers to follow their interests, and actively participate in meaningful activities. The project approach provides opportunities for more in-depth study, to move in different directions, and to have more diverse ways of documenting what learning has occurred. These approaches match what is known about how children learn and benefit from actively pursuing their interests.

 ## KEY TERMS

culminating activity
Developmentally Appropriate Practice (DAP)
emerging curriculum
High/Scope
human impulses

initiating activities
National Association for the Education of Young Children (NAEYC)
project approach
subject area
theme

 ## REFLECTION

1. How are themes or units selected for early childhood classrooms? PreK–K? Primary?

2. Explain the use of projects in an early childhood classroom. What are some of the strengths of this approach? Are there weaknesses?

3. Read more about the Reggio Emilia approach. Do you think this format promotes creativity? Explain why or why not.

4. Creativity and self-expression in this chapter are associated with what the children learn. How can you ensure that children's art products will all look different while they participate in many of the same activities?

✺ THINKING ABOUT THE OBSERVATION OF CREATIVITY

1. What was Darren interested in photographing?
2. How were photographs used to document a class project?
3. How did Darren's photography change after he observed and talked to the adult photographer?
4. How did Darren demonstrate that he was proud of his photographs?
5. How were the photos used to document the experience?

✺ POSSIBILITIES FOR ADULT LEARNERS

Activity: Unit Planning the Systematic Way
Goal: To develop a unit using a systematic plan.
Materials: Textbook with the directions for planning a unit.
Procedure:

1. Divide into small groups, teachers who are planning to work in PreK–K or with primary children.
2. Select a thematic unit that you might teach.
3. Use the steps outlined in the chapter to create curriculum planning webs by brainstorming and using the eight-cell planning tool.

Activity: To Teach Thematically or Not to Teach Thematically: That Is the Question
Goal: To observe the use of thematic units in an early childhood classroom.
Materials: Notebook and pen or pencil.
Procedure:

1. Visit a preschool, kindergarten, child-care center, or primary classroom.
2. Write down the schedule for the day.
3. Note times when thematic teaching is incorporated into the schedule, and if it is not, times when it could be incorporated.
4. Share your observations in class discussion.

✺ OPEN-ENDED ACTIVITIES FOR YOUNG CHILDREN

PreK–K

Activity: A New Baby in the Family
Goal: To use information about a baby in play.
Materials: Baby clothes, bottles, diaper bag, baby toys, audiotape of lullabies.

Procedure:

1. After the new baby's visit to the classroom, collect baby items.
2. Place the items in the housekeeping corner.
3. Observe the new play that occurs as children explore the roles of having a new baby in the family.

Kindergarten

Activity:	Building Homes for Families
Goal:	To construct homes representing places where families might live.
Materials:	Poster board, paste board, paint, small blocks, pieces of wood, glue, twigs, small stones, and other such items.

Procedure:

1. Read the book *My Great Grandpa* by Martin Waddell (1990).
2. Provide construction materials for the children to make houses.
3. Observe what kind of houses the children make.
4. Display their creations to be appreciated by all.
5. Some children may decide to make houses like Great Grandpa described; others simply may construct something associated with houses and neighborhoods.

Primary Grades

Activity:	What I Have Learned
Goal:	To identify ways to share what children have learned.
Materials:	Chart paper and other display materials.

Procedure:

1. How can children let others know what they have learned?
2. In a class discussion of the theme, note all the different concepts the class has learned.
3. Let the children decide how they might show others what they have learned through paintings, drawings, drama, photos, block displays, and the like.

ADDITIONAL READING

Allen, D. D., & Piersma, M. L. (1995). *Developing thematic units: Process & product.* Clifton Park, NY: Thomson Delmar Learning.

Altwerger, B., & Flores, B. (1994). Theme cycles: Creating communities of learners. *Primary Voices K–6, 2*(1), 2–6.

Bayman, A. G. (1995). An example of a small project for kindergartners that includes some 3Rs learning. *Young Children, 50*(6), 27–31.

Cadwell, L. (1997). *Bringing Reggio Emilia home: An innovative approach to early childhood education.* New York: Teachers College Press.

Chard, S.C. (1998). *Project approach: Developing the basic framework. Practical guide 1.* New York: Scholastic.

Chard, S.C. (1998). *Project approach: Developing curriculum with children. Practical guide 2.* New York: Scholastic.

Cornett, C. E. (1999). *The arts as meaning makers.* Upper Saddle River, NJ: Prentice Hall.

Dodge, D. T., & Colker, L. (1992). *Creative curriculum for early childhood.* Washington, DC: Teaching Strategies.

Edwards, C. P. (1993). Inviting children into project work. *Dimensions of Early Childhood, 22*(1), 9–12, 40.

Edwards, C., Gandini, L., & Forman, G. (Eds.). (1998). *The hundred languages of children: The Reggio Emilia approach—advanced reflections* (2nd ed.). Stamford, CT: Ablex.

Elgas, P. M., & Peltier, M. B. (1998). Jimmy's journey: Building a sense of community and self-worth through small-group work. *Young Children, 53*(2), 55–59.

Elliot, M. J. (1998). Great moments of learning in project work. *Young Children, 53*(2), 55–59.

Freeman, C. C., & Sokoloff, H. J. (1996). Children learning to make a better world: Exploring themes. *Childhood Education, 73*(1), 17–22.

Gandini, L. (1993). Fundamentals of the Reggio Emilia approach to early childhood education. *Young Children, 49*, 4–8.

Giffard, S. (1997). Theme studies and the arts. *Primary Voices K–6, 5*(2), 2–5.

Goldberg, M. R. (2000). *Arts and learning: An integrated approach to teaching and learning in multicultural and multilingual setting* (2nd ed.). New York: Longman.

Goldhaber, J. (1998). Oh, Miss Jones! Where did you get that beautiful butterfly? *Young Children, 53*(2), 60–63.

Hartman, J. A., & Eckerty, C. (1995). Projects in the early years. *Childhood Education, 71*(3), 141–147.

Helm, J. H., & Katz, L. G. (2001). *Young investigators: The project approach in the early years.* Washington, DC: National Association for the Education of Young Children.

Hendricks, J. (Ed.). (1997). *First step toward teaching the Reggio way.* Upper Saddle River, NJ: Prentice Hall.

Hohmann, M., Babet, B., & Weikart, P. (1979). *Young children in action.* Ypsilanti, MI: High/Scope Press.

Jones, E., & Nimmo, J. (1994). *Emergent curriculum.* Washington, DC: National Association for the Education of Young Children.

Leekeenan, D., & Edwards, C. P. (1992). Using the project approach with toddlers. *Young Children, 47*(4), 31–36.

Marcon, R. A. (1992). Differential effects of three preschool models on inner-city 4-year-olds. *Early Childhood Research Quarterly, 7*(4), 517–530.

Rankin, B. (1992). Inviting children's creativity: A story of Reggio Emilia, Italy. *Child Care Information Exchange, 85*, 30–35.

Sloane, M. W. (1999). All kinds of projects for your classroom. *Young Children, 54*(4), 17–20.

Trepanier-Street, M. (1993). What's so new about the project approach? *Childhood Education, 70*(1), 25–28.

Workman, S., & Anziano, M. C. (1994). Curriculum webs: Weaving connections from children to teachers. *Young Children, 49*(1), 4–9.

 ## CHILDREN'S LITERATURE CONNECTION

Family Thematic Unit

Brown, M. (1987). *Arthur's baby.* New York: Joy Street Books.
   Arthur isn't sure he is happy about the new baby in the family, but when his sister asks him for help in handling the baby, Arthur feels much better. (PreK–3)

Crews, D. (1991). *Bigmama's.* New York: Greenwillow Books.
   Banished to the hallway for disrupting the class on the day of a favorite author's visit, best friends Chris and Jeremy write the most outlandish apologies they can think of. (PreK–3)

Dragonwagon, C. (1990). *Home place.* New York: Macmillan.
   While hiking, a family comes on the site of an old house and finds some clues about the people that once lived there. (PreK–3)

Henkes, K. (1991). *Julius, the baby of the world.* New York: Greenwillow Books.
>   Lilly is convinced that the arrival of her new baby brother is the worst thing that has happened in their house, until Cousin Garland comes to visit. (PreK–3)

Hines, A. G. (1986). *Daddy makes the best spaghetti.* New York: Clarion.
>   Not only does Corey's father make the best spaghetti, but he also dresses up like Bathman and acts like a barking dog. (PreK–K)

Hoban, R. (1964). *A baby sister for Frances.* New York: Harper & Row.
>   When things change around the house after her baby sister is born, Frances decides to run away; but not too far. (K–3)

Morris, A. (1990). *Loving.* New York: Mulberry.
>   This book offers a look at families throughout the world and how they show love. (PreK–K)

Polacco, P. (1988). *The keeping quilt.* New York: Simon & Schuster.
>   A homemade quilt ties together the lives of four generations of an immigrant Jewish family, and remains a symbol of their enduring faith and love. (K–3)

Rylant, C. (1985). *The relatives came.* New York: Bradbury Press.
>   The relatives come to visit from Virginia and everyone has a wonderful time. (PreK–3)

Schlemmer, P., & Schlemmer, D. (1998). *Challenging projects for creative minds.* Minneapolis: Free Spirit.
>   Containing 12 self-directed enrichment projects, this book develops and showcases student ability. (Ages 6–10)

Shelby, A. (1995). *Homeplace.* New York: Orchard Books.
>   A grandmother and grandchild trace their family history. (PreK–K)

Simon, N. (1976). *All kinds of families.* Niles, IL: Albert Whitman.
>   This picture book is an essay on family love and communities. (PreK–3)

Tang, G. (2004). *Math fables: Lessons that count.* New York: Scholastic.
>   A book containing rhymes about animals that teach behaviors such as cooperation, friendship, and appreciation, while introducing children to counting and grouping numbers. (Ages 3–6)

Thompson, L. (2004). *Little Quack's Hide and Seek.* New York: Simon & Schuster Children's.
>   The story of a mother duck playing hide and seek with her ducklings. As she counts down from ten, each page has a "Quack-u-Lator" to help children count down with her. (Infant–PreK)

Waddell, M. (1990). *My great grandpa.* New York: G. P. Putnam.
>   Spending a memorable Sunday with her great-grandfather and her other grandparents, eight-year-old Deborah realizes that with good health, the elderly can live a rich and varied life. (K–3)

Wells, Rosemary. (2001). *World around us: Based on Timothy goes to school and other stories.* London: Puffin.
>   In this fun activity book, children learn about families, communities, and cooperation. (Infant–PreK)

"Cleaning Up Our Creek" Unit

Bang, M. (1996). *Chattanooga sludge.* New York: Harcourt Brace & Company.
>   John Todd attempts to clean the toxic waters of Chattanooga Creek with a Living Machine. (K–3)

Berger, M. (1992). *Look out for turtles!* New York: HarperCollins.
>   Describes the remarkable turtle, which can live almost anywhere, eat almost anything, ranges in size from tiny to gigantic, and lives longer than any other animal. (K–3)

Cone, M. (1994). *Come back, salmon: How a group of dedicated kids adopted Pigeon Creek and brought it back to life.* San Francisco: Sierra Club Books for Children.
>   An inspiring story of young scientists in action in Everette, Washington. These children worked with their teacher to clean up Pigeon Creek and reclaim it as a salmon spawning ground. (K–3)

George, W. T. (1989). *Box Turtle at Long Pond.* New York: Greenwillow Books.
>   On a busy day at Long Pond, Box Turtle searches for food, basks in the sun, and escapes a raccoon. (PreK–K)

Guilberson, B. (1992). *Spoonbill swamp*. New York: Henry Holt.
>In a tropical swamp, a spoonbill and an alligator care for their young throughout the day. (PreK–K)

Lewin, T. (1992). *When the rivers go home*. New York: Macmillan.
>An introduction to an exotic endangered habitat—the Pantanal—a vast swamp in central Brazil. (PreK–3)

Reiser, L. (1993). *Tomorrow on Rocky Pond*. New York: Greenwillow Books.
>Vacationing in the country, a child anticipates tomorrow's activities of fishing and hiking. (PreK–K)

Say, A. (1989). *The lost lake*. Boston: Houghton Mifflin.
>A young boy and his father become closer friends during a camping trip in the mountains. (PreK–K)

 For additional resources involving creativity and the arts with young children, visit our Web site at **www.earlychilded.delmar.com**

REFERENCES

Bredekamp, S. (1996). 25 years of educating young children: The High/Scope approach to preschool education. *Young Children, 51*(4), 57–61.

Bredekamp, S., & Copple, C. (1997). *Developmentally appropriate practice in early childhood programs*. Washington, DC: National Association for the Education of Young Children.

Bredekamp, S., & Rosegrant, T. (Eds.). (1992). *Reaching potentials: Appropriate curriculum and assessment for young children—Volume 1*. Washington, DC: National Association for the Education of Young Children.

Bredekamp, S., & Rosegrant, T. (Eds.). (1995). *Reaching potentials: Appropriate curriculum and assessment for young children—Volume 2*. Washington, DC: National Association for the Education of Young Children.

Cone, M. (1994). *Come back, salmon: How a group of dedicated kids adopted Pigeon Creek and brought it back to life*. San Francisco: Sierra Club Books for Children.

Dewey, J. (1902). *The child and curriculum*. Chicago: University of Chicago Press.

Dewey, J. (2001). *The school and society: And the child and the curriculum*. Mineola, NY: Dover.

Fitzhenry, R. I. (Ed.). (1993). *The Harper book of quotations* (3rd ed.). New York: HarperCollins.

Gardner, H. (1993). *Frames of mind: The theory of multiple intelligences* (20th Anniversary Edition). New York: Basic Books.

Healy, J. (1990). *Endangered minds: Why children don't think and what we can do about it*. New York: Simon & Schuster.

Helm, J. H., & Katz, L. G. (2000). *Young investigators: The project approach in the early years*. New York: Teachers College Press.

Hoban, R. (1964). *A baby sister for Frances*. New York: Harper & Row.

Hohmann, M., & Weikart, D. P. (1995). *Educating young children: Active learning practices for preschool and child care programs*. Ypsilanti, MI: High Scope Press.

Isbell, R. (1995). *The complete learning center book*. Beltsville, MD: Gryphon House.

Jalongo, M. R., & Isenberg, J. P. (2000). *Exploring your role: A practitioner's introduction to early childhood education*. Upper Saddle River, NJ: Merrill.

Jarolimek, J., & Foster, C. D. (1989). *Teaching and learning in the elementary school*. New York: Macmillan.

Jensen, E. (1998). *Teaching with the brain in mind*. Alexandria, VA: Association for Supervision and Curriculum Development.

Katz, L. G. & Chard, S. C. (2000). *Engaging children's minds: The project approach*. Norwood, NJ: Ablex.

Katz, L. G., & Helm, J. H. (2001). *Young investigators: The project approach in the early years*. Williston, VT: Teacher's College Press.

Kilpatrick, W. H. (1925). *Foundations of method: Informal talks on teaching.* New York: Macmilan.

Malaguzzi, L. (1993). History, ideas, and basic philosophy. In C. Edwards, L. Gandini, and G. Forman (Eds.), *The hundred languages of children: The Reggio Emilia approach to early childhood education* (pp. 41–89). Norwood, NJ: Ablex.

Morris, A. (1990). *Loving.* New York: Mulberry.

Moyer, J., Egertson, H., & Isenberg, J. (1987). The child-centered kindergarten. *Childhood Education, 63*(4), 235–242.

NAEYC. (1997). *Developmentally appropriate practice in early childhood programs serving children from birth through age 8: A position statement of the National Association for the Education of Young Children.* Washington, DC: NAEYC.

Ornstein, A. C., & Hunkins, F. P. (1988). *Curriculum: Foundations, principles, and issues.* Englewood Cliffs, NJ: Prentice Hall.

Raines, S. C. (1995). *Whole language across the curriculum: Grades 1, 2, 3.* New York: Teachers College Press.

Raines, S. C. (1997). Developmental appropriateness: Curriculum revisited and challenged. In J. P. Isenberg & M. R. Jalongo (Eds.), *Major trends and issues in early childhood education* (pp. 75–89). New York: Teachers College Press.

Raines, S. C., & Canady, R. J. (1989). *Story s-t-r-e-t-c-h-e-r-s: Activities to expand children's favorite books.* Mt. Rainier, MD: Gryphon House.

Raines, S. C., & Canady, R. J. (1990). *The whole language kindergarten.* New York: Teachers College Press.

Raines, S. C., & Canady, R. J. (1991). *More story s-t-r-e-t-c-h-e-r-s: More activities to expand children's favorite books.* Mt. Rainier, MD: Gryphon House.

Raines, S. C., & Canady, R. J. (1992). *Story s-t-r-e-t-c-h-e-r-s for the primary grades: Activities to expand children's favorite books.* Mt. Rainier, MD: Gryphon House.

Rinaldi, C. (1993). The emergent curriculum and social constructivism. In C. Edwards, L. Gandini, & G. Forman (Eds.), *The hundred languages of children: The Reggio Emilia approach to early childhood education* (pp. 101–111). Norwood, NJ: Ablex.

Rylant, C. (1985). *The relatives came.* New York: Bradbury Press.

Schweinhart, L. J., Montie, J., Xiang, Z., Barnett, W. S., Belfield, C. R., & Nores, M. (2004). Lifetime effects: The High/Scope Perry Preschool study through age 40. *Monographs of the High/Scope Educational Research Foundation, 14.* Ypsilanti, MI: High/Scope Press.

Silberman, C. E. (December 4, 1970). Crisis in the classroom: A diagnosis, with suggestion for remedy. (Speech given at the 85th Annual meeting). Boston: New England Association of Colleges and Secondary Schools. (ERIC Document Reproduction No. ED047412.)

Simon, N. (1976). *All kinds of families.* Niles, IL: Albert Whitman.

Smith, B. O., Stanley, W. O., & Shores, J. H. (1957). *Fundamentals of curriculum development.* New York: Wiley.

Snyder, S. (March 2001). Connection, correlation, and integration. *Music Educators Journal. 87*(5), 32–39, 70.

Wright, S. (1997). Learning how to learn: The arts as core in an emergent curriculum. *Childhood Education, 73*(6), 361–365.

INTEGRATING THE ARTS

CHAPTER 10

This chapter provides the rationale for the arts being interwoven into early childhood classrooms. Examples from centers, themes, and emerging projects will be presented. The chapter also explores the child's creative expression and enjoyment of art, music, movement and dance, drama, and storytelling in many forms.

After studying this chapter, you will be able to:
- Identify a "position paper," and explain how these support a child's right to the expressive arts.
- Distinguish teaching with the arts, about the arts, and through the arts.
- Describe how NAEYC (National Association for the Education of Young Children) Developmentally Appropriate Practices have an impact on the arts in the classroom.
- Collaborate with art specialists for the benefit of young children.
- Discuss the role of an atelierista in the early childhood program.
- Identify how the arts could be integrated into a unit of study.

OBSERVATION OF CREATIVITY

Inspired by dandelions blooming on the school lawn in April, several four- and five-year-olds picked the yellow flowers for their teacher. A white pottery coffee cup holding a bunch of dandelions was perched on top of a low bookcase in full view of the painting easel. Other dandelions lay wilting on top of the bookcase. Another bunch was placed in a styrofoam cup on the science table, accompanied by a chart that in large print asked, "Is it a flower or is it a weed? What do you think?" Two columns were drawn on the chart: one was labeled weed and the other flower. Green markers were provided for children to mark weed and yellow markers for those who chose flower.

Is it a flower or is it a weed? What do you think?	
WEED	FLOWER
I I I I	I I I I I I I I I I I I I

Without the teacher's prescription but with the teacher's inspiration, dandelions were painted the most. Many of the painters concentrated on painting yellow, white, and green, although there

WHAT WAS OBSERVED?

What does the creative episode tell us about the teacher, the children, and the organization of the classroom? Why did the teacher capitalize on the occasion of the dandelion gifts? The teacher in this PreK classroom provided time in the schedule and materials, and he planned for connections between the expressive arts and the curriculum. Although not a formal curricular topic, dandelions emerged as an interest when they surfaced on the lawn near the outside play area. The teacher could have accepted the bouquet of flowers as a gift from the children, but instead capitalized on the occasion and incorporated the dandelions into the classroom activities.

were many other colors in the paint tray of the easel. Several struggled with how to show the white cup on the nearly white paper. Most of the children painted huge renditions of the dandelions. Some of the older children in the group drew themselves picking the dandelions, then painted their pictures. One child made green lines and yellow splotches near the bottom of his paper to illustrate the wilting dandelions, but most of the children concentrated on the cup of flowers. The chart was true to their language; most believed that the dandelion was a flower.

DEFINITIONS AND RIGHTS OF THE CHILD FOR THE EXPRESSIVE ARTS

In the Association for Childhood Education International's (ACEI) position statement, "The Child's Right to the Expressive Arts: Nurturing the Imagination as Well as the Intellect," Jalongo (1990) writes, "The expressive arts—music, art, drama, dance, writing—are important because they are the means of communicating our creative productivity and imaginative thinking." The entire position statement can be found, along with the newest position paper, "The Child's Right to Creative Thought and Expression" (Jalongo, 2003), at the end of this chapter.

Children are constructors of language and of other representations of what they know, feel, and desire to express (Raines & Canady, 1990). The expressive arts give children multiple means of communication as they create with materials and as they examine the representations and creations of others. In 1902, John Dewey proposed that the early childhood curriculum should be driven by "the human impulses to socialize, to construct, to inquire, to question, to experiment, and to express or to create artistically" (Smith, Stanley, & Shores, 1957, p. 265). The human impulse to express oneself and create artistically is a time-honored tradition, worthy of continuing in the early childhood classrooms of today.

ACEI's position paper on "The Child's Right to the Expressive Arts" (Jalongo) gives educators a statement of seven rights that can guide classroom practice.

1. Every child has a right to opportunities for imaginative expression.
   Time, materials, and artistic instruction must be provided for all children, not just those dubbed as gifted and talented.

2. Educating the child's imagination is education for the future.
   We are told by futurists that tomorrow's children will need to be creative, flexible, imaginative, risk-takers, able to work with multiple images, see issues from different

A young child is painting on an easel outdoors.

perspectives, and enjoy change. The expressive arts can enhance each of these characteristics.

3. The educated imagination is the key to equity and intercultural understanding.

Creativity and the expressive arts lead us to explorations of our own self-expression and an appreciation of how others express themselves. From children's self-perspectives, they use their imaginations to identify with others, to interpret others' expressions, to see new cultural interpretations, and to build connections (Hansen, 1986; Hoffman & Lamme, 1989; Jalongo, 1990).

4. Children's creative productivity is qualitatively different from adults'.

Children grow in their ability to control media. While there are similarities among children in their productions in artistic expression, their originality and imagination should be appreciated instead of expecting that the renderings, music, and other productions should be like those of little adults.

5. Creative expression should permeate the entire curriculum.

Children's play, drawing, painting, sculpting, building, storytelling, movement, and music are available to children long before they can express themselves in the standards of reading and writing. Opportunities to express one's self and to understand others' expressions is central to the early childhood curriculum, and transcends the curricular areas.

6. Imagination is the key to artistry in teaching and excellence in our schools.

Dull and uninspired curriculum can come alive when children and teachers use their imaginations to express what they are learning. According to Kieran Egan (1988), the arts and creative expression are not alternatives to education, but rather a basic to all educational activity.

7. We must refashion our schools for creative expression.

Given our ambitions for education to provide opportunities for children to grow as thinkers, reflective decision-makers, risk-takers, and expressive human beings, our schools must change their view of the arts and creative expression as extras, and see them as basic to our human needs and desires.

✿ ORIENTATION TO THE ARTS

Bresler (1993) researched teachers' orientations to incorporating art experiences into daily classroom practices. They described three orientations to the arts curriculum:

1. the **little-intervention orientation**
2. the **product-oriented orientation**
3. the **guided-exploration orientation**

A brief review of the three orientations provides insight into appropriate integration of the arts. The little-intervention orientation is most often associated with the belief that if one provides the materials for artistic expression, time in the schedule, and the expectation that children will use the materials, then the children will express themselves creatively. This view most often is associated with the visual arts and is prevalent in early childhood classrooms.

Many primary classrooms are product-oriented, meaning children are expected to produce a product whether in the visual or performing arts. In fact, this view is often associated with music and drama productions.

In the guided-exploration orientation view, children are taught about art forms and aesthetic qualities found in the specialists' classroom or the classrooms of teachers with an interest in the arts. This view is also consistent with the Getty Center for Education in the Arts position paper, "Beyond Creating: The Place for Art in America's Schools" (1985). The visual arts guided-exploration orientation teaches children about line, form, shapes, balance, and color. Similarly, the language of music, theater, and literature are used to describe the artistic and creative expression of others, whether children's works or those of famous artists.

Teachers in the little-intervention orientation emphasize creativity, the child's exploration of materials, self-expression, and independence. Authors Stake, Bresler, and Mabry (1991) criticize early childhood classrooms for the lack of an aesthetic environment, little knowledge of the arts, and concern that children may miss meaningful learning when the substance of the arts is available mostly through raw materials. In this environment, children may miss opportunities to expand their understanding of the arts. However, children's products in the little-intervention classroom are highly individualized, which meets the goals in early childhood classrooms.

Product-orientation often results in uniformity, little self-expression or independence, and rather simplistic expectations. Copied materials for coloring result in rows of art products that look the same, much like craft patterns. In music and drama, children are expected to perform exactly as the material was written, with little creativity or self-expression. The children's products are mostly the same as craft productions.

The guided-exploration orientation classrooms includes a diversity of materials similar to the little-intervention orientation, but the teacher guides the children's explorations of the art forms, the associated symbols, and the development of concepts, skills, and knowledge of the arts. In the guided-exploration orientation, the children's products are more individualized, but there are more products associated with the study of the arts and art forms, as well as opportunities for self-expression.

In early childhood classrooms, there are opportunities to use several of these approaches, alone or in combinations. The children in the classroom, their level of development, and the activities influence the selection and level of guidance. When a material or activity is first introduced, there is an essential period of exploration. This is how the young child learns about the material's properties. Later, or in a more advanced level of work or activity, a child may request help or guidance from either the teacher or his peers. The teacher must observe and respond appropriately to encourage the child and his growing abilities in the arts.

Project work often includes group discussion and planning with the teacher.

✿ DEVELOPMENTALLY APPROPRIATE PRACTICES AND THE PROCESS VERSUS PRODUCT ISSUE

Early childhood educators are guided by long-held practices, recommendations from experts and professional associations, and their own experiences. Generally, emphasis is placed on the process versus the product, given that the young child has much to experience and learn (Dixon & Chalmers, 1990). An early childhood teacher who makes play dough available to children may expect, at the end of cleanup time, that all of the dough will be returned to the tubs, with no remaining product. As many teachers of preschoolers have noted, the children may paint a picture, then get caught up in the process of painting and completely cover the sheet of paper on the easel with one color of paint. During the process, the child created a painting but chose to paint over it. The process was more important than the product. Children often have difficulty finding their paintings at the end of the day when they are dry enough to take home. It was the process of painting that was important. As children progress in their experiences with various art media, they begin making products they want to keep.

✿ INTEGRATED CURRICULUM

Integration involves combining diverse fragments into connected learning experiences that are meaningful for children. The arts can play a very important role in integrating the different parts into a whole, which makes the children's learning more understandable and comprehendible. However, the arts must also maintain their integrity when woven into other curriculum areas. For example, drawing a picture after a science nature walk provides the opportunity to recall what has been seen and represent this in drawings. It does not, however, provide the time to explore the art tools and materials that are available to be used in the studio art area. The drawing is a way for the children to represent and revisit what they have seen; it should not replace the focused time that is needed to explore art.

The arts are often interwoven into activities, making it difficult to determine the content area. When a child cuts clay with a plastic knife, is the experience art, science, or small motor development? It is all three. As children experiment with clay, they are learning the properties of the materials (science); when they pound and cut, they are manipulating the clay with their hands (motor development); and when they make a design on a pot formed by pinching the clay (a pinch pot) or shape the clay, it is art. The arts provide a vehicle for students to integrate their learning and provide diverse opportunities to learn. These integrated experiences are similar to life experiences in which learning is not compartmentalized, but rather happening together. The addition of the arts into curricular areas is important. However, it does not eliminate the need for focused time for drawing, painting, drama, movement, or music. These longer periods of intense investigation allow children to build their understanding of the arts and appreciate that these elements are an essential part of their lives and the classroom. The integration of the arts into the curriculum varies from a teacher who uses only a small amount of time to the teacher who uses the arts as a major component of the classroom. Cornett (1998) identified some different ways classroom teachers integrate the arts into their classroom.

Teaching with the Arts

In this method, the teacher includes art because the children enjoy it, and it provides them an opportunity to be creative. The teacher may have a circle song, an art center, and provide time for the children to explore materials.

Teaching about and in the Arts

In this design, the teacher helps children learn about the arts. They also use the arts in their work. In this approach, the teacher wants the children to develop their creativity and their knowledge of the arts. For example, a class of first graders studies Eric Carle's illustrations and techniques. They focus on the illustrations by comparing and contrasting the illustrations from several of his books. The children use resources and reference materials to find out about Eric Carle, the person and artist. During this two-week investigation, the children experiment with the materials and techniques that he has used in his artwork.

Teaching through the Arts

The teacher who uses this approach views the arts as an essential part of the day, and includes them in routines as well as units of study. In this classroom, there is a great deal of attention given to creating an aesthetically pleasing environment. Since the arts are considered content areas in this design, they can serve as a basis for units of study, as well as support content learning in other areas such as math, science, and social studies. Teaching though the arts creates a classroom where children are immersed in the arts and live with the arts.

✿ CLASSROOM TEACHERS COLLABORATE WITH EXPERTS

Early childhood educators can benefit from collaborating with specialists in art, music, movement, and drama. These specialists can provide in-depth information that will help in designing enriched experiences in the curriculum for young children that include the arts. If early childhood educators understand the basics of the field and recognize the importance of the arts, they will strive to include them in their classroom and throughout the curriculum. Specialists can provide suggestions for materials, resources, and methods that can be used to support the development of a project or a unit of study. For example, a third-grade teacher might want to develop a study of Africa. The music teacher may suggest musical instruments or songs from Africa that could be woven into the study. The art educator might have pictures of masks that were made in Africa that could inspire children's art. The movement or physical education teacher might suggest a dance that would get the children actively involved during the study, as they learn about Africa. These additions to the study will help the children better understand the people, the cultures, and some of the forms of art they use. When this collaboration occurs, early childhood teachers and children benefit from the expertise of specialists, which is integrated into the curriculum. Ultimately, it is the early childhood teacher who selects the materials and activities to be included in the curriculum. She or he values the arts because they provide another way of knowing and challenging children's thinking.

In primary schools, where music and art teachers are more widespread, teachers may not attend each other's classes. If one is fortunate enough to have a music, art, dance, or movement teacher, he should attend the class with the children and provide opportunities during the week for children to use what they have learned from the arts educator. Collaborate with the specialist on how to support current projects and themes in the classroom. Use music, art, or drama activities occurring in special classes to enrich classroom experiences. The interweaving of the activities of the specialist and teacher helps children learn that the arts are for all people, not just a special few.

Artist-in-Residence Programs

Another source of expertise is the **Artist-in-Residence** program. Practicing artists, often supported by school districts or community arts councils, agree to spend some of their time with children, where they demonstrate their art, facilitate lessons, and help children learn about their profession. Few artist-in-residence programs have been adapted to very young children, yet children enjoy live performances and can learn the language of art, new concepts, and discover what skills are needed. Older children who have developed some proficiency in their art form, and adults who are hobby artists, also are excellent resources to provide expertise or performances in the early childhood classroom. A violinist may play music for the children, then let the children pluck the violin strings, try the bow, and feel the vibrations. A potter may throw a pot, then teach the children a simple coiling and shaping method. Opportunities to observe, interact, and appreciate an artist's work enrich children's learning and inspire their artistic abilities.

Atelier and the Atelierista in Reggio Emilia Programs

Reggio Emilia programs have prompted educators in the United States to reflect on the importance of the arts. Teachers have examined extensive murals and sculptures created by young children in Reggio Emilia and noted their highly individualized responses and connection to the project being studied. Educators recognize that young children are far more capable in the arts than was previously believed. *The Hundred Languages of Children* is an exhibit of children's work that tours around the world. This impressive display demonstrates children's different modes of expression through panels, photographs, sculptures, and inventions. This work documents the problem-solving, thinking, and insightful language of young children in the Reggio schools. When the exhibit first came to the United States, many educators were surprised by the level of symbolic representation, the descriptive language, and the unique works that the children had created over time. One of the basic principles of the Reggio schools is that teachers view young children as immensely capable. This belief in the children's abilities challenges the teachers to think about art, materials, and possibilities in a different way. They observe children outdoors as they are intrigued by the shadows their bodies make. After collaboration with the teachers, they create a shadow screen that builds on this interest while inspiring movement and experimentation. The teachers observe and support the children during this discovery process as they identify additional provocations that will lead to new challenges. What kinds of shadows can be produced when you place an overhead projector on a low table in front of a screen? What if the lamp used to create shadows is moved? What is the shadow like when you wear a costume? Or dance?

According to Edwards, Gandini, and Forman (1993), "the atelier is a workshop, or studio, furnished with a variety of resource materials, used by all the children and adults in a school." The atelierista is a "teacher trained in art education, in charge of the atelier, who supports teachers in curriculum development and documentation" (p. 313). The atelier is a special arts space, replete with materials and tools. Children and teachers move freely between the space and their classrooms. Instead of having a designated time to interact, the atelierista engages children in whatever topic or project they are currently investigating. The atelierista works together with the teachers to support children as they create. In

> "The delicate role of the adult is allowing the child to take the lead while also encouraging the child to wonder, notice, and make relationships that would allow a new level of understanding to develop."
>
> *L. B. Caldwell, 1997*

addition, the atelierista works to document the children's creative process. One example, given by Malaguzzi (1993), was of children using images such as turning a poppy into a spot, a light, a bird in flight, a lighted ghost, and a handful of red petals within a field of green and yellow wheat. The exploration of the arts, art forms, and study of the problems of artistic expression are supported by the atelierista and the atelier.

Loris Malaguzzi founded and directed the Reggio Emilia municipal early childhood programs (Edwards, Gandini, & Forman). Malaguzzi lists nine beliefs that guide the program:

1. Creativity should not be considered a separate mental faculty but a characteristic of our way of thinking, knowing, and making choices.

2. Creativity seems to emerge from multiple experiences, coupled with a well-supported development of personal resources, including a sense of freedom to venture beyond the known.

3. Creativity seems to express itself through cognitive, affective and imaginative processes. These come together and support the skills for predicting and arriving at unexpected solutions.

4. The most favorable situation for creativity seems to be inter-personal exchange, with negotiation of conflicts and comparisons of ideas and actions being the decisive elements.

5. Creativity seems to find its power when adults are less tied to prescriptive teaching methods, but instead become observers and interpreters of problematic situations.

6. Creativity seems to be favored or disfavored according to the expectations of teachers, schools, families, and communities as well as society at large, according to the ways children perceive those expectations.

7. Creativity becomes visible when adults try to be more attentive to the cognitive processes of children than to the results they achieve in various fields of doing and understanding.

8. The more teachers are convinced that intellectual and expressive activities have both multiplying and unifying possibilities; the more creativity favors friendly exchanges with imagination and fantasy.

9. Creativity requires that the school of knowing finds connections with the school of expressing, opening the doors (that is our slogan) to the hundred languages of children. (pp. 70–71)

The factors of time, space, adult interactions with children, and the extensiveness of the children's investigations differ from other models of early childhood education and the usual practice in the United States. Like Vygotsky and Piaget, Malaguzzi is a constructivist who is concerned about children constructing meaning. Interactions of the cognitive and affective are intertwined. Like Vygotsky, Malaguzzi points out "how thought and language operate together to form ideas and to make a plan of action, then for executing, controlling, describing, and discussing that action" (p. 79). In Reggio Emilia classrooms, the teacher's role is to assist the child in constructing his own learning using rich problem-solving situations. The arts are a major component of the Reggio Emilia schools and provide the languages that children use to investigate, explore, and demonstrate their learning.

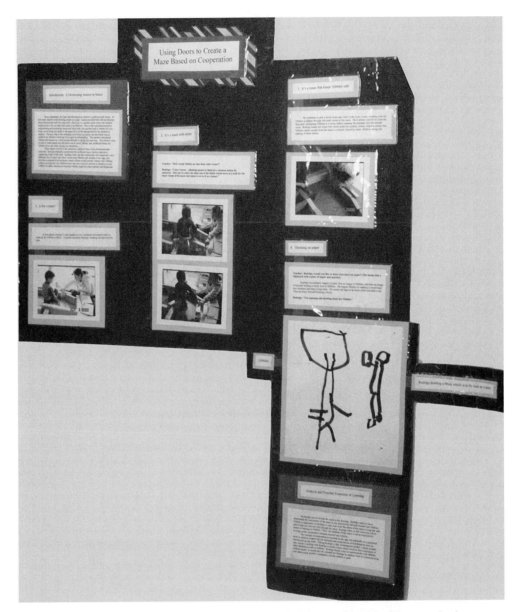

The panel represented here has elements that some educators in the United States, who have been inspired by the Reggio Approach, have decided are important. Panels include a background or project history, children's dialog and actions, teacher commentary, and steps for curriculum development. Teachers use documentation panels in a reflective manner, to help analyze children's learning and thinking, as well as their own interactions and interventions with children, in order to extend the learning process. In addition, the panels are a tool for effective communication with parents. The children's dialog and actions are essential components of all panels addressing children's thinking and learning. Without these elements, learning cannot be represented. The teacher commentary includes the background, ongoing analytic interpretations of the learning, and a conclusion that sums up the learning and incorporates the next curriculum steps.

A variety of bells produce different sounds.

✿ CREATING A CLASSROOM FOR THE EXPRESSIVE ARTS

Early childhood teachers design experiences for children in the expressive arts that provide:

- a plan based on the characteristics of young children as artists
- an understanding of the artistic process
- a positive atmosphere for experimentation
- time, materials, and background skills
- knowledge of the basic elements of the various art forms
- enthusiastic involvement in the arts by the children and the teacher (Raines & Canady, 1990, p. 157)

The artistic process in early childhood classrooms involves problem-solving, in which children select a medium of expression, manipulate materials, explore the possibilities of the medium, and create representations of their thoughts or feelings (Raines & Canady, 1990). The expressive arts occur best in a supportive learning environment where children are free to express themselves without an expected adult-like product. The teacher's positive attitude toward the arts and the aesthetic environment are an acknowledgment of the child's right to the expressive arts.

The Physical Environment

The early childhood classroom should be a beautiful place that is comfortable for both children and teachers. The walls of the space should provide a neutral background that serves as a canvas to draw attention to the work of the children and the colorful designs they create. Varied materials should be stored close to where the activity occurs and organized so the children can make selections independently. The space should be uncluttered, to help children focus visually and determine what they will use in their work. Art prints or regional crafts may be displayed to help the children appreciate these works and the artists who created them. There could be a special place for treasures that can be touched, manipulated, and enjoyed. Display an arrangement of fall leaves in a basket or a large rock with unusual patterns. Plants growing in the classroom provide opportunities for children to care for them. This makes the space more homelike and an inviting place where children know they can explore and experiment.

There should be natural light in the classroom or a variety of types of lighting that can be adjusted. In the space, there should be a balance of learning centers and open areas. The displays of children's art and projects should be planned and attractively designed to add interest to their work. Diversity is respected in the classroom, as shown by the pictures of people and their art, which represent different ages, races, ethnic backgrounds, sexes, and skin colors. This environment nurtures the belief that beauty is universal and comes in many different forms.

A classroom should also include a variety of textures—soft pillows in the library area, an area rug in the meeting place, and display boards covered with woven fabric. Having the opportunity to see, distinguish, and feel these textures encourages children to think about this element in their work and projects. The classroom environment communicates to young children what happens and what is valued in this place. If the space is immersed in the arts and designed to support children's way of learning, it tells children that they can be adventurous and try new things here. In this aesthetically pleasing classroom, they discover that their work with the arts is valued.

Centers, Themes, Projects, and Stories

> **"Every child is an artist. The problem is how to remain an artist once he grows up."**
>
> *P. Picasso*
> *(in Fitzhenry, 1993)*

Organizational vehicles for early childhood classrooms have been described throughout this book. For this discussion, descriptions of centers, themes, projects, and stories that support the expressive arts will be provided. These glimpses into the classroom are mere snapshots of a much richer context and include essential elements of the creative arts.

In early childhood classrooms, teachers often organize space and materials into learning centers. Art, music, blocks, construction, and drama areas are places where materials provide ready access for children to play, create, use as accessories, or construct representations of what they are learning. Adding centers and/or appropriate materials supports themes, projects, and stories that are part of the curriculum and program. An open-ended quality allows children of varying levels of development to successfully participate in creating, collaborating, and participating in the arts.

In the restaurant center a pizza delivery is ordered.

Integrating the Arts into a Study of Spring

In a preschool classroom, teachers look at how to integrate art, music, and story or children's literature into a unit on spring. The teacher has a variety of activities planned, including planting flowers in a window box, sprouting bean seeds, and observing trees in the atrium. One of the teacher's favorite books about spring is based on a folk song, *The Green Grass Grows All Around: A Traditional Folk Song* adapted by Hilde Hoffman (1968). This is the story of a little boy's city back yard and what happens in the spring when he plants a tree in the ground. The recurring refrain is, "And the green grass grows all around, all around, and the green grass grows all around." The story begins with a hole in the ground and ends with a back yard celebration of the boy's tree and a mother bird living there. Bright yellow and green illustrations include gleeful children of different ethnic backgrounds as they frolic, sing, and play (Raines & Canady, 1989).

The music center has rhythm instruments and a tape recorder stored on low shelves. It is near the group or circle time area rug. After reading the book, the teacher provides the children with the words to the song. The children decide which musical instruments will represent different parts of the song. When that word is read in the book or sung in the song, the child holding the instrument plays it. After some discussion about the sounds of the instruments, they decide that the bongo drum will signify the hole and shakers the roots. The tambourine will symbolize the tree and the long rhythm sticks the branch. The twig is represented by a clang of the cymbals and the sand blocks are the bird's nest. The bird is characterized by a run on the xylophone with the mallet and a tinkle of the triangle represents the feather.

As the teacher rereads the story, children play their instruments whenever they hear the word it represents. Since the refrain repeats the previous words, the children learn to listen closely and everyone sings, "And the green grass grows all around, all

Children are selecting an instrument to represent a character in a story.

around, and the green grass grows all around." The teacher then asks them what they could do to help remember the words. First, there is a hole in the ground, then roots in the hole, then a tree on the roots, then a limb on the tree, then a branch on the limb, then a twig on the branch, then a nest on the twig, then birds in the nest, then eggs in the nest, and ends with a feather on the bird. The children decide to draw pictures to help them remember the words. They understand that everyone's tree will be different, as will the nest, eggs, bird, and even the feather. The children have fun creating their versions of the song and combining art and music.

The value of a story as a means to connect the arts to the children's lived and vicarious experiences is written about eloquently by Kieran Egan (1997) in *The Arts as the Basis of Education*. In children's sociodramatic play, stories are enacted: some real, some imagined. After the children become comfortable with art materials and have explored possibilities, they begin to paint pictures and tell the teacher stories about an event depicted in their pictures. When children play with puppets, they recall and perform stories associated with that puppet, or they make up their own stories. Storytelling is another basis for drama productions, dance, opera, and theater. It is the story that helps organize children's thoughts because they include beginnings, endings, characters, and narratives. The story told allows children to change, enhance, and develop their creative thinking in the oral tradition. These drama techniques interweave the arts into programs for young children.

The Expressive Arts in a Study of "Life in the Sea: Real and Imagined"

Thematic units provide opportunities to integrate the arts into curricular studies, during which children learn about the arts at the same time. A glimpse inside the classroom of a primary teacher in California whose unit is "Life in the Sea: Real and Imagined" provides some examples of the integration of art, music and movement, and storytelling (Raines & Canady, 1992).

The teacher reads five different focus books dealing with the unit topic. *Ibis: A True Whale Story,* written and illustrated by John Himmelman (1990), is one of the focus books. Ibis and Blizzard are two whales that become so accustomed to the whale-watching boats that Ibis becomes entangled in a net. Blizzard pushes Ibis's body to the surface, where whale-watchers find a way to rescue her.

After reading *Ibis: A True Whale Story,* the teacher and children decide on an art project that follows the book. They examine the ways that John Himmelman illustrated his book with below the water, partially submerged, and above water scenes. Learning to see from different perspectives is an artistic concept. While the teacher merely calls attention to the illustrator's work, a wide selection of art materials for painting, drawing, and collage are made available to the children. Several children decide to team together and show the story of Ibis and Blizzard in three different scenes on a large poster board. They negotiate with each other about who will do what and finally decide to use water colors for the background, cut out the whales from poster board, and construct the hulls of the boats by painting forms they cut from a Styrofoam tray.

The drama of the story is compelling and some children decide to write a short version to dramatize. Later, they share their script with the other children in front of the large posters. Two children decide to write a song about Ibis and Blizzard to introduce the drama to the class. The song is adapted to the tune of Row, Row, Row Your Boat, and several children add movements to reinforce the words and rhythm.

In the reference materials at the end of *Ibis: A True Whale Story,* Himmelman refers the reader to the Center for Coastal Studies in Provincetown, Massachusetts. The children brainstorm some questions they would like to ask whale-rescuers and write them a letter. When the center sends the class materials, they thank the people in Massachusetts by returning snapshots of the children's posters and a tape of the children singing their Ibis rescue song.

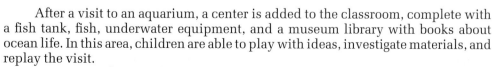

"Row, row, row your boat,
Out to see our whale,
Attach a float, attach a float,
Pull her on home.
Cut, cut, cut the net
Out our dear Ibis.
Swim, swim, swim away
Goodbye, Goodbye,
Goodbye, free Ibis"

(Raines & Canady, 1992, p. 144–145).

After a visit to an aquarium, a center is added to the classroom, complete with a fish tank, fish, underwater equipment, and a museum library with books about ocean life. In this area, children are able to play with ideas, investigate materials, and replay the visit.

Integrating the visual arts with the curriculum study of life in the ocean enriches the study. However, an arts educator might ask if there are other lessons that could have been included in the art activities. Some suggestions might include adding a display of maritime art to the classroom, mixing paints for different shades of blue, using lines to suggest the presence of a boat on the surface, or creating shadows of whales under the sea. The children are inventive with their selection of materials, but using a vocabulary of color terminology to describe the physical properties of water could have been added to the lesson with artistic terms such as *hue, value,* and *intensity.* The pattern of waves is illustrated in the children's painting by a rhythm of lines with strong and weak accents. Even the repetition of the wave patterns can be emphasized in the children's work and in descriptions of what is on the posters. Line, shape, contour, texture, and color are evident in the illustrator's work and in the children's renderings. To enrich the experience, the teacher can talk about what can be seen in Himmelman's illustrations and how the child artists have used similar design elements in their work.

ARTIST-IN-RESIDENCE INSPIRES MULTIPLE CREATIVE ACTIVITIES

An artist-in-residence, a local storyteller, visited a kindergarten classroom. The storyteller told the folktale of "The Lost Mitten With Tiny, Shiny Beads" (Raines & Isbell, 1999), an adaptation of an old Ukrainian folktale (the entire story can be found in Appendix C.) The storyteller wore a highly decorated vest, trimmed with embroidery, tiny buttons, and ribbons. He said it was a vest from the Ukraine and invited the children to create their own vests using a paper bag. The steps in the process included forming each vest by cutting out a neck hole and two arm holes on the sides, then cutting down the center of one side of the bag to make it open like a vest. The children glued buttons, ribbons, fabric, fringe, yarn, cotton, decorative trim, and braid on the vest. Although some were very ornate and others were simple designs, each was unique.

The next day when the storyteller returned, the children wore their vests and began to retell variations of the Ukrainian tale. At first, they thought of farm animals, zoo animals, desert animals, and tropical animals. Then they decided that the desert animals and the tropical animals would not be getting into a mitten to keep warm. How could they change the story if they included tropical animals? They decided to have the tropical animals get under a straw hat to shade them from the hot desert sun and a rain hat to shield them from the rain in the tropics. This provided opportunities for the children to elaborate on an idea and be flexible in their thinking as they used art and drama in their activities.

As an extension of the story, the artist-in-residence asked the children if they would like to act out the story of "The Lost Mitten

Books are an important element of the curriculum.

with Tiny, Shiny Beads." He encouraged them to discuss all the different events that occurred. They decided that a tablecloth could serve as a prop to represent the mitten. A child could enter the imaginary mitten by crawling under the tablecloth. The children selected the parts they wanted to play in the reenactment. The first child was the field mouse. Then came the frog, an owl, rabbit, fox, wolf, wild boar, bear, and finally the cricket. Then they exploded out of the mitten.

The drama and art were connected to the Ukrainian folktale. However, the richness of the experience was in the children's re-creation of the story. Using flannel board pieces, the children retold the story in their own special ways. After several days of interest in "The Lost Mitten with Tiny, Shiny Beads," the teacher brought in two different versions of the folktale. Until this time, the story was the one told by the storyteller. The children were anxious to compare the animals in the two versions to the ones in the storyteller's tale, and to find out if any animals from their stories were included. They compared Jan Brett's (1989) *The Mitten* and Alvin Tresselt's (1990) version of *The Mitten*. They discovered similarities and differences as they identified the characteristics of the stories. Their creative problem-solving and the generation of ideas led them into an expanded study of other folktales.

A Creative Project from a Reggio Emilia–Inspired Classroom

Breig-Allen, Hill, Geismar-Ryan, and Cadwell wrote about their experiences in the Clayton Schools' Family Center in St. Louis (1998). They were inspired by their observations of one child who noticed that his riding toy produced lines when he drove it through water and onto the pavement. This became the basis of an investigation of lines. The teachers followed this interest by providing many different materials and opportunities to create lines. The teachers asked provocative questions as the children experimented. Children drew, painted, rolled trucks through paint, created lines, and observed lines in nature. They experimented with making

Teacher and child are using puppets in their play.

"Teachers must think for themselves if they are to help others think for themselves."

The Carnegie Corporation (in Applewhite, Evans, & Frothingham, 1992)

long lines and big lines, and connecting objects to make lines of pipe cleaners, shreds of paper, and Cuisenaire rods (solid rectangular bars of various sizes and colors). At first, their lines were straight. Then they discovered curves, squiggles, and lines that appear in nature. They played with lines, connected lines, and displayed lines. The teachers used the children's interest to spark a project, provided the materials, trusted their questions, and provided a few provocations that the children would use to investigate the concept of lines. While the project may seem like a small one, for two- and three-year-olds the powerful observation of lines led them to create in new ways.

Following the child's interests, for example "lines," as a topic of study is based on the view of the emerging curriculum that may include the project approach. Often, children work in pairs, solve problems, and develop the habit of improving by systematically documenting their explorations of a topic (Wright, 1997). The teachers are participant-observers in what the children are learning. They talk with them as a means to provoke additional learning, but the questioning and interactions are background for what the child is doing. They are not directive in their interactions: they are resources for the learners.

 SUMMARY

All curriculum and content areas contain opportunities for creative thinking. The creative arts are recognized as being extremely important for young children's artistic expression, divergent thinking, and affective development. Recently, curriculum developers and early childhood educators have reappraised the value of the arts. They state that all children have the right to be involved in the arts and have begun to look for ways to make this a reality. The creative process involves cognitive events that include making choices, investigating interest, exploring materials, and collaborating with others. These experiences can occur in themes, units, projects, classroom environments, and in content areas where the arts are integrated into the total curriculum. This design helps children learn to see the arts as an essential part of their lives and a way of unifying a community of learners.

 KEY TERMS

Artist-in-Residence
guided-exploration orientation

little-intervention orientation
product-oriented orientation

 REFLECTION

1. The teacher provided many colors for painting, but the children primarily used yellow, white, and green. Why do you think the children made these choices? Discuss your ideas with a classmate.

2. From your observations, describe a creative episode such as the dandelion event in an early childhood classroom, during which the teacher seized an opportunity to inspire children's creativity.

3. Read Bresler's article on three orientations to arts education. Compare the little-intervention, product-orientation, and guided-exploration approaches. Give examples from your experience as a student or from your observations.

4. Consider your experiences in the expressive arts. Which art form gives you the most pleasure? Recall a time from your childhood and one as an adult. Discuss how you experienced the pleasure of artistic or creative expression.

THINKING ABOUT THE OBSERVATION OF CREATIVITY

1. What are some of the reasons the preschoolers picked the dandelions?
2. How did the chart help the children think in a new way about the dandelions?
3. Can you explain why young children categorized the dandelion as a flower instead of a weed?

POSSIBILITIES FOR ADULT LEARNERS

Activity: Bringing It Together
Goal: To relate content to the real world of children.
Materials: Graph paper, camera and film, measuring tape, pencil, and paper.
Procedure:

1. Visit a PreK, kindergarten, or primary classroom.
2. Diagram at least two of the following: the art area, blocks, music, storytelling, puppetry, or dramatic play.
3. Share your drawing with members of the class.
4. Discuss your observations of the different centers, children's participation, and the materials in each area.

Activity: Artist-in-Residence
Goal: To talk with an artist about his work with children.
Materials: Tape recorder, pencil or pen, and a note pad.
Procedure:

1. Interview an artist-in-residence.
2. Find out how he is funded, favorite ages of children, and how teachers can help the artists be more successful.
3. Answer any questions about the age of children you teach.

Activity: A Creative Unit
Goal: To develop a unit on a unique topic that would interest young children.
Materials: Paper and pencil or pen to record ideas and possibilities.
Procedure:

1. Work with a partner.
2. Brainstorm possible topics and continue to identify units that you have not seen.

3. Together, make your choice.
4. Brainstorm ideas that connect art, music, and drama to integrate the arts into the unit.
5. Research the topic.
6. Write down your ideas and share with the members of your class.

Activity:	Tell a Story
Goal:	To develop your ability to tell a story without the use of a book.
Materials:	Collection of stories, index cards to write the story outline, and tape recorder or video camera.

Procedure:

1. Select five stories from a collection of stories for young children.
2. Study, outline, and practice telling each story to friends and classmates.
3. Volunteer to tell the stories to children (see Isbell & Raines, 2000; Raines & Isbell, 1999).
4. Share your experiences with other students.

OPEN-ENDED ACTIVITIES FOR YOUNG CHILDREN

PreK–K

Activity:	Smell the Roses
Goal:	To develop an awareness of the world around you.
Materials:	Note pad, sketch pad, or camera.
Procedure:	

1. Enjoy a sensory walk.
2. Focus on the sights, sounds, and smells of your environment.
3. Plan a creative way to tell, show, or perform your feelings related to your sensory walk.

Primary Grades

Activity:	A Collection of Beautiful Things
Goal:	To find a creative way to represent objects that you appreciate.
Materials:	A collection of favorite items and the materials for creating a display such as fabric, photos, and drawings.
Procedure:	

1. Collect several favorite beautiful objects from around your house.
2. Determine how to demonstrate their significance to yourself.
3. Draw, photograph, or write about the collection and your feelings related to the objects.

THE NATIONAL STANDARDS FOR ARTS EDUCATION

These standards describe "what every young American should know and be able to do in the arts." These standards were developed by the Consortium of National Arts Education Associations, which includes the National Association for Music Education (MENC).

Dance/Movement (K–4)

1. identifying and demonstrating movement elements and skills in performing dance.
2. understanding choreographic principles, processes, and structures.
3. understanding dance as a way to create and communicate meaning.
4. applying and demonstrating critical and creative thinking skills in dance.
5. demonstrating and understanding dance in various cultures and historical periods.
6. making connections between dance and healthful living.
7. making connections between dance and other disciplines.

Music (K–4)

1. singing, alone and with others, a varied repertoire of music.
2. performing on instruments, alone and with others, a varied repertoire of music.
3. improvising melodies, variations, and accompaniments.
4. composing and arranging music within specified guidelines.
5. reading and notating music.
6. listening to, analyzing, and describing music.
7. evaluating music and musical performances.
8. understanding relationships between music, the other arts, and disciplines outside the arts.
9. understanding music in relation to history and culture.

Dramatic Arts (K–4)

1. script writing by planning and recording improvisations based on personal experience and heritage, imagination, literature, and history.
2. acting by assuming roles and interacting in improvisations.
3. designing by visualizing and arranging environments for classroom dramatizations.
4. directing by planning classroom dramatizations.
5. researching by finding information to support classroom dramatizations.
6. comparing and connecting art forms by describing theatre, dramatic media (such as film, television, and electronic media), and other art forms.

7. analyzing and explaining personal preferences and constructing meanings from classroom dramatizations and from theatre, film, television, and electronic media productions.

8. understanding context by recognizing the role of theatre, film, television, and electronic media in daily life.

Visual Arts (K–4)

1. understanding and applying media, techniques, and processes.

2. using knowledge of structures and functions.

3. choosing and evaluating a range of subject matter, symbols, and ideas.

4. understanding the visual arts in relation to history and cultures.

5. reflecting upon and assessing the characteristics and merits of their work and the work of others.

6. making connections between visual arts and other disciplines.

From *National Standards for Arts Education*, published by Music Educators National Conference (MENC). Copyright © 1994 by MENC. Used by permission. The complete National Arts Standards and additional materials relating to the Standards are available from MENC–The National Association for Music Education, 1806 Robert Fulton Dr., Reston, VA 20191. Telephone: 800-336-3768.

 | **ACEI POSITION PAPERS**

The Child's Right to the Expressive Arts: Nurturing the Imagination as Well as the Intellect

A Position Paper of the Association for Childhood Education International. By Mary Renck Jalongo–*Mary Renck Jalongo is Professor of Education, Indiana University of Pennsylvania, Indiana.*

When we describe someone as "imaginative," we usually mean the person can formulate rich and varied mental images, see beyond the obvious, or draw upon experience in inventive and effective ways. Most of us believe that childhood is the wellspring of adult imagination (Cobb, 1977). But have our schools really nurtured children's imagination? In 1935, Lois Meek observed:

> ... we have recognized that young children are active and free in imaginative play, that as they grow older they become more stereotyped in their behavior, and that in adult life, only the unusual person displays the ability to put old ideas and experiences into new forms. (p. vii)

Contemporary educators have arrived at much the same conclusion (Klein, 1984; Lindberg, 1980; Sutton-Smith, 1988). "What happened to imagination?" Greene (1988) wonders. "It has been discouraged by literalism, by complacency, by technical rationality, by obsessions with predictable results . . . [we need] to break through the fixities of our age . . . to look at things as they could truly be otherwise" (p. 55).

In response to these concerns about the child's right to creative expression, this Association for Childhood Education International position paper will:

- examine the contributions of creativity and imagination to the total learning of the child.
- offer counter arguments to myths that de-emphasize the arts in the curriculum.
- recommend ways of refashioning our schools to promote the expressive arts.

A Rationale for Imagination and Creativity

Contrary to popular opinion, imagination is not wild, irrational or self-indulgent (Degenhardt & McKay, 1988; Johnson, 1987; Vandenberg, 1983). The products of imagination are unusual, but they must also be effective (Barrow, 1988). As one of the leading educators of this century explained, imagination without knowledge is foolishness and knowledge without imagination is pedantry (Whitehead, 1929). It is useful to think of imagination in action as a kaleidoscope: knowledge is comparable to the bits and pieces in the kaleidoscope; imagination is what enables us to turn the drum and create new patterns (Parnes, 1963). Imagination "gives rationality life, color and meaning" (Egan, 1988, p. 118). Thinking imaginatively engages learners in "as-if" thinking, "if-then" thinking and empathic thinking (Tamburrini, 1984). Furthermore, imaginative thought functions simultaneously at three levels: as a stimulus, a material and a companion (Furlong, 1961).

The expressive arts—music, art, drama, dance, writing—are important because they are the means of communicating our creative productivity and imaginative thinking. Some of the benefits associated with an expanded role for the expressive arts in schools include:

- The expressive arts foster "learning from the inside out," authentic learning that changes behavior and encourages reflection (Heathcote, 1984; Hoffman & Lamme, 1989).
- The expressive arts enhance the child's ability to interpret symbols. It is the "symbolic ability of the child on which everything which is distinctly human will develop" (Smith, 1984, p. 28).
- The expressive arts are associated with growth in all areas of development, including academics (Courtney, 1982; Sylva, 1984; Wagner, 1988).
- The expressive arts regard the child as a meaning-maker and constructor, a discoverer and an embodiment of knowledge rather than a passive recipient of someone else's ready-made answers (Brunner, 1986; McLaren, 1986; Wells, 1986).

When imagination, creative productivity and the expressive arts are fostered in schools, we find children who are:

> ...becoming sensitive to or aware of problems, deficiencies, gaps in knowledge, missing elements, disharmonies, and so on; bringing together in new relationships available information; defining the difficulty or identifying the missing elements, searching for solutions, making guesses or formulating hypotheses about the problem or deficiencies, testing and retesting them; perfecting them and finally communicating results. (Torrance, 1969, p. vi)

Why Are the Expressive Arts Undervalued in Our Culture?

At least five popular myths are used to justify neglecting the expressive arts in classrooms.

1. First, some adults dichotomize children's academic achievement and artistic achievement, as if the former were nutritious vegetables and the latter, a rich dessert. But human beings must balance their need for objective truth with their need for aesthetic truth (McLaren, 1988), because facts stripped of images and feelings cannot be said to have meaning (Landau, 1985). The expressive arts complement academics; they are what makes knowing academics worthwhile. Educators must lead others to abandon this sort of either/or thinking. It is a major deterrent to innovation, not only in schools but also in society at large (Rickards, 1985).

2. A second explanation for reducing the importance of the arts is insufficient time in an already overburdened curriculum. But if teachers get caught in a mad race to "cover" everything, they may literally do just that—conceal the real purposes of learning from the child (Duckworth, 1972).

3. Third, it is sometimes argued that only a small percentage of children have exceptional artistic talent, so education in the arts is more expendable than education in other areas of development. But it is not our purpose in the expressive arts to be elitist, to "discover" stars. Adults have the responsibility of affirming and nurturing every talent in every child and giving all children opportunities to participate in authentic artistic experiences (Lamme, 1989; Teffinger, 1989).

4. A fourth common misconception is that parents will not support programs that emphasize the expressive arts. Ironically, parents flock to programs that highlight children's achievements in the arts, whether it is a single event (such as a school play) or an entire school curriculum with an arts curriculum (such as the Settlement House School or St. Augustine's in the South Bronx). Even those parents who are skeptical of the value of "nonacademic" subjects become converts when they see their children expressing themselves through the arts instead of racing through activities completely conceived and controlled by misguided adults. As one music educator remarked, school concerts that "elicit nothing more than remarks from parents that the performance was 'cute' are not good enough." Authentic experiences in the performing arts ". . . inspire children to actively pursue music as performers and consumers throughout their lives" (Moriarity, 1988, p. 22).

5. The fifth and final myth is that because there are socially trained teachers for at least some of the expressive arts (such as art, music and movement), they have complete responsibility for the expressive arts. But when regular classroom teachers delegate this authority to others, they are relinquishing a powerful educational and motivational tool. Most of the things we now use as motivational devices—tests, grades, privileges, the promise of future jobs—are "alienated from the act of learning now" (Shor & Freire, 1987, p. 5). The opportunity to participate in the expressive arts gives children a reason to learn today. And those opportunities will be far too limited if they are reserved for one class period per week.

ACEI Position

The Association for Childhood Education International believes that, in order to reaffirm the importance of the expressive arts in schools, educators must accept the following precepts:

Every Child Has a Right to Opportunities for Imaginative Expression. Imaginative expression is not the exclusive province of special programs for the gifted and talented. It is not a curricular "frill" to be deleted when time is limited. Nor is imagination synonymous with enrichment, something reserved for those children who have already completed their "work." Rather, imagination is a capacity in every child that should be nurtured. "If we think of imagination as part of our intelligence, then we must be ready to admit that, like the rest of human intelligence, it needs education" (Warnock, 1977, p. 202).

Educating the Child's Imagination Is Education for the Future. As we look ahead to the future, what will be required of tomorrow's children? Minuchin (1987) predicts they will need "resilience and flexibility, a creative and integrative way of thinking, and a certain psychological sturdiness in the way they face new circumstances in the company of other people" (p. 254). One thing we can be certain about in our culture is change. The "personal inclinations required by the arts" are well suited to the demands of a rapidly changing society. These include play with images, ideas and feelings, recognizing and constructing the multiple meanings of events, looking at things from different perspectives and functioning as risk-takers (Eisner, 1976).

The Educated Imagination Is the Key to Equity and Intercultural Understanding. Creative productivity can be social rather than isolationist and its outcomes need not be money-saving, labor-saving or even artistic. Imagination dramatizes the inner workings of our minds and is the undercurrent of human interaction (Rosen, 1980). As we gain insight into ourselves, we can use imaginative powers to identify with others (Hanson 1986). We can empathize with their situations, envision possibilities and enact creative solutions to social problems. These connections with others, forged by imagination, are the basis for intercultural understanding.

Children's Creative Productivity Is Qualitatively Different from Adults. We must resist "childism," the tendency for adults to look condescendingly upon children's ideas and feelings, to regard them as less real or important than their own (Lightfoot, 1978). One of the great assets of childhood is that young children are less constrained by convention, less literal in their thinking, less restricted by boundaries between and among subject areas (Gardner, 1983). "We don't really see what we take for granted," and children's creative productivity is no exception (Silberstein-Storfer & Jones, 1982). If adults overlook children's imaginative processes, then children are deprived of an authentic voice, both in the arts and in traditional subject areas.

Consider, for example, children's drawing. Too often, adults demand realism in art. But if we push this prejudice to its logical extreme, the essence of art is lost. Individuality is replaced by conformity and our "artists" are inferior to our copy machines. Likewise, if we insist on hurrying children into using the conventions of print, meaning is sacrificed to form. Eventually, the child's composing process functions like computer software designed to locate mistakes, rather than as a vehicle for creative expression. Children's imagination is just that: it belongs to children, not to miniature adults.

Creative Expression Should Permeate the Entire Curriculum. When we speak of basics in education, people immediately think of reading, writing and arithmetic. But is that what is basic? If basic means something that is fundamental to the experience of all children, then other things would surely be basic. Play would certainly be "basic" (Isenberg & Quisenberry, 1988). Telling and enacting stories would be "basic" (Nelms, 1988). Drawing, painting and sculpting would surely be "basic" because, even before children can read, write, or calculate, they are using these ways to communicate their ideas, emotions, and individuality. Music and dance are "basic" because even before children can speak, they can listen and move to music.

Clearly, a rigid, lackluster curriculum is an environment inimical to the basic expressive arts. Under regimented conditions, teachers become walking contradictions, like the teacher in a cartoon who announces to the class: "I expect you all to be independent, innovative, critical thinkers who will do exactly as I say" (Warren, 1989, p. 38).

Imagination Is the Key to Artistry in Teaching and Excellence in Our Schools. We keep searching for the panacea in education by creating artificial dichotomies. The '60s gave us the humanistic movement which was countered with back-to-basics. When the basics failed to improve schools, an excellence-or-else approach was lauded as the answer. Education may have traveled far, but the course has been a series of zigzags between opposites instead of straight and steady progress toward quality and equality.

Teachers are jaded by these bandwagons, tired of legislative mandates, weary of standardized tests that dictate the curriculum. What is worse, our schools have been sapped of their surprisingness—so much so that the overwhelming impression after thousands of hours of observation in classrooms is that they are routinized, predictable and "emotionally flat" (Goodlad, 1984).

Where does the solution lie? Many prominent educators state that our schools need artistry, creativity, intuition, insight, inspiration and reflection (Rubin, 1985; Schon, 1983; Sizer, 1984)—all intimately connected with imagination.

We Must Refashion Our Schools for the 21st Century. School reform must, in the view of the National Education Association, recognize that the Industrial Model is obsolescent in our Information Age (Futrell, 1989). We need to shut off the rapid assembly line of textbooks, tests, schedules and paper work in favor of "circles of learning" (Johnson et al., 1984) and projects go beyond tolerating imagination and begin to value and educate it. In schools for the 21st century, children will learn to make decisions, to reflect upon experience, and to understand their own imaginative processes as well as those of others (Ayers, 1989; Hatcher, 1987; Hoffman & Lamme, 1989; Paley, 1981).

Conclusion

A belief in the child's right to imaginative expression transforms the classroom. For too long, education has operated like a pupil postal system—we spend most of our time sorting and determining destinations. And, like the post office, we operate on the premise that environmental conditions should be ignored, that "the mail must go through." Never mind that junk mail addressed to "occupant"—the postal equivalent of a developmentally inappropriate curriculum—also gets delivered.

In a school committed to the expressive arts, children are active participants. They learn how to bring order out of chaos, to use their frames of mind, to interpret symbols, to be open to feelings, to develop a tolerance for ambiguity and to seek problems as well as solutions. If a school nurtures children's imagination and creativity, it means that children function more autonomously as they meet challenges in a supportive environment (Kamii, 1988). It means that teachers function as enablers who share their power and wisdom—inviting children to manage their own learning processes and giving them time to revise their tentative notions about the world (Isaksen & Treffinger, 1985), deferring judgement until children are satisfied with their work (Klein, 1984).

As Egan (1988) stated, developing the imagination "is not an alternative educational activity to be argued for in competition with other claims; it is a prerequisite to making any activity education" (p. ix). In the past, in the present and in the future, our most enlightened educational visions will be connected by the common thread of imagination, creativity and the expressive arts.

References

Ayers, W. (1989). *The good preschool teacher: Six teachers reflect on their lives.* New York: Teachers College Press.

Barrow, R. (1988). Some observations on the concept of imagination. In K. Egan & D. Nadaner (Eds.), *Imagination and education* (pp. 79–90). New York: Teachers College Press.

Bruner, J. S. (1986). *Actual minds, possible worlds.* Cambridge, MA: Harvard University.

Cobb, E. (1977). *The ecology of imagination.* New York: Columbia University.

Courtney, R. (1982). *Re-play: Studies in human drama and education.* Toronto: OISE Press.

Degenhardt, M., & McKay, E. (1988). Imagination and education for cultural understanding. In K. Egan & D. Nadaner (Eds.), *Imagination and education* (pp. 237–255). New York: Teachers College Press.

Duckworth, E. (1972). The having of wonderful ideas. *Harvard Educational Review, 42,* 217–232.

Egan, K. (1988). The origins of imagination. In K. Egan & D. Nadaner (Eds.), *Imagination and education* (pp. 91–127). New York: Teachers College Press.

Eisner, E. (1976). *The arts, human development and education.* Berkeley, CA: McCuthen.

Furlong, E. J. (1961). *Imagination.* London: George Allen & Unwin.

Futrell, M. H. (1989). Mission not accomplished: Education reform in retrospect. *Phi Delta Kappan, 71*(1), 8–14.

Gardner, H. (1983). *Frames of mind: The theory of multiple intelligences.* New York: Basic Books.

Goodland, J. (1984). *A place called school: Prospects for the future.* New York: McGraw Hill.

Greene, M. (1988). What happened to imagination? In K. Egan & D. Nadaner (Eds.), *Imagination and education* (pp. 45–56). New York: Teachers College Press.

Hanson, K. (1986). *The self imagined.* London: Routledge & Kegan Paul.

Hatcher, B. (Ed.). (1987). *Learning opportunities beyond school.* Wheaton, MD: Association for Childhood Education International.

Heathcote, D. (1984). In L. Johnson & C. O'Neil (Ed.), *Dorothy Heathcote: Collected writings on education and drama* (p. 104). London: Hutchinson.

Hoffman, S., & Lamme, L. L. (Eds.). (1989). *Learning from the inside out: The expressive arts.* Wheaton, MD: Association for Childhood Education International.

Isaksen, S. G., & Teffinger, D. J. (1985). *Creative problem solving: The basic course.* Buffalo, NY: Bearly Ltd.

Isenberg, J., & Quisenberry, N. (1988). Play: A necessity for all children. *Childhood Education, 64,* 138–145.

Johnson, M. (1987). *The body in the mind: The bodily basis of meaning, imagination, and reason.* Chicago: University of Chicago Press.

Johnson, D. W., Johnson, R. T., Holubec, E. J., & Roy, P. (1984). *Circles of learning: Cooperation in the classroom*. Alexandria, VA: Association for Supervision and Curriculum Development.

Kamii, C. (1988). Autonomy of heteronomy: Our choices of goals. In G. F. Roberson & M. A. Johnson (Eds.), *Leaders in Education: Their views on controversial issues*. Lanham, MD: University Press of America.

Katz, L., & Chard, S. C. (1989). *Enaging children's minds: The project approach*. Norwood, NJ: Ablex.

Klein, B. (1984). Power and control, praise and deferred judgement. *Journal of Creative Behavior, 14*, 9–17.

Lamme, L. L. (1989). Illustratorship: A key facet of whole language instruction. *Childhood education, 66*, 83–86.

Landau, J. (1985). The necessity of art in education. *World Futures, 21*, 29–51.

Lightfoot, S. L. (1978). *Worlds apart: Relationships between families and schools*. New York: Basic Books.

Lindberg, L. (1980). Child development and the arts. In *Proceedings of the ACEI Summer Seminar July 9–11* (pp. 74–77). Taipei, Taiwan, Republic of China: Association for Childhood Education International of the Republic of China. (ERIC Document Reproduction Service No. ED 231 499.)

McLaren, P. (1986). *Schooling as a ritual performance: Towards a political economy of educational symbols and gestures*. London: Routledge & Kegan Paul.

McLaren, P. (1988). The limited servant and the ritual roots of critical pedagogy. *Language Arts, 65*, 164–179.

Meek, L. H. (1935). Foreword. In F. V. Markey, *The imaginative behavior of preschool children* (p. vii). New York: Teachers College Press.

Minuchin, P. (1987). Schools, families and the development of young children. *Early Childhood Research Quarterly, 2*, 245–254.

Moriarity, K. (1988). Learning by doing: Lessons of a summer arts program. *Music Educators Journal, 75*, 18–22.

Nelms, B. (1988). *Literature in the classroom: Readers, texts and contexts*. Urbana, IL: National Council of Teachers of English.

Paley, V. (1981). *Wally's stories*. Cambridge, MA: Cambridge University Press.

Parnes, S. J. (1963). In C. W. Taylor & F. Barron (Eds.), *The identification of creativity and scientific talent* (pp. 225–255). New York: Wiley.

Rickards, T. (1985). *Stimulating innovation*. London: Frances Pinter.

Rosen, H. (1980). The dramatic mode. In P. Salmon (Ed.), *Coming to know* (pp. 152–169). London: Routledge & Kegan Paul.

Rubin, L. (1985). *Artistry in teaching*. New York: Random House.

Schon, D. A. (1983). *The reflective practitioner*. New York: Basic Books.

Shor, I., & Freire, P. (1987). *A pedagogy for liberation: Dialogues on transforming education*. South Hadley, MA: Bergin & Garvey.

Silberstein-Storfer, M., & Jones, M. (1982). *Doing art together*. New York: Simon & Schuster.

Sizer, T. (1984). *Horace's compromise*. Boston: Houghton Mifflin.

Smith, P. K. (1984). The relevance of fantasy play. In H. Cowie (Ed.), *The development of children's imaginative writing* (pp. 12–31). New York: St. Martin's Press.

Sutton-Smith, B. (1988). In search of the imagination. In K. Egan & D. Nadaner (Eds.), *Imagination and education* (pp. 3–29). New York: Teachers College Press.

Sylva, K. (1980). A hard-headed look at the fruits of play. *Early Child Development and Care, 15*, 171–184.

Tamburrini, J. (1984). The development of representational imagination. In H. Cowie (Ed.), *The development of children's imaginative writing* (pp. 32–48). New York: St. Martin's Press.

Torrance, E. P. (1969). *Dimensions in early learning: Creativity*. Sioux Falls, SD: Adaptation Press.

Treffinger, D. J. (1989). The potentials of productivity: Designing the journey to 2000. *Gifted Child Today, 12*(12), 17–21.

Vandenberg, B. (1983). Play, logic and reality. *Imagination, Cognition, and Personality, 3*, 353–361.

Wagner, B. J. (1988). Research currents: Does classroom drama affect the arts of language? *Language Arts, 65*, 46–55.

Warnock, M. (1977). *Schools of thought*. London: Faber & Faber.

Warren. (1989). Cartoon. *Phi Delta Kappan, 71*(1), 38.

Wells, G. (1986). *The meaning makers: Children learning language and using language to learn.* Portsmouth, NH: Heinemann.

Whitehead, A. N. (1929). *The aims of education and other essays.* New York: Macmillan.

Courtesy of the Association for Childhood Education International (ACEI). Copyright © 1990 by the Association for Childhood Education International ISBN 0-87173-120-7. Reprints are available from: ACEI, 11141 Georgia Ave., Suite 200, Wheaton, MD 20902 $1.75 each, members; $2.50 nonmembers; 10% discount on 10–49 copies; 20% on 50–99; 25% on 100 or more. Price includes postage and handling.

The Child's Right to Creative Thought and Expression

Mary Renck Jalongo is Professor of Education and Coordinator of the Doctoral Program in Curriculum and Instruction, Indiana University of Pennsylvania, and Editor, *Early Childhood Education Journal.*

ACEI'S Position on Creative Thought

It is the position of the Association for Childhood Education International (ACEI) that the definition of creativity needs to be enriched and enlarged to be consistent with contemporary theory and research. Furthermore, it is ACEI's position that creative expression depends not on talent alone, but also on motivation, interest, effort, and opportunity. The creative process, contrary to popular opinion, is socially supported, culturally influenced, and collaboratively achieved. In taking this position, ACEI acknowledges that several challenges must be addressed by educators throughout the world. First, we need to redefine creative teaching and confront misconceptions about creative thinking. Second, we need to provide students with role models of motivation and persistence in creative thought, and arrive at more capacious ways of assessing creative processes and products. Finally, educational institutions and the larger societies in which they exist need to reflect deeply on what they hope children will become. We need to do more than prepare them to become cogs in the machinery of commerce. The international community needs resourceful, imaginative, inventive, and ethical problem solvers who will make a significant contribution, not only to the Information Age in which we currently live, but beyond to ages that we can barely envision.

Adults often make reference to children's active imaginations; point out that children, particularly young children, are creative; or note that children seem to be naturally curious and playful. Is it accurate to say that children have active imaginations? To be imaginative means that a person formulates rich and varied mental images, sees beyond the obvious, and draws upon experience in inventive and effective ways.

Studies of the brain activity of preadolescent children offer empirical evidence that children do indeed have active imaginations (Diamond & Hopson, 1999). Even wide awake children experience theta wave activity, which mature adults primarily experience when their minds hover between being awake and falling asleep. Theta wave brain activity is more relaxed, freewheeling, and receptive to fleeting mental images. Eminent creative individuals in various fields report trying a host of techniques to capture theta wave activity, including meditation, keeping a lighted ink pen at bedside, and so forth (Runco & Pritzker, 1999). Thomas Edison used to go to sleep with ball bearings clutched in his hands and metal pie plates positioned below so that, as his hands relaxed, he would be freshly awakened by the clatter and could jot down the ideas that came to him in that half-awake/half-asleep state (Goleman & Kaufman, 1992). It would seem that with more access to this theta wave activity, children are adept at forming varied and unusual images. Although children may not be *more* imaginative, they certainly do have *active* imaginations.

How does creativity in children compare with that of adults? Adults may have the advantage when it comes to storing and retrieving information, drawing upon experience, and making judgments about what is appropriate and effective. Fishkin (1998) uses the term "germinal creativity" as a preferred descriptor for budding creativity in children. While germinal creativity produces unique ideas, the child may not yet have the ability to execute them well or communicate them clearly to others.

Children's creative thought is bolstered by the fact that "the young child is not bothered by inconsistencies, departures from convention, nonliteralness . . . which often results in unusual and appealing juxtapositions and associations" (Gardner, 1993, p. 228). The creative assets of childhood include a tolerance for ambiguity, a propensity for nonlinear thinking, and receptivity to ideas that might be quickly discarded by an adult as too fanciful to merit further consideration. Because children do not have a firm line of demarcation between fantasy and reality, ideas from one realm can slip through into the other. Thus, children may respond in ways that are nonstereotypic, a trait that many adults, particularly those in the arts, find enviable (Kincade, 2002). Interestingly, contemporary philosopher Chung-Ying Cheng (2001) contends that an essential task in adulthood is to accept the reality of unreality and the unreality of reality. This, he argues, is the path to enlightenment and wisdom. The capacity for blurring the lines between reality and fantasy originates in childhood. When Pablo Picasso was asked why his work improved as he grew older, he observed that it had taken him a lifetime to learn to draw as a child, and that "Every child is an artist. The problem is how to remain an artist once he grows up" (http://tqpage.com/).

Adults often seek to reconnect with childhood, a time before harsh critics, both external and internal, succeeded in reining in creative thought and discouraging the risk-taking that is necessary to generate fresh, original work. Children may not be, strictly speaking, "more" creative than adults; nevertheless, they certainly are differently creative from adults.

Are children naturally playful and curious? Here, the research is just beginning to catch up with anecdotal impressions of children's behavior. Imagine a group of preschoolers who are engaged in sociodramatic play, or school-age children who are making preparations to present a talent show in their neighborhood. In these childhood pursuits, we see intensity combined with playfulness, the very sort of "regulated curiosity" that empirical research associates with creative behavior (Kashdan & Fincham, 2002). Research on creative thinking often describes an ability to focus with such intensity that a person becomes "lost" in the work and time flies by unnoticed (Kashdan & Fincham, 2002). Eminent creative thinkers describe these times when their work is going well as times when their thinking proceeds more fluidly or "flows" (Csikszentmihalyi, 1990). Once the mind has been captivated by such an "optimal experience" it tends to pursue it again—even in the absence of external rewards (Csikszentmihalyi, 1996).

The child at play is the prototype for fluid-adaptive thinking that is simultaneously serious and playful (Rea, 2001). Fluid-adaptive thinking helps to explain why the work of the most brilliant scientists reflects the aesthetic attributes of art (e.g., an "elegant" theory) and why the work of the most brilliant artists possesses the control, order, and rigor of the sciences (e.g., a dance that "works"). Children are full of wonderment, capable of pursuing their interests with intensity and playfulness. If given the opportunity, they are naturally curious and playful (Isenberg & Quisenberry, 2002), and play during early childhood is predictive of later facility with divergent thinking (Russ, Robins, & Christiano, 1999). Even more to the point for educators is the finding that children who are actively engaged in learner-centered environments score higher on measures of creativity (Hyson, Hirsh-Pasek, & Rescorla, 1990; Rushton & Larkin, 2001).

Despite growing evidence that childhood is the well-spring for later creative pursuits, adults frequently fail to develop those rich resources of imagination, creativity, curiosity, and playfulness (Cobb, 1977; Martindale, 2001). Many experts have noted how children's creative thinking is stereotyped, romanticized, trivialized, and, at times, suppressed (Dacey & Lennon, 1998). If, as both classic and contemporary studies of talent development suggest, it takes nearly 17 years of training and preparation to contribute to a field, educators are in a unique position to influence creative development in human beings (Duffy, 1998). Consequently, it is unacceptable for creative thought and expression, a resource so valuable to society and vital to the individual, to be misunderstood, squandered, or squelched.

Every Child Has the Right to Creative Development

Educating children in ways that foster creative development is consistent with Fontana's (1997) notion of "education for being," which means offering children

> the right to express their own feelings, to give their view of events, to explain themselves, to reflect upon their own behavior, to have their fears and their hopes taken seriously, to ask questions, to seek explanations in the natural world, to love and be loved, to have their inner world of dreams and fantasies and imaginings taken seriously, and to make their own engagement with life. (cited in Craft, 2000, p. 13)

Opportunities for creative expression should not be reserved for children who "earn" them through obedience or because they display early glimmerings of star potential. This is a destructive practice. Take, for example, the development of musical talent. Schools routinely use tests to identify children with musical aptitude, who then will have access to the school's limited musical instruction resources, while children who do not test well are excluded from opportunities to acquire musical performance skills. Furthermore, as children mature, talent becomes less critical than the family's financial resources, including their ability to afford an instrument, private lessons, appropriate attire, and travel to musical performances and events. Both at home and at school, then, resources are the driving consideration.

Like the medical profession, educational systems have an obligation, first and foremost, to do no harm. Not only is it harmful to label children as devoid of musical potential, it is also very likely to be inaccurate. Quick-scoring tests do not address such important variables as motivation or interest. Usually, musical aptitude tests emphasize the ability to hear various notes, match them, or discriminate among them. At the very least, the school should uphold every child's right to enjoy and participate in music, and should make their musical resources accessible to all students.

Creative thought is domain specific and affected by the particulars of the situation (Han & Marvin, 2002). A person who is highly creative in one domain and environment—such as preparing a meal in a well-equipped kitchen—may appear to be lacking in creativity in another situation—such as leading a meeting of investment bankers in a corporate boardroom. Therefore, children need to experience a wide range of interesting activities in order to discover their particular creative assets. Creative thinking is not the exclusive province of special programs for the gifted and talented. It is not a curricular "frill" to be deleted when time is limited. Nor is it the same thing as enrichment, something reserved for those children who have already completed their required work. Rather, creativity is a capacity of every child that ought to be valued and extended across the lifespan.

All children have the right to have their interests and abilities affirmed and nurtured; all children deserve opportunities for creative thought and expression (Isenberg & Jalongo, 2001). Predictions about which children will become highly creative and productive as adults are notoriously inaccurate, because such gifts and contributions develop over time and are influenced by purpose, play, and chance (Gruber & Davis, 1988). Therefore, it is incumbent upon all who work with children not only to see the genius in every child but also to advocate for every child's creative development (Armstrong, 1998).

Creativity: ACEI'S Call for Redefinition

For decades, creativity has been hindered by a stale debate filled with contradictions. It is common to say that "everyone is creative," yet focus exclusively on inventors whose products revolutionized society; it is typical to argue that creative thinking is an asset to be cultivated, yet dwell on stories of geniuses at the brink of madness; and it is customary for business, industry, and governments to publicly extol the virtues of innovation, all the while succumbing to habit, preferring routine, and seeking the comfort of conformity (Horibe, 2001). Furthermore, even when people are convinced of the valuable contributions of creative thought in adult society, creative thought in children too often is treated as aimless, frivolous, and counteractive to the attainment of academic standards.

Misconceptions about creativity are prevalent among educators as well as the general public (Jalongo, 1999). In a study of over a thousand teachers' attitudes toward creativity (Fryer & Coilings, 1991), only about half of the teachers regarded divergent thinking as an element of creative thought. In sharp contrast, experts on creativity regard breaking stereotypes as a critical feature of creative thought, and consider the need to engage in "what if" and "as if" types of thinking as the very essence of imagination (Egan, 2003; Weininger, 1988). It is ACEI's position that creativity needs to be reconceptualized along at least five dimensions.

A first step in clearing up the confusion about creativity is to *use the word "creative" in combination with "thought"* (Webster, 1990). This helps to dispel the common misconceptions that creativity is elusive and defies description, that creative individuals are ineffectual free spirits, or that creative teaching and learning is antithetical to rigor and quality. In fact, creativity is a key component in Sternberg's (1998) theory of successful intelligence, which he defines as "a set of mental abilities used to achieve one's goals in life, given a sociocultural context, through adaptation to, selection of, and shaping of environments" (p. 65). Sternberg's triarchic theory of intelligence combines analytical thinking (e.g., analyzing, comparing/contrasting, evaluating, explaining) with creative thinking (e.g., creating, designing, imagining, supposing) and practical thinking (e.g., using, applying, implementing). Both Sternberg (1998) and Gardner (2000) provide a much more expansive definition for intelligence, one capable of moving far beyond the popular, yet inaccurate, notion that the word "creative" is another word for "unusual." Rather, creative thought is synonymous with productive thought, because it relies on complex reasoning processes (Marzano, Pickering, & McTighe, 1993) such as "comparing, classifying, inducting, deducting, analyzing errors, constructing support, abstracting, analyzing perspectives, making decisions, investigating, inquiring, problem solving, and inventing" (Beattie, 1997, p. 5).

A second key approach to sorting out the definition of creative thought is to *recognize that creative potential alone is insufficient to bring ideas to fruition.* Just as athletic abilities can lie dormant due to lack of opportunity, be undermined by overzealous or misguided attempts to accelerate them, or be destroyed by bad decisions, creative capacities can be underdeveloped, diminished, and ruined. Creativity is a complex developmental system that is shaped by at least seven influences: 1) cognitive processes; 2) social and emotional processes; 3) family aspects, both while growing up and current; 4) education and preparation, both informal and formal; 5) characteristics of the domain and field; 6) sociocultural contextual aspects; and 7) historical forces, events, and trends (Feldman, 1999, pp. 171–172).

A third useful direction in redefining creativity is to *differentiate between "big C Creativity," or the eminent creativity of celebrated geniuses, and "little c creativity," or the problem-solving ability that is more widely distributed among people* (Craft, 2000; Nakamura & Csikszentmihalyi, 2001; Ripple, 1989; Runco, 1996). To think only in terms of mature creative genius underestimates the contributions of creativity during childhood, and puts a price tag on creativity that makes it valuable only when it saves time, labor, or money. Society needs to value the "little c creativity" that teachers use to plan a successful lesson or that parents use to stretch their budgets. The contributions of everyday problem solving may not be spectacular, yet they are significant.

A fourth strategy in redefinition is to *gain a multi-cultural and global perspective on the concept of creativity.* Western ideas about creativity tend to emphasize invention, individual achievement, and linear problem-solving processes (Lubart, 1990, 1999). Interestingly, other cultures pursue creativity as a contribution to the good of the group. For example, everyone in Bali is expected to sing, dance, share stories, craft objects, and so forth—not just those chosen few judged to be talented. To the Balinese, being singled out as particularly talented in the arts would be a source of embarrassment rather than pride. This notion is quite a departure from the Western way of thinking. Becoming enlightened about creative thought, therefore, involves broadening our viewpoint beyond the immediate context and adopting a perspective that can embrace creative endeavors at different times, in other places, and within various cultures. In order to achieve this, we need to abandon what Jerome Bruner (1996) refers to as the "computational" view of thought in which the mind merely processes (e.g., inscribes, stores, sorts, retrieves, manages) information, and replace it with a cultural view in which the mind itself is a cultural artifact. From the computational view, the development of mind is an inside-out operation; from the cultural view, the development of mind is an outside-in operation (Roeper & Davis, 2000), as individuals share the symbol systems, modes of discourse, and ways of being in the world with their respective communities. As Meador (1999) points out, creative thinking is part of a common language that has the capacity to transcend "race, country, culture, and economic level" (p. 324). Speaking that common language is one important way to reconceptualize what it means to be creative.

A fifth important step in redefining creative thinking is to *acknowledge that capturing the essence of creative endeavors demands a blurring of traditional disciplinary boundaries and varied methods of representation.* Creative thought is in no way limited to the fine arts. When the personnel of the Nobel Museum decided to create the museum's first international exhibit to commemorate the 100th anniversary of the Nobel Prize, they were confronted with the challenge of capturing and communicating creative eminence. Clearly, the exhibit would need to embrace an array of disciplines and employ multiple means of representation, including innovative use of film, archival objects, interactive exhibits, photography, computer databases, and the Internet (Gelescke, 2001). Representing creativity in schools also requires interdisciplinary approaches. "Picturing a Century," a project to chronicle the history of Finnish art education, resulted in a CD-ROM that synthesized teaching materials, photographs, text and sound recordings, interviews with art educators, and archives of student work submitted between 1939 and 1981 to the National Board of Education in Finland (Pohjakallio, 1998). Efforts such as this one to represent the creative process require moving beyond subject matter boundaries and communicating what we know and can do in a variety of ways.

Motivation, Interest, and Effort Are As Important As Talent

In 1925, giftedness was operationally defined as ranking in the top one percent in terms of intelligence. Today, theories on giftedness focus on other traits as well, such as interest, motivation, planning, attention, persistence, creativity, leadership, self-confidence, and self-esteem (Amabile, 2001; Naglieri, 2001; Robinson & Clinkenbeard, 1998; Ryan & Deci, 2000). As Li (1996) explains:

> Everybody has gifts; giftedness is a potential. . . . Education can enhance creativity and giftedness because creative thinking . . . can be taught and learned. It is necessary to make a distinction between child giftedness and adult giftedness. A gifted adult is not a simple continuation of a gifted child. Many gifted children do not produce creative works when they become adults and many gifted adults do not have their gifts recognized as children. A lot of complicated extra-intellectual factors affect adult giftedness and accomplishment. (p. 209)

Stunning creative thought does not simply appear. Rather, it is the product of years of learning, thought, and preparation (Weisberg, 1992). In fact, many contemporary psychologists downplay the role of innate talent, and instead emphasize deliberate practice (Ericcson & Charness, 1994). Such a perspective would call into question the "talent scout" mentality that often operates in schools. If it is talent we seek, then we must actively develop it rather than merely take notice after it has emerged. History is replete with examples of creative individuals who were not highly regarded by their teachers when they were students, yet nevertheless made monumental contributions to society as adults. The appropriate role of education is to provide all children with a host of thoughtfully designed experiences in creative representation, beginning in early childhood (Brickman, 1999; Chenfeld, 2002) and continuing throughout school (Torff, 2000). Creative abilities contribute to the quality of life both inside and outside of school; therefore, any discussion of lifelong learning must include attention to creative thought and expression.

The Creative Process Is Collaborative

When asked to describe a creative individual, people from Western cultures often offer stereotypic portrayals, such as the lone genius who remains a fiercely independent outsider and is misunderstood, unappreciated, or even feared by the power group—the "writer in the garret" archetype. Contrary to popular opinion, however, bringing creative thought to fruition requires more than personal ability or even individual determination; it requires social support (Cszikszentmihalyi, 1988; Gruber & Wallace, 1999; Zimmerman & Zimmerman, 2000). Whether the work is a technological breakthrough, a paradigm-shifting scientific theory, an aspiring singer's first CD, or an elementary school child's drawing and story, successful innovation requires some access to social capital. Social capital refers to a range of resources that are intellectual, economic, cultural, and institutional in nature (McLaughlin, 2001), and that are differentially distributed and allocated depending on an individual's circumstances in society, access to these resources, and ability to elicit appropriate support. In fact, an "investment" theory of creativity depicts the creative process as "buy low" and "sell high," taken to mean that the creative individual invests in an idea with rather humble origins, persuades others of its importance, then leaves that idea and goes on to another one that requires development (Sternberg & Lubart, 1996). It is no accident that many highly creative individuals throughout history have been particularly adept at convincing others to marshal the social capital necessary to transform an idea into a reality.

A creative product, no matter how cutting edge, is ultimately a unique recombination of elements that already exist. It bears the markings of what was invented previously; it is not entirely new. For this reason, if for no other, we need to replace the metaphor that characterizes creativity as a bolt out of the blue and replace it with something completely different, such as the metaphor of a circuit board. The circuit board metaphor would characterize creative processes and tasks as a network of interconnected elements bound together by a shared background, which would represent, to extend the analogy, the cultural backdrop against which creative ideas, tasks, and products are played out.

We need only to look around to see that our actions reflect a belief in social networks capable of stimulating creative thought, as well as a conviction that some environments are more conducive to innovation than others. For example, students leave home to attend college, corporations invest millions in think tanks, and scientists work together in laboratory settings, all based on the assumption that particular environments and forms of interaction yield more creative outcomes. Rather than urging children to be creative in quiet solitude, we need to look at how creativity is nourished outside of schools. Educators need to abandon the misconception that creativity flourishes only in isolation and only at the margins of society. Consider, for instance, the intellectual networks that have fostered stunning achievements—the Impressionist School of Artists, Frank Lloyd Wright's community of architects, or the thousands of creative thinkers who have contributed to the Internet. Likewise, education at its best uses creative, collaborative processes to generate work that builds relationships. In one such example, an art and history program in Florida promoted more positive ethnic relations between African American and Latino preadolescents (Cruz & Walker, 2001). Indeed, from a sociological perspective, intellectual innovations are not properties of individuals or ideas, but rather of dynamic networks and organizations (Collins, 1998).

Challenges for Educators

Educators bear a major responsibility as advocates for children's creative thought and expression. Fulfilling this important role often involves unlearning common assumptions and replacing them with more enlightened perspectives. Educators and educational organizations that promote creative thought operate on the assumption that "everyone has creative potential but developing it requires a balance between skill and control and the freedom to experiment and take risks" (Robinson, 2001, p. 45).

Confront Misconceptions about Creative Thinking

What implicit theories do you hold about creative thinking? As teachers, even nuances of belief can affect expectations for children and the details of daily practice. Thus, teacher behavior can be either "facilitative or inhibitive" of children's creative thought and expression (Runco & Johnson, 1993, p. 91). Many parents and teachers, for example, confuse precocity (early emergence of abilities) with creativity (development of original and useful processes and products) (Fishkin & Johnson, 1998; Nicholson & Moran, 1986). Others mistakenly regard creativity as a synonym for eccentric, inappropriate, or even self-destructive behavior. Nettle (2001) points out, however, that disorganized and damaging behavior is an anathema to creative productivity. Educators at all levels need to reconcile rigor and creativity, and to treat them as compatible, coexisting dimensions of intelligence. Educators also need to communicate these ideas to parents, families, and community members so that they can begin to challenge prevailing assumptions about creativity and talent (Kemple & Nissenberg, 2000; Rotigel, 2003). Several other erroneous assumptions about creativity are both prevalent and persistent (Kindler, 1997):

- *Erroneous Assumption 1: Creativity is naturally unfolding.* Actually, creativity, like any other ability, needs encouragement and guidance. The notion that it naturally unfolds too often results in laissez-faire approaches that reduce the teacher's role to distribution of materials. Children need gentle coaching. Skilled guidance is the purpose of artist-in-residence programs around the globe. Young children in Reggio Emilia created a guidebook to their city (Davoli & Ferri, 2000); Scottish children, ages 10 to 14, constructed three-dimensional art projects intended for public display (Coutts & Dawes, 1998); and adolescents in Brooklyn used their skills in critical thinking and the graphic arts to make powerful statements about their identity and the violence, drugs, and gangs in their environment (Simpson, 1995). In these cases, creativity did not unfold predictably like a lima bean seed germinating under time-lapse photography; rather, the children were apprenticed into understanding the repertoire of skills necessary to attain excellence, and were given the opportunity to practice those skills alongside helpful, observant professionals and peers.

- *Erroneous Assumption 2: Creativity is all about process.* In truth, the creative mind that fails to generate anything can hardly be expected to make a contribution. Although it is true that the process needs to be valued, it is not an end unto itself. In virtually every depiction of the creative cycle, the culmination involves evaluation of a product. Take, for example, written composition. Although the child's writing process needs to be valued and supported, the writer also needs opportunities to share writing with others. When children are urged to languish at the process stage, based on some adult's misguided ideas about process, they are being denied the satisfaction of bringing work to a conclusion, which is surely one of creativity's great rewards.

- *Erroneous Assumption 3: The creative process is a safety valve.* Although creative works are forms of self-expression, this does not mean they are purely ways of "letting off steam." One look at an Irish step dance class contradicts the idea that jumping around to release excess energy is the reason for dance. Rather, the dance movements are planned, controlled, and practiced. The tendency to treat the arts as emotional outlets distances creative work not only from the cognitive and physical processes used to attain excellence, but also from the cultural contexts in which creative works are produced (Duncum, 2001; Freedman, 2000). Take, for example, the art form of Vietnamese water puppetry. In this performance art of the rice fields, which dates back to 1121, water is used to move the puppets in ways that complement a story element (e.g., violently during a battle, gently undulating during a quiet scene) and to conceal the operational apparatus below the surface (Contreras, 1995). Reducing this work to a safety valve strips it of its power. Art is much more than an emotional outlet. In the case of Vietnam's water puppetry, it is an expression of traditional values, a source of national pride, and, for those outside the culture, a way of promoting intercultural understanding.

Confronting misconceptions about creativity cannot stop at the level of the individual child, teacher, and family. Such misconceptions about children's creative thought and expression need to be addressed at the school, district, national, and international levels.

Redefine Creative Teaching

What does it mean to be a "creative" teacher? Some people mistakenly believe that it means generating better than average lesson plans or visual aids. If an educator's effectiveness is determined by her or his ability to develop creative thought and expression in children, however, much more is necessary. In her 1996 study of 1,028 teachers in the United Kingdom, Fryer arrived at some essential characteristics of creative teaching. The top five included teachers' commitment to:

- Deepen learners' understanding of the world
- Believe in the creative ability of all students
- Adapt the curriculum to meet children's individual needs
- Encourage empathy in learners
- Value creative expression in learners, and teach in ways that facilitate it.

These findings suggest that creative teaching involves dispositions as well as pedagogical skills. Perhaps the most important disposition in educators who strive to become creative teachers is, as Fritz (2002) argues, the determination to "find the balance between stifling the students within a limited set of skills and letting them loose with endless horizons but ill equipped with skills and knowledge to realize their ideas" (www.21learn.org/arch/articles/fritz.html). The arts have always been focused on "mixtures and balances." Creative teaching can do no less, for it too relies on an appropriate blend of structure and freedom for students, teachers, and curriculum. In China, where 178 million children attend elementary and secondary school, the official purpose of art in "the national curriculum is to foster patriotism, morality, and socialism"; however, the teachers also recognize their responsibility to enlarge children's vision and allow them to create according to their imaginations (Perry, 1998). Such dichotomies are not unique to China, nor are they resolved by either/or thinking. It takes both commitment to children and political savvy to negotiate such conflicting views. It takes mixtures and balances.

Furthermore, the focus of creative teaching needs to be as much, if not more, on the learner than it is on the teacher. According to Stanko (2000), teachers can function more creatively in three basic ways: 1) by teaching the skills and attitudes of creative thinking to students; 2) by orienting students to the creative methods of various disciplines; and 3) by creating a "problem friendly" classroom in which lines of inquiry, with relevance for the learners, can be pursued through multi-disciplinary methods. A classroom that promotes creative thinking takes a "problem finding" approach, differentiating between superficial mental exercises (in which the teacher typically knows the answer in advance) and genuine inquiry. In order to function at full creative capacity, children need the freedom to pursue questions that captivate them, and to work in learning environments that offer a blend of high support and high expectations (Rea, 2001). Amabile (1986) describes certain "creativity killers," including inflexible schedules, intense competition, reliance on extrinsic rewards, and lack of free time. Although a certain amount of "breathing room" is necessary in order to develop creative potential, studies of school arts in the United States suggest that the power of art is diluted by teacher practices being guided by the following constraints: 1) time (e.g., choosing quick projects to conform to a 30-minute time block); 2) materials (e.g., using inexpensive materials, since high-quality art materials are not supplied); 3) physical environment (e.g., being concerned about neatness and clean up); and 4) presentation (e.g., lack of space and resources for appropriate display of children's art) (Bressler, 1998).

Provide Children with Role Models of Motivation and Persistence in Creative Thought

From a psychological perspective, high skill and low challenge leads to boredom (Csikszentmihalyi, 1996), a dynamic that helps to explain why so many highly creative adults were considered troublesome as school children. Conversely, low skill and high challenge leads to frustration, a dynamic that helps to explain the angry and destructive student. When the media covers stunning creative achievements, they often gloss over the struggles and disappointments along the way. It is important, however, for children to see that the road to innovation is not always apparent or easy, and that having a mind stocked with ideas and a growing repertoire of skills—rather than being blessed with pure luck—is the surest route to making a creative contribution.

It is helpful for children to see how people who have accomplished personal goals—peers, parents, family members, community members, and professionals from various fields—think about their work and refine it, whether it is a teacher sharing a piece of writing that she hopes to polish for publication, or an illustrator sharing dissatisfying first efforts as well as the ones that were chosen for publication and explaining the reasons for those choices. Children need adult role models who rebound from discouragement, whose work is their avocation, and who persist at a task until a high-quality result is achieved. The creative individual is challenged by ambiguity, is comfortable with multiple perspectives, and often addresses the "same" problem across a series of works or experiments, even if these efforts are not always successful (Lindstrom, 1997).

It is equally important for parents, families, and the larger community to encounter these role models. Participation in the arts—namely, those subjects with undeniable connections to creative processes, such as art and music—is clouded by stereotypes, gender bias, and prejudice. In a qualitative study of parental attitudes toward arts education for children, most parents considered the arts to be feminine, frivolous, and non-essential in terms of getting ahead in the "real world" except as a mechanism for acquiring self-discipline (e.g., through regular practice of a musical instrument). They were conflicted about ways in which the arts affected social status; in one study, even families who strongly supported arts education preferred that it be an extracurricular activity, in order to preserve the exclusivity of their child's training (Gainer, 1997).

Call for Appropriate Assessment of Creative Processes and Products

At one time, assessing creativity was fairly straightforward. The main characteristic under consideration was novelty, and that could be measured, even quantified, by statistical rarity. Today, experts in the field have added appropriateness, usefulness, and value as desirable qualities. Consequently, assessment of creative products is now far more difficult. There is the practical difficulty of deciding how to respond to students' aesthetic engagement and how to assess their work, as well as the broader issue of different beliefs in different subject areas about what qualifies as creativity, how to determine the cultural value of work, and the language used to communicate these important and powerful ideas.

Appropriate assessment of creative tasks and processes is a challenge for at least four reasons. First, creative works are multi-faceted, multi-layered, and do not yield a single, correct, and easy-to-score response. Second, creative processes that are highly productive in one discipline may be ill-suited to another domain. Third, creative processes and tasks are context-specific and are greatly affected by the particulars of the situation in which the work was brought to fruition. Fourth, although numerous psychometric tools exist—Fishkin and Johnson (1998) reviewed over 60 different instruments for assessing creativity in school-age children—no single measure can predict a child's creative potential or assess a person's creative capacity.

It is a truism that, in schools, work that is not linked to standards and assessed in some systematic way is treated as less important and less vital to educational purposes. When work is not assessed, it is treated as if it does not "count." Such work also can be expected to be on the endangered list when resources are in short supply—witness the almost constant threat to school art and music programs in the United States. Fortunately, several national organizations have generated standards and guidelines that can provide a framework for assessment in the arts, including the National Advisory Committee on Creative and Cultural Education (1999) in the United Kingdom and the Consortium of National Arts Education Associations and National Committee for Standards in the Arts (1994) in the United States. In their book on evaluating creativity, editors Sefton-Green and Sinker (2000) contend that evaluation is the crux of the matter. Increasingly, the emphasis rests on the contribution of the creative product or response as judged by an appropriate group of observers; in other words, a consensual process is used to assess creativity (Amabile, 2001; Priest, 2001). Alternative assessment provides numerous examples of a consensual process used to evaluate creative products, such as a team of elementary school teachers evaluating children's writing portfolios, or a panel of secondary educators scoring a student's senior project. It is critical that creative processes and products be part of the overall assessment plan in the curriculum.

Appropriate assessment of creative efforts:

- Is founded on expanded definitions of intelligence and creativity
- Is fair (e.g., gives all students an equal opportunity to participate) and adapted to the special needs of individual students

- Is oriented toward students but planned and monitored by teachers who can clearly state the purpose of the assessment, identify the domain to be assessed, understand the assessment strategy or task, prepare the actual task or exercise, devise a scoring plan, and make a plan for reporting the results
- Is integrated with the curriculum (e.g., supports instruction and course objectives)
- Is committed to evaluating creative work at multiple levels and from multiple perspectives
- Is continuous and focuses on providing ongoing feedback
- Is focused on "real world" tasks and considers the particulars of the context in which creative works are generated
- Includes both informal and formal assessment strategies
- Considers not only the products but also the processes
- Provides opportunities for students to revisit the work, refine, and revise
- Is responsive to knowledge of disciplinary content, skills, and processes of a discipline, requisite motor skills in a discipline, appropriate procedures in particular contexts, self-appraisal of strengths and weaknesses in a discipline, and insight into the dispositions and values associated with achievement in a domain
- Is concerned with determining students' preconceptions and changing their misconceptions
- Is linked to standards and referenced to criteria
- Is supportive of collaborative and cooperative learning. (adapted from Beattie, 1997)

Educators throughout the world are grappling with ways of designing curriculum and assessing it in ways that promote creativity, such as the Japanese Ministry of Education's attempt to define expressive education in early childhood (Mori, 1996). As part of this reconceptualization of assessment, teachers need to rethink the practice of using contests and tangible rewards. Growing support in the literature for the social-cognitive perspective argues that overreliance on conspicuous rewards may actually diminish the desired behavior (Fawson & Moore, 1999). This consequence is thought to occur in two major ways: partly by constraining the response (e.g., a student chooses a less innovative response to avoid rejection), and partly by diverting attention from the intrinsic rewards of the task (e.g., a student becomes focused on the prize instead of the process) (Joussement & Koestner, 1999). Thus, it is possible to assess creative processes and products, but only if educators are willing to challenge the customary ways of evaluating children's work.

Reflect on Our Hopes and Dreams for Children

In a recent interview (Cramond, 2001) with E. Paul Torrance, one of the pioneers-in creativity research, Torrance talked about his 30-year study of what he referred to as the "beyonders," those individuals whose creative achievement was remarkable in a particular domain (Torrance, 1993). The characteristics that these individuals shared were: a delight in deep thinking, a tolerance for mistakes, a passion for their work, a clear sense of purpose and mission, an acceptance of being different and a level of comfort with being a minority of one, and a tendency to ignore admonitions about being "well-rounded." Based on this research, Torrance and his colleagues (Henderson, Presbury, & Torrance, 1983) advised children to pursue their interests with intensity, work to their strengths, learn to self-evaluate, seek out mentors and teachers, and learn to be interdependent. Such advice, based on studies of those who excelled in their chosen fields and functioned at very high levels of creativity, is suggestive of the type of changes that need to be made in schools and programs to make them places in which creative thought can grow.

An environment for creativity would have to go against the grain of prevailing ideas about creativity and emphasize critical judgment. One important reason for this emphasis is that creative thought is not inherently "good." Creative processes and products can be put to destructive ends. Therefore, it makes sense to guide children in examining the underlying values of creative work. In fact, many of the activities that are used to teach media literacy take this approach (Semali & Watts Pailliotet, 1999). An advertiser might spend hundreds of thousands of dollars on a creative idea for promoting a product. But whose interests are being served? Who is most likely to be taken in by the appealing advertisement? What are the consequences for society at large if questionable claims and business practices are allowed to proliferate? Society is inundated with unstructured problems like this one, not by the neat, predictable, and orderly kinds of questions too often presented in school. If we seek to prepare children for the future, we must devote attention to the thoughtful critique of creative products in society. We also must think beyond what is customary, orthodox, and conventional if the genuinely important potential of creativity—the ways in which it is used to capture the very essence of its culture—is to be realized.

Conclusion

As Robinson (2001) argues,

> Developing creative abilities calls for sophisticated forms of teaching and for relevant forms of assessment and accountability.... As long as the debate in education is seen simplistically as a contest between traditional and progressive methods, creativity or rigour, the fundamental objective of developing an education system for the twenty-first century will be thwarted. These are not simply questions of standards or accountability but of purpose and vision. (p. 49)

A belief in the child's right to creative thought and expression transforms the classroom. In the past, in the present, and in the future, our most enlightened visions of education will be connected by the common thread of imagination, creative thought, and enhanced opportunities for creative expression. As we look ahead, it will no doubt be possible to trace society's greatest innovations and achievements back to an abiding respect for creative thought processes during childhood. For when we value creative thinking and creative expression in society, it becomes part of our social consciousness and social capital. Society then protects its reserves of creativity by fashioning networks of support that are capable of instilling confidence, promoting resilience, and multiplying ways of being intelligent in every person, commencing in childhood and continuing throughout the lifespan.

References

Amabile, T. M. (1986). The personality of creativity. *Creative Living, 15*(3), 12–16.

Amabile, T. M. (2001). Beyond talent: John Irving and the passionate craft of creativity. *American Psychologist, 56*, 333–336.

Armstrong, T. (1998). *Awakening genius in the classroom.* Alexandria, VA: Association for Supervision and Curriculum Development.

Beattie, D. K. (1997). *Assessment in art education.* Worcester, MA: Davis.

Bressler, L. (1998). "Child art," "fine art," and "art for children": The shaping of school practice and implications for change. *Arts Education and Policy Review, 100*(1), 3–10.

Brickman, N. A. (1999). *Creative representation: High/Scope preschool key experiences.* Ypsilanti, MI: High/Scope Educational Research Foundation.

Bruner, J. S. (1996). *The culture of education.* Boston: Harvard University Press.

Chenfeld, M. B. (2002). *Creative experiences for young children* (3rd ed.). Portsmouth, NH: Heinemann.

Cheng, C. (2001). "Unity of three truths" and three forms of creativity: Lotus sutra and the process of philosophy. *Journal of Chinese Philosophy, 28*(4), 449–456.

Cobb, E. (1977). *The ecology of imagination.* New York: Columbia University.

Collins, R. (1998). *The sociology of philosophies: A global theory of intellectual change.* Cambridge, MA: Harvard University Press.

Consortium of National Arts Education Associations and National Committee for Standards in the Arts. (1994). *National standards for arts education: What every young American should know and be able to do in the arts.* Reston, VA: Music Educators National Conference.

Contreras, G. (1995). Teaching about the Vietnamese culture: Water puppetry as the soul of the rice fields. *Social Studies, 86*(1), 25–28.

Coutts, G., & Dawes, M. (1998). Drawing on the artist inside: Towards 1999. *Journal of Art and Design Education, 17*(2), 191–196.

Craft, A. (2000). *Creativity across the primary curriculum: Framing and developing practice.* London: Routledge.

Cramond, B. (2001). Interview with E. Paul Torrance on creativity in the last and next millennia. *Journal of Secondary Gifted Education, 12*(3), 116–120.

Cruz, B. C., & Walker, P. C. (2001). Fostering positive ethnic relations between African American and Latino children: A collaborative urban program using art and history. *Multicultural Perspectives, 3*(1), 9–14.

Csikszentmihalyi, M. (1988). Society, culture, and the person: A systems view of creativity. In R. J. Sternberg (Ed.), *The nature of creativity* (pp. 325–329). New York: Cambridge University Press.

Csikszentmihalyi, M. (1990). *Flow: The psychology of optimal experience.* New York: Harper and Row.

Csikszentmihalyi, M. (1996). *Creativity: Flow and the psychology of discovery and invention.* New York: Harper and Row.

Dacey, J. S., & Lennon, K. H. (1998). *Understanding creativity: The interplay of biological, psychological, and social factors.* San Francisco: Jossey-Bass.

Davoli, M., & Ferri, G. (Eds.). (2000). *Reggio Tutta: A guide to the city by the children.* Rome: Ministry of Education.

Diamond, M., & Hopson, J. (1999). *Magic trees of the mind: How to nurture your child's intelligence, creativity, and healthy emotions from birth through adolescence.* New York: Penguin.

Duffy, B. (1998). *Supporting creativity and imagination in the early years.* Buckingham, UK: Open University Press.

Duncum, P. (2001). Visual culture: Developments, definitions, and directions for art education. *Studies in Art Education, 42*, 101–112.

Egan, K. (2003). Start with what the student knows or with what the student can imagine? *Phi Delta Kappan, 84*(6), 443–445.

Ericsson, K. A., & Charness, N. (1994). Expert performance: Its structure and acquisition. *American Psychologist, 49*(8), 425–747.

Fawson, P. C., & Moore, S. A. (1999). Reading incentive programs: Beliefs and practices. *Reading Psychology, 20*, 325–340.

Feldman, D. H. (1999). The development of creativity. In R. J. Sternberg (Ed.), *Handbook of creativity* (pp. 169–186). New York: Cambridge University Press.

Fishkin, A. S., Cramond, B., & Olszewski-Kubilius, P. (Eds.). (1998). *Investigating creativity in youth: Research and methods.* Cresskill, NJ: Hampton Press.

Fishkin, A. S., & Johnson, A. S. (1998). Who is creative? Identifying children's creative abilities. *Roeper Review, 21*(1), 40–46.

Fontana, D. (1997). Cited in Craft, A. (2000). *Creativity across the primary curriculum: Framing and developing practice* (p. 13). London: Routledge.

Freedman, K. (2000). Social perspectives on art education in the U.S.: Teaching visual culture in a democracy. *Studies in Art Education, 41*, 315–329.

Fritz, A. (2002). *Keynote address for IDATER '98—Creativity: From philosophy to practice.* Retrieved August 28, 2002, from www.21learn.org/arch/articles/fritz.html.

Fryer, M. (1996). *Creative teaching and learning.* London: Paul Chapman.

Fryer, M., & Collings, J. A. (1991). Teachers' views about creativity. *British Journal of Educational Psychology, 61*, 207–219.

Gainer, B. (1997). Marketing arts education: Parental attitudes toward arts education for children. *Journal of Arts Management, Law & Society, 26*(4), 253–268.

Gardner, H. (1993). *Frames of mind: The theory of multiple intelligences* (10th anniversary edition). New York: Basic Books.

Gardner, H. (2000). *Intelligence reframed: Multiple intelligences for the 21st century.* New York: Basic Books.

Gelescke, K. (2001, April 28). What is creativity and can it be exhibited? *The Lancet, 357*, 1373–1374.

Goleman, D., & Kaufman, P. (1992). The art of creativity. *Psychology Today, 25*(2), 40–47.

Gruber, H. E., & Davis, S. N. (1988). Inching our way up Mount Olympus: The evolving-systems approach to creative thinking. In R. J. Stemberg (Ed.), *The nature of creativity* (pp. 243–270). New York: Cambridge University Press.

Gruber, H. E., & Wallace, D. B. (1999). The case study method and evolving systems approach for understanding creative people at work. In R. J. Sternberg (Ed.), *The handbook of creativity* (pp. 93–115). New York: Cambridge University Press.

Han, K., & Marvin, C. (2002). Multiple creativities? Investigating domain-specificity of creativity in young children. *Gifted Child Quarterly, 46*, 98–109.

Henderson, M., Presbury, J., & Torrance, E. P. (1983). *Manifesto for children.* Staunton, VA: Full Circle Counseling.

Horibe, F. (2001). *Creating the innovation culture: Leveraging visionaries, dissenters and other useful troublemakers in your organization.* New York: Wiley.

Hyson, M., Hirsh-Pasek, K., & Rescorla, L. (1990). The classroom practices inventory: An observation instrument based on NAEYC's guidelines for developmentally appropriate practices for 4- and 5-year-old children. *Early Childhood Research Quarterly, 5*, 475–494.

Isenberg, J. P., & Jalongo, M. R. (2001). *Creative expression and play in early childhood* (3rd ed.). Upper Saddle River, NJ: Merrill/Prentice Hall.

Isenberg, J. P., & Quisenberry, N. (2002). Play: Essential for all children. *Childhood Education, 79*, 33–39.

Jalongo, M. R. (1999). How we respond to the artistry of children: Ten barriers to overcome. *Early Childhood Education Journal, 26*(4), 205–208.

Joussement, M., & Koestner, R. (1999). Effect of expected rewards on children's creativity. *Creativity Research Journal, 12*(4), 231–239.

Kashdan, T. B., & Fincham, F. D. (2002). Facilitating creativity by regulating curiosity. *American Psychologist, 57*(5), 373–374.

Kemple, K. M., & Nissenberg, S. A. (2000). Nurturing creativity in early childhood education: Families are part of it. *Early Childhood Education Journal, 28*(1), 67–71.

Kincade, T. (2002). The child's heart in art. *American Artist, 66*(716), 12.

Kindler, A. M. (1996). Myths, habits, research, and policy: The four pillars of early childhood education. *Arts Education Policy Review, 97*(4), 24–30.

Li, R. (1996). *A theory of conceptual intelligence: Thinking, learning, creativity, and giftedness.* Westport, CT: Praeger.

Lindstrom, L. (1997). Integration, creativity, or communication? Paradigm shifts and continuity in Swedish art education. *Arts Education Policy Review, 99*(1), 17–24.

Lubart, T. I. (1990). Creativity and cross-cultural variation. *International Journal of Creativity, 25*, 39–59.

Lubart, T. I. (1999). Creativity across cultures. In R. J. Sternberg (Ed.), *Handbook of creativity* (pp. 339–350). New York: Cambridge University Press.

Martindale, C. (2001). Oscillations and analogies: Thomas Young, MD, FRS, genius. *American Psychologist, 56*, 342–345.

Marzano, R. J., Pickering, D., & McTighe, J. (1993). *Assessing student outcomes: Using the Dimensions of Learning Model*. Alexandria, VA: Association for Supervision and Curriculum Development.

Meador, K. (1999). Creativity around the globe. *Childhood Education, 75*, 324–325. (Special Theme Issue, Creativity Around the Globe.)

McLaughlin, N. (2001). Optimal marginality: Innovation and orthodoxy in Fromm's revision of psychoanalysis. *Sociological Quarterly, 42*(2), 271–287.

Mori, K. (1996). Expressive education in early childhood. *Arts Education Policy Review, 97*(4), 31–34.

Naglieri, J. A. (2001). Understanding intelligence, giftedness and creativity using the PASS Theory. *Roeper Review, 23*(3), 151–156.

Nakamura, J., & Csikszentmihalyi, M. (2001). Catalytic creativity: The case of Linus Pauling. *American Psychologist, 56*, 337–341.

National Advisory Committee on Creative and Cultural Education. (1999). *All our futures: Creativity, culture, and education.* United Kingdom: DfEE.

Nettle, D. (2001). *Strong imagination: Madness, creativity, and human nature.* New York: Oxford University Press.

Nicholson, M. W., & Moran, J. D. (1986). Teachers' judgments of preschoolers' creativity. *Perceptual and Motor Skills, 63*, 1211–1216.

Perry, P. (1998). Art in a million schools: Art education in China. *Journal of Art and Design Education, 17*(3), 311–314.

Pohjakallio, P. (1998). New and old: Multimedia as a tool for providing interpretation and meaning: Reflections on the Finnish Art Education History Project. *Journal of Art and Design Education, 17*(3), 303–310.

Priest, T. (2001). Using creativity assessment to nurture and predict compositional creativity. *Journal of Research in Music Education, 49*(3), 245–257.

Rea, D. (2001). Maximizing the motivated mind for emergent giftedness. *The Roeper Review, 23*(3), 157–164.

Ripple, R. E. (1989). Ordinary creativity. *Contemporary Educational Psychology, 14*, 189–202.

Robinson, A., & Clinkenbeard, P. R. (1998). Giftedness: An exceptionality examined. *Annual Review of Psychology, 48*, 117–139.

Robinson, K. (2001). Mind the gap: The creative conundrum. *Critical Quarterly, 43*(1), 41–45.

Roeper, B., & Davis, D. (2000). Howard Gardner: Knowledge, learning and development in drama and arts education. *Research in Drama Education, 5*(2), 217–233,

Rotigel, J. (2003). Understanding the young gifted child: Guidelines for parents, families, and educators. *Early Childhood Education Journal, 30*(4), 209–214.

Runco, M. A. (1996). *Eminent creativity: Everyday creativity and health.* Norwood, NJ: Ablex.

Runco, M. A., & Johnson, D. J. (1993). Parents' and teachers' implicit theories on children's creativity. *Child Study Journal, 23*(2), 91–113.

Runco, M. A., & Pritzker, S. (1999). *Encyclopedia of creativity.* San Diego: Academic Press.

Rushton, S., & Larkin, E. (2001). Shaping the learning environment: Connecting developmentally appropriate practices to brain research. *Early Childhood Education Journal, 29*(1), 25–34.

Russ, S. W., Robins, A. L., & Christiano, B. A. (1999). Pretend play: Longitudinal prediction of creativity and affect in fantasy in children. *Creativity Research Journal, 12*(2), 129–139.

Ryan, R. L., & Deci, E. L. (2000). Self-determination theory and the facilitation of intrinsic motivation, social development, and well-being. *American Psychologist, 55*, 68–78.

Sefton-Green, J., & Sinker, R. (Eds.). (2000). *Evaluating creativity: Making and learning by young people.* London: Routledge.

Semali, L. M., & Watts Pailliotet, A. (Eds.). (1999). *Intermediality: The teachers' handbook of critical media literacy.* Boulder, CO: Westview.

Simpson, J. W. (1995). Choices for urban art education. *Arts Education Policy Review, 96*(6), 27–30.

Stanko, A. J. (2000). *Creativity in the classroom: Schools of curious delight* (2nd ed.). Mahwah, NJ: Lawrence Erlbaum.

Sternberg, R. (1998). Principles of teaching for successful intelligence. *Educational Psychologist, 33*(2/3), 65–72.

Sternberg, R., & Lubart, T. (1996). Investing in creativity. *American Psychologist, 51*(7), 677–686.

Torff, B. (2000). Encouraging the creative voice of the child. *NAMTA Journal, 25*(1), 195–214.

Torrance, E. P. (1993). The beyonders in a thirty-year study of creative achievement. *Roeper Review, 15,* 131–134.

Webster, P. R. (1990). Creativity as creative thinking. *Music Educators Journal, 76*(9), 22–28.

Weininger, O. (1988). "What if" and "as if": Imagination and pretend play in early childhood. In K. Egan & D. Nadaner (Eds.), *Imagination and education* (pp. 141–149). New York: Teachers College Press.

Weisberg, R. W. (1992). *Creativity: Beyond the myth of genius.* New York: Freeman.

Zimmerman, E., & Zimmerman, L. (2000). Art education and early childhood education: The young child as creator and meaning maker within a community context. *Young Children, 55*(6), 87–92.

Courtesy of the Association for Childhood Education International (ACEI). Copyright © 2003 by the Association for Childhood Education International ISBN. Reprints are available from: ACEI, 11141 Georgia Ave., Suite 200, Wheaton, MD 20902 $1.75 each, members; $2.50 nonmembers; 10% discount on 10–49 copies; 20% on 50–99; 25% on 100 or more. Price includes postage and handling.

Jalongo, M. R. (2003, Summer). The child's right to creative thought and expression. *Childhood Education 79*(4), 218–228.

 ## ADDITIONAL READING

Arnold, A. (1997). Stories & art: Creating multiple levels of meaning. *School Arts, 96*(8), 22.

Ascbacher, P. (1996). A FLARE for the arts. *Educational Leadership, 53*(8), 40–44.

Balke, E. (1997). Play and the arts: The importance of the "unimportant." *Childhood Education, 73*(6), 355–360.

Barrentine, S. J. (1996). Engaging with reading through interactive readalouds. *The Reading Teacher, 50*(1), 37–43.

Bolen, L. (1989). The importance of the arts in early childhood curriculum. *Dimensions of Early Childhood, 18*(1), 11–14.

Bouleris, J. (1991). Measuring up: Teaching geometry through art. *School Arts, 91*(3), 22–24.

Bresler, L. (1995). Introduction to the symposium on the integration of the arts into the curriculum reform. *Arts Education Policy Review, 97*(1), 9–10.

Cameron, L. (1997). Draw a story . . . write a picture. *School Arts, 96*(8), 20–22.

Demetrulais, D. M. (1992). Developing intellectual creativity through children's literature for preschoolers through third grade. *Education 112*(3), 464–469.

Dunn, P. C. (1995). Integrating the arts: Renaissance and reformation in arts education. *Arts Education Policy Review, 96*(4), 32–37.

Fauth, B. (1990). Linking visual arts with drama, movement, and dance for the young child. In W. Stinson (Ed.), *Moving and learning for the young child.* Reston, VA: American Alliance for Health, Physical Education, Recreation, and Dance.

Gandini, L., Hill, L., Cadwell, L., & Schwall, C. (Eds.). (2005). *In the spirit of the studio: Learning from the Atelier of Reggio Emilia.* New York: Teachers College Press.

Giles, C., Andre, C. D., & Pfanneenstiel, V. (1998). Talking about books: Connections through literature using art, music, and drama. *Language Arts, 76*(1), 67–75.

Irwin, R. L., & Reynolds, J. K. (1995). Integration as a strategy for teaching the arts as disciplines. *Arts Education Policy Review, 96*(4), 13–19.

McCall, A. L. (1999). Speaking through cloth: Teaching Hmong history and culture through textile art. *The Social Studies, 90*(5), 230–235.

Mills, H., & Clyde, J. A. (1992). Using art and mathematics to tell a story. *Dimensions of Early Childhood, 20*(3), 28–29, 40.

Nevinskas, N., & Pizer, C. H. (1998). Art in motion. *School Arts, 97*(9), 40–42.

Nicholas, R. A. (1992). Drawing from life: Helping children preserve culture through art. *Dimensions of Early Childhood, 20*(3), 5–7.

Parr, N. C., Radford, J., & Snyder, S. (1998). Kaleidoscope: Building an arts-infused elementary curriculum. *Early Childhood Education Journal, 25*(3), 181–188.

Pinciotti, P. (1993). Creative drama and young children: The dramatic learning connection. *Arts Education Policy Review, 94*(6), 24–29.

Reimer, B. (1989). A comprehensive arts curriculum model. *Design for Arts Education, 90*(6), 2–16.

Schon, D. A. (1983). *The reflective practitioner.* New York: Basic Books.

Seefeldt, C. (1993). *Social studies for the pre-school primary child.* New York: Macmillan.

Stinson, W. J. (Ed.). (1990). *Moving and learning for the young child.* Reston, VA: American Alliance for Health, Physical Education, Recreation, and Dance.

Walczak, J. (1994). Escher tesselations. *School Arts, 93*(7), 29–31.

CHILDREN'S LITERATURE CONNECTION

Alexander, M. (1983). *How my library grew.* New York: H. W. Wilson.
Neither Dinah nor her Teddy Bear have ever been to the library, but when one is built just down the street, she looks forward to the opening day and works to complete a special present for the new library. (PreK–1)

Anderson, J. (1990). *Harry's helicopter.* New York: Morrow Junior Books.
One day, Harry's bright red cardboard helicopter takes off with him in a gust of wind and gives him a thrilling ride. (PreK–1)

Cooney, B. (1990). *Roxaboxen.* New York: Lothrop, Lee & Shepard.
A hill covered with rocks and wooden boxes becomes an imaginary town for Marian, her sisters, and their friends. (Primary)

Engel, D. (1988). *Josephina the great collector.* New York: Morrow Junior Books.
Josephina's passion for collecting anything and everything finally drives her sister out of the room they share. Josephina develops a creative plan to reconcile with her sister. (PreK–2)

Himmelman, J. (1990). *Ibis: A true whale story.* New York: Scholastic.
A survival story of two friendly whales. (Primary)

 For additional resources involving creativity and the arts with young children, visit our Web site at **www.earlychilded.delmar.com**

REFERENCES

Applewhite, A., Evans, W. R, III, & Frothingham, A. (Eds.). (1992). *And I quote.* New York: St. Martin's Press.

Breig-Allen, C., Hill, J., Geismar-Ryan, L., & Cadwell, L. B. (1998). The language of lines. *Young Children, 53*(4), 64–66.

Bresler, L. (1993). Three orientations to arts in the primary grades: Implications for curriculum reform. *Arts Education Policy Review, 94*(6), 29–34.

Brett, J. (1989). *The mitten: A Ukrainian folktale.* New York: Putnam.

Caldwell, L. B. (1997). *Bringing Reggio Emilia home.* New York: Teachers College Press.

Cornett, C. E. (1998). *The arts as meaning makers: Integrating literature and the arts throughout the curriculum.* Upper Saddle River, NJ: Merrill.

Dixon, G. T., & Chalmers, F. G. (1990). The expressive arts in education. *Childhood Education, 67*(1), 12–17.

Edwards, C., Gandini, L., & Forman, G. (1993). *The hundred languages of children: The Reggio Emilia approach to early childhood education.* Norwood, NJ: Ablex.

Egan, K. (1988). The origins of imagination. In K. Egan & D. Nadaner (Eds.), *Imagination and education* (pp. 91–127). New York: Teachers College Press.

Egan, K. (1997). The arts as the basic of education. *Childhood Education, 73*(6), 341–345.

Fitzhenry, R. I. (Ed.) (1993). *The Harper book of quotations* (3rd ed.). New York: HarperCollins.

Getty Center for Education in the Arts. (1985). *Beyond creating: The place for art in America's schools.* Los Angeles: J. Paul Getty Trust.

Hansen, K. (1986). *The self-imagined.* London: Routledge & Kegan Paul.

Himmelman, J. (1990). *Ibis: A true whale story.* New York: Scholastic.

Hoffman, H. (1968). *The green grass grows all around.* New York: Macmillan.

Hoffman, S., & Lamme, L. L. (Eds.). (1989). *Learning from the inside out: The expressive arts.* Wheaton, MD: Association for Childhood Education International.

Isbell, R. T., & Raines, S. C. (2000). *Tell it again 2: Easy-to-tell stories with activities for young children.* Beltsville, MD: Gryphon House.

Jalongo, M. (1990). The child's right to the expressive arts: Nurturing the imagination as well as the intellect. *Childhood Education, 66*(4), 195–201.

Jalongo, M. R. (Summer 2003). The child's right to creative thought and expression. *Childhood Education 79*(4), 218–228.

Malaguzzi, L. (1993). History, ideas, and basic philosophy. In C. Edwards, L. Gandini, & G. Forman (Eds.), *The hundred languages of children: The Reggio Emilia approach to early childhood education* (pp. 41–89). Norwood, NJ: Ablex.

Raines, S. C., & Canady, R. J. (1989). *Story s-t-r-e-t-c-h-e-r-s: Activities to expand children's favorite books.* Mt. Rainier, MD: Gryphon House.

Raines, S. C., & Canady, R. J. (1990). *The whole language kindergarten.* New York: Teachers College Press.

Raines, S. C., & Canady, R. J. (1992). *Story s-t-r-e-t-c-h-e-r-s for the primary grades: Activities to expand children's favorite books.* Mt. Rainier, MD: Gryphon House.

Raines, S. C., & Isbell, R. T. (1999). *Tell it again: Easy-to-tell stories with activities for young children.* Beltsville, MD: Gryphon House.

Smith, B. O., Stanley, W. O., & Shores, J. H. (1957). *Fundamentals of curriculum development.* New York: Harcourt Brace Jovanovich.

Stake, R., Bresler, L., & Mabry, L. (1991). *Customs and cherishing: Art education in the United States.* Urbana, IL: Council of Research in Music Education.

Tresselt, A. R. (1990). *The mitten: An old Ukrainian folktale.* New York: William Morrow.

Wright, S. (1997). Learning how to learn: The arts as core in an emergent curriculum. *Childhood Education, 73*(6), 361–365.

Appendix A

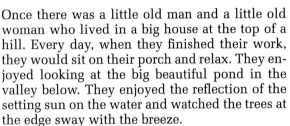

The Ducks That Could Not Swim

Once there was a little old man and a little old woman who lived in a big house at the top of a hill. Every day, when they finished their work, they would sit on their porch and relax. They enjoyed looking at the big beautiful pond in the valley below. They enjoyed the reflection of the setting sun on the water and watched the trees at the edge sway with the breeze.

One evening, as they were enjoying the pond, they decided that their view would be more beautiful if they had some white ducks to swim in the pond. They began to check the newspaper for ads of ducks to be purchased. One day they found an advertisement, "Ducks for Sale." They called and got directions to the place where the ducks were for sale. All the while, they imagined how beautiful the white ducks would be swimming in their pond.

The little old man and little old woman drove their truck up into the mountains, around curvy roads, higher and higher. At last, they reached the place where the white ducks were for sale. The owner took them to a big chicken house where the ducks had lived their entire life. The couple was thrilled with the beautiful white ducks and bought five of them. They lifted them into a cage in their truck. They drove home, over the mountains and around the curves with the ducks quacking all the way.

When the little old man and woman arrived at their home, they couldn't wait to take their five white ducks to the pond. They drove their truck to the edge of the pond and unloaded the cage. The white ducks ran out of the cage, but did not go into the water. They stood at the edge and walked around the pond, but, they did not go in the water. The little old man began to shoo the five white ducks toward the pond. The ducks only circled the edge of the water. They did not place their webbed feet in the pond. The ducks looked at the water but made no attempt to swim in the pond.

The little old man and the little old woman were very puzzled. Why were the ducks afraid of the water? Of course ducks know how to swim. Each day the man and woman would walk to the pond and try to get the ducks to swim in the water. Each time the ducks would simply walk around and around the pond, but they never entered the water. Once, the man ran a duck to the edge of the water. The duck's foot touched the water but he quickly removed it—almost like the water was hot. Months passed and the white ducks never swam in the pond, they simply walked around and around the edge of the water. The ducks never swam in the pond. And to this day, these five white ducks do not know that they can swim. They simply walk around and around the edge of the beautiful pond.

Based on a true story by Rebecca Isbell.

Appendix B

Rhymes and Finger Plays

All By Myself *(Adapted Traditional)*

> There are many things I can do
> All by myself. (*point to self*)
> I can comb my hair and lace my shoe
> All by myself. (*pretend to comb hair and lace shoe*)
> I can wash my hands and wash my face
> All by myself. (*pretend to wash hands and face*)
> I can put my toys and blocks in place
> All by myself. (*pretend to arrange objects*)

My Friends *(Adapted Traditional)*

> My friends are gaily waving, (*have everyone wave*)
> Waving, waving.
> My friends are gaily waving,
> And I will wave at them. (*wave back*)
> My friends are sweetly smiling, (*have everyone smile*)
> Smiling, smiling.
> My friends are sweetly smiling,
> And I will smile at them. (*smile back*)

Floppy Rag Doll *(Adapted Traditional)*

> Flop your arms, flop your feet, (*do action as rhyme indicates*)
> Let your hands go free.
> Be the floppiest rag doll
> You ever did see.

Reach for the Ceiling *(Adapted Traditional)*

> Reach for the ceiling. (*do actions as rhyme indicates*)
> Touch the floor.
> Stand up again,
> Let's do some more.
>
> Nod your head,
> Bend your knee.

Shrug your shoulders
Like this, you see?

Reach for the ceiling,
Touch the floor.
That's all now,
There isn't anymore.

Jack-in-the-Box *(Author Unknown)*

Jack, Jack, down you go,
Down in your box, down so low. (*crouch down*)
Jack, Jack, there goes the top.
Quickly now, up you pop! (*jump up*)

Magic Feet *(Adapted Traditional)*

Have you seen my magic feet, (*do the action as rhyme indicates*)
Dancing down the magic street?
Sometimes fast, sometimes slow,
Sometimes high, sometimes low.

Come and dance along with me,
Dance just like my feet you see.
First we'll slide and then we'll hop,
Then we'll spin and then we'll stop.

Dig a Little Hole *(Traditional)*

Dig a little hole, plant a little seed,
Pour a little water, pull a little weed.
Chase a little bug—Heigh ho, there he goes!
Give a little sunshine, grow a little rose.

Five Little Babies *(Traditional)*

One little baby rocking in a tree.
Two little babies splashing in the sea.
Three little babies crawling on the floor.
Four little babies banging on the door.
Five little babies playing hide and seek.
Keep your eyes closed tight, now,
Until I say . . . PEEK!

Carefree Cruising Bubbles *(Author Unknown)*

Five little bubbles cruising through the air. (*Hold up all five fingers then close fist.*)
The first bubble said, "I haven't a care!" (*Hold up index finger.*)
The second bubble said, "It's warm in the sun." (*Hold up middle finger.*)
The third bubble said, "I'm having such fun!" (*Hold up ring finger.*)
The fourth bubble said, "It's great to be free." (*Hold up little finger.*)
The fifth bubble said, "I'm happy as can be!" (*Hold up thumb.*)
A bird flies by. (*Flap hands.*)
Its wings go flop.
Five little bubbles go Pop! Pop! Pop! Pop! Pop! (*Hold up hand and flip bubbles off.*)

Appendix C

Stories to Dramatize with Young Children

Three Billy Goats Gruff *(A Norwegian folktale adapted by Raines & Isbell, 1999)*

Once upon a time, there were three billy goats whose family name was Gruff. The three brothers were Little Billy Goat Gruff, Middle-Sized Billy Goat Gruff, and Great Big Billy Goat Gruff. They grazed on the lush green grass that grew on the hillsides. Middle-Sized Billy Goat and Great Big Billy Goat often warned Little Billy Goat not to wander far from home.

"Don't go across the bridge. There is a mean old troll who lives under the bridge. He eats little billy goats. Always stay on this side of the bridge."

Little Billy Goat, being an obedient little brother, always listened to the advice of Middle-Sized Billy Goat and Great Big Billy Goat Gruff. But one day, he grazed all the green grass on the little hillside near their home. He nibbled the grass on the little hillside near their home. He nibbled the grass right up to the edge of the wooden bridge.

When he looked across the bridge, there on the other side was a grassy hillside with green, green grass. He thought to himself, "If I could just graze on that green, green grass, I could grow big and strong like my middle-sized brother, maybe even as big and strong as my great big brother." He looked longingly across to the hillside and glanced down under the bridge. He didn't see the troll, so he decided to cross the bridge.

Trip-trap, trip-trap, trip-trap. Little Billy Goat Gruff came trip-trapping across the wooden bridge.

Suddenly, he heard the troll say, "Who is that trip-trapping across my bridge?"

"It is Little Billy Goat Gruff."

The troll replied, "Little Billy Goat Gruff, I love to eat little Billy goats and I am going to eat you up!"

Little Billy Goat Gruff, being a smart little goat, answered, "Oh, Mr. Troll, you don't want to eat me. I am just a little billy goat. Wait for my brother, who is much bigger than I am. Then, you would have more to eat."

The troll, thinking how nice it would be to have a big meal of billy goat, replied, "But, how do you know your brother will come to my bridge?"

"Mr. Troll, when my brother cannot find me, he will come looking for me. When he sees me eating the green, green grass across this bridge, he will come to fetch me home."

And so Mr. Troll waited while Little Billy Goat Gruff trip-trapped, trip-trapped, trip-trapped across the wooden bridge and up the hill to the green, green grass on the other side.

Soon, Middle-Sized Billy Goat Gruff spotted his little brother eating the green, green grass across the bridge. He decided to go get his little brother, to bring him home.

Trip-trap, trip-trap, trip-trap, Middle-Sized Billy Goat Gruff came trip-trapping across the wooden bridge.

Suddenly, he heard the mean old troll say, "Who is that trip-trapping across my bridge?"

"It is Middle-Sized Billy Goat Gruff."

The troll growled, "Middle-Sized Billy Goat Gruff, I love to eat middle-sized goats and I am going to eat you up!"

Middle-Sized Billy Goat Gruff, being a smart middle-sized goat, answered, "Oh, Mr. Troll, you don't want to eat me. I am just a middle-sized billy goat. Wait for my brother, who is much bigger than I am. Then, you would have more to eat."

The troll, thinking how nice it would be to have a great big meal of billy goat, said, "But how do you know your brother will come to my bridge?"

"Mr. Troll, when my brother cannot find me, he will come looking for me. When he sees me eating the green, green grass on the hillside across the bridge, he will come fetch me home."

And so Mr. Troll waited and waited, while Middle-Sized Billy Goat Gruff trip-trapped, trip-trapped across the wooden bridge and up the hill to join his little brother and eat the green, green grass on the other side.

Soon, Great Big Billy Goat Gruff, spotting his two brothers grazing on the green, green grass across the bridge, decided to go get his little brothers to bring them home.

Trip-trap, trip-trap, trip-trap, Great Big Billy Goat Gruff came trip-trapping across the wooden bridge.

As expected, the troll growled, "Who is that trip-trapping across my bridge?"

"It is Great Big Billy Goat Gruff."

The troll growled, "Great Big Billy Goat Gruff, I love to eat great big billy goats and I am going to eat you up!"

Great Big Billy Goat Gruff, being a quick-thinking great big billy goat, answered, "Oh, Mr. Troll, I don't think you are going to eat me. Just come up and see how big I am and how tough I would be to eat."

The mean old troll crept up the banks of the creek and over the edge of the bridge. Great Big Billy Goat Gruff stood in the middle of the wooden bridge and lowered his head. He butted the mean old troll off the bridge, up into the air, and far, far down the river.

When the troll landed, he ran off to another bridge and another hillside.

Now, every day, the three Billy Goats Gruff cross the wooden bridge to graze on the green, green grass on the hillside.

I can just hear them now, crossing the bridge.

Trip-trap, trip-trap, trip-trap, trip-trap, trip-trap, trip-trap, trip-trap, trip-trap.

Nail Soup (*A Czechoslovakian folktale adapted by Raines & Isbell, 1999*)

Once upon a time, a tramp, with his bundle slung over his shoulder, walked along a lonely road. As night approached, the tramp saw a small cottage at the edge of the woods. The sunset reflecting on the windows of the cottage gave it a welcoming glow.

So, the tramp walked up to the door and knocked. An old woman answered the door. She scowled as she said, "Don't ask for any food, because I have none."

Seeing the fire burning in the fireplace, the tramp asked if he could come and sit by the fire and warm himself. The old woman replied, "Oh, all right. I guess it won't hurt anything. The fire can burn for two as easy as it can for one."

So the tramp put his bundle in the corner and sat upon the stool near the warm fire. In a few minutes, his stomach began to growl. He was very hungry. But the old woman said, "There is no food to eat."

The tramp took a nail from his pocket and held it up in the light of the fire as if to admire it. "What is that nail for?" asked the old woman.

"Well, Madam, you may never believe it, but last night, I ate the finest soup I've ever eaten, and the main ingredient was this nail."

"Nail soup? Nail soup? That is ridiculous!" the woman scoffed, but she was curious.

"Yes, Madam, it is true. I boiled this nail in a pot of hot water. It was delicious," he assured her.

"Delicious? Delicious? How can you make delicious soup from a nail? I must see how it is done," she said, as she went off to get the pot for boiling water.

The old woman handed a big pot over to the tramp. He filled it half full of water and placed it on the stove. Then, he lifted the lid and dropped in the nail. With much ceremony, he put the lid back on the pot, then returned to sit on his stool by the fire.

He waited patiently. When he heard the water boiling, he lifted the lid. "Nail soup, delicious nail soup. Madam, when I cooked the soup last night, all it needed was some salt and pepper. I don't suppose you have a bit of salt and some pepper, do you? The batch of soup that I made last night just needed some salt and pepper to make it just right."

"Salt and pepper? I might just have some salt and pepper left in this empty cupboard," she said.

The tramp ceremoniously added the salt and pepper into the bubbling water with the nail. He put the lid back on the large soup pot and returned to sit on his stool by the fire.

The old woman, curious about the soup, lifted the lid to check inside. Just as she lifted the lid, the tramp asked, "Madam, might you have just half an onion to add to the delicious nail soup? The batch of soup that I made last night just needed half an onion to make it just right."

"Half an onion? I might just have half an onion left in this cupboard," she said. As she cracked open the door and slid out the onion, the tramp spied other vegetables upon the shelves, but he pretended not to notice. Instead, he replied, "Yes, half an onion will make it just right." He slipped the onion into the pot of boiling water, with the salt and pepper, and one gleaming nail.

When the onion had been cooking in the pot and the aroma filled the little house, the old woman lifted the lid to check inside. Just as she lifted the lid, the tramp asked, "Madam, might you have just a few carrots to add to this delicious nail soup? The batch of soup that I made last night just needed a few carrots to make it just right."

"A few carrots? I might just have a few carrots left in this cupboard," she said. When she went to the cupboard, cracked open the door, and slip out the carrots, the tramp spied other vegetables. Again, he pretended not to notice. Instead, he replied, "Yes, a few carrots will make it just right."

He slipped the carrots into the pot of boiling water, with half of an onion, the salt and pepper, and one gleaming nail.

The tramp returned to sit on his stool by the fire. The old woman was getting hungry now. She went to check the soup. Just as she lifted the

lid, the tramp asked, "Madam, might you have just a few small potatoes to add to this delicious nail soup? The batch of soup that I made last night just needed a few potatoes to make it just right."

"A few potatoes? I might just have a few potatoes left in this cupboard," she said. She went to the cupboard, cracked open the door, gathered up the potatoes, washed them, diced them, and brought them to the tramp. He said in quite a matter-of-fact way, "Yes, a few potatoes will make it just right." He plopped the potatoes into the pot of boiling water, with a few carrots, half an onion, some salt and pepper, and one gleaming nail.

The tramp returned to sit on his stool by the fire. The old woman was ferociously hungry now. She went to check the soup. Just as she lifted the lid, the tramp asked, "Madam, might you have a cabbage, even just a little head, to add to this delicious nail soup? The batch of soup that I made last night just needed a small head of cabbage to make it just right."

"A small head of cabbage? I might just have a small head of cabbage left in this cupboard," she said. She went to the cupboard, cracked open the door, and lifted a small head of cabbage from its place in the corner. She brought the cabbage to the tramp. He said in quite a matter-of-fact-way, "Yes, a small head of cabbage will make it just right." He peeled the cabbage leaves into the pot of boiling water, with the potatoes, a few carrots, half an onion, some salt and pepper, and one gleaming nail.

The tramp returned to sit on his stool by the fire. Now, the soup was bubbling and churning with good vegetables. The tramp invited the old lady to stir the soup and smell the delicious aroma. Although she agreed that it smelled delicious, she said, "A bit of meat is what we need to add to this batch of soup to make it just right."

The old woman returned with some cooked roast beef and chopped it into small pieces. "Yes," she said, "a bit of roast beef will make it just right." She dropped the roast beef into the pot of boiling water with the small head of cabbage, some potatoes, a few carrots, half an onion, some salt and pepper, and one gleaming nail.

The old woman and the tramp returned to sit by the fire. Soon, the old woman asked, "Shall we eat? The soup smells ready." The tramp looked around at the lovely cloth she was stitching, the candlestick on the mantel, and two beautiful bowls that sat upon a shelf.

"Madam," he said, "since you added the lovely pieces of roast beef, this delicious soup is now fit for a king and queen. Shall we set the table like royalty?"

With a smile on her face, the old woman placed the beautiful cloth on the rough kitchen table. She took the candlestick from the mantel by the fire. She brought lovely silver spoons from a drawer. She took down the beautiful bowls that sat upon the shelf and filled them with the delicious soup.

The tramp looked at the table fit for a king and queen and said, "Madam, the batch of soup that I made last night would have been just right, if we had a loaf of bread to accompany our delicious nail soup."

"A loaf of bread? I might just look in the bread box to see if a crust of bread might remain." She went to the bread box and opened it. There was a lovely loaf that looked like it had been baked that very day.

The tramp clasped his hands together and declared, "Dear Madam, I shall be honored to share my delicious nail soup with you."

They sat at the lovely table, ate their delicious soup, and talked of many journeys the tramp had made all across the country. It was a delightful evening, but the old woman was warm from the soup and tired from her gardening. Reluctantly she decided it was time to go to bed, but not before she invited the tramp to sleep in front of the warm fire.

The next morning, at breakfast, they ate another bowl of soup. The old woman said, "I don't know when I ever enjoyed an evening more than last night or have eaten a better bowl of soup."

As the tramp rose to leave, the old woman said, "Thank you for showing me how to make nail soup."

"No, no, it is I who must thank you," said the tramp. "It was what you added that made the difference!"

The old woman stood at the cottage door with a smile on her face.

And the tramp walked on down the road, whistling as he went. He paused just a minute and patted the nail in his pocket just to make sure it was still there.

The Lost Mitten with Tiny, Shiny Beads
(An old Ukrainian folktale adapted by Raines & Isbell, 1999)

Once upon a time, a grandmother and her grandson lived together in a little house beside a great wood. One cold winter morning, the grandmother said, "Grandson, please go and find some kindling for the fire, so that I might make some porridge."

The boy, being an obedient boy, dressed in his warmest winter snowsuit. He pulled on his fur-lined boots. He wrapped his warm scarf around his neck. He pulled his warm hat over his ears. Then he put on his mittens.

The mittens were ones his grandmother had made him. She knitted them, stitched in warm fur, and sewed tiny, tiny beads on the outside. The boy loved his beautiful mittens.

He planned to fill his sled with kindling from the forest. Even with the howling wind, the swirling snow, and the gray skies, he liked walking in the woods.

The snow was so deep that it was difficult to find the little broken branches or to find the spot where the woodcutters often left scraps of wood. The boy pulled his sled deeper and deeper into the forest, searching for the kindling. Each piece of kindling he found he put on his little sled.

Once, when the boy stopped to pick up a piece of kindling, he saw a beautiful icicle hanging from the bough of a majestic evergreen tree. The boy took off one of his mittens and laid it carefully on the sled. He touched the icicle and a few drops of water melted onto his hand.

The icicle glistened in his hand. Just ahead, he spotted a place where the woodcutter had worked. There would be some kindling there. He rushed ahead, pulling his sled behind him. The little boy did not notice that his beautiful furry mitten, with tiny, shiny beads stitched on the outside, dropped from the sled and fell onto the snow.

When the boy reached the clearing, he picked up the small pieces of kindling the woodcutter had left behind. He was so busy that he did not notice that his beautiful furry mitten, with tiny, shiny beads stitched on the outside, was missing.

When the sled was loaded, he started back home. His hand felt cold. He stopped to get his mitten from the sled, but he could not find it. He looked under each stick of kindling on the sled, but he could not find his beautiful furry mitten, with tiny, shiny beads stitched on the outside.

The boy looked for the beautiful mitten everywhere. The wind continued to howl, and the blowing snow made it hard to see. He could not even see the tracks from his sled. With a heavy heart, he realized that he could not find his beautiful furry mitten, with tiny, shiny beads stitched on the outside.

So, the little boy put his cold hand into his pocket and started for home. With the swirling snow and his search for the mitten, he had gotten off the path and did not know which way was home. He was so cold and getting more frightened by the minute. Then he remembered some advice the woodcutter had given him: follow the tall row of evergreens that line the path. The little boy searched until he found the evergreens that lined the path and made his way back to the little house beside a great wood.

Meanwhile, his beautiful furry mitten, with tiny, shiny beads stitched on the outside, lay upon the snow. It seems that the little boy was not the only one who was cold that morning. Field Mouse had been out searching for dried seeds, and he became so cold. He spied the beautiful furry mitten, with tiny, shiny beads stitched on the outside. Field Mouse wiggled inside and felt the warm fur. He decided that he would wait out the snowstorm inside this beautiful furry mitten, with tiny, shiny beads stitched on the outside. Just as Field Mouse was about to take a little nap, he heard someone outside the mitten. "Croak, croak, it is so cold outside. Please, may I come in?"

"Who is that croaking voice outside in the cold?" the warm field mouse asked. "It is I, Frog, and I am so cold." Field Mouse, recognizing the croaking voice of Frog, said, "Yes, of course, there is always room for one more." So, Frog hopped inside the beautiful furry mitten, with tiny, shiny beads stitched on the outside.

Just as Field Mouse and Frog were about to take a little nap, they heard someone outside the mitten. "Hoot, hoot, it is so cold outside. Please may I come in?"

"Who is that hooting voice outside in the cold?" the warm field mouse and frog asked. "It is I, Owl, and I am so cold." Field Mouse and Frog, recognizing the hooting voice of Owl, said, "Yes,

of course, there is always room for one more." So, Owl flew inside the beautiful furry mitten, with tiny, shiny beads stitched on the outside.

Just as Field Mouse, Frog, and Owl were about to take a little nap, they heard someone outside the mitten. "Sniff, sniff, it is so cold outside. Please may I come in?"

"Who is that sniffing voice outside in the cold?" asked the warm friends. "It is I, Rabbit, and I am so cold." Field Mouse, Frog, and Owl, recognizing the sniffing voice as Rabbit, said, "Yes, of course, there is always room for one more." So, Rabbit hopped inside the beautiful furry mitten, with tiny, shiny beads stitched on the outside.

Just as Field Mouse, Frog, Owl, and Rabbit were snuggling up to take a little nap, they heard someone outside the mitten. "Growl, growl, it is so cold outside. Please may I come in?"

"Who is that growling voice outside in the cold?" asked the warm friends. "It is I, Fox, and I am so cold." Field Mouse, Frog, Owl, and Rabbit thought it was getting very crowded inside. But, recognizing the growling voice of Fox, said, "Yes, of course, there is always room for one more." So, Fox crowded inside the beautiful furry mitten, with tiny, shiny beads stitched on the outside.

Just as Field Mouse, Frog, Owl, Rabbit, and Fox were settling down and trying to make room for each other inside the tight space, they heard another voice. "Snarl, snarl, it is so cold outside. Please may I come in?"

"Who is that snarling voice outside in the cold?" asked the warm friends. "It is I, Mountain Lion, and I am so cold." Field Mouse, Frog, Owl, Rabbit, and Fox yelled back, "No! It is too crowded in here. We can barely move. Mountain Lion, you are too big. You cannot come in."

Mountain Lion was so cold and he began to snarl, cry, and shiver. "Friends," he begged. "Please make room for me. It is so cold outside that my paws are freezing." So the warm friends crunched closer and said, "Yes, of course, there is always room for one more." So Mountain Lion crawled inside. The mitten was stretching, and stretching, and stretching. Finally, he was inside. The beautiful furry mitten had stretched so big that most of the tiny, shiny beads had popped off the outside, but the friends were warm inside the very tight space.

Just as they were settling down in close company inside the mitten, they heard another voice. "Chirp, chirp, it is so cold outside. Please may I come in?"

"Who is that chirping voice outside in the cold?" asked the warm friends stuffed inside. "It is I, Cricket, and I am so cold." Field Mouse, Frog, Owl, Rabbit, Fox, and Mountain Lion thought, if we can get a great big mountain lion inside this beautiful fur-lined mitten, we can stretch it a little more to get a tiny cricket inside. So they said, "Yes, of course, there is always room for one more." So Field Mouse, Frog, Owl, Rabbit, Fox, and Mountain Lion drew in their breaths to make room for Cricket.

The beautiful fur-lined mitten stretched and stretched. This time, it stretched so far that the stitches holding it together broke, and the beautiful fur-lined mitten burst open.

Field Mouse, Frog, Owl, Rabbit, Fox, and Mountain Lion tumbled out onto the cold snow. While they had been inside, the wind had stopped blowing, and the sun was peeking through the clouds. So Field Mouse, Frog, Owl, Rabbit, Fox, and Mountain Lion felt the warmth of the sun and rushed back to their homes in the great woods.

Only Cricket was left. Finding a piece of the beautiful furry mitten, with one tiny, shiny bead left on the outside, Cricket said, "This will make me a nice, warm home, to wait out the winter, until spring comes." And so he did.

One day, the following spring, the little boy was playing along the path where the evergreens lead into the big woods, when he found a scrap of woven cloth. It reminded him of his beautiful furry mitten, with tiny, shiny beads stitched to the outside. In fact, there was one tiny, shiny bead stitched on the scrap of woven cloth. When he picked it up, he heard a voice inside.

"Chirp, chirp, who is moving my warm house?"

"It is I, Little Boy, who lives in the house beside the big woods. How did you come to have this scrap of woven cloth for your house?" asked the boy.

"Chirp, chirp, now that is quite a story, chirp, chirp. Sit here on this stack of kindling and let me tell you about a cold day last winter."

So, Cricket hopped upon the shoulder of the little boy and told the story of how the beautiful furry mitten, with tiny, shiny beads stitched on the outside became his home for the winter.

The Four Musicians (An adaptation of the work of Jacob and Wilhelm Grimm by Raines & Isbell, 1999)

Once there was a donkey who had worked for many years, day in and day out, carrying heavy sacks of grain for his master. Now that the donkey was older, his master decided to get rid of him. The donkey heard of his master's plan and decided to run away.

Years before, in the city of Bremen, the donkey had heard bands playing music. The donkey said, "I make a very loud noise when I bray. I can be a musician like those in the band." So the donkey set out to become a street musician. As he was walking down the road he saw a dog lying on the ground. He looked very tired and he was panting.

"Why do you look so tired?" asked the donkey.

"I am not strong enough to go hunting, so my master doesn't want me anymore," said the dog.

"Come go with me. I am going to Bremen to be a street musician," said the donkey. The dog thought that was a very good idea. They both walked down the road together, the donkey and the dog.

Much farther down the road they saw a cat sitting by the road. The cat looked very sad. Her sorrowful meowing broke the hearts of the donkey and the dog.

The donkey asked, "Whatever made you so sad, cat?"

The cat explained that her teeth were no longer very sharp and she had trouble catching mice. What was she to do?

"Come go with us. We are going to be street musicians. You can sing and make night music with our band of musicians." The cat was pleased that they thought she could sing, so she joined the band of the donkey and dog. They walked down the road together, the donkey, the dog, and the cat.

The group walked for many miles before they came to a barnyard. On the fence was a rooster, crowing with all his might.

The donkey asked the rooster, "Why are you crowing so loudly?"

The rooster said, "I have just heard the most awful news. Company is coming on Sunday and my master wants to put me in the soup."

"Come go with us. We are going to Bremen to be street musicians. You have a very loud voice. Please join our band of musicians." The rooster was proud of his fine voice, so he flew down from the fence and joined the band. Now there were four musicians who walked down the road together: the donkey, the dog, the cat, and the rooster.

It was a very long way to the city of Bremen, and they needed a place to rest for the night. The rooster flew up in a tree and spied a house nearby. He flew to the house and saw a warm fire in the fireplace. Together the four animals, the donkey, the dog, the cat, and the rooster, decided that the house would be a good place for them to stay for a night.

When they came to the house, the donkey, who was the tallest, looked in the window to see what was inside. The donkey saw a table filled with good things to eat and drink. He noticed bags of gold and silver stacked around the table. He also saw a group of robbers eating the food and enjoying themselves. The four musicians, the donkey, the dog, the cat, and the rooster, devised a plan to scare the robbers away. After the robbers were gone they would eat the delicious food and have a place to stay for the night.

The donkey stood on his hind legs with his front feet on the window. The dog stood on the donkey's back. The cat climbed onto the dog's back. The rooster flew to the very top and stood on the cat's back. Then they all began singing together. The donkey brayed. The dog barked. The cat meowed. The rooster crowed.

When they sang together, they made so much noise that the windows of the house shattered.

"What a horrible noise! It must be a terrible monster," said the robbers, who were so frightened that they ran away and left all the wonderful food and drink behind for the musicians. The donkey, the dog, the cat, and the rooster ate and ate and ate until they could eat no more. The four musicians liked the house and food so much that they decided to stay for the night. The donkey lay down in the yard. The dog lay down behind the door in the house. The cat curled up by the fire. The rooster flew to the top of the roof. They were all so tired from their long trip that they fell asleep very quickly.

The robbers had been hiding outside in the woods. When they saw the lights go out, they decided to go back to the house and try to find out what had made the horrible noise. One of the robbers went to the house to see if anything was inside. He went into the house. It was very dark. He saw the green eyes of the cat by the fire and this startled him. But when he struck a match to see better, the cat jumped at him and scratched him. As he ran to the door the dog, who was sleeping by the door, barked and bit him on his leg. In the yard the donkey kicked him and the rooster screamed loudly, "Cock-a-doodle-do!"

The man was so frightened that he told the other robbers, "There is a horrible monster in the house. It has green eyes that glow in the dark, long arms with sharp nails, big white teeth, strong steel legs, and it makes a terrible screaming sound." When the robbers heard the story about the monster, they all ran away. They never returned to the house again.

The four musicians had found themselves a good home. They had enough silver and gold to buy food and drink to last for the rest of their lives. They decided not to go to Bremen but to make music together in their new home.

They are probably still there today making music: the donkey, the dog, the cat, and the rooster.

The Fisherman and His Wife (An adaptation of the work of Jacob and Wilhelm Grimm by Isbell & Raines, 2000)

Once upon a time, there was a fisherman and his wife. They lived together in a hut on the top of a high hill. Every day, the fisherman went to the ocean and fished all day long. Some days, he caught many fish, and other days, he didn't catch any fish at all.

One day, after fishing for many hours without catching anything, he suddenly felt a powerful tug on the end of his line. After much pulling and tugging, he reeled in an enormous fish. The fisherman was delighted at his catch. To his surprise the big fish began to talk.

The fish pleaded, "Please don't keep me. I won't taste very good because I am a magic fish. Please throw me back into the water so I can swim away."

The man said, "You are indeed a very special fish because you can talk. I will throw you back into the water and you can swim away."

The man returned home to his wife in the hut at the top of the hill. He told her about his day fishing. He explained that all he had caught was a magic fish that could talk. Because the magic fish was so special, he had thrown him back into the water.

His wife was very angry with him. She said, "A magic fish that could talk? Didn't you ask the fish for a magic wish?"

The man shrugged. "I didn't ask for anything. There is nothing that I really want," he said.

The wife said sharply, "We live in a shabby hut and you can't think of anything to wish for? Go back to the ocean and tell the magic talking fish that you want a house to live in."

So the man went back to the ocean. He called, "Magic fish, magic fish, we have a wish."

The magic fish swam up to the top of the water and asked, "What is your wish?"

"My wife doesn't want to live in a shabby hut any more. She would like to live in a house."

The magic fish said, "Go back and see what you find."

When the fisherman returned home, he found a lovely cottage with a living room, bedroom, and a kitchen. Behind the house was a little garden with ducks and chickens. He and his wife were very pleased. They agreed that this was a very nice house and garden. Yet, after a week had passed, the wife became very discontent. She told her husband, "This house is much too small. We don't have enough room. It is too crowded. The garden is too small. The magic fish could give us a much larger house. Go back and ask the magic fish for a castle."

The man didn't want to go back, but his wife insisted. When he got to the ocean he called, "Magic fish, magic fish, we have a wish."

The fish came swimming up out of the water. He asked, "What do you want?"

The man said, "My wife thinks the house is too small and wants a castle instead."

"Go home and see what you find," said the magic fish.

When the fisherman returned home, he saw a huge castle sitting on the top of the hill. His wife invited him inside to see the magnificent castle. Inside were many rooms: living rooms, dining rooms, kitchens, and fifteen bedrooms with baths. Each room was filled with fancy furniture that was finished in gold. Behind the castle was a big pasture with horses and cows. In front of the castle was a beautiful garden.

The man said, "This is wonderful! Let's live in this beautiful castle and be happy."

The very next day the wife woke up early. She looked at the beautiful castle and the wonderful land. She woke her husband up and said, "You should be King of this country." The fisherman explained that he didn't want to be King.

She said, "If you don't want to be King, then I will be Queen. Go tell the fish that I want to be Queen of the castle."

The man slowly walked to the ocean. He didn't want to ask the fish to make his wife the Queen of the castle, but he called, "Magic fish, magic fish, we have a wish."

The fish slowly came swimming out of the water and asked, "What do you want?"

The man hesitated and then said, "My wife wants to be Queen."

The fish replied, "Go home and see what you find."

When the man returned home he was amazed at what he saw. The castle was bigger and much grander than before. It was behind golden gates with fancy ironwork. Soldiers in bright red uniforms were outside the gate and castle. Inside the castle were marble floors and walls covered in gold. In one of the enormous rooms, his wife was sitting on a golden throne. She wore a diamond and ruby crown on her head and a velvet cape trimmed in white fur around her shoulders.

The man said, "Now you are Queen. You have a fine castle, gardens, horses, and soldiers. You have all you have ever wished for."

The wife thought a moment and then quickly demanded, "Well there is one more thing I would like. I would like to be ruler of the universe." The man felt very sad. He could not believe that his wife still wanted more. He did not want to ask the magic fish for anything else, but his wife insisted.

So, he slowly walked back to the ocean. This time the water was not clear and blue, as it had been before. The ocean water was black and rough with many waves. The wind was blowing and the trees were shaking.

The man called, "Magic fish, magic fish, we have a wish."

The magic fish did not come, so he called again, "Magic fish, magic fish, we have a wish."

The magic fish still did not appear, so he called again, "Magic fish, magic fish, we have a wish."

Slowly the magic fish came out of the water and asked, "What do you want now?"

"My wife wants to be ruler of the entire universe," the man said.

The fish replied, "Go home and see what you find."

When the man returned home, there were no soldiers, no horses, no cows, no garden, and no castle. Nothing was left but a shabby hut. And to this day, the man and his wife live in that same shabby hut on top of the hill.

The Great Lion and the Tiny Mouse *(An Aesop's fable adapted by Isbell & Raines, 2000)*

Once upon a time, a Great Lion was king of the jungle. He ran where he wanted to run. He ate what he wanted to eat. And he slept where he wanted to sleep.

No one bothered Great Lion. The monkeys did not bother him. The zebras did not bother him. The water buffalos did not bother him. The giraffes did not bother him. Even the elephants did not bother the Great Lion.

One day, Tiny Mouse was hurrying home to his tiny burrow. Because he was in a hurry, he was not looking where he was going. He ran over the paw of Great Lion while he was sleeping. Tiny Mouse tickled Great Lion's paw as he ran over it, and Great Lion awoke. He slapped his huge paw down and caught Tiny Mouse by the tail.

"Well, what do we have here?" Great Lion said in a huge booming voice.

"Oh, please, Great Lion, please let me go. Do not hurt me. I am just a tiny little mouse."

"Just a nice little afternoon snack for me, I should think," boomed Great Lion.

"Oh please, Great Lion, please let me go. If you let me go, some day I will do a favor for you," squeaked Tiny Mouse.

"A favor, a favor for me? You will do something good for me some day?" laughed Great Lion. "Well, I don't think a great strong lion like me will ever need a little mouse like you to do me a favor, but I'm not very hungry, so I'll let you go." And Great Lion lifted his great paw.

Tiny Mouse ran away, as fast as he could, but he yelled back to the lion, "I always keep my promises. Some day, I will do something good for you. I will do you a favor."

But Great Lion was already sleeping, making great snoring sounds. He didn't even hear Tiny Mouse. From that day on, tiny Mouse was careful to stay away from sleeping lions.

Not long after Great Lion spared Tiny Mouse's life, Tiny Mouse thought he heard something in the far distance. It sounded like the Great Lion's roar. Sure enough, Great Lion was roaring. He was roaring and clawing, stretching and straining, trying to get loose. Great Lion had been caught in a trap. Some trappers had rigged a net to fall on Great Lion. The more Great Lion stretched and strained, rolled and tumbled, the more he became entangled in the ropes of the net.

Great Lion roared and roared, calling for other animals to help him. The monkeys came to see what all the commotion was about. But they just stared at Great Lion, laughed at him caught in the ropes, and swung back into the trees, chattering all the while.

Great Lion roared and roared, calling for the other animals to help him. The zebras came to see what all the commotion was about. But they just stared at Great Lion, laughed at him caught in the ropes, and trotted on back to their grazing.

Great Lion roared and roared, calling for the other animals to help him. The water buffalos came to see what all the commotion was about. But they just stared at Great Lion, laughed at him caught in the ropes, and went on down to the watering hole to drink.

Great Lion roared and roared, calling for the other animals to help him. The giraffes came to see what all the commotion was about. But they just stared at Great Lion, laughed at him caught in the ropes, and went back to nibbling leaves from the treetops.

Great Lion roared and roared, calling for the other animals to help him. The elephants came to see what all the commotion was about. But they just stared at Great Lion, laughed at him caught in the ropes, and went back to swinging their trunks and herding their babies along the path.

Tiny Mouse was rushing, as fast as he could, in the direction of the roaring lion. He passed the monkeys swinging in the trees. He passed the zebras grazing on the grass. He passed the water buffalos by the watering hole. He passed the giraffes nibbling leaves from the treetops. He passed the elephants herding their babies along the path.

Finally, Tiny Mouse reached Great Lion. He saw him caught in the ropes, but Tiny Mouse did not laugh at Great Lion. He told him to be still and rest. Then, Tiny Mouse gnawed and chewed, chewed and gnawed, until he gnawed right through one rope. Then he gnawed right through another rope. Finally, he gnawed a hole in the ropes big enough for Great Lion to escape.

Tiny Mouse said, "I always keep my promises. I promised you that one day I would do something good for you. I promised you that if you let me go, I would do you a favor."

Great Lion lay his great paw down on the ground gently. Tiny Mouse stepped on it. Great Lion lifted Tiny Mouse up to his great strong back and they walked away. And, to this day, if you ever see a great sleeping lion, look for a tiny mouse. He is sure to be close by.

Jack and the Magic Beans (An adaptation of the traditional folktale, Jack and the Beanstalk)

Once upon a time, a little boy named Jack lived with his mother in a run-down house. They were very poor and had little food to eat.

One day, Jack's mother said, "We are going to have to sell our only cow so we will have money for food." Jack did not want to sell the cow, but they had no other choice.

As Jack was walking down the road with the cow, an old man appeared in front of him. The old man told Jack he had "magic beans" that would grow to the sky. He bargained with Jack, telling him he was willing to trade the magic beans for the cow.

Jack was intrigued by the idea of magic beans, so he gave the old man the cow, and took the magic beans. Jack was so excited about the magic beans that he ran home to show his mother what he had traded.

When he arrived home, Jack's mother asked, "Where is the food you were supposed to buy?" He explained that he didn't have any food or any money. What he did have were three magic beans.

His mother was very angry. She scolded him and said, "Three magic beans, for a good cow?" She snatched the beans from Jack's hand and threw them out the window. Then, she sent Jack to his room, because he had done such a foolish thing.

"I can't believe it!" she said, "A cow for three magic beans!"

That night it rained, and the beans began to sprout. They grew out of the ground—higher and higher—right up to the sky.

When Jack woke up the next morning, there was a huge beanstalk outside his window. He was so excited that he began climbing up the high beanstalk.

When Jack got to the top of the beanstalk, he found a castle. He went to the door of the castle, but it was so tall that he couldn't reach the doorknob.

Jack could smell food, so he crawled under a small opening in the door. He followed the smell of the food and found a huge feast atop a massive table. Jack climbed up onto the table and began to eat the food from gigantic bowls. There were bowls of chicken, mashed potatoes, beans, pudding, and bread.

Just as Jack was eating a big bite of food, an enormous woman entered the room. Jack was very scared, so he hid behind a bowl of chicken. The woman saw Jack and said, "I have always wanted a little boy. What's your name?" Then, she picked Jack up from behind the food.

All of a sudden, there were loud sounds, boom, boom, boom. Jack asked fearfully, "What's that?" The woman said, "Oh, it's just my husband, the giant," and dropped Jack into her apron pocket.

As the giant came in, he began to chant, "Fe, Fi, Fo, Fum, I smell the blood of a little boy. Be he alive or be he dead, I will grind his bones to make my bread."

His wife explained that he just smelled the chicken she had fixed for dinner, and the giant sat down at the massive table to eat. While the giant was eating, Jack jumped out of the wife's apron pocket and escaped from the room.

In the next room, Jack found a hen that was laying golden eggs. Jack spoke to the hen, and asked who her owner was. She explained that it was the man who had traded with Jack for the magic beans.

Jack grabbed the hen, ran from the castle, and climbed down the beanstalk.

When Jack showed his mother the hen that laid golden eggs, she was impressed. "But, Jack," she said, "you must go back up the beanstalk, and rescue the magic harp that the giant stole from the old man."

Jack was not anxious to return to the giant's castle, but he did what his mother wanted. He climbed the tall beanstalk, walked back to the castle, and slid under the door.

When he got inside, he found that the giant was in his enormous bed, asleep. Jack went from room to room inside the castle, until he finally found the magic harp.

As Jack approached, the harp screamed, "Who are you?" The harp was confused, and yelled, "Help, a thief is trying to steal me!"

All of the screaming and yelling woke the giant, and he pounded toward the room where Jack was with the magic harp. Boom, boom, boom. When the giant came in, Jack grabbed the harp and ran as fast as he could, out the door, to the beanstalk.

Jack held the harp and climbed down the beanstalk. His mother was waiting at their front door. When she saw him, she said, "Oh Jack, I am so happy you are back, and you have saved the magic harp!"

Jack and his mother rushed to get an axe. Together, they chopped down the beanstalk, which fell to the ground with a loud boom.

Jack and his mother had the hen that laid golden eggs, and the magic harp that played beautiful music.

And, they all lived together forever and ever.

The Hat Salesman *(An adaptation of the traditional folktale, Caps for Sale, as represented by Esphyr Slobodkina, 1947)*

Once there was a salesman who sold hats throughout the town. He carried all of his hats on top of his head, as he walked around on the streets. He had many different styles of hats on his head.

First, his own striped hat.
Next, he had six brown hats.
Then, five green hats.
Then, four blue hats.
On the top, he had three yellow hats.

As he walked though the town, he carried the hats very carefully, so they would not fall off. As he walked, he called out. "Brown hats, green hats, blue hats, and red hats for sale. A real bargain. One hat for one dollar."

One day, he walked though the streets and called out, "Brown hats, green hats, blue hats, and red hats for sale. A real bargain; one hat for one dollar."

But on this day, no one wanted to buy his hats, and he did not earn any money.

He was very discouraged and decided to take a walk in the country. He walked a very long way and was very careful not to knock his hats of his head. He was very tired. So, he found a big shade tree and decided to rest.

Before he went to sleep, he checked his hats: Six brown hats, five green hats, four blue hats, and three yellow hats. They were all stacked on top of his head.

After sleeping for a long time he woke up. As he stood up, he checked to make sure all the hats were on top of his head. To his surprise, there were no hats on his head. He looked all around the tree—but, no hats. He continued looking.

The last place he looked was up in the tree. In the tree were monkeys wearing his hats. The monkeys were wearing his six brown hats, his five green hats, his four blue hats, and his three yellow hats.

The salesman did not know what to do. The monkeys were wearing all his hats. He was very angry, so he waved his hand at the monkeys. The monkeys waved their hands at him, too.

The salesman became angrier and shook both hands at the monkeys. The monkeys laughed and shook their hands at him, too.

The salesman was so angry that he threw his striped hat on the ground. And, to his amazement, the monkeys threw their hats to the ground, too.

The salesman picked up his hats.
First, the six brown hats.
Then, his five green hats.
Then, his four blue hats.
And, finally, the three yellow hats.
He made sure the hats were straight on his head and walked back to town. He called, "six brown hats, five green hats, four blue hats, and three yellow hats. A real bargain. One hat for one dollar."

References

Raines, S. C., & Isbell, R. T. (1999). Nail soup. *Tell it again!: Easy-to-tell stories with activities for young children* (pp. 52–62). Beltsville, MD: Gryphon House.

Raines, S. C., & Isbell, R. T. (1999). The four musicians. *Tell it again!: Easy-to-tell stories with activities for young children* (pp. 132–139). Beltsville, MD: Gryphon House.

Isbell, R. T., & Raines, S. C. (2000). The great lion and the tiny mouse. *Tell it again! 2: Easy-to-tell stories with activities for young children* (pp. 48–63). Beltsville, MD: Gryphon House.

Isbell, R. T., & Raines, S. C. (2000). The fisherman and his wife. *Tell it again! 2: Easy-to-tell stories with activities for young children* (pp. 38–46). Beltsville, MD: Gryphon House.

Raines, S. C., & Isbell, R. T. (1999). The lost mitten with tiny, shiny beads. *Tell it again!: Easy-to-tell stories with activities for young children* (pp. 120–130). Beltsville, MD: Gryphon House.

Raines, S. C., & Isbell, R. T. (1999). Three Billy goats gruff. *Tell it again!: Easy-to-tell stories with activities for young children* (pp. 36–44). Beltsville, MD: Gryphon House.

Slobodkina, E. (1947). *Caps for sale.* New York: W. R. Scott.

Appendix D

Primary Thematic Unit: Icky Sticky Fun!

Adapted from a unit developed by Amy Carmichael, Carolyn Kent, Stacy Larsen, and Shelley Notter

CHALLENGE TO STUDENTS

Create a unit that focuses on a theme you have never seen used in an early childhood classroom. Include all of the creative arts in the unit and include an open-ended learning center in the plan.

GOALS FOR THE UNIT

The children will:

- Learn about materials in their environment through exploration and experimentation.
- Use the creative arts to expand their understanding of substances in their world.
- Develop problem-solving skills as they investigate different materials.
- Work cooperatively to find answers and create work.
- Discover new ways to learn about materials and their properties.

OVERVIEW

Children will learn about "stickiness" through art, music, movement, dramatic arts, creative thinking, literature, and a "sticky" learning center.

List of Lesson Plans

1. Design: Turning Sticky Mud into Houses (Visual Arts)

2. Pantomime of Sticky Situations (Dramatics)
3. What Is This Sticky Stuff? (Creative Problem-Solving)
4. Don't Get Stuck! (Movement)
5. Sticky Recipes (Visual Arts: Small Motor)

Design of Unit

Children learn best through meaningful activities and hands-on experiences. The "sticky" learning center and many "sticky" activities in the areas of art, music, movement, dramatics, literature, and problem-solving will provide open-minded, experiential, and creative activities to assist children in constructing their understanding of the properties of stickiness.

The sticky center will consist of a wide variety of sticky and nonsticky materials that students can explore. Additional materials will be provided for constructing creative objects as children practice using glue, tape, contact paper, and other sticky materials. The center will contain choices of activities allowing students to explore their interests at their own pace.

Additional Activities

Additional activities will provide support for the student developing understanding of stickiness. Each activity and the learning center will be described in full detail within this unit plan.

Introducing the Unit

The K-W-L chart will be used as the introductory activity for this unit of study. Using either a chalkboard, paper, or dry erase board, create three categories with the word STICKY across the top. The first category is What We Know. The second category is What We Want to Know, and the third is What We Learned. Begin by asking the children to tell you what they know about the word *sticky*. Record every response by writing it in category one on the chart. Talk about their responses and ask them to share their ideas about what they would like to learn about sticky. Record these responses in the second category. At the end of the unit, revisit the K-W-L to record what has been learned.

Follow up this activity by asking the children to look around the room for anything that is sticky. Supply them with Post-It notes to "tag" the sticky items they found. Record these items on an additional sheet or section of the board. In addition, send a letter home to parents to introduce the new sticky learning center and unit. Ask the parents to look around the house with their child and create a list of sticky things at home. Allow everyone to share his list with the entire class the following day. The letter is also a good time to ask for sticky donations, if needed.

Letter to Parents

Dear Parents,

In class today, we discussed the word "sticky." We made a list of everything sticky we know and identified sticky things in our classroom. As you can probably tell, we will be spending some time in class exploring things that are sticky, finding out why they are sticky, and discovering what sticky things can do.

Please take some time to look around your house, and with your child's help, create a list of the sticky things you found. The bathroom and kitchen are a good place to start. We will share this list on Wednesday during morning meeting.

If you have anything sticky to add to our learning center, we would appreciate it. Please feel free to call with any questions or drop by to see the sticky learning center.

Thank you.

ART CENTER

The art center will be set up in the classroom during the unit study. Children will be able to select, question, explore, and discover the properties of sticky materials.

Objectives for the Center

The children will:

- discover the properties of sticky as they manipulate the materials.
- question how stickiness is produced.
- investigate the use of sticky materials in an art project.
- combine materials in unique ways.

PURPOSE. To allow children to question, discover, explore, and learn about the properties of things that are sticky.

MATERIALS. Sticky things such as all sorts of glue and tape, Post-It® note pads, Velcro®, honey, molasses, syrups, food coloring, contact paper, sugar, vanilla, oil, paints, Kool-Aid®, Jell-O®, and bubbles. Nonsticky things such as water, cornstarch, soap shavings, paper, markers, scissors, stapler, rubber bands, material, sponges, brushes, containers, wood pieces, sand, magnets, and straws.

SETUP. The art center can be available for the children to explore every day. The materials can be changed periodically and the children can bring items from home to contribute. This center will have a facilitator on hand at all times for safety purposes and the proper handling of potentially harmful materials (when applicable). This center provides materials and space for any creative endeavors the children construct throughout the day pertaining to sticky stuff, and should remain free and open-ended for their discoveries and interests.

STICKY WALL. Attach a long piece of clear contact paper to the wall of the art center. Remove the covering on the sticky side, and turn the paper so the sticky side is away from the wall. This will produce a sticky wall that can be used to attach materials selected by the children in the center. This wall can be used in the art center throughout the study, to allow more integrated designs to be created. Children may also bring materials from outside or home to add to the growing "sticky" mural.

✿ | LESSON PLAN 1: TURNING STICKY MUD INTO HOUSES (VISUAL ARTS)

OVERVIEW. A long time ago, house builders throughout the world discovered that soil mixed with straw and water would harden into bricks with the sun's help. Mud could be used to hold the bricks together for building long-lasting homes. This technique is still used today and can be replicated in the classroom.

OBJECTIVES. The children will:

- investigate the history of using adobe for building.
- construct a three-dimensional structure using straw, water, and soil.
- work cooperatively on a building project.
- learn about proportions, shape, and texture.
- develop language that relates to the construction.

MATERIALS. The items needed for this project include plastic quart bags, empty pint milk cartons trimmed to about one inch high, dirt (with clay base helps), dried straw or grass from the yard, water, and a large tub for mixing. This project is great for outdoor play.

PROCEDURE

1. In the mixing tub, mix the soil with water until it is the consistency of pancake batter. Add the dried grass clippings or straw. It will pour better if the straw is cut into small pieces before mixing.

2. As you mix, talk about the importance of the water as a mixing agent, and how dirt and water can be poured. Why do you mix the dirt and grass? The grass holds dirt together.

3. Where does the water go? Place a plastic quart bag over one carton of adobe. Water should collect at the top of the bag, showing it escaped the mud by means of evaporation.

4. Place a similar bag, though not completely, over the carton. No water should appear. Would the adobe be a good way to build a house in your area? Why or why not?

5. After mixing, spoon the mixture into the milk cartons. Tamp the container so that the mud slides down. That way, the surface of the brick will be flat for later stacking.

6. Place the containers in the sun to bake and dry. This will take several days, depending on the humidity. You may remove the bricks from their molds (cartons) as soon as the mixture sets in order to reuse the containers.

7. Build a simple adobe structure using mud as your mortar (glue). Plaster it with more mud for smooth walls. A wet sponge can be used to smooth stacked blocks. Let the structure dry thoroughly before using for play.

EXTENSION

1. Other substances can be used to make different structures. Make concrete in the cartons using cement, gravel, and water. The proper proportions for mixing should be listed on the bag of cement. This shows how water mixes with a solid to form another solid. Concrete, like bricks, will require mortar to keep things in place.

2. Ice cubes can be frozen into blocks that later can be turned into an icehouse. For an ice structure, you will need a day with temperatures around freezing, and a wet sponge or sprayer filled with water to help form a solid structure from ice blocks. Packing snow into containers would provide another building material.

VOCABULARY

adobe	investigate	properties
architecture	liquid	proportions
construct	mix	solid
design	mixture	straw
evaporation	overlap	texture

CONNECTIONS TO ART

1. Have the children create blueprints of what they want their structure to look like. Use real examples, invite architects to speak about design, take walks to look at buildings in the neighborhood, and bring in construction workers to discuss building procedures and safety. Visit a building or home that is currently under construction.

2. Provide magazines and books about homes and building for reference and reading materials.

3. Encourage the children to talk about the properties of the building material and construction process. Record their thoughts and ideas in books, with drawings.

LITERATURE CONNECTIONS

Barton, B. (1981). *Building a house.* Boston: Greenwillow.

Burton, V. (1942). *The little house.* Boston: Houghton.

Crosbie, M., & Rosenthal, S. (1993). *Architecture shapes.* Washington, DC: The Preservation Press.

Devlin, H. (1964). *To grandfather's house we go: A roadside tour of American homes.* New York: Parent's Magazine Press.

Lillegard, D. (1986). *I can be a carpenter.* Chicago: Children's Press.

Malone, N. (1988). *A home.* New York: Bradbury Press.

Martin, C. (1984). *Island winter.* Boston: Greenwillow.

Penner, F. (1985). *A house for me.* Boston: Greenwillow.

✿ LESSON PLAN 2: PANTOMIME OF STICKY SITUATIONS (DRAMATICS)

OBJECTIVES. The children will:

- develop their imaginations in creating a pantomime.
- determine the situation presented by another child.
- critique the pantomime of other children participating in the activity.
- learn that pantomime can be used to communicate ideas.

MATERIALS. Imagination, children, and idea cards in a bag.

PROCEDURE

1. Make several sticky idea cards before starting to play. Ask students to help. Examples may include some of the following ideas.

   You have just stepped on a piece of gum that is sticking to the bottom of your shoe.

   Your hands have been glued together and won't come apart.

   Someone put glue on your chair, and now you can't get up.

   Your lips have been glued shut, and you are trying to order a meal at the drive-through.

   You are eating something really sticky like honey, marshmallow fluff, taffy, or the like.

2. Ask everyone to make a big circle and sit down.

3. Ask for a volunteer and let him pick a sticky idea card from the bag.

4. Everyone in the circle can chant the volunteer's name until he starts to pantomime his sticky idea.

5. The volunteer begins his pantomime, and the first person to guess what is going on has the next turn.

6. If nobody guesses correctly, allow the volunteer to tell the audience what he was acting out and let him pick the next person.

✿ LESSON PLAN 3: WHAT IS THIS STICKY STUFF? (CREATIVE PROBLEM-SOLVING)

OBJECTIVES. The children will:

- use their sensory skills to determine sticky materials.
- develop their problem-solving abilities as they investigate sticky materials.
- improve their use of questions to find answers.
- work with others to cooperatively find solutions.

MATERIALS. Containers to hold sticky stuff, scarves, wet wipes, and a number of sticky items such as honey, plastic wrap, hair mousse, liquid soap, maple syrup, contact paper, tree sap, molasses, marshmallows, hair gel, bubbles, peanut butter, toothpaste, chewing gum, cotton candy, shaving cream, sugary water, taffy, Velcro®, fruit juice, Jell-O®, pudding, tape, and glue.

PROCEDURE

1. Have children participate in this activity during center time or in small groups.

2. Place the materials into plastic containers ahead of time.

3. Blindfold the children and allow them ample time to inspect and explore the various materials as they try to guess what it is. Encourage them to use their senses. "What does it smell like?" "How does it feel?"

4. Record the children's responses and share their answers with them afterward. This information can be tallied and graphed by the children.

LESSON PLAN 4: DON'T GET STUCK! (MOVEMENT)

OBJECTIVES. The children will:

- develop spatial understanding as they participate in movement activities.

- use problem-solving to connect and form a circle.

- learn to cooperate with others in untangling the "pretzel."

MATERIALS. A large, open space.

PROCEDURE

1. Have the children stand in a circle and join hands with people in the circle, either across the circle or beside them.

2. The only rule of this game is that they cannot join both hands with the same person. They must join one hand with one person and the other with another person.

3. After everyone has joined both of their hands, ask the children to try and untangle themselves and get into one circle again, with everyone still holding hands.

4. This requires a great deal of teamwork, spatial understanding, and trial-and-error problem-solving. The first time you use this activity, break the children into small groups and let them practice before attempting to do it with the entire class.

LESSON PLAN 5: STICKY RECIPES (VISUAL ARTS, SMALL MOTOR)

(Children will choose the recipe to make and use while in small groups.)

OBJECTIVES. The children will:

- follow directions to make recipes.

- explore and determine the properties of the substances.

- gain confidence in their abilities by making the recipes.

- use "childmade" products to create artwork.

FINGERPAINT

Ingredients

½ c. cornstarch	2 c. boiling water
1 c. cold water	food coloring or poster
1 package unflavored	paint
gelatin	

Procedure: In a saucepan, mix cornstarch with ¾ c. cold water to a smooth paste. Soak gelatin in ¼ c. cold water. Set aside. Pour boiling water slowly over cornstarch mixture, stirring. Cook over medium heat, stirring constantly, until mixture boils and clears. Remove. Stir in gelatin. Cool and divide into separate, small, screw-top jars. Add color and use. Refrigerate to store. Paint is transparent, strong, and durable with a high-gloss finish. May be used on dry and wet paper.

SILLY PUTTY

Ingredients

½ c. liquid starch	½ c. Elmer's® glue

Procedure: Mix the starch and glue together until it feels like silly putty. Store in an airtight container in the refrigerator.

CLASSROOM PASTE

Ingredients
1 c. non-self-rising wheat flour
1 c. sugar
1 c. cold water
4 c. boiling water
1 tbsp. powdered alum

Procedure: Combine flour and sugar in a large pot. Slowly stir in cold water to form paste. Slowly add boiling water, stirring vigorously to break up clumps. Bring mixture to a boil, stirring constantly, until thick and clear. Remove from heat and add alum. Stir until mixed well. Store in airtight container Makes about 1½ quarts. Classroom paste is a good, all-purpose paste, especially appropriate for work with children. This paste will keep for several weeks. If it gets too thick, it can be thinned with hot water for easy spreading.

DECOUPAGE GLUE

Ingredients
3 parts white household glue
1 part warm water

Procedure: Combine glue with water in a jar or bottle with a screw-top lid. Shake until mixed well. To make a collage, brush a thin layer of glue on the back surface of paper scraps or pictures. Smooth them onto a piece of cardboard. Brush on a thin layer of glue to coat the surface.

❋ LITERATURE CONNECTION

These children's books and references can be used to stimulate thinking about sticky materials. The books can be added to the library area of the classroom so that children can select the books that interest them.

Bennet, S., & Bennet, R. (1993). *365 outdoor activities you can do with your child.* Holbrook, MA: Adams Media Corporation.

Bently, D. (1999). *The icky sticky frog.* New York: Piggy Toes Press.

Bree, L. T., & Bree, M. (1993). *Kids squish book: Slimy, squishy, sticky things to do that should only be done when wearing your oldest clothes.* New York: NTC/Contemporary Publishing.

Carle, E. (1981). *The honeybee and the robber.* New York: Putnam Publishing Group.

Matthews, M. (1997). *Icky sticky gloop.* New York: Troll.

Miller, R. (1999). *Sloppy, slimy, sticky, soggy, dripping, moving science.* New York: Scholastic.

Numeroff, L. (1998). *If you give a pig a pancake.* New York: HarperCollins.

Sattler, H. R. (1987). *Recipes for art and craft materials.* New York: William Morrow.

Stevens, C. (1996). *Paper craft school.* New York: Reader's Digest.

Warbrick, S. (1996). *What is sticky?* Portsmouth, NH: Heinemann.

Wilt, J. (1977). *Touch! 48 tactile experiences for children, plus 34 art media recipes to make and use.* Waco, TX: Creative Resources.

EVALUATION OF UNIT

1. Are children actively participating in the activities related to the unit?

2. Do the materials stimulate creative thinking?

3. Are the arts being integrated into meaningful activities?

4. What changes are needed to make the unit and/or activities more effective?

5. Is documentation being used to record the children's work during the process?

6. Can new ideas and extension be observed as the children are involved in the study?

EVALUATION OF CHILD(REN)

1. Did the child(ren) learn about the materials in the environment? Which ones? How did this occur?

2. Was problem-solving used in the selection of materials and solutions to activities?

3. Did the child(ren) use the arts to learn about stickiness? In what way?

4. Did the child(ren) work cooperatively to create projects, make recipes, or determine conclusions?

5. Were the children able to create and use new combinations of materials? Example?

6. Was confidence developed while building, making recipes, and participating in the unit?

Glossary

A

abstract — In visual arts, "abstract" generally refers to artwork emphasizing shapes, colors, lines, and texture over subject matter.

accommodation — The part of adaptation in which new schemas are created and old ones are adjusted to produce a better fit with the environment.

action songs — The combination of melody and movement.

active listening — The act of responding to sounds that are heard.

aesthetics — In the arts, aesthetics relates to a knowledge and awareness of ideas about beauty. These ideas change and evolve over time. Therefore, art education programs engage students in discourse about aesthetics through a study of art history that also involves the student's critical development of his or her own sense of aesthetics, to guide artistic creations.

appreciation — This refers to the listener enjoying the sounds of music.

art center — A specific area of the classroom designed to serve as the hub of artistic creation.

art education — Art curriculum with specific goals and standards taught by art educators who have specialized training related to the content of art.

Artist-in-Residence — Practicing artists, often supported by school districts or community arts councils, who agree to spend some of their time demonstrating their art, facilitating lessons, and helping children understand their profession.

assimilation — That part of adaptation in which the external world is interpreted in terms of current schemas.

associative play — A form of social participation in which children are engaged in separate activities, but they may interact briefly by exchanging toys and commenting on one another's behavior.

atelier — A workshop, or studio, furnished with a variety of resource materials, used by all the children and adults in a school.

atelierista — A teacher trained in art education, in charge of the atelier, who supports teachers in curriculum development and documentation. The art specialist who provides the catalyst for artistic expression in the Reggio Emilia schools of Northern Italy.

atmosphere — The prevailing tone of a place or classroom.

auditory awareness — Being conscious of sounds in the environment.

auditory discrimination — The ability to distinguish between sounds that are heard.

auditory sequencing — The ability to remember the order of sounds heard.

autocasmic play — A type of play defined by Erikson as involving self, people, and things.

Autoharp — A stringed instrument that produces chords by pressing buttons. Can be used to accompany children's singing.

B

basic form stage — At three to four years of age, a child's drawing begins to exhibit form and organization. Repeated patterns and the use of basic forms and lines define this stage of art development.

behaviorist theory — An approach that views directly observable events as the focus of study and the development of behavior as taking place through classical and operant conditioning.

bodily-kinesthetic intelligence — Includes physical movement and awareness and/or wisdom of the body; the body is used to solve problems, make things, and convey ideas and emotions.

body awareness — Recognition of how much space the body occupies and how to control movements.

brainstorming — A technique widely used as a way of producing many ideas.

C

cephalocaudal — The usual pattern of physical development, which progresses from the head down to the toes.

chant — The repetition of phrases and/or words in a rhythmic pattern.

characters — The people who carry out the story and action. Often the characters use dialog as they communicate with each other.

children's theater — This indicates a formal dramatic production that is directed, for which dialog is memorized, and that is performed for an audience.

collaboration — A tool used to assist children or adults in working together on projects, sharing ideas, clarifying thinking, and mediating problems.

collage — A combination of different elements that can be either two- or three-dimensional.

color — Primary and secondary hues created by light and pigments.

composition — Arrangement of the design and space.

construction play — Play in which children manipulate and/or combine objects to build something.

constructivist theory — The position, based on Piaget's theory, that people interpret objects and events that surround them in terms of what they already know, so that one's current state of knowledge guides processing.

controlled scribble — The second step of the scribble stage of artistic development that occurs approximately between birth and two years of age. This step demonstrates the beginning awareness of cause and effect as children begin to experiment with the different marks they can make: zigzags, lines, circles, and suns.

convergent thinking — The generation of a single correct answer to a problem.

cooperative play — A form of true social participation, in which children's actions are directed toward working together.

cooperative work — Being able to work with a group of people and adjusting personal ideas during the process.

creative drama — An informal technique that includes spontaneous acting, without rehearsals and props.

creative movement — Using one's body to move in nondirected ways to express feelings and thoughts.

Creative Problem Solving (CPS) model — Developed by Osborn and Parnes, this model focuses on the generation of creative ideas, with an emphasis on divergent thinking.

creative process — The creative act and the methods or procedures used during the process.

creativity — The production of novel thoughts, solutions, and/or products based on previous experience and knowledge.

creativity training — A planned training program to increase the production of creative ideas.

critical periods — Times when the brain is primed for certain types of learning to take place.

culminating activity — A celebration, event, or product that occurs at the end of a project, to represent what was learned.

cultural creativity — An act, idea, or product that has an impact on the world or how it is viewed. This type of creativity is rare.

D

Developmentally Appropriate Practices (DAP) — Education that is based on both typical development and the unique characteristics of a given child.

display — An attractive arrangement of products for others to view.

divergent thinking — The generation of multiple and unusual possibilities when faced with a task or problem.

documentation — Evidence of what is occurring in an experience or project that involves children and their teachers. Documentation includes transcripts of children's words and photographs of their work that makes visible the learning that was occurring.

documentation panel — A display panel that tells the story of specific experiences and the learning that was taking place. Documentation panels often include photographs, materials, and dialog. The panel provides a tool for children, teachers, and parents to use in communicating about the investigations that were taking place.

Drama in Education (DIE) — The use of drama as a way of teaching other subjects in school. It can be used to study a specific topic and learn more about the area.

duets — Two people or two instruments performing together.

dynamic balance — Maintaining equilibrium while moving.

dynamics — The volume of sounds—soft or loud.

E

egocentric speculation — Thinking that does not take into account the viewpoints of others.

elaboration — A component of the creative process identified by Torrance. "Elaboration" is taking an idea and expanding it to make it more intriguing and complex.

emerging curriculum — Curriculum based on the child's interests and exploration of a topic.

empirical evidence — Findings and conclusions that are supported through research studies. It is sometimes called "research-based practices."

energy — The force that is used to show intentions.

environment — The physical space in which the teacher and children live.

existentialist intelligence — The ability and tendency to consider questions about life, death, and basic truths.

F

fiber art — Art forms that use fibers or materials created from fibers.

fine motor skills — The use of small muscles like those in the hands and fingers.

finger play — Song, story, or chant accompanied by the movement of hands and fingers.

flexibility — A component of the creative process identified by Torrance. "Flexibility" is the ability to change directions or think in another way.

flow — A term coined by Dr. M. Csikszentmihalyi, whereby there is focus on a creative activity that demonstrates intense concentration.

fluency — A component of the creative process identified by Torrance. "Fluency" is the generation of many different ideas.

focus — Concentrating on the drama and staying involved in the process.

folk art — Refers to art created by individuals who are self-taught. Their art is not developed in response to a study of art, but derives out of the experiences of their lives and the materials available that they prefer.

form — Three-dimensional quality, which includes height, width, and depth.

G

general space — The shared space in which children move. Indoors, it is usually limited by floors, walls, and ceilings.

gross motor skills — The use of large muscles like arms, legs, and trunk; also referred to as large motor skills.

group process — A group of people working together to solve an identified problem.

group projects — Projects done by a group of children working together to plan, discuss, and create work.

guided-exploration orientation — An orientation to the art curriculum in which children are taught about art form and aesthetic qualities.

guitar — A stringed instrument that can be used to play chords or melody.

H

harmony — The blending of sounds. These may be produced by two or more sounds performed at the same time.

High/Scope — An early childhood program that focuses on the development of cognition through key experiences.

holistic — A term used to refer to the development of the whole child physically, cognitively, emotionally, socially, and creatively.

hue — The quality of color, as it progresses from whiteness toward blackness.

human impulses — Children's desire to construct when provided with multiple opportunities for learning.

humanistic theory — The theory that contends that people have a natural capacity to make decisions about their lives and control their behavior while striving to be a self-actualized person.

I

illumination — The third step in the creative process defined by Wallas. This step is often described as the moment of "Aha!" or "Eureka!" because a new idea or combination appears that meets the requirements of the problem.

imagination — The ability to form rich and varied images or concepts of people, places, things, and situations when they are not present.

incubation — The second step in the creative process defined by Wallas. This step involves a period of abstinence, when the problem is not considered.

initiating activities — Teacher-initiated activities used to generate an interest in an event, project, or unit.

interpersonal intelligence — An intelligence that deals with person-to-person relationships and communication, working effectively with others, understanding people, and recognizing their goals, motivations, and intentions.

intrapersonal intelligence — An intelligence that involves self-reflection and metacognition or the understanding of one's own emotions, goals, and intentions.

intrinsic motivation — Participation in something by choice, without the need for external reward.

J

junior theater — In junior theater, young actors perform well-rehearsed productions for an audience.

K

keyboard — A musical instrument that can be used to play a melody. It could be a piano, organ, or synthesizer.

kinesthetic-bodily intelligence — An intelligence that includes physical movement and awareness or wisdom of the body. The body is used to solve problems, make things, and convey ideas and emotions.

kinesthetics — Use of the body to gain control and learn about physical capabilities, develop body awareness, and gain understanding of the world. It is another way of knowing and feeling.

L

learning centers — A way of organizing the classroom into areas designed for specific learning to occur. Provides opportunities for small groups to work together.

left hemisphere — The left hemisphere of the brain specializes in logical operations.

line — A mark made by using a tool across a surface (can be vertical, horizontal, diagonal, or curved).

little-intervention orientation — An orientation to art curriculum most often associated with the belief that if one provides the materials for artistic expression, time in the schedule, and the expectation that children will use the materials, then the children will express themselves creatively.

locomotor skills — Body motions such as walking, running, marching, jumping, hopping, galloping, and skipping.

logical-mathematical intelligence — An intelligence that includes deductive or inductive reasoning and recognizing and manipulating abstract reasoning.

M

macrosphere play — A form of play, identified by Erikson, that involves sharing play with others.

manipulative skills — Gross motor skills involving an object—e.g., reaching, grasping, releasing, throwing, catching, and striking.

melody — The tune of music and the pattern of sound that makes up a musical composition.

microsphere play — Using small items to represent the world in play. For example, small plastic family dolls.

mobile — Three-dimensional art that moves when suspended in space.

motor development — The development and coordination of large and small muscles for movement purposes.

multicultural education — A form of education in which the goal is to develop an understanding of original cultures.

multisensory — The use of several different ways of learning, combined into an experience.

musical intelligence — An intelligence that deals with the recognition of tonal patterns, environmental noise, sensitivity to rhythm and beats, and responsiveness to the emotional implications and elements of music.

N

National Association for the Education of Young Children (NAEYC) — A professional organization for people who work with young children from infancy through age eight.

naturalistic intelligence — An intelligence with the capacity to recognize flora and fauna, make distinctions in the natural world, and use this ability productively.

nonlocomotor skills — Stationary actions that include stretching, bending, swaying, and shaking.

novel — New, unique, and different.

O

observation — A focus of attention on the actions of children participating in an activity.

onlooker play — Action in which children simply watch others at play, but do not actually participate themselves.

open-ended — An activity that allows for many different responses to a problem; divergent thinking is needed.

oral language — Language that is expressed verbally.

originality — A component of the creative process identified by Torrance. In order for something to be original, the idea must be truly unique.

P–Q

painting — The use of tempera, watercolor, oil, or acrylic paint to produce a creative product.

pantomime — The use of movement and gestures to express ideas or feelings.

parallel play — A form of limited social participation in which the child plays near other children with similar materials but does not interact with them.

pattern — The repeat of design, lines, or shapes in the artwork.

perceptual theory — Relates to creations developed relative to how objects/subjects are seen through observation. This differs from an artist rendering things according to imaginative thoughts or ideas about how things function.

percussion instruments — Instruments played by striking.

personal creativity — Doing something new for the individual, something he or she has never done before. This type of creativity can be seen in everyday happenings and accomplished by ordinary people.

personal experimentation — An individual's exploration.

personal space — The personal or shared area that is used by the body during movement. This includes the levels of high and low and directions, such as forward, backward, up, and down.

perspective — Point of view created by techniques such as size and overlapping.

pictorial stage — When drawings are recognizable to the viewer and artist.

pitch — The highs and lows of musical sound patterns.

play — The spontaneous activity of young children that is enjoyable.

playfulness — The ability to play with ideas, experiment, and try interesting things.

pleasure principle — The primary reason for an activity is the enjoyment it brings to the participants.

plot — The sequence of events in a drama that creates the meaning. Setting the place where the action occurs.

practice theory — A theory developed by Gross, who believed play was an intrinsic activity that continues to develop as the child matures.

preoperational play — The second stage of Piaget's constructivist theory. It is dominated by the development of symbolic representation.

preparation — The first step in the creative process defined by Wallas. This step involves exploration, gathering information, finding available resources, and getting acquainted with the "problem" or "issue."

preschematic stage — The third stage of artistic development that occurs at approximately four to seven years of age. Children begin to use symbols, in an attempt to represent objects in their own perspective.

print making — A form of art that involves making a copy of something.

process — Exploring and playing with tools, techniques, and materials throughout the creative process.

product — The final result of the creative process.

product-oriented orientation — An orientation to the art curriculum in which children are expected to produce a product, with little self-expression or independence.

project approach — A curriculum approach that allows children to study a topic of interest for an extended period of time.

proportion — Refers to the relationship (ratio) of the size and scale among objects. Used to compare objects and convey the relationship of parts to whole objects.

proximodistal — Pattern of physical growth from the center of the body outward.

psychoanalytic theory — An approach to personality development introduced by Freud that assumes children move through a series of stages in which they confront conflicts between biological drives and social expectations. The way these conflicts are resolved determines psychological adjustment.

psychologically safe environment — An environment that meets the child's basic needs, supports ideas, and provides respect for individual differences.

puppetry — A drama technique that allows children to take on the role of another, with the use of a prop.

R

readers' theater — Children read scripts of a story or play with rehearsal and props.

realism — The fifth stage of artistic development that occurs approximately from nine to twelve years of age. Children become more concerned about realism in their art through size, proportion, placement, shape, color, and perspective.

Reggio Emilia — A city in Italy with having early childhood programs that have received international attention for their excellent practices.

rehearsal — Practicing a presentation, story, or song until it can be performed at a higher level.

relaxation theory — Developed by Patrick, who believed play was a way to recover from fatigue or hard work.

representational — In visual arts, representational refers to images that look like the object(s) they represent, if not realistically, at least through identifiable characteristics or components that relate to the object(s) that the artist has in mind.

resonator bells — A set of bells, arranged by the musical scale, with soundboards under each, to produce a beautiful tone.

rhythm — The beat of music, including tempo and meter.

rhythm instruments — A group of instruments, such as rhythm sticks, bells, and tambourine, used to play the rhythm of a song.

right hemisphere — The right hemisphere is the visual-spatial portion of the brain.

rounds — When a musical composition is played or sung, with groups beginning and ending at different times.

rubbing — Paper is placed on an object, then, a crayon, charcoal, or marker is used to rub the paper and reproduce the outline of the object.

S

scale — The relationship of representations to the perception of their size: identification of the object (subject of the painting) in relation to parts of the whole or the surrounding contexts of the subject, the scale of the object — large or small. Large scale representations show things as large, in relation to other things in the image, even if placed on a small piece of paper or canvas. Small-scale representations show things as small, in relation to other things in the image, even if placed on a large piece of paper or canvas.

schemas — In Piaget's theory, a specific structure or organized way of making sense of experience; it changes with age.

schematic stage — The fourth stage of artistic development that occurs approximately from seven to nine years of age. Children continue to develop symbols to represent the world "realistically" and experiment with detail, placement, and materials.

scribble stage — The early stage of artistic development that includes scribbles produced by a young child.

sculpture — Three-dimensional art made from wood, clay, metal, and/or found objects.

self-actualized — Maslow defines the self-actualized person as one who has become all that he or she is capable of being.

self-assessment — The process of evaluating one's own work.

sensorimotor development — Using the five senses and motor development in a coordinated way.

sensory development — Seeing, hearing, touching, tasting, and smelling.

sensory exploration — The use of the senses to examine an object or experience.

sensory-motor play — The first stage of Piaget's cognitive theory. In infancy young children learn by acting on their world through their senses.

sewing — Connecting fabric or materials with thread, yarn, or ribbon.

shape — Configuration, contours, or outline.

small motor coordination — The use of the eye and hand to complete a task. For example, putting together a puzzle.

social competencies — The collection of social skills that permit individuals to perform successfully in social settings.

social constructivist theory — Vygotsky's interpretation of constructivism that sees the process as influenced by the social world.

social play — Participating with others in play activities.

social skills — The ability to work with others, using techniques such as sharing or collaboration.

sociodramatic play — Children imitate the actions and people that they have experienced in their play. They repeat, solve problems, and relive these experiences.

solitary play — Play on one's own; others are not involved in the activity.

space awareness — The recognition of near, far, over, under, up, down, and proximity and distance between objects and/or one's body.

spatial relationship — Refers to the association among things in space, whether these are lines or shapes on a page, or among objects or parts of objects in three-dimensional space.

static balance — Staying balanced while remaining still.

story dramatization — Creating an improvised play, based on a story or piece of literature.

story line — The events and conclusions that make up the form of the story.

storytelling — The sharing of a story, without the use of a book.

subject area — A content area of the curriculum, such as science or mathematics.

surplus energy theory — Earliest theory of play, developed by Spencer, who thought that children release their excess energy through play.

T

teachable moment — Spontaneous opportunity for teachers to expand on a child's interests.

texture — The way an object feels or how the grain might feel when touched.

thematic unit — A curriculum approach that focuses on a specific topic and includes an integration of content areas and the arts.

theme — A concept or idea that is used to organize curriculum and activities in an early childhood classroom.

Theory of the Mind (TOM) — The theory that pretend play uses mental representation and role-playing as a way of understanding others.

three-dimensional — Refers to objects represented with media that can be manipulated and seen from many perspectives in space. The artist and viewer can see the object from many sides, and often from the top and/or bottom.

timbre — The tone of the sound, for example, the uniquely different qualities produced by a log drum or a steel drum.

time — This includes rhythm, speed, emphasis, and duration of the movement.

two-dimensional — Refers to images represented on flat surfaces with any combination of marking tools: pencil, pen, marker, crayon, paintbrush, photograph (ink), etc.

U

uncontrolled scribble — First step in the scribble stage of artistic development that occurs between the ages of birth and two. These first marks are typically uncontrolled, unrefined, and show little concern for the final product.

unoccupied play — Not involved in any play.

use of body — The coordination of the body to communicate in drama. Use of gestures, facial expressions, and movement.

V

value — The quality of color as it progresses from light to dark.

verbal expression — Speaking clearly and effectively, using volume, tone, pitch, and pauses. It includes the ability to improvise dialog.

verbal-linguistic intelligence — A form of intelligence related to words and language, which produces language with sensitivity to the nuances, order, and rhythm of words.

verification — This is the fourth step in the creative process, as defined by Wallas. Trying out the solution and determining if the ideas will work occurs during this step.

visual-spatial intelligence — An intelligence that relies on the sense of sight and being able to visualize an object. It also involves creating visual–spatial representations of the world and transferring them mentally or concretely.

W–X–Y

weaving — The process of interconnecting fibers in a systematic pattern.

whole child — A theory of child development that focuses on the emotional, social, physical, creative, and cognitive growth of a child.

Z

zone of proximal development (ZPD) — In Vygotsky's social construction theory, a range of tasks that the child cannot yet handle alone but can do with the help of an adult or more skilled partner. The gap between the point of being able to do something with assistance and the point of being able to do it alone.

Index